BRITISH
LIGHT
CARS
1930-1939

BRITISH LIGHT CARS 1930-1939

by
Bruce Hudson

ISBN 0 85429 167 9

First published September 1975, reprinted April 1979

©Bruce Hudson 1975, 1979

A FOULIS Motoring Book

Published by
Haynes Publishing Group
Sparkford, Yeovil, Somerset, BA22 7JJ, England

Distributed in North America by:—
Haynes Publications Inc
861, Lawrence Drive, Newbury Park, California 91320, USA

Editor Tim Parker
Jacket Design Edward Piper

Printed in England by Haynes Publishing Group, Sparkford, Yeovil, Somerset

Preface

In this companion volume to *Postwar British Thoroughbreds* the reader is invited to look back fondly to an earlier era, a formative space of ten years wherein the legacy of the Vintage car as a 'motor carriage' evolved the seeds of modern motoring, shared by millions to-day.

At last it would appear that the post-Vintage 'stigma' is fast fading; cars made since 1930 are nowadays appreciated for what they are, and not viewed sceptically because they were manufactured after a certain somewhat arbitary date. This book casts an affectionate eye on prewar British motoring as a whole, and the multiplicity of light cars built during a fascinating decade. None are singled out for preferential treatment at the expense of others; be it Ford or Frazer Nash, Singer or Squire, an equal place has been found for each.

Due to the enormity of the subject, limitations of space have meant that certain more obscure makes of light car such as the A J S, Trojan and Swift have been omitted, and it must be stressed that this volume is not intended to serve as a definitive history of the smaller 1930s' motor-car, nor as a comprehensive manual for 'old car' restoration. Also, whilst every care has been taken to supply accurate information throughout the book, its use and interpretation is entirely at the risk of the reader and no responsibility will be accepted by the author or his publishers for consequent loss or damage.

The Car Club movement is growing year by year, and this more than anything ensures that older cars are correctly maintained and carefully 'pampered' - as often they need to be, because of the ravages of time. No museum piece, however resplendant and glittering, can rival the sight of its 'double' driving along a modern motorway. Rust, grime and cobwebs can hide what soon becomes more a way of life than a mere car, and often it is here that membership of a club catering for a certain prewar make is so valuable. Club technical officers and the like are acquainted with the problems and idiosyncrasies of each model and can guide the novice over the frustrating pitfalls that beset someone working 'alone' without recourse to sympathetic advice.

In my own researches into the more obscure details of the hosts of prewar light cars that were manufactured, I too have been glad to consult several Car Club historians among whom I must include R.A. Cox (Alvis), A.M. Feather (Aston Martin), R.K. Taylor (British Salmson), B.E. Smith (BSA and Lanchester), G. Lee (Crossley), N. Sands (M G), A.J. Wood (Lagonda Rapier), P. Pringle (Lea-Francis) and C. Watson (Triumph).

All of the above mentioned have supplied photographs for the book, as have P.S.W. Pearce (Armstrong-Siddeley), I. McGregor (Aston-Martin), the Ford Motor Company and Mrs. C. Harris (Ford), D.A. Thirlby (Frazer Nash), A.B. Demaus, Chrysler UK Ltd and the Olyslager Organisation (Hillman, Humber, Singer and Talbot), A. Pluckrose, P. Crosby, D.B. Mitchell and Dr. O.J. Follows (Jowett), A.B. Price and K.A. Tricker (Lea-Francis), Miss Georgina Tree and B. Lacey-Malvern (MG), P.H.G. Morgan (Morgan), D.G. Styles (Riley), I. Elliott of British-Leyland, Austin-Morris Ltd (Morris), S. Banting of British-Leyland Rover Ltd

(Rover), K. Mayfield, A.M. Lake (S.S.), Mrs. H. Pengelly of Triumph Motors (Standard), E.H. Bavenstock, G. Binns and R.J. Broad (Triumph), and Mrs. C. Harris, M. Selby-Lowndes, B.W. Young, R. Burrows, N.E. Ballard, H. Cooper (Wolseley). Also the *Hemel Hempstead Evening Echo*, the Hillman Aero Minx Register and Mr. D.W.T. Bell have to be acknowledged. Certain photographs have also been supplied by the Montagu Motor Museum, Beaulieu, and others reproduced from the late Gregor Grant's book *British Sports Cars* by kind permission.

I am grateful, too, for the practical help afforded by my wife in typing the manuscript, by Miles Marshall, who kindly loaned me his collection of prewar *Autocar* magazines, and by Tim Parker of G.T. Foulis & Co Ltd, whose constant attention to the progress of the book has been most welcome.

The fascination of old cars is exerting an increasing influence, as is evidenced in the growing membership of owners' clubs and wider interest in rallies, competitions, museum collections and the like. Perhaps, then, there is room for one more book such as this on an expanding 'Motoring' bookshelf.

Bruce A. Hudson

Bacton, Suffolk
August 1975

Contents

List of illustrations

BRITISH LIGHT CARS

Part One

Chapter One   Fundamentals: the light car and you

Austin 7, Morris 8, Riley 9 - mere horsepower ratings, merely humble numerals, but to-day endowed with such magical portents! The long tapering bonnet of the M G Magna or the bull-nosed dummy radiator of the Morgan Aero Sports peer out from the mists of forty years ago through yellowing headlamps - spelling 'magnetism' to the motoring romantic! Alongside any contemporary blatantly-functional fastback GT saloon, a prewar square-set 'Brooklands Replica' strikes an attitude of worldly defiance, its glistening alloy bonnet and open mudguards hypnotically turning the clock back to an earlier era of dusty roads, sunny countrysides and excitement: the pure joy of a full-throated open exhaust note, the friendly smell of ageing leather and benzol mixture, the cool polished texture as one grips half-nonchalantly the massive black steering-wheel — the highway empty but for the distant outline of a Hyper Lea-Francis slowly but surely drawing nearer in the driving mirror!

And once that 1933 Ulster Special is finally and painstakingly acquired, it's little wonder that technicolor handout for this year's 'Valenza GT' has found itself tucked under the front seat to give added support to those elderly seat-springs. That "car for 1984 available now" could well begin to symbolize all that is decadent in the modern motor car, for what could be more sensible than black enamelled rather than cellulosed wings in orange fireflake, and how could pressed stainless-steel wheel covers ever supercede glistening heavily-chromed Rudge-Whitworth knock-off hubs...?

In 1914 both Morris and Singer produced light 10 hp four-cylinder two-seaters contrasting sharply in performance with contemporary 'runabouts' and 'voiturettes' with their single-cylinder engines and heavy bodywork. But neither drew very wide attention until after the 1914-18 war, when a taxation system based on horsepower and size of cylinder bore turned the motorist away from the 15 to 20 hp range, creating overnight a demand for a car with a small engine but good road performance. This new vogue heralded the establishment of the light car in its own right, - a vehicle of 17 to 14 hp with an economical engine of small cylinder dimensions, powering a chassis and body of fairly light weight (to limit this book by rigidly adhering to the classic definition of a light car as having a maximum engine capacity of 1500cc seemed far too 'purist' for no definite reason, and so models of light car up to 1700cc have also been included).

'Light' cars meant light bodywork and hence light running costs, and these 'Minis of the Twenties', born out of the benefits of early mass-production, offered the average family-man a chance to buy a car he could afford to run; soon the monstrous and over-bodied coupes-de-ville, limousines and coupe-cabriolets found themselves languishing in the garage far more often, their glossy aura of 'sheer size and strength makes the better car' becoming obscured by gathering dust and cobwebs.

Now four people plus luggage could be transported from A to B at the same cost as a single railway ticket. Petrol varied in price and grade from 1s to 1s 6d per gallon, and costs per mile from 1d to 3d only, according to the size of light car in question. Purchase prices varied from

£100 to £600, the latter representing a virtually hand-built specialist model. Generally, though, the average price for a semi-mass produced and unpretentious light car by 1930 was less than £200 (the mythical price of a *fully-equipped* light car at a mere "£100 brand new" ceasing to be a myth just after the mid-30s with the appearance of the Ford Eight).

By the end of the 1920s many British light cars were on the market: AC, Alvis, Austin, Clyno, Frazer Nash, Hillman, Humber, Lea-Francis, Morris, Riley, Rover, Singer, Standard, Swift, Trojan and Wolseley all offered small-engined cars of 7,8,9,10 and 11 horsepower. Most of them could carry four people, returning a very adequate road performance at low fuel costs; also they could go on providing service for several years, covering many thousands of miles.

Building on the experience of the previous decade, light cars of the 1930s became far more reliable, powerful and comfortable. Engine output increased some twenty per cent over the years before the Second World War, the quality of fuel progressively improving , and technical development making possible more efficient engine designs.

Open two-seaters and four-seaters remained as popular as the saloons and certain manufacturers even introduced six-cylinder overhead-valve or overhead-camshaft engines for their light cars, the Wolseley Hornet being a good example of this, although it did suffer later from weight-distribution problems due to the engine overhanging the front axle! But in general the makers still favoured the four-cylinder side-valve layout with its inherent reliability and long periods of service between overhauls. Dry-disc clutches and helical-toothed gearboxes, coil ignition, electric fuel pumps, rubber engine mountings, downdraught carburetters, stiffer chassis, lower centres of gravity, low-pressure tyres, hydraulic shockabsorbers and eventually independent front suspension all gradually became adopted and made for better cars.

To-day quite a movement has built up of enthusiasts interested in restoring and putting back on the road all types of light cars manufactured from about 1920 onwards. But cars of the 1920s represent fifty years of history, and over these five decades the mists of time are

beginning to close - these early and obscure cars seem more the province of the professional restorer. By 1928, radical improvements began to appear and by 1930 there emerged cars with more obviously 'modern' features, less obscurities and idiosyncrasies, less downright 'awkwardness', particularly as regards the enthusiastic amateur or hobbyist of to-day who wishes to chance his hand and 'have a go' at rebuilding. For this reason, light cars of 1930-39 offer a far more realistic task in their renovation, and although breakers' yards and suchlike will not be much help with spare parts, many specialists and workshops, and of course one-make Car Clubs, now offer advice and practical assistance in just this field.

There is prejudice in cars, just as much as in other walks of life, but in this book the author steers clear of any differentiation: be it Alvis or Ford, Riley or Vauxhall, all have their good points and bad, and all an undeniable character or charm. 'Thoroughbred' and 'utility' rub bumpers in these pages, for with the passage of some forty years, the prewar social distinctions attached to such cars have little validity. Their very 'elderliness' makes each one 'respectable' and equally desirable nowadays.

First things first

How does one begin to start looking for such a car to-day? First must come one's own truthful self-assessment. How keen are you? Not from the fireside armchair, 'dreaming' of yourself at the wheel of a resplendent 1935 X Y Z, but in the cold light of morning, faced with an assemblage of 'dead metal' needing many months of your strained enthusiasm and energy, and possibly many pounds in hard cash to 're-incarnate'?

You must have some mechanical aptitude and a flair for improvization. You must have determination to succeed, even in those 'darkest hours', plus plenty of allotted time. You will need space to work - the street is not the best 'workshop' for most of us. And you must never be tempted to fix a definite time-limit for that 'first run to the coast' - for it may well take place in the depths of February of the *next* year! These facts are on the debit side.

The 'credits', of course, are in far-more-than-equal magnitude; the realisation of an ambition; the sense of accomplishment (together with perhaps nostalgically-tinged and affectionate memories of crises that turned into triumphs); the deep satisfaction and pride in your own final success. And the comradeship enjoyed as a member of a fanatically-keen Car Club will never be forgotten, either.

Which?

Next, which particular car is best for you? This is a combination of personal preference and availability, tempered by one's exchequer. By definition, all light cars when fully restored will provide sensible and, it is hoped, enjoyable transport for two to four persons at a thoroughly realistic fuel consumption figure, so choice of maker is not too vital at first. But obviously a very rare model will prove more difficult to restore than others, of which many thousands were manufactured. Also models of the early 1930s will have mechanical brakes and beam front axles, whereas those of 1936 onwards may well have hydraulic brakes and independent front suspension; a 'crash' gearbox on an early model may have developed synchromesh by the end of the decade. Technical features like this need consideration - for example, the dictates of the MOT test must be met in full by your prewar vehicle before it may be used on the roads, and in this case alone mechanical brakes must be fully restored to complete effectiveness in order to satisfy the retardometer the tester uses. 'Crash' gearboxes, too, require mastery - not much fun in a modern traffic jam. Early suspensions can prove quite a shock on a rough road that your Mini makes light of. The car's powerplant is certainly a vital part of the car, and when it stops, so does your pleasure. Perhaps the standard four-cylinder side-valve engine represents the simplest type to rebuild and maintain. A single carburetter makes for ease of tuning and a mid-30s semi-synchromesh gearbox for ease of driving. Hydraulic shock-absorbers give added travelling comfort, and coil ignition seems to be less 'temperamental' compared to a magneto, particularly in damp weather.

Non-runners and their failings

The car you definitely do *not* want is a 'non-runner' with a decayed chassis or with early monocoque construction where the floor has rusted away. Yes, welding *seems* a solution, but remember that you cannot weld to rusty metal - the welding torch will turn into a cutter if you try it and your vital fragments of what was left of the foundation will burn away. In fact the condition of the chassis is the most vital factor you will face - is it sound, restorable, or a 'write-off'? Soundness may be quickly checked by jabbing the frame-members with a screwdriver. You should feel a firm, clear impact - if you hear a crunch and it goes straight through, the chance is that the old car will never ride the highways again. Of course, a chassis that's generally solid but with cross-members in an early stage of corrosion can be treated against further rusting and rebuilt, a rivetted chassis can be repaired and new sections re-rivetted in place; but any elderly car with a badly decayed chassis is certainly not a sensible investment, however romantic its outer appearance. Monocoque or unit-construction was a feature of, for example, the Vauxhall Ten and Twelve of 1938, and these models were literally trend-setters - nowadays unit-construction is the rule rather than the exception. But absence of an independent chassis frame indicates the need for great care in the preservation of the floor and sub-frame (as witness the short lives of many modern cars). The engines and other features of these late-30s Vauxhalls were quite advanced, the performance being lively, and the ride comfortable due to the inclusion of independent front suspension, but these innovations, married to unit-construction, spelt doom for the thousands of Tens and Twelves produced during this era. Very few survived for more than a couple of years after the war as the floors decayed and made the cars unsound; but despite this the Vauxhall Ten or Twelve is certainly worth restoring, should one come upon an example which has been stored in a dry atmosphere, or used regularly and meticulously preserved. But to recap finally - if the chassis or all-important floor and sub-frame is badly decayed, look for another car.

Two typical, although vastly different, small light cars of the early-mid thirties. At the top is a 1933 Morris Minor Two Seater embodying all that was cheap and simple, whilst below is a 1934 BSA Saloon equipped with 'four wheels', Daimler 'fluid flywheel' and self-changing gearbox, and that speaks for itself

Chapter Two   Head start: the 'runner'

What does one do if a car is being sold as a 'runner'? Well, different pros and cons apply in this case. By definition a 'runner' is driveable and *should* have satisfied the MOT test in all respects. The owner too should have maintained the car in reasonable overall condition (but one can never be sure). Deterioration accelerates when elderly cars are stored away - conversely, keeping them in use in effect helps to preserve them, so a 'runner' may be a far better proposition, but it will cost far more to purchase - no chance of 'getting it for a song'. Motoring journals such as *Motor Sport* contain column after column of advertisements, and you need to study these each month until you have decided (1) which model will suit you best, and (2) a reasonable figure to pay for it. If you have a fair working-knowledge of modern-car mechanics, then go out and inspect one of two advertized cars, keeping your eyes open for obvious defects. Wear overalls or old clothes, and a beret, and clamber underneath each one before you're tempted to gaze into the hypnotic glitter of those massive headlamps. Shine your torch around and jab your screwdriver at the chassis as hard as you can - don't do it gently, in the hope of perhaps fooling yourself, because the result could be a lot of hard cash thrown away. If sound, inspect the engine and bodywork and go for a test drive (described soon).

A genuine novice, or not?

If you are brave enough to admit that you are very 'green' when it comes to sizing-up an old, but loveable car, then do not act rashly and in haste. It could be the beginning of a costly and frustrating enterprise and you could be embittered by your experiences. First try to find out more about the complexities of your favourite model, and the possible problems you may well have to face. Having read Part 2 of this book first, you'll be sure you've made a good choice - a model suitable for *you*. For example, the Austin Seven is a far better bet than, say, a BSA Scout if you are not rich, nor very skilled. An early Riley Nine Monaco is quite a different thing from a 1936 Ford Eight with its honest, down-to-earth simplicity; in fact many prewar Ford Eights are to be seen giving regular day-to-day service, not necessarily in the hands of enthusiasts, and this goes for many other mass-produced cars from the more orthodox 1930s car companies. Anyway, if you are a genuine novice avoid 'jumping-in head first' and decide carefully. Perhaps the derilicit 'non-runner' is not a wise choice to take on as a first attempt. The 'runner' can be far more encouraging and yield much first-hand experience which may prove invaluable should you decide to rebuild a 'non-runner' next. You may well have to pay far more, of course, but don't be tempted to 'economize' by seeking a virtual wreck instead of patiently saving for something better.

One-make clubs

One approach is to join a one-make Car Club some time before you decide to purchase (see Part 2 for club addresses) and by studying their quarterly bulletin thoroughly, acquaint yourself with the good and bad points of the model you particularly fancy, if it is not described in Part 2. This way you will learn too about the numbers of your car still on the road and the availability of spares. You may get to chat with present owners and even arrange a deal with a club member. Very often there are only the Car Clubs left to fall back on. Some makes and models are now so rare and obscure that no generally-available literature exists; you must contact the appropriate club or you'll never get out of the 'mist' that surrounds the legend. And very often the best-condition models change hands in the privacy of a Car Club; they are not advertized in the motoring journals, and deliberately so. Also if you can obtain old copies of the prewar journal *The Light Car* they could provide much information and help you to make your decision.

Vetting a 'runner'

Should you learn of a sale through a public advertisement, firstly see whether the price asked is realistic when related to the year and condition described. Don't be surprised if you find on arrival that the rarer 1933 model you expected turns out to be the 1935 model with its notorious leaky rear axle! Very often the most ardent enthusiast can be blinded by his very enthusiasm, and unwittingly be under a deeply-rooted misconception, particularly if the log-book is an elderly 're-copy' with the year of manufacture copied in error. Only the chassis number will provide definite proof, because the engine could be a replacement.

Having decided that 'that long journey into Herefordshire' is worth it, it may be better to take only a suitable small deposit with you. Should you decide to have the car, be certain to obtain a signed receipt for the deposit, with the registration number written somewhere in the agreement. Very often in retrospect one has second thoughts, and it's better to sacrifice a small deposit than buy something outright in the heat of the moment, only to find large mechanical problems looming up shortly after you got the car home.

Chassis comes first

Anyway, check that chassis first. Next ask to see the car's current MOT certificate, looking for cunningly subtle alterations to extend its 'validity'. Even a valid MOT certificate may not be sufficient proof that the chassis will pass the tester next time, and it is best to make one's judgement by a first-hand examination. Look out for layers of fibreglass plugged into the decay spots, cleverly camouflaged with 'artificially aged' underseal or what-have-you, or for a 'back-yard' welding repair with no actual strength whatever. Poke around with a sharp object, particularly in corners, butt joints and inaccessible crevices. And whilst underneath take a glance at the exhaust system, brake linkages and anchorage points for the body, particularly if it has a fabric-covered wooden framework as in some light cars of the early 1930s. Knowing what can happen to mild steel in forty years, it's easy to imagine the effect of those forty long years on humble ash spars and the like. Ply floorboards, too, cannot last for ever, but are more easily renewed.

Apart from the chassis (and perhaps you may even be prepared to accept slight decay spots that have not spread too far), vetting the rest of the car entails personal decisions only: the engine may be 'wheezing', the gears 'chattering', but still you're prepared to overlook these points in order to secure the car's chassis as a sound basis for rebuilding. In fact one may be obliged to overlook quite a lot - a 100% restored, mechanically perfect prewar model could fetch a 'sky-high' price, and so this somewhat more humble, less costly version will almost certainly be far from perfect. And trying to make it tend towards the 'perfect' is going to be half the fun of the thing for you, surely?

Those extra spares

We come now to that extra £50 tacked on to the price to cover 'spare engine and boxes of parts', the phrase you so gleefully read at the foot of the advertisement. The author has always been extremely sceptical of such things, and anyway, stockpiling for example dozens of boxes of say, wheel nuts, is ridiculous. In fact accumulating a garage full of spare parts, some rusty, some already badly worn, some deteriorating month by month is quite futile. Often the 'spare engine' you paid so much for is found never to be required; it in fact was in worse condition than the spluttering 'dead beat' that dragged the car home. Sometimes you may take a brass drain-cock off to replace one that's leaking on the car, or pick off a plug washer or a nut here and there. But generally that heavy block of corroding metal just lies there year after year until in the end the local scrap merchant offers to take it away. Crankshafts and pistons can rarely be just 'swapped over' - the tolerances are so fine in an efficient engine that such a practice may produce even negative results, compression disappearing completely, and oil pressure dropping to zero! When for example crankshaft bearings and journals are badly worn, the crankshaft is reground and new bearings fitted: you cannot simply swap the spare crankshaft over and hope it will cure the trouble, - it never does. Hence 80% of that spare engine is doomed to remain 'spare' for ever. Those originally gleaming alloy rocker-covers get more and more corroded each winter they remain imprisoned in the garage: glittering cog-wheels in those spare gearboxes steadily film over with rust; that spare silencer will be found to crumble to pieces when you finally hook it out from the bottom of the pile.

Be realistic

Expendable spares — plugs, points, dynamo brushes, Bendix starter springs, brake linings and the like - yes, by all means keep a stock handy, wrapped in sealed polythene bags and tucked away on the garage shelf. But that certain mania we all go through of snapping-up box after box of elderly 'spares' must be suppressed. Don't hoard them up, - wait until you're sure that you're going to need, say, another rear axle. And don't then buy three 'just in case', because they were there temptingly propped-up at the back of some barn. But should you know, through your

Car Club, that spares for your model are non-existent, you may have to stockpile a little.

Looking more closely

You may be wondering how, in fact, to judge the condition of the car, in detail. You may very well not be prepared to accept a solid chassis while 'overlooking' certain points, but want a car in good overall condition. So what do you look for? Well, if you have been underneath the car, you will know more about the condition of the wooden body-frame (if there is one) and whether its anchorages to the chassis are sound or otherwise. Without doubt, wood (in this case ash, or you can substitute cheap grades of mahogany) is far more easy to work with than, say, mild steel, and replacement of the body-frame will be nearer simple carpentry than engineering. And the old spars can be used quite simply as patterns for the new ones (see Chapter 10), so a decayed wooden frame is not too alarming.

Fabric bodies

Cars of the early 1930s often had a part-fabric covering to the body. When elderly and in need of replacement this is obvious to detect: the fabric is brittle, wrinkled and far from attractive, even torn in places - or missing in others. You'll quickly be able to decide if it's going to need a new 'skin' and this too isn't an insurmountable problem, but it is fairly skilled work if you are expecting a neat, close-fitting job.

Alloy bodywork

Bodies covered in aluminium panels have an inherently long life. Unlike pressed steel, alloy cannot rust; eventual decay appears as a white powder (basic aluminium oxide) and the panel crumbles away. Of course, the salt used on icy roads in winter accelerates the process, acting in effect like an acid and eating away the aluminium far more quickly, as aluminium

The 1930s produced some of the finest and beautiful light sports cars ever seen. This 1935 Riley Nine Imp Two Seater is a superb example

chloride. The lower edges of alloy panels should be carefully inspected for atomspheric corrosion, particularly those adjoining the steel chassis. Here 'sacrificial corrosion' may be apparent - the alloy has 'sacrificed' itself to preserve the steel, and repair will be necessary.

If the owner has repaired parts of the bodywork with fibreglass paste, note this too. Careless finishing may be evident here, and you can certainly improve on this by (1) stripping the paste off and starting again, or (2) rubbing-down the repair with far more care, perhaps patching it up as you go.

Dents may be quite simply knocked out from alloy panels, the metal is quite soft and without much 'spring', but you will need a set of panelbeater's 'dollies' and some bumping and dinging hammers, *not* the domestic variety. 'Pop' rivets can work wonders too, and rapidly anchor down 'flapping edges'.

Peeling cellulose on alloy is a common problem on elderly cars. If you spot this, rest assured that there are methods to refinish such peeled areas satisfactorily (see Chapter 10).

Steel bodywork

Rust has always been the enemy of the car renovator. You will soon notice it if it's there, but you may have to kneel down to spot it, as it's the lower sections of the bodywork that become affected first. And as with alloy, salt water attacks steel viciously and rust can 'creep through' a steel panel, invisibly at first, then making itself noticed as it finally 'bubbles up' the paintwork. Evidence of bad body rusting is a sign to stop and ponder carefully. A bit of rust here and there you can ignore, whereas mudguards barely attached and 'hanging by a thread' are not going to be so funny when it comes to working out how to resecure them. And of course, as mentioned in Chapter 1, evidence of widespread rusting of the lower bodywork of a unit-construction car is extremely serious, as the stressed-skin of the body and floor substitutes the conventional chassis altogether.

Polyester resins and pastes ('fibreglass' pastes) are one modern solution to the rust problem. But only if the decay is not in the actual structure of the body i.e. only if the paste or resin-impregnated fibreglass cloth takes the place of flat areas of panel etc. Body anchorage points cannot be 'reconnected' with clods of polyester paste - you'll have to make new brackets or metal fittings first and secure the body mechanically with nut-and-bolt construction before worrying about 'appearances'.

Welding, too, is another solution - but one generally beyond the realm of the amateur. Rust must be cut out by removing part of the panelling with an oxy-acetylene cutter, and welding-in the new piece of panel requires skill, too. 'Home' arc-welding kits are available fairly cheaply; yet arc-welding demands more skill than gas welding, and cheap arc-welding kits demand plenty of flair and much practice before achieving even semi-professional results. More often than not one gets not a welded join when working with thin-gauge panelling, but a 'burn'; even on a low amperage, a 'home' arc-welder can easily cut a series of holes along the entire length of a seam, much to the distress of the operator. Once this has occured, all one can then do is to try to mask the unsightly join with very heavy layers of primer-filler, and this is rarely successful. In fact you have replaced one problem with yet another.

Think carefully if you find a lot of rust decay in the body. Should the car be a two-seater with a canvas hood in poor overall condition, this is only a small problem as there are several specialist firms who supply new hoods to pattern, some even from stock. In fact very often a two- or four-seater convertible light car represents a much more realistic restoration project as virtually 50% of the 'bodywork' is canvas; it's far easier to fit a new canvas hood than restore a badly rusted saloon roof.

Other external details

Now look round at the chromework, wheels and tyres. Badly pitted chromium plating can be restored, but at a price. Nickel plate, which lacks the crisp, bright sparkle of chrome, can also be renovated. If the underlying metal is brass there will be little problem, either; but deep pitting demands a lot of grinding right down to the basic steel or alloy-metal before plating new metal on to the surface, the resulting smooth-ness of this ground surface dictating with complete finality just how brilliant a replate you'll get. Scimp this very laborious grinding and your 'new chrome' will in fact look just like rather poor nickel.

It's doubtful whether many light cars of 1930 onwards were finished with nickel bright parts. By the end of the 1920s chromium had virtually superceded it completely, so don't worry about nickel plating - that rather dim and filmy gleam is very likely to be dulled chrome.

Plating works and suchlike exist in most cities and large towns and will usually undertake small jobs such as your door handles. Or you can try a type of non-electrical chemical plating which can be done at home (for details of plating works and 'home chrome' suppliers see the Appendix).

Headlamps reflectors are not chromium plated. A thin coating of aluminium is applied to the concave surface by an anodizing process nowadays; in the 1920s and early '30s silver plate was employed but later superceded by aluminium because of the rapid tarnishing of silver. Dim reflectors, therefore, will need either a new plating of silver or aluminium; abrasive metal polishes immediately ruin reflectors, and previous owners could quite well have resorted to this in sheer desperation, only to discover that the underlying brass makes a very poor re-flector! Another possible alternative is the adaptation and substitution of a new reflector in each headlamp.

Wire wheels should be checked over for soundness. Any signs of rusty spokes will certainly indicate the need for immediate attention. 'Artillery' pressed-spoke wheels, too, can be far less sound than they look and you should examine the areas where the two halves of the wheel come together to make up the 'spokes': the metal can be nearly wafer-thin here due to internal corrosion, invisible from the out-side, more particularly beneath layers of old paint. Rusty rims may be found, and the same danger signs apply to disc wheels.

Balding tyres are now illegal. Several companies nowadays cater for the 'old car' enthusiast in that they can supply tyres to fit the now-obsolete larger rims of 17, 18 and 19 inch diameter (see the Appendix for details). One point - beware buying ancient tyres that appear to have seen very little use - the sort offered to you with that 'spare engine' for example. The treads look perfectly all right from the outside, and fitting them on the car would be extremely authentic (real 'vintage' tyres no less!), but in fact all rubber ages and breaks down structurally, becoming soft and tending to crumble; you'll find you get a disappointingly short term of service from old tyres like this. It's always best to buy new, and present-day re-moulds are perfectly satisfactory as regards quality.

Interiors

The interiors of old cars have a smell all their own — a blend of antique leather, gentle decay, and oil fumes from the crankcase breather-pipe which have permeated every fibre. The appearance can also be quietly 'aged', and certainly very 'lived-in', and this is after all how it should be. This car has been somebody's joy for nigh on forty years, through thick and thin, year in year out, fair weather and foul. Often it's a pity to spring-clean the interior of an old car to such a degree that you destroy all the character and charm it ever possessed, but on the other hand too much downright 'grime' is understandably intolerable. That ancient head-lining probably hides more dust than you could ever imagine! And down the backs of those sticky faded-blue-leather seats lurk curios, coins and small souvenirs innumerable! Headlinings can be repaired or restored, upholstery rebuilt and door panels re-covered (as Chapter 10 explains); but do consider the number of man-hours entailed in this - a vacuum cleaner will barely make a scratch of difference, and polishing the dashboard won't get rid of that certain unlocatable 'smell' that could be coming from under the unexplored rear carpet!

The engine

Now, at last, is the time to open the bonnet and start up the engine. As the bonnet slowly and reverently rises, so will your hopes - but do be prepared to be let-down. This is a vehicle still in use on to-day's far-from-antiseptic roads, and it will show.

There is an indefinable sense of 'rightness' on looking at an engine which is original and complete in every detail. Everything seems to drop into place; there is a degree of symmetry and balance. Should you, on first inspection, sense this, then you have before you a prewar car that has been cherished. But if, on the other hand, as you peer here and there, you begin to get the notion that the bonnet conceals a host of 'make-do-and-mends', start peering more carefully.

Layers of grime, corroded alloy castings, oil oozing from old gaskets, water seeping from frayed hoses, white powder all over the top of the battery, rusty throttle linkages, tatty wiring, odd-make spark plugs, a cracked distributor cap, a missing oil-filler cap, a threadbare fan belt, the bulkhead eaten away by slopping battery acid... just a few points making-up a total picture of 'predestined trouble'. But a picture as black as this would be black indeed, and more often than not 50% of the overall to-be-maintained components of an engine should be found in fair condition - grime and dust on the outside can have no effect whatever on internal workings in most cases. A car as neglected as the one described above could never give more than a few minutes' reliable service per week, let alone be advertised as an 'MOT'd runner' priced quite probably at a couple of hundred pounds.

You may have to decide about some obvious 'adaptations', for example a non-original and home-made exhaust system, the fitting of a more modern carburetter or distributor and so on. There may be no way around the adaptations either - unless Car Club spares officers are having certain unique parts specially made, then tracing, say, the authentically built 'correct' exhaust system could prove impossible in the 1970s. Here we are on the border-line dividing 100%-authentic renovation from 80%-authentic; the owner may be able to clarify for you just why certain things are no longer as depicted in the yellowing pages of the rather soiled manual. You too may have to come to this vital decision at a later date - 'to run or not to run' may well be the question!

Now ask the owner to start the engine. Does he use the handle? Or pull the starter? The starting-handle was certainly there to be used before the war, as batteries and other electrics were nowhere near so perfected as they have been in recent years, and should the battery be genuinely flat then starting on the handle is essential, other than a 'push' start. But his mumbled excuses about resorting to the handle may be deliberately schemed to hide the fact that the teeth of the ring-gear are so worn that starting on the button is 'out', and were he to try you'd hear the most agonizing grinding sound from the starter motor! New ring-gears are shrunk on to the flywheel in the same way that the village blacksmith fitted iron rims to wooden cart wheels, heating the rim to red-heat so that it just slipped over the wheel's diameter. As metal cools, so it contracts, and like the iron rim the cooling ring-gear grips extremely tightly round the edges of the flywheel. But unlike cart wheels, flywheels are inaccessible objects. The engine needs to be completely removed from the car first, before you can begin to get at it - quite a Herculean task in some cases - so tackle the owner about why he hasn't used the starter-pull; your studies of the model should aid you in assessing such responses as: 'You always started these on the handle', 'The starter cable's snapped', 'I reckon the old solenoid's had it, don't you?', 'Starter's a bit groggy, that's all', 'Never got time to refit the starter', 'Yes, funny noise, wasn't it?' etc., etc.

A quick start and rapid burst of power is always very impressive, and quite rightly. It speaks of reliability at all times, correct maintenance, and mechanical skill. But should it be a winter morning, give the chap a chance. Elderly, low-compression engines sleep very soundly at night!

A rhythmic ticking noise, louder as the engine warms up, could be the tappets out of adjustment (or simply noisy tappets); 'lumpy' tickover indicates a worn or badly-tuned carburettor; a definite rythmic knock is more serious, i.e. wear in the big-end bearings (pull off each plug lead in turn - if the knock stops, that's the cylinder with the worn bearing); worse still is a rumble when the engine is revved up - this could be main-bearing wear, quite an expensive noise to quieten. Odd clickings and rattles could easily come from loose mountings or, say, the fan belt slapping the side of the bonnet, or a creaking water-pump.

As the engine is revved up, look back at the tail pipe for a cloud of blue smoke, more evident when the engine is thoroughly warm and the throttle smartly opened after a few minutes' tick-over. If the pastoral view behind suddenly 'disappears in the fog' you've conclusive proof that engine oil is being burnt by the engine somehow, either through valve-guide or cylinder wear. This is certainly not a crisis, but remember the cost of oil per pint nowadays and the bother that gummed-up plugs can cause. However, until you can get the time and money to put it right, burning oil for a month or two won't matter much, and valve-guide replacement is a fairly simple job, anyway. Special piston rings can also be fitted to help take up cylinder wear without resorting to a full rebore.

Dashboard clues

Should the dashboard sport an oil-pressure gauge, check the reading at medium revs i.e. the speed of an average engine pulling a car at 30-40 mile/h. A reading of from 40-70 lb/in^2 is perfectly satisfactory for most prewar light cars; oil-pressures were not always as high as they are in modern cars, and 40 lb/in^2 could represent the 'showroom' oil-pressure of this particular model. Others had even lower pressures, so your researches should be bearing fruit in cases like this. More often than not 'utility' light cars with simple side-valve engines were not fitted with an oil-pressure gauge or even a warning light, and here you may have to be trusting or even take a gamble; but should one be fitted leave reading the oil pressure until the engine is thoroughly warmed up. Bear in mind too that tick-over pressure was often very low in a prewar engine at working temperature; conversely, be prepared for an amazingly high 'freak' reading with the engine cold - thick, cold oil and a lazy pressure-release valve can whizz it up to around 90 lb/in^2 with no trouble.

Check also the ammeter - does it show that the dynamo is charging or not? A zero reading here could indicate a burnt-out dynamo or inoperative gauge, a 'minus' or discharge reading definitely indicating that the dynamo needs attention.

Don't bother to read the mileage meter; the car could well have been 'round the clock', that's to say has covered 99,999+ miles once, and may even be on the way to covering the same mileage again. Or (1) this is a replacement speedometer, (2) it's broken, (3) it's been disconnected for the past twenty years. The only true indication of mileage covered will be the overall mechanical and structural condition you can glean by looking hard. And if the owner has spent many years rebuilding so that once again everything appears brand new and glittering, you can expect him to demand a pretty 'glittering' price for his efforts - if you want 'A1 condition' in a car forty years old, you have to pay for it nowadays.

A test drive

Having judged the overall soundness of the engine, ask for a 'run out' in the car, as long as you are sure that your insurance covers you adequately. But first, before you actually take the wheel, let the owner drive. After all, he knows the car far more intimately, and by anticipating its idiosyncrasies can obtain smoother operation of the car as a whole; and if he is desirous to sell he'll certainly do his best to create a good impression. Of course, a little genuine deception may enter into it, but on the other hand you'll get a fairly good idea of what can be done by a driver who has particular experience with this car. And all 'elderly' cars need to be 'coaxed' to give of their best, anyway.

Now move into the driver's seat, readjust the rear-view mirror (if fitted), start up the engine, depress the clutch fully and select first gear. Silky? Or was there a nasty crunch before the gear went in? Back to neutral and try again, this time making sure the clutch pedal has been pushed right down to the floor. Better? If not, reluctance on the gearbox's part may be due to the clutch-pedal linkage being out of adjustment or the clutch friction-material worn out - this latter neccessitating quite a lot of overhaul work. By the early 1930s the single dry-disc clutch faced with 'Ferodo' material had superceded the leather-faced cone clutch of earlier years. Fierceness of action was a typical problem of the cone clutch, dressing the leather with 'Collan' oil effecting a remedy if you were lucky. And should that '1935 model' have in fact turned out to be the 1925 version due to a misprint in the advertisement, you could well be faced with clutch fierceness due to hardened leather. But not all 'snatch and grab' clutches belong to the Twenties - the omnipresent Austin Sevens of the 1930s are notorious for fierce take-up of the drive, a mere ¼-inch of travel in the clutch pedal separating 'clutch in' from 'clutch out'! So if it's an old 'Seven' don't be alarmed if you find yourself moving rapidly forward from halt in a series of kangaroo jumps.

Once in first gear, slowly release the clutch pedal and pull away. Fierceness here in a dry-disc clutch indicates that the 'Ferodo' clutch lining is worn down to the minimum, requiring replacement, a quick check being the amount of travel in the clutch pedal from fully-in to fully-out. Excepting the 'Seven' and very few others, a clutch in good condition provides about one full inch or more of latitude as it engages. A minute movement and a fierce 'snatch' both augur extreme clutch wear.

From first gear, move swiftly (but not jerkily) through all the gears and into top. Probably the centrally-situated gearbox will have the conventional 'floor change' gear-lever and 'H'-type gate; four-speed gearboxes will provide a speed on each leg of the 'H', whereas with a three-speed box one of the legs will be reverse; reverse in a four-speed unit being selected by pulling the gear-knob up and across, then down into a fifth position. First, and quite possibly second, gear will not necessarily be synchromesh, so allow for one or two 'crunches' due more to your own inefficiency than the car's. But if after quite a few gear-changes you begin to find it impossible to change sweetly, than it would appear to indicate definite clutch or gearbox trouble. Your 'enthusiast' owner may even be running with a dry gearbox.

Whilst moving along in top gear, take an occasional glance at the speedometer to check that it's working, and at the oil-pressure gauge. Once the engine is really hot, verify that the 'under-load' oil-pressure is fairly good, while at crossroads you'll have a further chance to read the tick-over pressure and compare it with information you may have picked up from club members.

Next, having checked that it's safe to do so, stop the car by applying a firm and increasing pressure to the brake pedal. Don't try to get a screeching skid, of course, but judge the effective retardation and whether the car keeps on a straight course or tends to veer to one side. Poor retardation, and this latter fault, will indicate impending attention in the very near future. New brake linings, and not merely adjustment, may well be necessary; oily linings or scored brake drums are far from 'ten minutes' work'; brake snatch may be the result of severe wear where the brake-lining rivets are contacting the scored surface of the drums. All is well should the pulling-up effect be satisfactory, coupled with an effective handbrake; prewar non-hydraulic brakes in good order can still prove quite adequate for modern driving, as long as allowance is made for the fact that their total efficiency can never quite approach that of a modern hydraulic system. All leverages, too, are directly mechanical, and your right foot has to do a certain amount of extra work to overcome the inherent friction in the linkages. The MOT test stipulates 65% retardation with the foot-brake and 35% with the handbrake, both checked by the Tapley retardometer from a steady speed of 20 mile/h and if possible without any skidding - so prewar rod or cable brakes can 'sail through' the test if correctly adjusted and maintained.

Vibration in the transmission or a hum from the rear axle *en route* are both warning signs of the approach of future bother for you. The axle will probably go on humming for a year or two and quite merrily at that, whereas shaft vibration really gets on your nerves and you'll soon be forced to attend to it one none-too-distant Saturday afternoon.

The Morris, MG and Wolseley factories all fitted hydraulic brakes to their cars from about 1930 on, so should it be a model from one of

In ten years of the British light cars, the contrast was staggering. In 1931 there were cars like the Alvis 12/50 Drophead Coupe (top) whilst in 1939 many looked like the Morris Twelve Series III Saloon (below)

these stables, expect to find brakes of near modern efficiency. 'Spongy' action of the brake pedal plus a indecisive brake-action speak of air bubbles in the system and the need for bleeding (fairly simple, though time-consuming). Veering over to one side could be a corroded brake cylinder on a front wheel; poor slowing-up perhaps indicating corrosion all round or bad adjustment of the mechanical side of the system. If you find yourself desperately pumping the brake pedal in order to miss that stray cat, the need for more than just immediate bleeding is imminent - you could find a fractured Bundy tube somewhere and most of the brake fluid left behind on the road. In general though, hydraulics that receive some yearly maintenance should prove more than adequate for the Seventies, even should they have seen some forty summers.

How much play did you notice in the steering? About one inch of circumferential play at the steering wheel is allowed by the MOT test - so beware of that 'rubbery' feeling on corners, as if the steering were operated by elastic - an indecisive, 'remote' feeling as you negotiate bends or try to steer a straight course. Wear in the steering gear can often only be remedied by the replacement of new or reconditioned parts, but even a thorough greasing can take up what was apparent sloppiness and make a tremendous difference in ease of driving. Don't expect light steering - quite a lot of weight was centred over the front wheels in those days, and worm-and-wheel or cam-and-lever steering gear so in vogue before the war gave a heavy, low-geared feel, markedly so as total bodywork weight increased progressively from around 1936 when pressed-steel bodies began to come in. If your present car has rack-and-pinion or even powered steering then you're going to notice the difference. Really stiff steering however, heralds the call of the grease-gun.

When you climb out of the car (often literally with some cars of the era) ask, if it isn't clamped to the back of the body, to have a look at the spare wheel. We all know that 'every car has five wheels' and it's that invisible fifth one we so depend on at times - so be firm and get him to rummage around in the shed to find it. Absence of a spare could mean that you're grounded for

weeks or even months while you write dozens of letters trying to get hold of one.

Nowadays prewar wheels are becoming scarce even with the specialists; minute variations in hub-fittings can prove exasperating, too, as you climb piles of wrecked cars at the local breakers'! One temporary way out is to get new tyres fitted and carry an extensive repair outfit just in case.

Be realistic

Finally - the price. If you have gone to the trouble of researching into the market price of the model now offered for sale, in various degrees of preservation, you'll have a fairly clear 'ceiling price' in mind, having looked the car over. But a missing spare wheel and evidence of 'backyard modifications', or worse, of the demon rust steadily gnawing its way through the underside, are all haggling points definitely in your favour. Keep calm, and push any romantic notions of a glittering renovation accomplished by you in a very short time well back into their true perspective. All elderly cars need careful nursing, and a diet of all your free time well-mixed with quite a large helping of hard cash.

So try to visualize all the work you feel will be necessary to get the car back into the kind of overall condition you'd like. Add this on to the initial price he's asking, then tot up the pros and cons.

Never buy blindly - fight that compulsive inner voice coaxing you into believing that 'car No.1 is it - what could be easier?' It's too simple to confuse fact with fantasy and just give in to yourself. How many other Swift Six Coupes have you looked at? There may well be several others for sale within a hundred miles radius of you, and they could be in better shape, too. So don't 'plunge in' and regret it later; know what you're looking for. And if you're not too sure, any unscrupulous owner (thankfully very few and far-between) may rapidly latch on to this and begin to pull the wool over your glazed eyes!

Should he be open and honest with you, then give him a chance, too. Don't strike too cautious a pose. Just imagine if you were in his shoes -

'old cars' are by definition old, and a little weary. Precision tolerances and a crisp, functional performance will most probably be absent, and if he tells you quite openly that 'of course, she burns a bit of oil', and 'crunches second, I'm afraid', then give him credit for not trying to trick you. If you're new to old cars, be receptive to that indefinable bond that is easily struck once you get talking to someone who is really in love with the prewar aesthetics of motoring. Then, and only then, can the right climate prevail for genuine bargaining.

Chapter Three New lease of life: the 'non-runner'

Cobwebs and corrosion can make a picturesque sight of an old abondoned wire-wheeled two-seater, slumbering almost unnoticed amid the dust of some rickety outbuilding. The romance of sunnier days and an earlier, more exciting age floods into the imagination.

But it's pure fantasy. The last time that engine ran was in 1946, on perhaps a precious gallon of rationed 'Pool' petrol, possibly even laced with a little ether to pep it up a bit. And how it played havoc with the valves - came 1948, and her last reincarnation simply ended in a cough and a splutter - so she was pushed into a derilict shed and forgotten.

These are the realities behind the golden legend. Hibernation sets-in very deeply as the years roll on, and machinery standing idle can rapidly deteriorate, sometimes beyond repair. Steel rusts, alloy and chromium corrode, rubber decays, wiring rots. And unless someone can think back and remember exactly why the car was garaged all those years ago, you can't even be sure that, say, the engine isn't wrecked internally, there being no possibility of ever making it run again. A dry storage space with a dusty earth floor bodes a certain degree of promise; corrosion will have proceeded only slowly and superficially, often merely to the detriment of outer appearance. But a leaking roof and a dank feeling everywhere will have already cut short any dreams of her ever gracing the highways again. Sometimes a lot of time, money and engineering can save a virtual wreck (even Parry Thomas's 'Babs' has been recently excavated from beneath Pendine Sands, where it has lain for forty-eight salty and highly-

corrosive years) but how many of us have extensive workshops at home? It's best to play safe and not fill your garage with a rusty epitaph that after a brief stay is dragged off to the hydraulic press, to emerge as a rusty cube. 'Non-runners' are extremely tricky to size-up unless you've worked on quite a few of them before, and very often only X-ray eyes can detect what's lurking within old crankcases and beneath corroded rocker-covers! Who knows, it could be pieces of a bronze bush scattered here and there, or a fragment of piston ring that many moons ago did a 'Grand Tour' of the entire engine, scoring bores and wrecking bearings.

But should you want to chance your luck with a 'non-runner', do inspect what you can see of the chassis first; and if the car is of unit-construction, where the floor-cum-door-pillars provide a structural basis for the engine and transmission mountings, look very hard indeed.

What price should one pay? This is of course relative to the rarity of the model, but in general don't give very much for a very dormant and rusty hulk. The total weight of metal cannot be worth more than a few pounds and if you and several others don't want it, then this is all that the average breaker will offer - again, beware of paying to indulge your sense of pathos - you can't argue with forty years of corrosion.

Once you have purchased your 'non-runner' you're going to need some tools for tinkering, and today's AF and Metric spanners will prove of little use. A full set of BSF/Whitworth open-ended spanners, some ring spanners, and small and large screwdrivers will provide a good start. To these can be added a new adjustable spanner, a 14/18 mm double-ended spark plug box-spanner, a sharp cold chisel, a hammer, and so on. Also take along some clean rags, an oil can, a tin of Plus Gas, another of Redex, a funnel, and even possibly a blow-lamp for dealing with badly seized nuts. PVC-coated work gloves, too, can often allay much of the unpleasant grime and oil from getting all over the hands and deep under the fingernails.

Rusted cylinder bores

It's natural to want to try and get the engine to go first. But certain factors need to be considered before you do. Often it's far safer to devote the first weekend to removing the spark plugs and pouring half an eggcupful of Redex into each cylinder bore. This done, leave the lubricant for seven days to loosen the cementing action of any rust there may be between the piston rings and the cylinders. If you rashly start applying leverage to the starting-handle regardless of whether the engine may be rusted solid, then something is bound to give, particularly if you force the issue. You could well do severe damage, rewarding your impatience with a large bill for new engine parts.

So try the handle very gently - and should there be the slightest sign of resistance, leave well alone until the Redex has had a chance. Should you suspect rusted valve-gear, warm up the valve-guides with the blow-lamp and then apply lubricant. Main bearings cannot rust solid as they are of a non-rusting soft alloy, and neither can big-end bearings or little-end bronze bushes; areas of the engine that can rust solid are where two ferrous metals contact each other closely.

Should you discover rusted-in spark plugs, apply Plus Gas, then the blow-lamp and then some smart blows from your hammer via the cold chisel against a corner where two 'flats' meet on the plug. Always allow time for the rust solvent to act.

Frost damage or leaks

Choose, if possible, the warmer part of the year for tinkering. Trying to coax an old engine to fire on frosty February mornings, and groping for tools with frozen fingers, can be agony. If it has to be winter, then certainly dress up for the job, keeping the small of your back warm in particular (trying to straighten up after hours of bending over a dingy bonnet can be painful!) Look around for signs of frost damage, such as core-plugs forced out by ice in the water-jacket, or far worse, a cracked block. When the cylinder block is cast in a sand mound, holes have to be left to remove the 'core' of sand from the hollow passages after casting. In the assembled engine, core-plugs (domed discs, hammered into the holes) seal the cylinder jacket so that it retains the cooling water; when accidentally frozen, the core-plugs are forced out allowing a certain amount of expansion, and if you're lucky the block doesn't crack. Severe freezing can easily split the block open - hence the need for antifreeze. (It's a myth, by the way, that manufacturers fit core-plugs to prevent split blocks, although they can act as a safety device in a case of mild freezing!)

Blocks cracked by frost can be repaired by welding, but are the realm of a specialist since cast iron is very tricky to weld. Core-plugs cost little more than a few pence, and after scraping the lime out of the bevelled edge of the hole the plug is pressed squarely into its recess and then struck smartly once or twice with a hammer. As the domed plug flattens, so it spreads and seals the aperture. An application of Hermetite will guarantee a perfect seal, but is not generally necessary.

An engine that has been lying idle for many years with a bone-dry cooling system can often suffer from gasket shrinkage, particularly the one under the cylinder head. So try filling the radiator and inspect for water seepage. Old hoses, too, will be perished and leaky, so on the first weekend be content with preparing to start the engine in a week's time - measure the old hoses for diameter using calipers (Fig. 1) and during the week purchase new ones. Radiator leaking? Another job for the specialist (see the Appendix), as often Bar's Leaks won't cure it. But you'll still be able to run the engine for a short time without any coolant, so don't despair; just remember to switch off after a

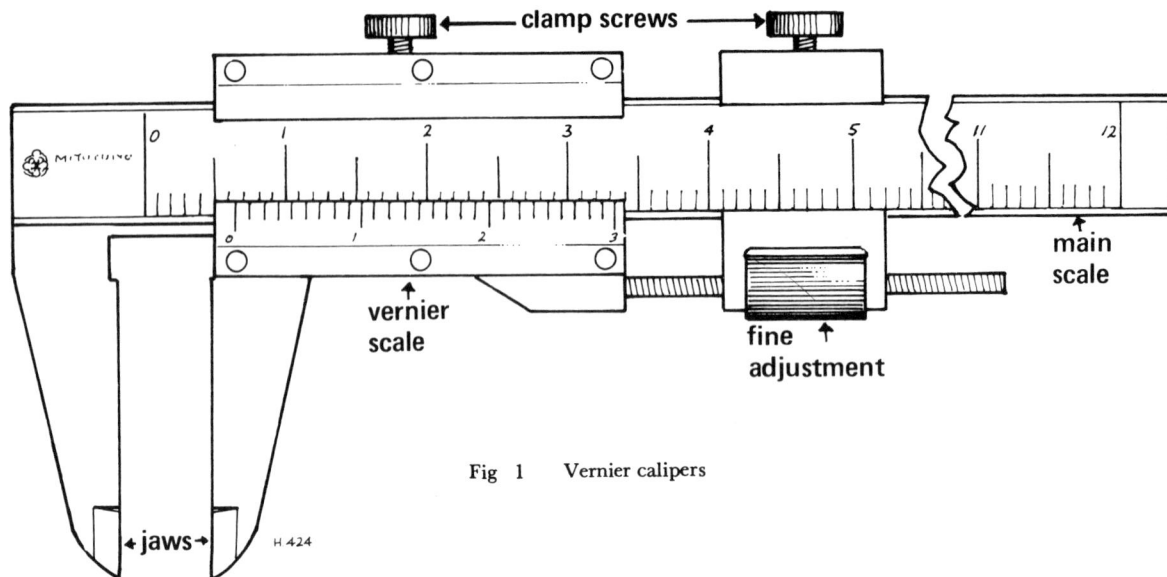

Fig 1   Vernier calipers

couple of minutes, no matter how delighted or amazed you are to hear her running.

Leaving the cooling system filled for a week can be risky in the depths of winter, so drain it, or fill with an antifreeze mixture. Better to drain it off, as you'll be using hot water next time in order to get a quick start.

Charged battery essential

Before you go, take a look at the battery. Not too lovingly though, as it will be completely sulphated and useless after all those years. You'll need to obtain a replacement, fully charged, of the correct voltage. Look again at the old one - three filler-plugs means a six-volt, six filler-plugs show it's a twelve-volt battery. Sometimes two six-volt batteries were connected together to give a total of twelve volts, and were hidden under the back seat, astride the transmission shaft. Here the connecting-cable will be badly corroded, so rinse it in hot water and see whether you'll need to get a new one made up. Always take the old one along as a pattern. An alternative for starting-experiments is the substitution of a single twelve-volt battery of the correct total amp-hour capacity.

Should the battery be missing, inspect the serial-number plate fixed to the generator. Lucas have always stamped the output voltage either on this plate or in the casing; scratch off the old black enamel in the latter case. Failing this for some reason, glance at the cap of the SU petrol pump, should one be fitted; here again the operating voltage will be given and this applies to the entire electrical system, so if it reads '6v' then you need a six-volt battery, and so on. If you're still stuck, take out a headlamp bulb and trace the voltage this way.

Most important to avoid frustration - your new battery must have the correct terminal posts to suit the size and type of clamps on the car's battery leads. And one final reminder - make sure the battery's fully charged. You may have to go down to the last milliamp before she fires, so the larger the amp-hour capacity the better. Something the size of a tea caddy is barely worth bringing unless you're expert with a starting handle.

Should the existing spark plugs look very weary, buy a new set, again taking one along as a pattern. Get the thread size and the reach right. Casually popping a long-reach plug into a short-reach plug recess can spell disaster when piston crown and plug come into contact. Large 'fat' plugs will probably be 18 mm and could mean a delay while the shop are trying to get you some.

If the sump oil-level was low, buy a gallon of multigrade 20W/50 oil for topping-up. Don't be too fussy about getting a 'straight 20 or 30 SAE' oil, just because the manual says so. A nice modern detergent multigrade oil will act as a wonderful tonic, and in winter will give the starter motor far less load.

Week number two: turning her over

Having allowed some days for that Redex to act, bring along those new hoses, the battery, a couple of gallons of fresh petrol and the gallon of oil. Don't forget those BSW spanners and other tools - or the clean rags; you'll also need a fair supply of both patience and determination. Pour about 1½ gallons of petrol into the tank, keeping the rest in reserve. Next top-up the sump. Slip the gear lever into neutral, reach for the starting handle and very gently try turning the engine. You could well hear some odd noises as any internal rust gives way and frees the rings in the cylinders, but should the engine still feel 'locked', do all you can to find out why, before even thinking of 'brute force'. Broken crank-shafts or piston rings don't like to be disturbed! Your only plan is to strip the engine down - a long, and perhaps not very worthwhile task. But such are the trials and tribulations of the 'old car' enthusiast; it's very rarely plain sailing, and this could be the first time your ardent enthusiasm has to stand the test. You will know whether you want to pursue your 'gamble' any further or not.

But this is the blacker side, after all. Most probably you'll feel a sweet, supple swing on the handle and then the reassuring resistance as one of the cylinders comes up to compression. Next remove the old plugs and turn her over ten or twenty times to loosen things up, fit the new set of plugs (gapped at about 0.020 in.) and re-place the HT leads, in the correct order. Most four-cylinder engines fire 1-3-4-2 and six-cylinder 1-5-3-6-2-4, number one cylinder being at the front nearest the radiator. Prewar Alvises, Rileys, Fords and Rovers were 'odd men out', firing 1-2-4-3; Jowetts fired 1-4-2-3, however.

Fuel system troubles

Use your spare petrol to fill the float-chamber(s) of the carburetter(s) by hand. This can give a quick start and 'short circuit' any petrol pump problems. These can be sorted out later! Signs of rust and muck inside a float - chamber dictate the need for a thorough clean-out before proceeding any further; jets, too, may need cleaning (unscrew them and hold up to the light) but never use a piece of wire - blow through them hard to dislodge specks of grit, rinse in petrol, then refit. Zenith and Solex jets machined with a square recess are removed using the square-ended float-chamber bolt as a jet key: early '30s bronze Zeniths require a tool resembling a large clock key to remove the jets, as they are machined with a square protrusion. The jet on an SU carburetter is located beneath the instrument and held in position by a hexagonal nut. After thorough cleaning (the piston and suction-disc may be badly corroded and will need freeing - see Fig. 20), top-up the dash pot with a thimble full of Redex. A punctured float, which is quite rare however, will reveal itself upon replacement. If you're suspicious about it, you can check it in two ways: (1) after leaving in the float-chamber for a few minutes remove it and shake close to your ear - petrol splashing inside the float is one clue, (2) place the float in a cup of hot water and look for a stream of small air bubbles from the leak. Repairing a float by soldering must be done very delicately, and having ensured that all trapped petrol has evaporated, the very minimum of solder must be employed or the float will be unbalanced and petrol-level radically disturbed. It's often far easier to pick up a good float from a breaker or friendly garage; floats are fairly standardized, although early '30s carburetters designed for gravity-feed via an Autovac had specially-made types with different overall dimensions. Here also check that the tiny bob-weights under the float-chamber lid are free to pivot under the rising action of the float; if they are corroded the needle cannot cut off the petrol supply and you'll get bad flooding. You must treasure that old bronze carburetter - if you lose or break parts you'll find it almost impossible to get replacements! Badly corroded jets with rounded-off keyways will have to be gently cleaned with thin brass wire, or can be removed using a small 'Eze-Out' stud-extractor (see Fig. 2) so long as you have another jet to replace each with. A suitable hole is drilled through the jet, the extractor screwing-in anticlockwise. Gentle heat and Plus Gas will aid the process.

Bolt up the carburetter(s) again and replace the throttle linkage, taking care in the case of twin carburetters to reset the distances exactly as they were originally, otherwise the petrol-air mixtures will no longer be synchronized. Now connect up the battery and switch on the ignition. Fig. 3 explains how to get round the problem if you have no ignition key.

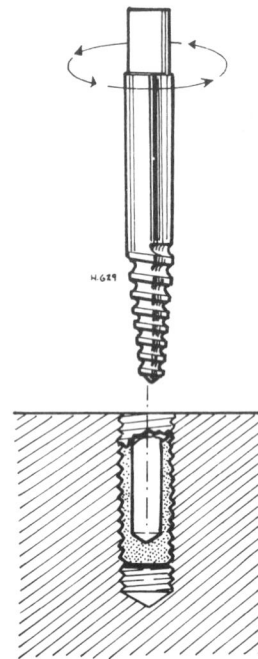

Fig 2   'Eze out' stud extractor

Fig 3   Bypassing the ignition key

Fig 4   Polythene 'squeeze' bottle

An immediate clicking sound indicates an electric SU petrol pump or an early Petrolift, its direct forerunner. All being well, the clicking will soon slow down and stop, the fuel line from the tank to the carburetter(s) now being full, together with the float-chamber(s). If the noise fails to stop, switch off - the pump valves are bone dry and because of an inadequate seal cannot produce suction. Disconnect the fuel pipe at the carburetter inlet and squirt some petrol via a 'squeeze bottle' (Fig. 4) along the petrol pipe and into the pump. As soon as the pump valves are moistened they will function properly and provide suction as soon as you switch on again. If the electric pump is situated under the bonnet you may be able to loosen both the inlet and outlet connections on the pump body itself and prime the pump far more directly. With the SU Petrolift, undo the cap at the top and pour a little petrol into the top chamber; by then lifting the cork float up and down you should be able to hear the solenoid actuating, and clicks coming from the electrical contacts inside the unit.

If you turn the key and hear nothing, you may have a faulty electric petrol-pump, or on the other hand the carburetter may be fed via a mechanical pump. There are two alternatives in this case. If it's an early '30s car an Autovac may be fitted, working from manifold vaccum: from about 1934 onwards the Autovac was superceded by an early type of AC pump operated by a rocker arm driven by an eccentric cam on the engine. The Autovac is, (see Fig. 23) like the Petrolift, a farily bulky instrument, located under the bonnet, and linking the tank to the carburetter. If it has run dry it's best to prise off the brass elbow-joint at the top marked 'Petrol Inlet' and with a small funnel partly fill the upper chamber with petrol; this will moisten the valve seatings and top-up the fuel level in the carburetter. Or you can fill the float-chamber of the carburetter, and by running the engine, get the Autovac to operate on manifold vacuum in the normal way. The gaskets on an Autovac may, however, be cracked or shrunk, and it will not operate unless all joints are hermetically sealed - here you must dismantle, clean thoroughly, lubricate the valves, and reassemble with new gaskets cut from thickish gasket paper and sealed with red Hermetite compound. Check too that the vacuum pipe from the manifold to the top of the Autovac isn't blocked by engine sludge.

The AC mechanical petrol-pump, still widely in use to-day, is a smaller unit, situated low down at the side of the crankcase. Early types are easily spotted due to their glass filter-bowl. As with many early niceties, this was soon deleted, later pumps being a very utilitarian all-metal affair - but nonetheless extremely efficient and trouble-free. As stated above, this type of pump operates from an eccentric cam affixed to the camshaft, a rocker arm actuating a rubber diaphragm and producing suction by means of spring-loaded valves. If the valve seatings are dry, they need wetting with petrol, injected into the pump through the pipe connections. Lack of operation may then be due to a punctured diaphragm, accessible by removing the cap at the top of the pump casing. After replacement with a new part, reassembly is best carried out with the pump removed from its mounting; the diaphragm must be fully flexed before bolting the cap down, and this is done by pulling the rocker arm upwards to its fullest extent while the screws are tightened up. The diaphragm cannot be flexed with the pump fitted to the engine.

All petrol pumps are fitted with filters - don't overlook the possibility of one being blocked. Scrub the gauze clean with an old toothbrush moistened with petrol; (don't prod it with a needle which can open the mesh wide enough for particles to then pass through and block the smaller carburetter jets).

One of the earliest and simplest methods of petrol supply was by gravity feed. An early or 'unadventurous' model may sport a scuttle tank at the rear of the bonnet - not the best place to carry petrol, and one which prompted designers to develop an efficient fuel pump so that the tank could be located at the rear and dangerous accidents involving fire avoided. But a model with a scuttle tank will be older and rarer, and normal usage should afford no hazards whatever, of course - you could well be the envy of your Car Club! With a 'non-runner' all you need to check is that the petrol tap and filter are not blocked, and that any layers of rust particles are cleaned out from the bottom of the tank.

Should the tank filler-cap be missing, investigate the interior of the tank first. Don't waste six gallons of petrol by pouring the golden liquid into a tank full of dead leaves or chicken feathers! Loosening the drain plug can often be difficult (or downright impossible) - you could try tipping-in half a gallon first, loosening the sludge by raking about on the bottom with a flexible Bowden cable, and then sucking the petrol back via the 'squeeze bottle' fitted with a length of neoprene tubing. Alternatively, remove the tank by loosening the tank straps, pour in some petrol plus a handful of small clean pebbles and shake the tank hard for as long as you've patience for. Then tip out, repeat the process, and replace the tank.

Be very wary of old, stale petrol - that heavy, foul-smelling liquid often to be found in the tanks of old, 'forgotten' cars. Ancient petrol degenerates into something not far removed from paraffin, and it is absolutely useless for starting. Get rid of it and replace with fresh. Many are the hours that have been wasted due to stale petrol and dormant engines!

Getting her started

Now into the driver's seat, switch on once more and pull the starter, often marked with an 'S'. A burst of life? No - well try again, with a bit of choke this time. A few splutters...clouds of smoke... and she's running! Stay where you are and keep blipping that throttle till she warms up. Now you can take your foot off and enjoy the satisfying sound of a perhaps erratic, but willing tick-over. Check the exterior of the engine for oil or water seepage and if all's well, with plenty of water in the cooling system, leave her running at tick-over speed for five minutes or so. The oil-pressure gauge will tell you about the oil pump and whether prolonged running is wise or not, and the ammeter will indicate any charge from the dynamo.

No luck

In the author's experience, using the starter-motor to turn the engine over rapidly often guarantees far greater chances of getting an old engine to start than breaking your back on the starting handle. A fast cranking-speed brings up both compression and oil pressure, and the momentum of the flywheel actually conserves battery power once the engine is revolving fairly fast. So first try her quite a few times on the starter, pausing occasionally to allow the battery to clear of polarisation caused by hydrogen bubbles collecting on the plates and reducing the effective current. Hot water in the cooling system and a viscostatic grade of oil will help things too, as will a good battery with plenty of charge.

But after quite a few pulls on the starter it's best to conserve the battery and resort to the handle. Bring it up to the top and just against compression, then smartly swing it down, keeping the thumb tucked into the palm of the hand. Endeavouring to whirl the engine round and round is exhausting, and quite pointless. A sharp pull is most effective, and you can go on for far longer. Try a 'push' start? Here again it's little more than a gamble, and a tiring one at that. Flat tyres need to be pumped up first, and a long spell of pushing often leads to frayed tempers and a feeling of despair. Far better to save your energy and take things calmly. Once she's run down that hill, how are you going to get her back?

Should it be winter, then you've chosen the very worst time for tinkering. Even the highest octane petrol is reluctant to inject life into frozen cylinders. One tip is to prime the engine with Ether Solvent, an extremely volatile and highly inflammable liquid, available at most chemists. Four fluid ounces will be ample: pour some of it into the 'squeeze bottle' or a small oil can that's free of oil and you're ready to prime the engine. In the Twenties and early Thirties sluggish aero engines were often primed with ether for a quick start; one failing with modern aerosol 'quick start' preparations is the admixture of upper-cylinder lubricant with the ingredients, which rapidly accumulates on the plugs and kills what may well be a weak spark. Pure ether cannot foul plugs, but cigarettes must be stamped out in the interests of safety, ether vapour being even more hostile towards naked flames than petrol.

Remove the air cleaner on the carburetter (if fitted) or the small domed metal cover clamped over the air-intake on certain prewar Zenith and Solex units. Now inject a small amount of ether into the throat of the carburetter and open the throttle so that the liquid vaporizes in the manifold. Give the starting handle a good swing over compression; if the ignition is functioning correctly and the timing is set accurately you should soon get her to fire and finally pick up. Make sure the ignition isn't fully advanced. Early cars with an ignition lever on the steering-wheel boss were generally started fully retarded (marked 'R') and en route were advanced (position 'A'), retarding the ignition on hills or long uphill gradients. It's best to set the lever half-way at first, particularly if priming with ether, so as to avoid sharp, and sometimes painful, kick-backs. Carry on priming with ether until the cylinders get warm enough for the engine to catch on petrol; you can only expect short, unsustained bursts of power from the ether, but it will fire even in sub-zero conditions. If you use nearly all the ether and still can't get a single 'cough' it points very definitely to ignition trouble.

You might even be adventurous enough to try warming the engine up not on petrol, but on Calor gas. Fit a very fine metal jet at the end of the gas lead, crack open the gas valve a small fraction, and direct the jet of gas into the carburetter intake. A petrol engine will fire on butane gas, and if the gas-air mixture is carefully regulated, will run for sufficiently long intervals for the cylinders to warm up. In fact, correctly adjusted, no carburetter is necessary; it may be removed and the gas directed straight into the manifold (at the correct distance for air to be drawn in as well, of course). In cases of carburetter trouble, this method could prove a quick substitute and minimize the number of troublesome 'variables'.

No spark

Old magnetos, ignition coils and condensers are bound to deteriorate through corrosion, their insulation breaking down when stored for years in damp conditions. Non-functioning coils and condensers cannot be repaired, but an electric hair-dryer is invaluable for drying-out damp electrical systems and often it is found that ignition troubles are due to damp more than decay. So before ripping out the coil and condenser, thoroughly dry out the entire ignition circuit - spray it with an aerosol water-repellent, if you like. One such dispersent is called WD 40, and can prove very effective and rapid-acting.

Having tried drying-out the electrics but to no avail, should you suspect the coil or condenser then substitute it with one that you know is in good order. Check that it's of the right voltage for the car. All coils are stamped with either '6v' or '12v' and a six-volt coil will burn out if operated at twelve volts. Condensers simply retain very high voltages for extremely short periods of time to avoid burning at the contact-breaker points; here battery voltage is arbitrary.

Coils may be tested for broken circuits by means of a test lamp and the battery (see Fig.5). The primary winding connects the 'SW' terminal with earth, likewise the secondary winding connects the 'CB' terminal with earth (the outer casing of the coil, in both circuits), 'SW'

meaning switch wire, and 'CB' standing for contact-breaker. To test either circuit for breakdown, earth one lead of the test lamp (the bulb should be, say, a small dashboard type of either six or twelve volts) to the casing of the coil and connect the other lead to the appropriate terminal. The bulb failing to light indicates a broken circuit, and since coils are sealed, you'll need a replacement. Condensers cannot be effectively tested, and anyway are relatively cheap.

Magnetos, so long beloved by the Brooklands racing fraternity, are however very susceptible to damp, and produce their weakest spark at low rotational speeds. So cranking-over a senile engine fitted with an elderly and rather damp magneto can prove especially futile and exceptionally frustrating! Having first carefully marked with chalk the exact position of the drive coupling to the engine, remove the magneto and dry it out thoroughly. Clean all terminals, the commutator, contact-breaker points etc. (see Chapter 6 for more details), and then reassemble. If you don't mind mild 'shocks', flick the magneto over in your hand,

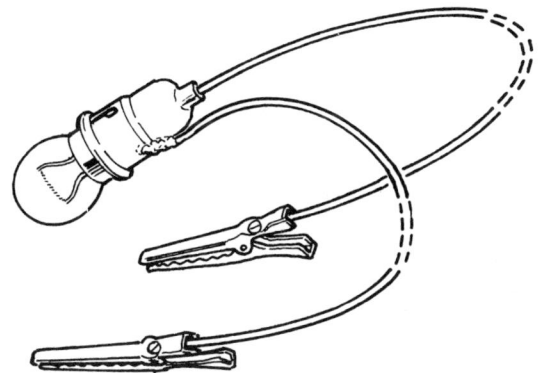

Fig 5   Simple test lamp

touching one terminal with a finger. A magneto in fair condition will certainly make you jump, and should you be working at the kitchen table, try connecting a short length of HT lead to a spark plug, earthing it to the magneto casing. Again, a good magneto will give an audible, blue spark even when spun over by hand. Under compression, though, the HT voltage from a magneto has much more to do than jump an open air-gap, and this is where a damp or rickety magneto fails, particularly if operating at very low cranking-speeds. Magnetos only come into their own at high speeds, and here the strength of spark increases with speed, hence their wide use in prewar racing cars - but back to your car - is it only damp that can cause trouble?

Unlike the distributor used with coil ignition, a magneto employs a certain number of shafts and gear-wheels to govern the operation of the contact breaker and gear down the speeds of certain of the internal components. Teeth get broken, bushes wear oval, magnet-strength decays, ebonite cracks, and eventually you're left with a impressively-engineered but very dead electrical 'dodo'. Often, however, completely dismantling, cleaning and relubricating the magneto can work wonders - this, plus a thorough drying-out usually rekindles the spark.

Checking the spark

Coil ignition can only be checked *in situ* on the engine. First remove one of the spark plugs, wipe the ceramic insulator clean and lay the plug down on the cylinder-head, where it has good earth contact, reconnecting the HT lead (see Fig.6). To conserve manpower, take out all the remaining plugs so you can crank the engine easily. Switch on the ignition, turn the engine and observe the plug gap. Your aim should be a fat, blue, snappy spark timed at a certain regular interval. Pink, feeble sparks are not good enough to overcome the compression in the cylinders; there could still be damp present, so leave the bonnet open in the sun if possible. Coil ignition gives a spark of constant strength irrespective of distributor revs, so cranking-speed doesn't matter. And if in doubt, substitute with a brand new plug - they, too, don't last for ever.

Dirty contact-breaker points adversely affect both magneto and coil ignition. Open the gap with the tip of a screwdriver and clean them with either fine carborundum paper or a petrol-soaked lintless rag. All traces of oil must be removed too from under the contact-breaker and around the condenser earthing-connection. Check all wiring from the coil, through the distributor, to the HT leads and plugs. With magneto ignition, simply check the leads and the plugs - if the magneto remains absolutely 'dead', entrust it to a specialist for repair (see Appendix).

A spark without fire

If you have a healthy spark but no life from the engine, even if primed with ether, there are four possible explanations: (1) burnt valves, corroded or fractured piston rings, or perforated piston crowns - all reducing compression markedly, (2) HT leads connected to the plugs in the wrong order (3) ignition - or, (4) valve timing incorrect. Number one is quite simple to put right - regrind the valve seats or fit new valves (plus inserts if necessary) and replace

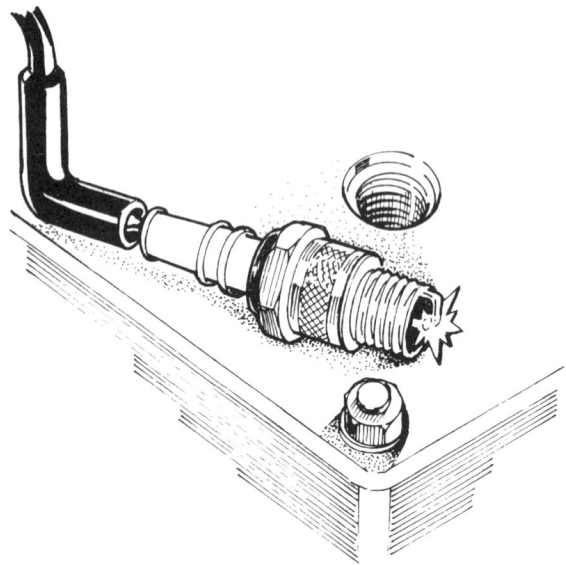

Fig 6   Testing the spark

other faulty parts with new. Number two can be corrected by referring to Part 2, and having traced the correct firing order, reconnecting the leads accordingly. As was stated previously, a common firing-order for four-cylinder engines is 1-3-4-2, and for six-cylinder engines 1-5-3-6-2-4; in general the cylinders are numbered with No.1 nearest the radiator. (Riley, Rover Alvis and Ford cars differed in that their firing-order was 1-2-4-3.) Remove all the plugs, reconnect the leads, and lay the plugs flat down on the top of the cylinder head so that each is well earthed. With the ignition on, turn the engine over slowly by hand and observe the sparks at the plugs and the order in which they occur. If wrong, swap over the leads so that the correct firing-order is restored. Once corrected, mark the leads so as to avoid confusion in future. Incorrect ignition timing may be due to a loose distributor pinch-bolt (Fig. 7) or incorrect setting by a previous owner. Loosen the pinch-bolt and experiment in moving the distributor body a few degrees at a time either in, or against, the direction of the rotor. The former retards the ignition, the latter advances it. You can do this either on your own, swinging the engine over after each adjustment to see if the engine will fire, or with an assistant pressing the starter button and keeping it depressed while you slowly rotate the distributor. But if you are adverse to trial-and-error, you can locate Top Dead Centre (tdc) in cylinder No. 1 and then set the ignition timing relative to this. Having traced the manufacturer's setting by reference to the manual, your Car Club, or Part 2 of this book, tdc may be ascertained in several ways. The most direct method is to find some kind of marking on the rim of the flywheel, visible on lifting a small inspection plate at the rear of the engine and usually mounted in the floorboards. It may be in the form of a short die-punched line and can bear the numbers '1-4' or '1-6'. When this mark is at its highest point on the 'crest' of the flywheel, cylinders 1 and 4 (or 1 and 6) are at tdc i.e. the piston is at its highest point of travel. But most important is to ensure that the piston is rising on the compression stroke, with both inlet and exhaust valves closed, as the spark has to occur at this particular instant. The flywheel mark also appears when cylinder No. 1 is at tdc on its

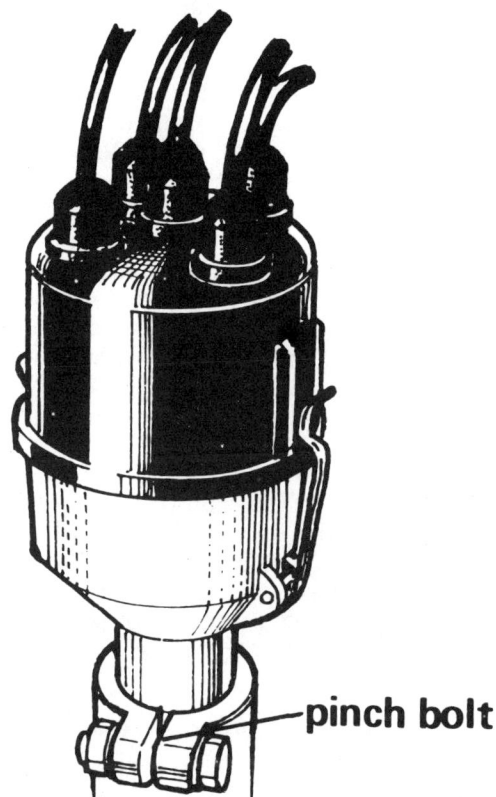

Fig 7   Distributor pinch bolt

exhaust stroke (the exhaust valve will be open in this case), but this position should not be confused with the tdc point on the compression stroke.

Let us imagine that the correct ignition timing is 10° before Top Dead Centre (10° btdc) or perhaps described as '1/16 in. btdc' as is found in many prewar manuals. By making a circular cardboard disc marked off in degrees around the circumference (or you can buy a plastic degree disc from motor-cycle shops) and fixing it to the fan pulley (or equivalent) at the front of the engine, the position at which the pulley's rotation is 10° before the 'zero point' i.e. 0° btdc or tdc, may be easily judged. At this instant the contact-breaker points should just be beginning to open, so rotate the body of the distributor until this is effected, lock the pinch-bolt, and the ignition timing is now correct.

Should there be no visible tdc markings on the flywheel or fan pulley, tdc may be found by inserting a foot length of wooden dowel through a spark plug hole and rotating the engine until the dowel, resting on top of the piston, rises to its highest point. Never, by the way, insert any metallic object into the cylinder as it may jam and cause internal damage (tdc indicators can be purchased cheaply from motorcycle dealers). Sometimes, however, cylinder-head formation precludes the 'dowel' method and another technique must be employed. For this one needs an old spark plug with the ceramic insulator chipped away so that it may be further loosened and removed. This done, screw the metal body of the plug into No. 1 cylinder's plug seating and bring the engine up to just before tdc. Now apply a film of liquid detergent across the open end of the plug body and rotate the engine further: a bubble will be produced, increasing in size until maximum volume is reached when the piston is at tdc. At this point make a suitable mark on the flywheel

or fan pulley. By means of the cardboard disc marked in degrees, 10° btdc may be pinpointed. One further method of verifying the ignition timing is by marking the 10° btdc position on the fan pulley with chalk and using a neon stroboscope.

As mentioned above, prewar manuals often gave the timing in fractions of an inch and not degrees. In the case of, say, '1/16 in. btdc' the 'wooden dowel' method must be employed, a pencil mark being made on the dowel at tdc and the engine turned back so that a line 1/16 inch *above* the tdc mark is now aligned against your chosen datum-point, (Fig 8). Should the manufacturer's manual give the ignition timing as, say, '2½ inch btdc' then this does not refer to piston travel, but to flywheel rotation, measured along its circumference. Fractions of an inch apply only to the movement of the piston; larger measurements, like the example given above, must be marked on the rim of the flywheel 'in advance' of the tdc position, and the ignition timing set accordingly, (Fig. 9).

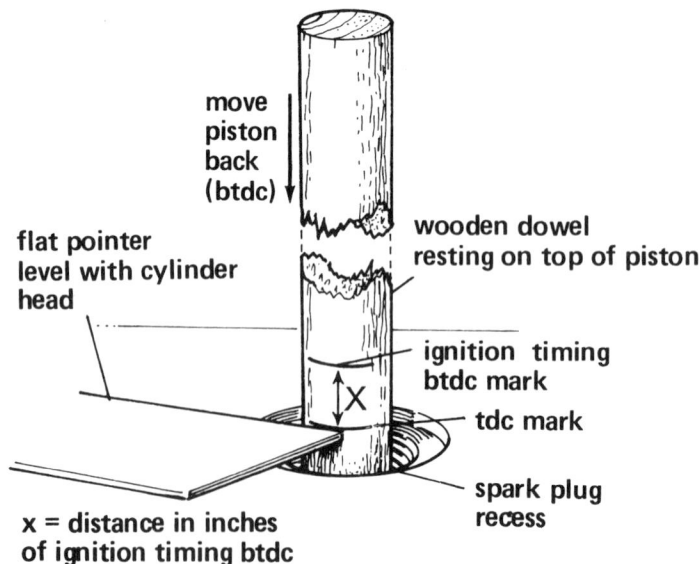

Fig 8   Setting ignition timing via a wooden dowel

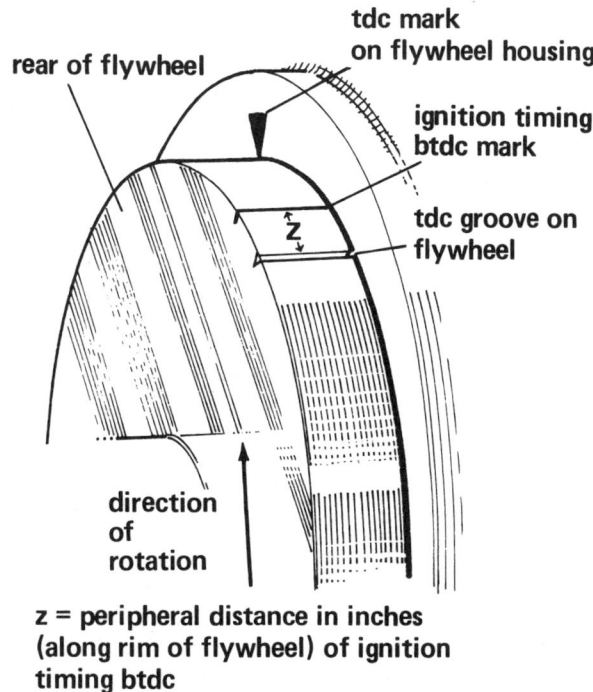

Fig 9   Setting ignition timing via flywheel marks

Resetting valve timing

Problem No.4, incorrect valve timing, entails rather more work. The valves open and close automatically as the camshaft rotates, but the correct timing is governed by a pre-arranged setting linked with the point of opening of No. 1 inlet valve. Should this initial setting be wrong, then the whole timing is thrown out. Once set correctly, it is extremely rare for the valve timing to 'slip'; usually misguided tinkering throws the valve timing out, as it is only by partially dismantling the engine that it can be altered. The front timing-case contains the valve-timing mechanism; it may consist of sprocket-wheels and a chain, or gears. In either case the correct valve timing is restored by aligning the mechanism by means of markings stamped on each component during manufacture. It is very rare to find the valve timing not indicated by markings. Usually they take the form of bright spots, nicks or punch marks.

A new timing chain, if obtainable, may well be fitted at this point before resetting the timing, as a worn chain can no longer provide crisp timing. Having removed the front timing-case, the camshaft sprocket-wheel should be detached next, timing marks looked for, and the assembly cleaned of sludge etc. The new chain is slipped over the lower sprocket(s). Now reset the tappet clearances to a wider gap and rotate the engine until it reaches tdc. Should the valve timing be, say, 15° btdc i.e. the inlet valve of No. 1 cylinder is just about to open when the flywheel is 15° in advance of tdc on the induction stroke, you will need to position the flywheel by turning the engine back to this point. Once accomplished, re-align the markings on the camshaft and crankshaft sprockets, refitting the new chain and the camshaft sprocket together, as the latter is slid into position on the camshaft. After locking up all retaining nuts etc., refit the timing case and restore the tappet clearances to normal. Following this, the ignition timing may need to be reset. Helical gearing greatly simplifies the setting of the valve timing as it entails merely realigning the gearwheels so that the markings coincide. With an overhead camshaft that is chain-driven or actuated by a train of gearwheels, the procedure for resetting the valve timing is similar in overall principle, but may be more complex. Noisy operation in the valve-gear of an ohc engine can prove costly to put right in that only the substitution of new moving parts will fully eradicate the trouble, there being no cure other than this for 'gear whine' or 'clatter', both symptoms of advanced wear.

Adverse engine noises

Once the engine is running, and the occasional backfire and splutter has disappeared, listen very carefully to the internal workings. Easiest to detect is a rythmic clicking coming from beneath the rocker cover of an ohv unit - the tappets are either badly worn or out of adjustment.

A long screwdriver will serve as a stethoscope to locate deeper engine noises, should their origin be none too evident, (put the handle to your ear and touch the crankcase with the tip). A regular, deep knock may come from a worn big-end bearing or two; you can rapidly pinpoint the culprit cylinders by pulling off the HT leads in turn - should the knock disappear on doing so, that particular cylinder has a worn bearing. New big-end bearings can often be fitted with the engine still in the chassis, however - much more serious is a low-pitched rumble on revving-up the engine, indicating overworn main bearings. Here the engine must be removed from the car before renovation can start. Low oil pressure, too, can accompany this latter fault. Noisy timing gear can be silenced by fitting new parts, but remember that a prewar high-performance engine embodying an overhead camshaft may never have been particularly silent in operation, even when new. In contrast, side-valve engines should be silky, and beyond a faint ticking from the tappets nothing else should be audible.

If you find a noise that is hard to locate on the engine, inspect the dynamo, water pump and other accessories for worn bearings. Or perhaps the fan blades are contacting the underside of the header tank. Luckily not all 'ominous noises' demand stripping down the engine.

Decayed exhaust system

Locating engine noises may well prove impossible should the exhaust be 'blown'. And often a hole in the pipe close to the exhaust manifold can completely upset the scavenging effect of the system, creating an impression of poor overall performance - with the exhaust rebuilt it could well feel like a different car. Elderly systems are always nearer than they appear to 'collapse', and it's best to rebuild the entire layout as soon as is convenient.

You may like to employ a specialist to make you an accurate replica, using the old pieces as patterns. Stainless steel systems are also available nowadays (see Appendix). A copper tail-pipe will give a sports car that added 'bark' on acceleration - but beware of too many decidels, for legal reasons! Most important is to keep to the same internal diameter of pipe, silencer box type and location, and length of the entire system. The manufacturer knew best. Flexible exhaust tubing of good quality, employing copper wire as well as asbestos to seal the coils, may be employed to connect-up the manifold with the silencer and tail-pipe. Use Holts Firegum and U-clamps, or get the assembly brazed together (welding will burn the flexible tubing).

Choice of silencer will depend on what you find already fitted to the car, should this prove original equipment. A 'straight through' design will minimize back-pressure and need not be at all noisy, but for sedate saloons track down a silencer of 'labyrinth' design incorporating baffles.

When installing the new exhaust, allow for engine movement on tick-over by including rubber bushes somewhere in the mounting. Never route the exhaust pipe too near to the tank or hydraulic system, and extend the tail-pipe a sufficient distance beyond the rear of the car to obviate fumes being drawn into the car interior due to air currents.

Testing the clutch

Once the engine is running fairly well the transmission can be checked. Should the tyres be flat, inflate them or repair any punctures. Old tyres with less than 1 mm tread are only suitable for short test runs on private ground.

With a manual gearbox select neutral, set the engine at tick-over speed, depress the clutch pedal fully, and engage first gear; procedure with a preselector gearbox and automatic clutch is to depress the clutch, move the gear lever to the position marked '1' and release the clutch - upon speeding-up the tick-over the car will begin to creep forward. Once in first gear, release the handbrake and, with a manual gearbox, slowly release the clutch to take up the drive. If all is well, continue to change up through all the gears and into top.

Failure to get into first gear may be due to a variety of troubles: a mechanically-operated clutch may be wrongly adjusted, badly worn or damaged; oil-soaked friction material will slip badly and render gear-changing a 'hit-or-miss' affair; an older model with a 'wet' clutch could lack lubrication or be badly worn; a hydraulic clutch (rare, however) may need 'bleeding' of air bubbles; or the clutch plates could be seized by rust.

First check the clutch-operating rod for slackness or play. One inch free travel is all that is necessary before the clutch begins to actuate, so look for sloppiness in the clutch pedal. Worn-out clutch plates are indicated if the range of opening movement is very small and the clutch moves 'in' or 'out' with the barest touch of the pedal (though this was normal with the Austin Seven!)In the case of severe wear or damage, replacement is the only cure and the engine must be removed from the car. A clutch penetrated by oil seepage also demands replacement of the friction plate. Hydraulic clutches were rare during the Thirties - should the pedal feel 'spongy' the system will require bleeding, as with hydraulic brakes (see p. 78)

Failure of the clutch to disengage can arise through internal rusting, the friction plate becoming bonded to the flywheel surface by rust. Pedal pressure, no matter how fiercely applied, will not effect disengagement, but a certain amount of work under the car can remedy the trouble. First locate the inspection cover at the base of the flywheel housing, remove it, and hence gain access to the flywheel and clutch. Now loosen all the clutch-cover bolts in turn, and having done so, apply leverage between the friction plate and the flywheel with a stout screwdriver. The bonding effect of the rust will be broken, but not visibly, because the power of the clutch springs will maintain all surfaces in close contact; all that needs to be done now is retighten the clutch-cover bolts. Work diagonally with progressive tightening, marking the bolts with a touch of chalk to identify them. The clutch cover must be pulled down equally to avoid distortion and ensure correct alignment.

Very occasionally one may encounter a car with a clutch of the Hele-Shaw pattern, a multi-plate metal-to-metal type running in oil. Obviously, lack of lubrication in storage will result in internal rusting. Complete dismantling is the only approach in this case. But should this type of clutch be known to be operative, an added trouble may be encountered due to clutch 'drag' in cold weather - here the cure is to depress the pedal and rev up two or three times to break the oil film.

A faulty 'fluid flywheel' generally lacks transmission fluid; top-up with the correct fluid only, never engine oil. While Lanchester, Daimler and some BSA models had fluid flywheels, cars such as the Armstrong-Siddeley were fitted with the Newton centrifugal clutch, complemented by a Wilson epicyclic gearbox. Breakdown in a centrifugal clutch is generally of a mechanical nature and repair should be entrusted to a specialist, as should a Wilson gearbox.

The prewar Talbot Traffic Clutch, also of centrifugal type, conveyed friction via semi-circular shoes instead of plates. Faults here could well be due to internal corrosion plus lack of lubrication, and inefficiencies in the friction material due to oil seepage or severe wear.
Trying the gearbox

Trying the gearbox

First top-up with the correct grade of oil and

allow time for it to penetrate parts that may have run dry. Change gear carefully at first, as there may be no synchromesh on some of the lower gears and you may not be used to this. To effect smooth changes, either double-declutch (see p. 88) or 'time' your change in sympathy with appropriate engine speed. A faulty or wrecked gearbox will prove only too evident - and will have to be stripped down. Models built around 1930 will have noisy meshing due to 'straight cut' gears; helical gears came later, around 1935 or so. A 'silent third' and, later, synchromesh on second gear were only brought in during the late Thirties, so gear-changing will not prove as effortless as in a modern car. Faults in automatic gearboxes should be left to an expert, or remedied by installing a substitute known to be in good condition.

In fact, gearbox overhaul is best left to those fully aquainted with the subject. Swopping-over the odd gearwheel here and there, rarely rids the unit of that annoying 'hum' or 'whine' - only new gears can be closely run-in to mesh silently with each other, and anyway 'with the lid off' a gearbox often presents a bewilderingly complex mass where only an expert can detect faults. To a beginner, the internals of any gearbox look 'perfect'; it is beneath the glitter of smoothly machined gearwheels and selector forks that 'invisible' troubles may lurk. But should you wish to do some of the work yourself, then Motolympia of Welshpool may prove very helpful. Rather than diagnose the faults by guess-work, post suspect parts to them and they will offer advice as well as replacements. Their full address is given in the Appendix.

Rear axle troubles

As with the gearbox, first top-up with the correct grade of gear oil. If you are unsure use an SAE 90 oil, but never engine oil. A pronounced hum from the axle could prove to be maladjustment only - the manual will state the degree of tooth-contact necessary for silent running and will indicate how it may be adjusted.

Far worse is no drive at all to the rear wheels due to broken parts such as a fractured half-shaft, sheared gear teeth and the like. Violent vibration at certain periods or road speeds arises through imbalance or distortion of the transmission shaft. Frayed fabric couplings also cause this. It is best to replace both these components, although a Jubilee clip secured at the right point on the shaft can sometimes remedy slight imbalance. Perished axle seals can allow oil to seep on to the rear brake linings, rendering them useless.

Checking the steering

Stiffness in the steering is due to lack of lubrication. A thorough greasing of all moving parts is first called for, and may reveal other faults, as you search for greasing-points. Top-up a dry steering box with SAE 140 oil, and check for loose mountings. With the car stationary, first look for play at the steering wheel. More than one inch circumferential play here is indicative of advanced wear, which may result in failure of the MOT test if not rectified. In an old car the wear in each linkage adds up to a fairly alarming total as revealed at the steering wheel! Often replacement of the worn parts with new is the only remedy, although a good supply of grease can minimize the effect of permissible wear.

The wear-pattern of the front tyres also indicates the condition of, and any maladjustment in, the steering. Part 2 gives the toe-in setting for many prewar models, and your local garage can check this. Incorrect tracking considerably reduces the useful life of the front tyres. Severe misalignment may even be due to chassis crash-damage, and this may prove impossible to correct.

Steering bias, where the car pulls to the left or right, can be checked with the car in motion, as can the dynamic balance of the front wheels. This latter will produce wheel wobble at certain speeds, sometimes caused by unequal wear in the tyres. Wheels are best balanced after the fitting of new tyres.

Brake assessment

Adequate brakes are vital in modern traffic

conditions. One can overlook the appearance of the bodywork and lack of vitality in the engine, but the ability of your prewar car to come to an abrupt halt if required is a vital factor, both legally and as regards personal safety. Poor brakes will fail the MOT test; also mechanically-operated brakes demand regular maintenance to preserve efficiency - in contrast, poorly maintained hydraulic brakes can easily outperform mechanical brakes, and 99% of cars entered for the MOT test do have hydraulic brakes, thus setting a fairly high standard. So poor brakes cannot be lived with nowadays, and there is no room for romanticism either in the MOT test or in safety.

With the exception of Morris, MG, Singer, Wolseley and one or two makes of luxury light car, most prewar models were fitted with mechanical brakes, operated by rods or cables. Other than renewing brake linings and maintaining certain adjustments, little can be done to improve the braking efficiency other than rebuilding the entire system with new parts. Kept in good trim, prewar mechanical brakes are perfectly adequate on today's roads.

Hydraulic brakes, although inherently more efficient, also demand maintenance, and the hydraulic system of an old car could well be in poor condition if it has stood idle for many years. Leakage of fluid will have enabled air to enter the system, producing 'sponginess' at the brake pedal and an impositive action. Rubber seals will decay and the fluid absorb water, rendering it dangerous in use and a cause of brake fade; Bundy tubing, the small-bore piping which conveys the fluid, can corrode, and fracture. A thorough overhaul will entail fitting new sections of Bundy tubing, new rubber seals (and perhaps wheel cylinders) throughout, filling the system with fresh brake fluid, and finally 'bleeding' it of air bubbles (see p. 78). Brake drums which are badly scored or worn oval must be skimmed, and of course, new brake linings will be needed.

Readjustment of the footbrakes will generally restore the efficiency of the handbrake, brake, although an old handbrake cable will be stretched beyond further usefulness.

The rough or the smooth?

Dry, unlubricated leaf-springs can never function correctly, and may even fracture if so neglected. A broken spring will reveal itself on your first longer run. Most prewar light cars depended solely on the leaf-spring for suspension. Very few mass-produced models sported independent front suspension; Hillman, Singer, Standard and Vauxhall did, however, introduce it during the decade. The Vauxhall Twelve and Fourteen models of 1934 first embodied ifs, and by 1938 it was featured throughout the entire Vauxhall range, from the Ten to the Twenty-five. Standard models with ifs were called the Flying Standard range.

In general, all-round leaf-springing will be encountered, and therefore inspection and lubrication will be necessary. Having jacked-up a particular wheel the springs will open slightly, and with the aid of a stout screwdriver may be further prised open. Plus Gas should now be injected between the spring layers, mud that has caked around the springs being first removed. Following this, penetrating oil or light engine oil should be applied to the springs. Should leather spring-gaiters be fitted, first remove them for inspection of the springs. Here medium grease, applied using a grease gun, is injected into the gaiters after refitting.

Wear in the shackle pins will cause rattles; new pins should be fitted and kept adequately lubricated. In contrast, shackle pins running in rubber bushes must never be oiled; should the rubber be perished, new bushes are needed.

Never attempt to dismantle a leaf-spring without having taken certain precautions. Sudden release of spring tension can be violent and dangerous.

Shockabsorbers were of several types. Earliest designs were of 'friction disc' pattern, and should the friction material be badly worn, the unit will prove inoperative. Rubber 'spring snubbers', fitted to the ends of the springs, may be perished, or the rubber soft so that it merely transmits shocks directly to the chassis.

Hydraulic shockabsorbers, of the vane or piston type, are found fairly frequently and could well be in poor overall condition after such long periods of service, or standing idle.

Correct fluid and correct fluid-level are vital here; stale fluid must be replaced. Shock-absorber mountings should be checked for looseness, or in the case of rubber-bushed assemblies, for decay and softening of the rubber. Prewar 'sports' suspension was generally rather firm, so allow for this; even 'saloon' suspension could rarely compare with the comfort taken for granted to-day. But a downright rough ride is most probably due to overall excess wear in the shockabsorbers.

Volts versus ohms

Electrical failure in a prewar car is fairly common due to decay of the insulation. Unfortunately the colour-coding of the wiring may well be indescernible, making the tracing of 'short' circuits difficult. Worse still, previous owners may have added to, or removed part of the wiring, thus making the tracing even of a simple circuit a Herculean task!

Whatever the problem, one cannot start work without first getting hold of the manufacturer's wiring diagram. Your Car Club may well be able to supply one (even if merely on loan). Early '30s cars had simple circuits, and sometimes 'double pole' wiring. 'Earth return' via the chassis came later with the 'negative earth' system, which gave way to 'positive earth' around 1936. If you are uncertain which battery terminal should be earthed, a rough guide is: pre-1936 negative earth, post-1936 positive earth; but this should not be applied too literally. The horn will not sound correctly with its polarity reversed, so this may prove a way of determining which pole should be earthed. But if in doubt do not leave the battery connected for more than a few seconds. Confusion cannot arise if non-interchangeable terminal clamps have been fitted; but check for a corroded earthing-strap connection to the chassis, as a high resistance can be set up here.

With the aid of a wiring diagram, faults may be found by a process of elimination. Decayed insulation, exposing bare wires, can give rise to short circuits which can take hours to trace - often the 'short' is under the bulkhead or below the floor and can only be located by systematic testing of each wiring-branch from the terminal box to the appropriate component. You can employ a sophisticated circuit-tester or a simple test lamp (Fig. 5). A fuse repeatedly blowing will narrow down the source of the trouble to the basic, or 'auxiliaries' circuit. Check also for correct fuse values - not all were of 35 amps.

A headlamp which will not come on will sometimes do so if struck smartly with the hand. Here bad earthing is indicated. Either remove all rust from the earthing connection or relocate it on part of the mudguard better protected from tyre spray. Corrosion of bulb terminals is simply removed with very fine carborundum paper, and the markings on bulbs is the first place to look if in doubt as to whether the replacement battery (if the original battery is missing) should be of six or twelve volts.

The next stage

Once your 'non-runner' has had its initial overhaul, and is even serving as regular day-to-day transport, you should begin to plan a more thorough restoration of the interior and bodywork. Perhaps the summer months are the best time for this, as you will need plenty of space, beyond the narrow confines of a garage. Warm weather and longer daylight hours will make the work far more pleasurable, and often much can be done out of doors, where one has the benefit of fresh air. Quite a lot of dust and grime will be discovered as the work gets under way, so claustrophobic conditions should be avoided. Later chapters explain how 'appearance restoration' should be carried out, and here the project offers much wider scope in that one's artistic visualisation of the car, rather than its mere mechanical efficiency, is involved.

Chapter Four   Motive force: car engines in the Thirties

By 1930, the light-car engine was more sophisticated, reliable and powerful than its ancestors of the previous decade. Developed directly from them, it offered higher power/weight and power/capacity ratios, was free of oddities and unnecessary complexities and ran for longer periods between services.

If you had opened the bonnets of twenty light cars at any one instant in time during, say, 1935, you would have found in nineteen cases out of twenty that the engine was of four-cylinder in-line side-valve pattern. This was, in effect, the archetype for light-car powerplants during the Thirties, overhead valve-gear being far less common. Although in theory less efficient, the side-valve engine was easier and hence cheaper to produce; it could also remain more trouble-free and required far less attention to keep it in tune. Improvements in steels were finally to make overhead valve-gear as reliable as side-valve, but for the large part of the decade the side-valve engine proved predominant. Four cylinders, too, offered few problems with regard to crankshaft length and periodic vibration, as did the addition of cylinders to produce in-line 'sixes' and 'eights'. Only the eventual evolution of a V-formation for the cylinders was to rationalize this.

Good, all-round 'utility' saloons and tourers of around 1½-litre capacity and under were in general, therefore, fitted with four-cylinder, in-line side-valve engines of simple and robust construction, with detachable cylinder heads and a unit-construction 3- or 4-speed gearbox. Occasionally the cylinder head of an ohv engine was of aluminium, a metal of high thermal conductivity, permitting a higher compression

ratio of around 8 or 9:1 to be used. But usually lower compression ratios of 5 to 6:1 were employed, coupled with a narrow cylinder bore and longer stroke of the piston. Hence peak rev/min were restricted to 3,500 - 4,500 and the power output of an average 1½-litre sv engine to around 35 bph at 3,500 rev/min, providing a top speed of 50-60 mile/h.

One example of increasing the power output of a modest side-valve engine is the mere 28 bhp at 3,400 rev/min developed by the 1550 cc Morris Cowley unit of the 1920s, affording 25 mpg; by 1932, its successor, a 1292 cc engine, could produce 30 bhp at 3,200 rev/min, while giving 32 mpg. Such increases in available power enabled such 1¼-litre engines to propel cars formerly driven by 1½-litre engines.

In contrast, an expensive sports-car engine such as that fitted to the 1½-litre Aston Martin developed 80 bhp at 5,250 rev/min, the top speed being over 100 mile/h.

Formulae against facts

The narrow bore, and hence necessarily long stroke of 'saloon' engines originated directly from the introduction in 1921 of the Roads Act which placed a tax on motors of £1 per RAC horse-power rating. This rating was not found by practical testing on the bench, but was arrived at mathematically from the formula $D^2N/2.5$, where D represents the cylinder diameter in inches and N the number of cylinders. The smaller D, the lower the RAC rating, and this led to manufacturers reverting to engines of narrow bore in order to attract custom through the low Road Tax on their vehicles. Note that the stroke of the engine finds no place in the RAC's formula: in order to increase cylinder capacity, a narrow bore needed to be complemented by an abnormally long stroke, yet this was directly at variance with the contemporary developments in engine design. Improved design produced increased crankshaft speeds, and hence higher piston speeds - the natural product being the 'square' engine, where bore and stroke were equal. In this latter design the shorter stroke helped reduce piston speed, and Continental manufacturers such as FIAT, unhampered by official formulae, took full advantage of new developments, offering cars powered by 'square' engines in 1934. In Britain, however, designers tailored their engines to fit the public purse, and natural development was held back (or 'post-poned' - in fact to the Ford 'Consul' and 'Zephyr' of 1951, with their engines of 1:1 bore/stroke ratio).

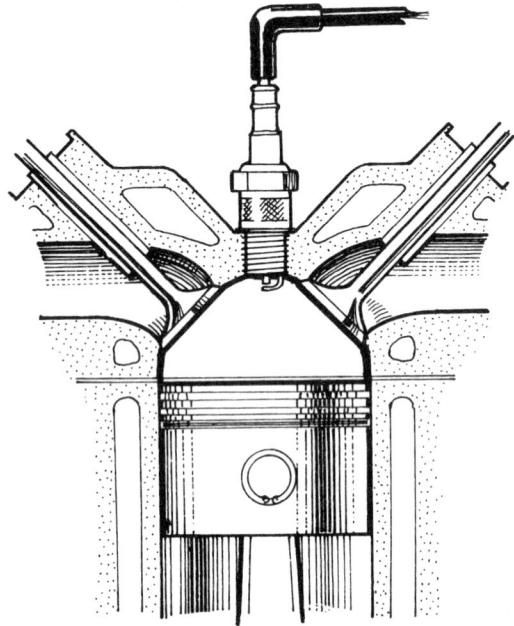

Fig 10   Hemispherical combustion chamber layout

Henry Ricardo

The development of light-car engines during the early Thirties owed much to the foundation laid by the researches of Henry R. Ricardo in the previous decade. Thanks to his work, high-octane fuels became generally available in 1924, permitting manufacturers to build engines with higher compression ratios. Sustained crankshaft speeds of up to 5000 rev/min became common in sports car engines, 30 bhp per litre being a typical average power output.

Ricardo was also the first designer to realise that turbulence within the combustion space increases the combustion-speed of the inspired charge. Even 'ideal' combustion-chamber designs embodying a hemispherical form (Fig.10) were found to generate insufficient turbulence for perfect combustion. The charge, although drawn into the cylinder smoothly and effectively, remained congealed into a single mass which ignited relatively more slowly than a charge swirling around the cylinder, activated by eddy currents.

Fig.11 shows the form of the 'Ricardo head' as applied to an orthodox side-valve engine. As the fresh charge is drawn through the open inlet valve via an annular space between the valve and its seat, complex eddy currents are set up, the mixture swirling all round the cylinder during the inlet stroke. The turbulence produced is strong enough to persist right through the subsequent compression stroke, facilitating a more homogeneous blend of fuel and air and promoting a much faster and steadier flame-speed throughout the burning mixture.

Ricardo also showed that low-octane fuel limited the power of an engine, giving rise to 'pinking' or 'knocking' (pre-ignition of the charge). He found that higher-octane fuels permitted the use of higher compression ratios, and there was less tendency for 'pinking' to occur. Taken further, it was found that the aromatic hydrocarbon benzene (or 'benzol'), if mixed with petrol served as an 'anti-knock' additive. Soon '50/50 Benzol Mixture' came on

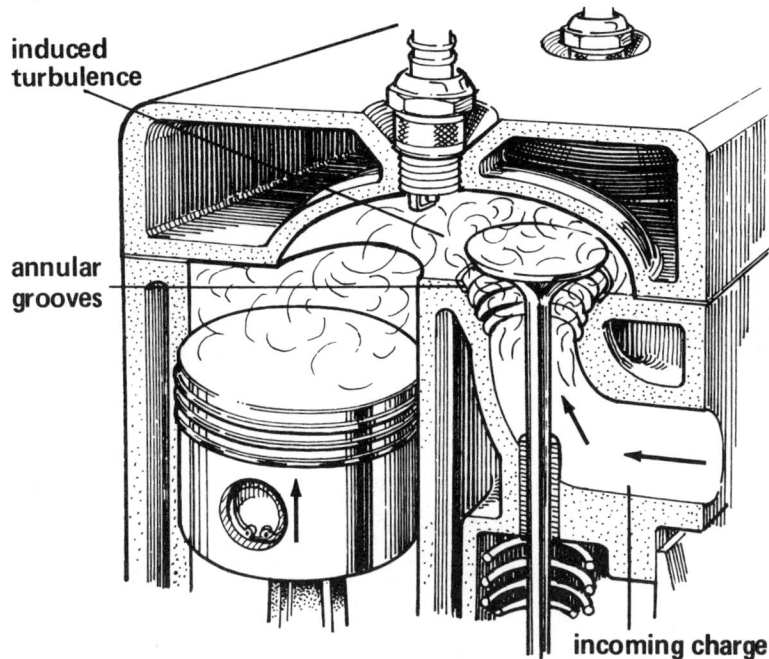

Fig 11   Ricardo cylinder head on sv engine

the market and later, in 1928, 'Ethyl Petrol', pioneered by General Motors' Research Corporation and containing tetra-ethyl lead as its anti-knock additive. Alcohol was also blended with petrol, serving as an ideal fuel for high-compression engines, and sold under the name of 'Discol'.

Having shown by research that the quality of fuel and the way its vapour is dispersed in the cylinders are both important factors of power output, Ricardo then concentrated his efforts in developing the mechanical aspects of engine design. Aircraft manufacture had set the future pattern in the widespread adoption of aluminium alloys for aero engines; better grades of steel and new alloy steels became more generally available, and were to prove equally applicable in the development of the motor car engine. Higher crankshaft speeds, produced by more efficient engine design, led to correspondingly higher piston speeds, particularly now that the 1921 Roads Act virtually dictated the retention

of an abnormally long stroke. Also a higher percentage of heat developed by more powerful engines demanded more efficient dissipation, and here the high thermal conductivity (and low density) of aluminium was to prove so valuable.

Heavy cast-iron pistons and steel connecting rods had been the norm up until the early Twenties, both metals being of high density, and in the case of cast-iron, fairly low thermal conductivity (it should be remembered that much of the heat of combustion is conveyed directly to the piston crown, from where it dissipates through contact with oil splashing against the underside of the piston or through the rings to the cylinder wall). Following aero engine practice, Ricardo and other researchers such as M. Henry introduced the application of light alloys to car engines. Aluminium pistons in 'L8' or 'Y' metal (two alloys specified by the Air Ministry of the mid-20s) and connecting rods in duralumin made their appearance, and by 1930 the practice was general, the use of cast-iron for pistons completely dying out.

Piston design

Some typical piston designs are shown in Fig 12. Together with types fabricated solely in one metal or alloy (A) and (B), there emerged experimental composite designs (C) and (D), the former being of aluminium and bronze, the latter having an aluminium crown screwed into a cast-iron skirt; but few of these unusual innovations served any long-term application.

Most interesting is type E, the Ricardo slipper piston. Here his insistence on the inherent lightness of reciprocating parts is evidenced to the full, 50% of the piston skirt being cut away so that the side-thrust of the piston is transmitted only where necessary, the large circular holes allowing adequate oil drainage and affording a further reduction in weight.

The different types of piston in use throughout the Thirties are too numerous to described here in full, but Fig.13 shows the three main classes of piston in use during the period, (1) the full-skirted type, (2) the truncated type, and (3) the slipper racing piston.

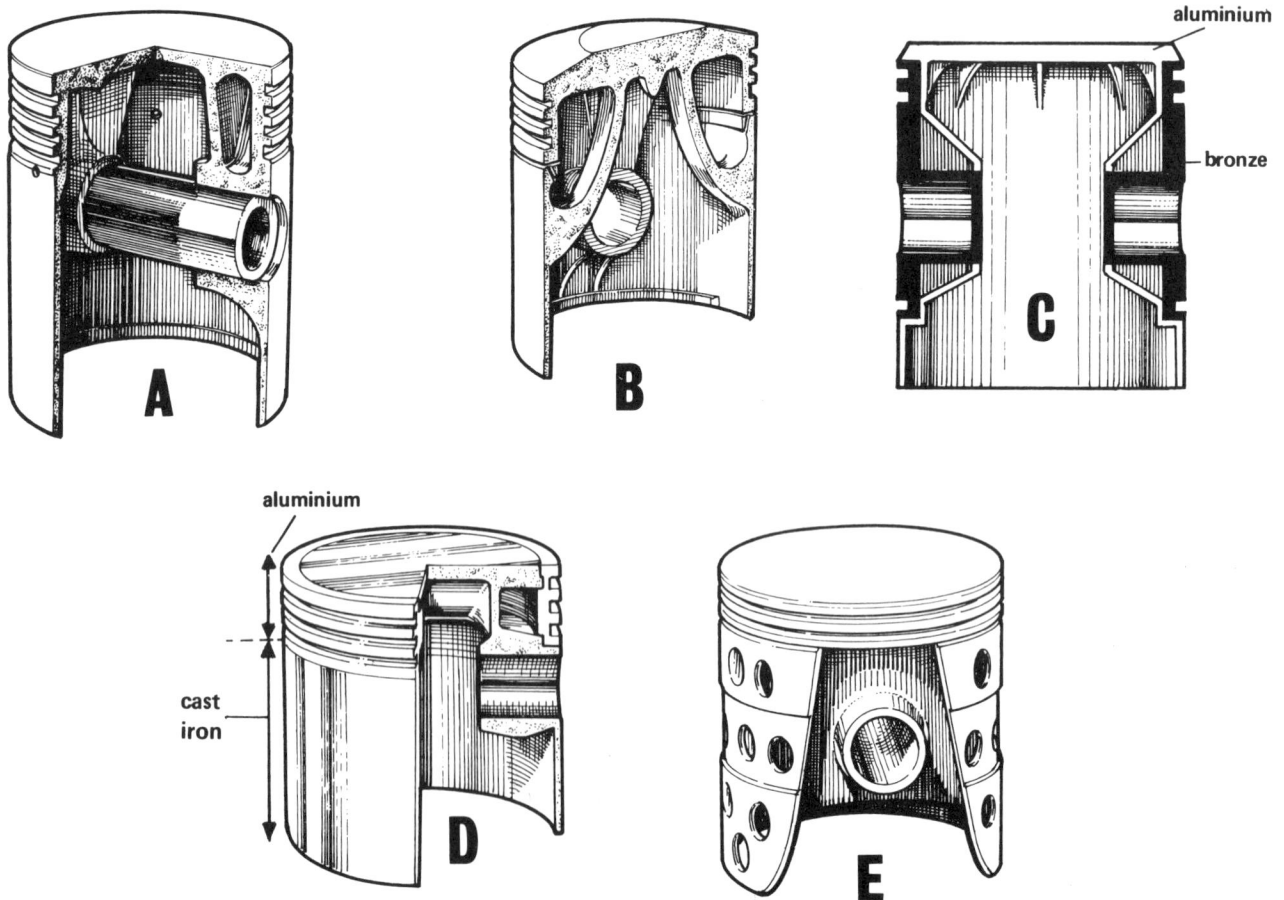

Fig 12   Various piston designs

Die-cast aluminium pistons employ strengthening ribs below the inside of the crown, connected to the gudgeon-pin bosses, where the explosive thrust is received and transmitted. The sides or 'walls' of pistons give way lower down to the 'skirt'; between these two areas are located the ring grooves in which rest the piston rings, separated into layers by the 'lands'.

Due to varying expansion and contraction, a smooth-sided 'lapped' aluminium piston cannot maintain an adequate cylinder seal, hence the need for fine-grained cast-iron piston rings which spring out and press against the cylinder walls. Upper rings are termed compression rings, while

those lower are described as scraper rings; narrow rings became most favoured, but each manufacturer of pistons had individual ways of arranging the number and type of rings. In Fig.14 several typical types of ring are shown in cross-section. From top to bottom they are: compression, slotted scraper, stepped scraper, bevelled scraper and oil scraper. During the '30s piston manufacturers were fairly numerous, among them Aerolite, Laystall, B.H.B., Hepolite, Wellworthy, Cords, M & H, and Jaegar. Nowadays Hepolite-Wellworthy and Cords only remain to serve the enthusiast, and even the latter are unable to help with prewar spares. But

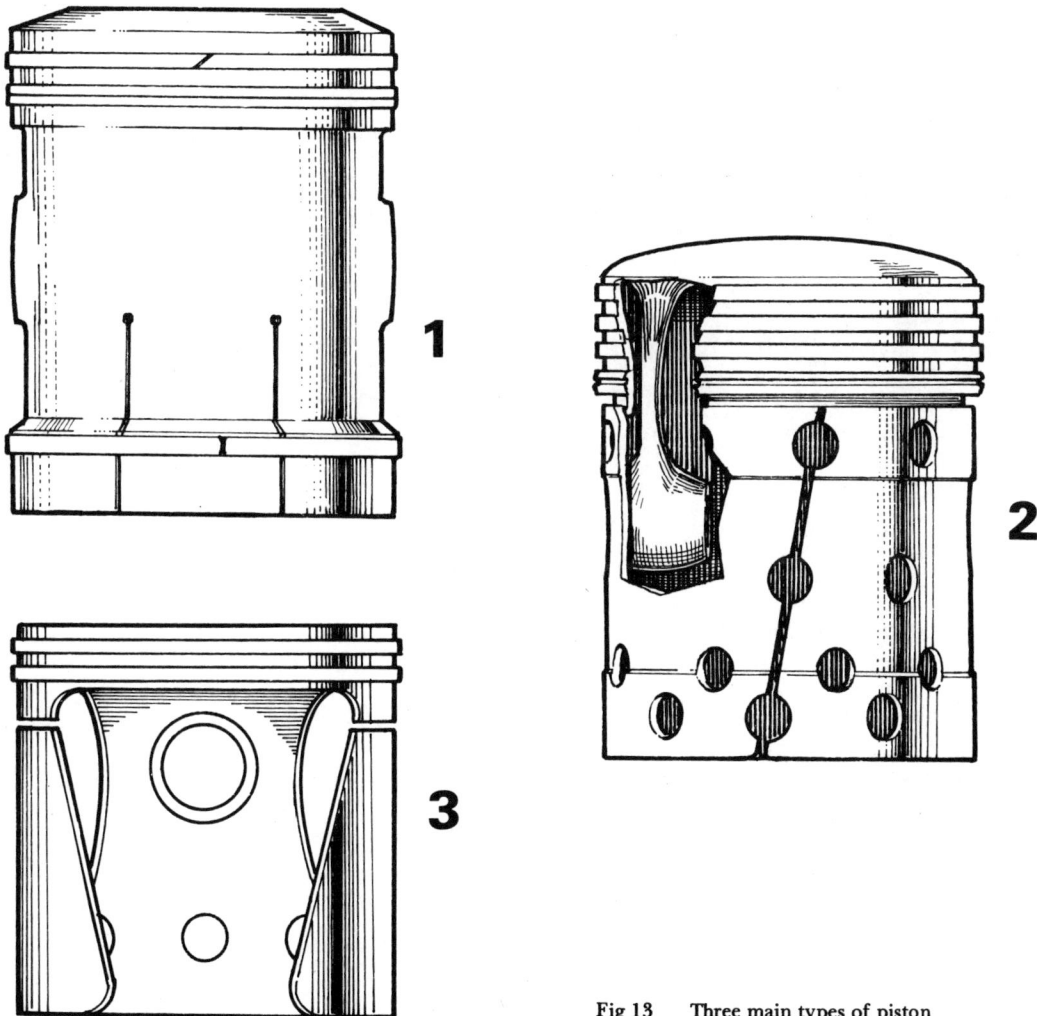

Fig 13   Three main types of piston

both Hepolite and Cords offer special rings to combat cylinder wear and conserve oil in a worn engine - the Cordsflex ring nowadays incorporating a stainless steel spacer/expander between the layers of a 'double' coiled ring. Before the war, Wellworthy offered a similar device called the Duaflex ring, and M & H also manufactured a special sealer-ring, but both relied on orthodox spring-steel for the 'crimped' expander.

Ring friction, and piston-crown temperature (220-380°C) represent two sources of heat in an engine which must be effectively dispersed to prevent seizure. Since much of the heat of combustion is conveyed by the piston rings to the cylinder walls, and to it must be added the heat produced by ring friction, one can appreciate that to minimize piston speed is to effectively reduce internal heat transfer. Henry Ricardo pointed out that 30-45% of the total engine friction is produced by the piston rings when the engine is running at full load; at light load, however, he demonstrated that ring friction increased to 65-70% of the total. Piston manufacturers were therefore set large problems to solve, piston speeds increasing during the 1930s as long-stroke engines began to develop full power at higher revs. The piston of an engine of four inches stroke, turning at over 4000 rev/min, attains a speed of half a mile a minute at a certain interval, and this under a temperature of nearly 400°C and extremely high cylinder pressures. In a racing engine these factors are even more pronounced.

Modern researches can now elaborate on Ricardo's early work regarding heat-dissipation by the piston. It has been found that the proportions are as follows: rings 40%, lands 30%, bearing face of piston 20%, lower skirt and underside of crown 10%. The wide adoption of aluminium alloy with its high thermal conductivity for the manufacture of pistons effectively solved the problems of overheating in high-performance car engines. Coupled with low reciprocating weight, these qualities in light-alloy engine parts enabled more of the available power to be harnessed, thus opening up a whole new vista of higher speeds with lower fuel **consumption.**

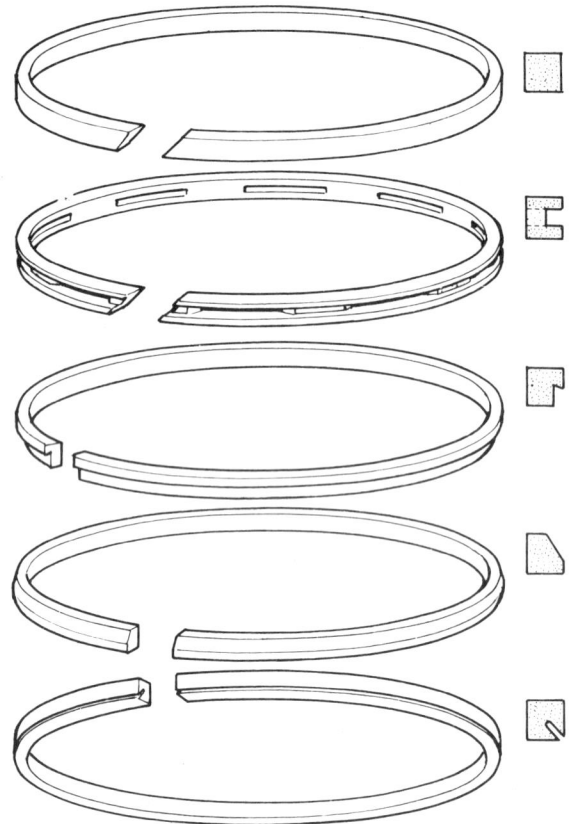

Fig 14   Various piston ring types

50

Valve and cylinder-head design

It is said that the exhaust valve is the hardest-worked component of an engine, opening and closing thousands of times per minute and operating at red heat under full throttle. This again affords some idea of the research and development entailed over the past fifty years in producing valves of to-day's high quality.

As is well known, the mushroom-shaped 'poppet' valve proved in the long term the most efficient device for metering the inlet and exhaust strokes. Cuff- and sleeve- valve mechanisms enjoyed only a brief span of popularity in the luxury car field due to problems involving the maintenance of very fine working tolerances and an inherent need for adequate lubrication.

By the early Twenties, poppet valves constructed with a cast-iron head fixed to a stem of mild steel had been superceded by an integral design in nickel steel. Soon superior alloy-steels, first used in racing engines, became available. It had been found that the addition of chromium, cobalt, vanadium and molybdenum to carbon-steels produced alloy-steels offering greater strength and heat resistance. Such developments were eventually to make possible the record-breaking run made by 'Goldie' Gardiner's stream-lined 1106 cc MG which attained speeds of over 200 mile/h during May and June of 1939.

Not of least importance in such high-performance racing engines was the internal form and contour of the combustion space. An overhead camshaft and supercharger were facets of racing design fully assimilated by 1939; good porting, Ricardo's 'turbulence' (supplied *gratis* by a supercharger), inertia scavenging, high compression ratio, light reciprocating weight of pistons and connecting rods, etc. were all incorporated to worthwhile effect. Yet in saloon and tourer engines, which lacked many of the above refinements, the internal design of the cylinder head and the arrangement of the valves became paramount factors regarding performance.

Three designs of inlet valve are depicted in Fig. 15. Type A is as was used in most '30s touring cars; B with the flat head and longer curve of the stem, enabled smoother flow of the incoming mixture at high speeds. Consistent with the practice of reducing the weight of reciprocating parts, C represents a 1930 racing valve with metal scooped out of·the head and seat width reduced to a minimum. Sodium-cooled valves with hollow stems were also used in racing engines.

As mentioned previously, the 'ideal' shape for the combustion space was, in the case of overhead valve-gear, hemispherical. With side valves, the deflection of the charge entering the combustion space generated a swirling effect, aiding combustion. 'Squish' and 'deflector' heads, sometimes in aluminium, were developed also to this end. The inherent inclusion of a 'pocket' in side-valve heads remained a detrimental factor, however.

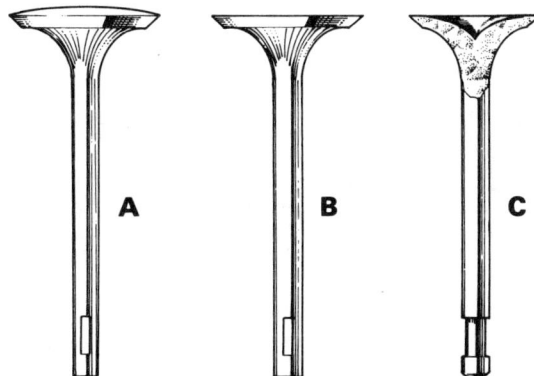

Fig 15   Three designs of inlet valve

Alternative valve layout

Fig. 16 shows a range of valve configurations and combustion-space shapes to be encountered in cars of the 1925-39 era. The top row are three ohv layouts of varying degrees of efficiency, tempered, from left to right, by ease of manufacture: the 'ideal' setup is progressively modified until the third design arrived at, though cheapest to produce, loses nearly all the advantages of ohv gas-flow. The bottom row consists of three alternative designs; the 'inlet-over-exhaust' or ioe pattern, the sv twin camshaft and the sv L-head. The L-head setup is cheapest to produce in that only one camshaft is needed to operate both inlet and exhaust valves. As for the twin camshaft sv layout, this proved uneconomic and became obsolete by 1930. Humber favoured the ioe arrangement during the 1920s, and it appeared again in the 1122cc Coventry Climax engine which powered both the 1933-37 Triumphs and the Morgan 4/4 of 1936-39. An added benefit with this latter design is that the inspired charge passes across the head of the exhaust valve and assists in cooling it.

A close relative of the ohv engine, the ohc powerplant has its camshaft mounted above the valves. In this way inefficiencies due to play in the valve gear are minimized and far crisper timing is possible. Examples of light cars with ohc engines are the early 847 cc Morris Minors and MG Midgets, the Frazer Nash TT Replica, the 1104 cc dohc Lagonda Rapier, the MG Magna and 1100 cc Magnette and the Wolseley Hornet. Efficient and sprightly ohv engines were fitted to such models as the Riley Nine, Singer Nine, Alvis Firefly and the Wolseley 12/48. Trusty, hard-working sv engines powered a host

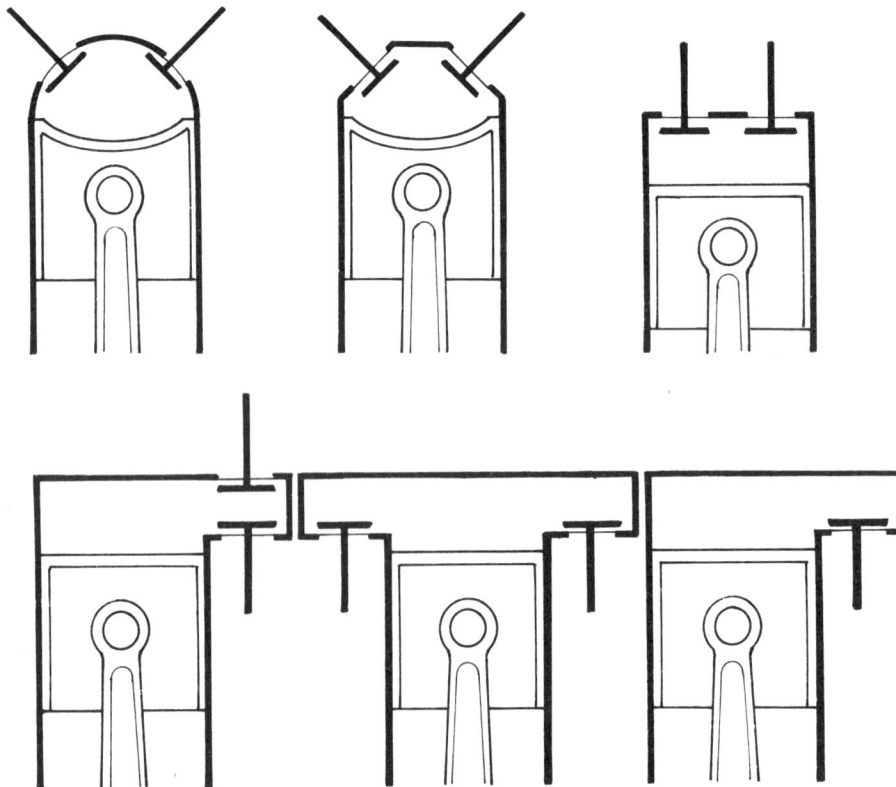

Fig 16   Various valve configurations

of cars, notable among them the Austin Seven, Morris Eight, Ford Eight and Ten, Standard Little Nine, Jowett Eight and Ten, the Hillman Minx and Talbot Ten. Three-wheelers of the period such as the Morgan retained twin-cylinder motorcycle engines up to 1939, manufactured by such enterprises as JAP and Matchless. These engines were of 1000 cc V-twin configuration, either air- or water-cooled, and of ohv or sv layout. The BSA three-wheeler featured front-wheel drive; its original engine, an air-cooled ohv V-twin of 1932, yielding a year later to a water-cooled four-cylinder design of 1075 cc. Morgan began to fit Ford four-cylinder engines in 1934.

Cylinder arrangement and design

Jowett remained unique in their adherence to a small-capacity flat twin engine with horizontally opposed cylinders. Of sv form, it powered their faithful Seven from the early years of the century right up to 1954, when due to liquidation, production of their Bradford van ceased. In the late '30s a sv 'flat four' was developed to power their ten-horsepower Jason.

Four-cylinder in-line engines were, however, predominant, of sv, ohv or ohc type, their compactness and ease of production outweighing problems of inbalance due to the uneven disposition of power- and exhaust-strokes. Impossible to balance perfectly, the four-cylinder in-line engine suffers through the two ascending pistons travelling faster than the two descending, due to the inclination of the connecting rods. The flat four is far superior in reciprocating balance to the in-line four, in the same way that the flat twin excels the V-twin.

Small capacity six-cylinder in-line engines, sometimes termed 'straight sixes', were introduced into the light car field with the advent of such cars as the Wolseley Hornet and MG Magna. The Wolseley engine had its origins, rather remarkably, in the Hispano-Suiza aero engine made by Wolseley under licence to power the SE5 fighter of 1916. Scaled down, and adapted to motor car practice, this serviceable 1271 cc engine was squeezed into a modified version of the Morris Ten chassis. By mounting it further forward than normal, only small modi-

fications were necessary to the frame, although the car proved nose-heavy and the chassis suffered from flexing. The Hornet was the direct ancestor of the MG Magna also of 1271 cc, MG retaining a vertical shaft to drive the camshaft, while their longer chassis afforded more room for the engine. In order to shorten the unit, Wolseley replaced the shaft by a chain-drive system in their later models which gave rise to tensioning problems as power output was increased; a two-stage drive, fitted to the Hornet Special engine, later solved this.

In general, cylinders were bored through an iron casting of 'monobloc' construction, separate cylinders, visible externally, having disappeared in the late '20s. A core of sand employed during casting made possible the inclusion of hollow water-passages running through the cylinder block close to the cylinders. Some more advanced designs of engine incorporated separate cylinder liners fabricated in special steels, called 'wet liners' when the coolant circulated directly around them. 'Dry liners' were occasionally employed by some manufacturers when a rebore was due, the thin liner being fitted into the cylinder after reboring oversize.

Connecting rods

Another highly-stressed component, the connecting rod is estimated to withstand tensile and compression stresses of several tons as it rotates.

By the mid-20s the steel connecting rod, with its high density and hence sizeable reciprocating weight, began to yield to a new type of rod cast in a lightweight alloy, duralumin. An alloy of 90% aluminium with copper, manganese and magnesium, this new alloy could, like steel, be drop forged. Further machining of an H-sectioned drop forging produced a rod with a 50-60% saving in weight.

In contrast to the more common H- or I-sectioned connecting rods (Fig.17), tubular designs were employed for a time, but were found to fracture around the big-end bearing boss. Plain cylindrical-sectioned rods did not survive long, due to high reciprocating weight. In racing circles further lightness was achieved by machining holes in the less-stressed sections of the connecting rod, or sometimes the complete web was removed.

General practice involved the fitting of a plain phosphor bronze small-end bearing allied to a hardened steel gudgeon pin. This latter could be of 'fixed' or 'floating' type. 'Fixed' gudgeon pins were clamped into the small-end and were a working fit in the piston bosses. 'Floating' types were a working fit in both the piston bosses and the small-end bush, side travel being restricted by means of circlips, or alloy end-pads in what was called the 'fully floating' pin, (Fig.18).

Throughout the 1930s white metal served as the most common material for the bearing surfaces

of big-ends. With a steel connecting rod, the white metal could be cast directly into the bearing recess; thin brass shells carrying the metal were fitted into the bearings of duralumin rods. Of varying composition, white metal (or Babbitt metal) is an alloy of tin, lead, copper and antimony, being fairly soft compared even to brass or aluminium. Although of very low tensile strength, white metal provides a perfect bearing surface for the high speeds of a crankshaft, minimizing friction and giving very long service. For high-speed use an alloy of 80% tin may be used, the lead content being omitted, whereas for general 'utility' bearings a composition of 60% lead and 20% tin will prove satisfactory. Before the white metal can be cast into the bearing (or on to brass shells) each must

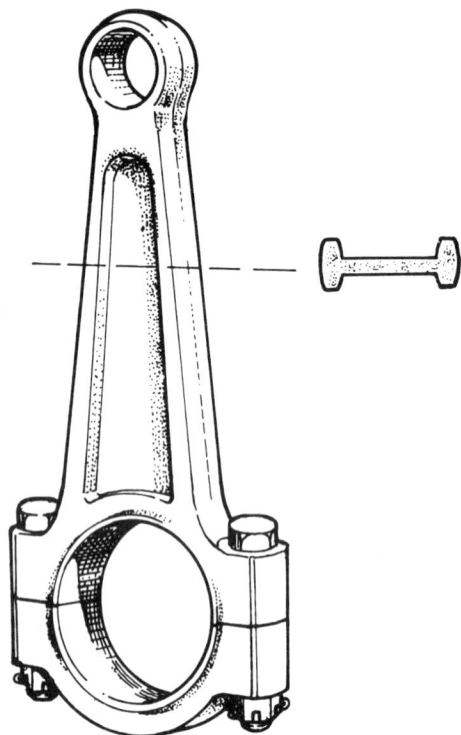

Fig 17   Typical connecting-rod cross-section

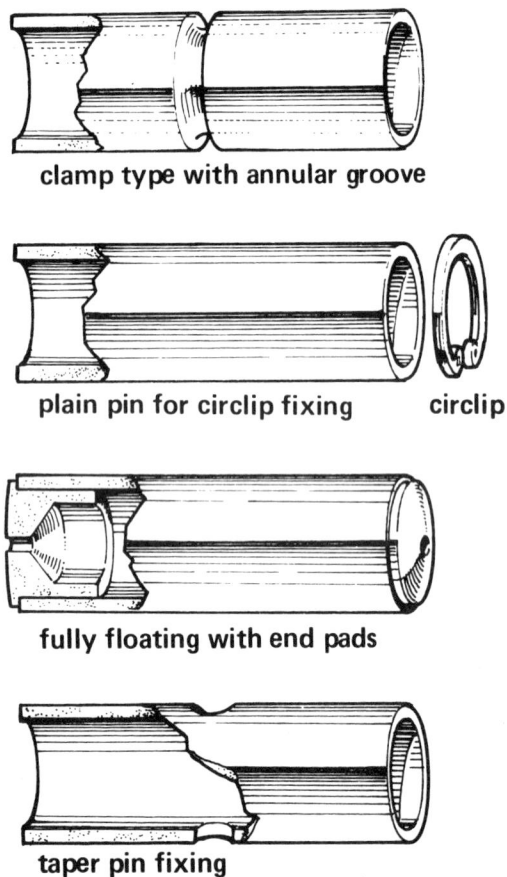

clamp type with annular groove

plain pin for circlip fixing   circlip

fully floating with end pads

taper pin fixing

Fig 18   Various types of gudgeon pin

first be tinned with solder to form a foundation to which the alloy can adhere. Prior to fitting into the engine, the rough-cast bearings were machined down to 0.002 in. undersize and then scraped by hand to an exact working fit; oilways were also cut by hand. Brands of white metal available during the decade were Hoyts, Ibis, Magnolia and Vulcan, among others.

Roller and ball bearings were also used in small engines instead of white metal, most notable being that of the Austin Seven which was served by a two-bearing crankshaft from 1923 to 1936; here a roller bearing was employed at the rear of the crankshaft with a ball-and-roller type at the front. Other large-capacity motorcycle engines, such as that fitted to the earlier version of the BSA three-wheeler, also relied on roller big-end bearings.

Crankshaft design and fabrication

Most common was a crankshaft forged in alloy- or carbon-steel and accurately machined to as near perfect static and dynamic balance as possible.

Disposition of the cranks dictates the firing sequence, and in the in-line four they are set at 180° with pistons 1 and 4, and 2 and 3 moving in parallel - when 1 and 4 are at tdc, 2 and 3 are at bdc, and vice versa. In such an arrangement the power strokes follow each other in succession but cannot overlap; in contrast, the disposition of the cranks at 120° in a six-cylinder engine does afford a degree of overlap, resulting in far greater smoothness of operation.

As stated previously, a flat twin performs more smoothly than a V-twin, and a flat four than an in-line four because of the better inherent balance of reciprocating parts when moving along a horizontal axis, the effect of gravity being reduced to a minimum.

The modern practice of fabricating crankshafts in cast alloy steel, pioneered by the Ford Motor Company, was, during the '30s, not widely adopted; a large amount of machining from the crude forging was necessary, and hence costly. Nowadays accurate casting keeps the amount of final machining to the minimum, and

although cast shafts are somewhat heavier than their forged counterparts, they are otherwise equal in every way.

Nitride-hardening was introduced during the early '30s, and a 'nitrarded' crankshaft was fitted to the engine of the supercharged TT Replica Frazer Nash. In this (then new) process, the shaft is heated to 500°C in an atmosphere of nitrogen gas, part of which is absorbed by the surface of the steel to form an extremely hard 'skin'. AFN, the manufacturers of Frazer Nash cars, had found the Meadows 4ED engine inadequate when supercharged, and under the aegis of Albert Gough developed their own engine, the shaft of which, while massive in overall proportions, was further strengthened by 'nitrarding'. This latter step produced a crankshaft well able to withstand the extra stresses imposed by fitting a high-pressure blower.

But most mass-produced engines had crankshafts of modest dimensions, machined from a forging in relatively unsophisticated steels and untreated by any new-fangled hardening process. As for the number of bearings, this did increase during the decade as average power output became greater. Small 7- and 8-horsepower engines made do with only two bearings during the early '30s but by the middle of the decade the number was increased on average to three by the addition of a centre bearing to reduce 'whip'. For example, in 1930 the engines of both the Morris Minor and MG Midget M-type had only two main bearings, while their successors, the Morris Eight and MG Midget T-type of 1936 both had three. Engines of 1 to 1½ litres, such as those powering the Triumph Gloria, Wolseley Wasp and Crossley Regis, also had three main bearings, while the six-cylinder units of the Wolseley Hornet and MG Magna had four. The need for added support in racing crankshafts is evidenced in the five-bearing shaft of the 1667cc Blackburne-engined TT Frazer Nash, which developed 90 bhp, roughly twice the figure for a contemporary 'saloon' engine of equal capacity. Other interesting examples of increased power brought about by detailed research and development come from the Austin and MG stables. In the case of their Austin Seven Racer of 744cc dohc supercharged type, its tiny engine was coaxed to give 80 bhp at 12,000 rev/min, while the MG Midget Q and R-types of 746cc developed over 100 bhp at 7200 rev/min, giving a top speed in excess of 120 mile/h.

Perhaps the most startling example of high power: capacity ratio is found on glancing across at Continental development during the end of the decade. Fantastic as it may seem for the time, the 1939 German Mercedes W 165 racing car engine of 1½-litre V-8 form, in two-stage supercharged trim, could develop 254 bhp at 8000 rev/min.

New bearing alloys

Research into more efficient substitutes for white metal continued through the Thirties and new and more sophisticated alloys were developed, such as lead-bronze, lead-indium, nickel-cadmium and silver-antimony. Nowadays lead-indium is a common bearing metal, available in the form of steel-backed thin shells, fitting into the bearing recess. The practice of casting white metal *in situ* is now virtually obsolete, although certain specialists still offer this service.

Camshafts, valve-timing and overlap

Camshafts were made in a similar way to crankshafts. Driven either by a train of gears, a chain and sprockets, or a vertical shaft with helical gearing, it bore the cams which actuated the inlet and exhaust valves. In a side-valve engine it was situated at the base of the cylinder block; ohv camshafts were also located here or, in the case of 'high camshaft' engines, in a position nearer the cylinder head. Ohc engines, of course, have camshafts sited above the valves. Twin camshafts were fitted in engines of higher performance, one actuating the inlet and the other the exhaust valve. This layout also enabled the fitting of valves inclined at an included angle of 90⁰ - the 'ideal' configuration when coupled with a hemispherical combustion chamber.

An example of an engine of dohc (double overhead camshaft) design is the 1104 cc unit fitted to the Lagonda Rapier of the mid-30s. Capable of developing 45 bhp at 4500 rev/min in standard form (a very good figure for a 1100 cc engine in 1934), supercharged versions were capable of 90 mile/h, the open four-seater proving the fastest. Production of this remarkable little car was continued later by Rapier Cars, Ltd.

Cam profiles dictate the crispness of action of the valves, 'touring' camshafts bearing cams of smooth profile where the valves open and close relatively gradually, while 'quick lift' cams, used in high-performance engines, snap the valves open and closed in a 'less leisurely' way, affording far more positive metering of the inlet and exhaust periods (Fig. 19).

Increasing the diameter of the inlet port, port polishing, and accurate mating of manifold junctions to remove any tendency for 'stepped' joints, were all found to yield power increases. Duplex valve springs i.e. a spring within a spring, helped to cure valve bounce.

Experiments with 'exaggerated' timing, which bore significant fruit in racing circles, paved the way for manufacturers of sports cars and sports saloons to adapt new valve-timing techniques to their engines. 'Overlap', where both the inlet and the exhaust valve remain open at the same time, was thought incongruous in the early days of motoring. It was found, however, that thanks to the inertia and momentum of gases, valve 'overlap' could be used to considerable advantage.

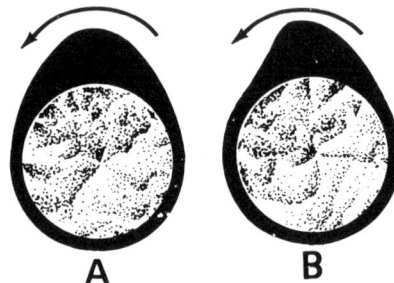

Fig 19   Normal (A) and 'quick lift' (B) cam profiles

Once a congealed mass of gas has been set in motion i.e. its inertia has been overcome, it then tends to continue moving under its own momentum. Under the extreme forces prevalent in an internal combustion engine, such fast-moving 'lumps' of gas entering the inlet port and leaving the exhaust port can provide a valuable pumping action of their own, both with regard to thorough scavenging of the exhaust gases and to a suction effect thus generated in the inlet port. By arranging the timing to 'overlap', this suction may be used to draw fresh mixture through the part-open inlet valve - thus the new charge can begin to enter the cylinder even before the added suction of the descending piston comes into play.

'Freak' timing, as it was then called, embodied not only 'overlap' but also a far longer interval of opening for the inlet valve. Often, with a racing-pattern camshaft, the inlet valve was set to open 20-30° btdc - in contrast with contemporary 'saloon' timing set sometimes even at 0° btdc. One can appreciate in this latter case that none of the advantages of 'inertia filling' were operative and hence maximum potential performance never realised.

Fortunately, however, these new timing techniques infiltrated the mass-produced car world, and by the mid-'30s virtually every engine embodied 'early' opening of the inlet valve, if not 'overlap' or large-area inlet ports. A poignant example of increased power in a re-worked engine is a comparison between the bhp figures of the mid-30s Riley 1½-litre models in standard and Sprite trim. In roadster form, the inlet valve was set to open at 0° btdc, the engine giving 45 bhp at 4500 rev/min. It contrast, the Sprite engine, with 20° btdc inlet timing, twin carburetters, high-compression head, a high-lift camshaft and extra large inlet ports could be made to yield 60 bhp at 5500 rev/min. Despite the 'extras', the exaggerated inlet-valve timing proved a salient feature, without which the high compression and special camshaft would have been far less potent. It is interesting to note that apart from the alteration in inlet-valve timing, both engines were identically timed.

Supercharged engines, with force-fed fuel induction, were found to perform perfectly adequately with more 'normal' timing while racing engines relying on orthodox aspiration benefitted most from a special camshaft and 'freak' timing.

Wet-sump lubrication

Circulation of oil in most engines was achieved, as it is to-day, by the 'splash-and-pressure' system, the sump acting as a reservoir for the oil. The lubricant was pumped to the bearings by means of a mechanical pump driven off the camshaft, the rotation of the big-ends splashing oil up under the pistons while oil mist found its way to the valve gear, etc. In most cases the oil pump was of the gear type, but individualists such as Riley developed their own 'double plunger' design (see Riley section in Part 2). Some type of filtering device was incorporated by the end of the decade, by which time the changeable paper filter-cartridge was in wide use.

Dry-sump lubrication

Only rarely used, even in racing cars, this system incorporated an external oil tank mounted at the front of the car to which hot oil was returned for cooling by a scavenger pump. A full-pressure pump delivered cooled oil to the engine bearings and other moving parts.

Distinctive by its reliance on this excellent but more complex system was the 1½-litre Aston Martin, a 2½-gallon oil tank being mounted between the dumb-irons.

Oil pressure

Lower than those prevalent to-day, oil pressures did increase throughout the decade as performance improved. An average figure is difficult to formulate, in that high and low oil pressures were employed by different manufacturers, and high performance did not always go hand-in-hand with high oil pressure. (The Jowett 10, a conventional saloon as regards performance, had an oil pressure of 40-45 lb/in^2, wheras the Triumph Dolomite, capable of 90 mile/h, made do with a mere 20 lb/in^2. Pressures were found ranging from 20-50 lb/in^2 (60-70 lb/in^2 being an average figure in a modern car). The Austin Seven once again is noteworthy in that its normal 'top-speed' oil pressure could, to quote from the 1933 Owners' Manual, "fall as low as 1 lb/in^2 once the oil has become more fluid on warming-up...this, however, is sufficient" !

Oils and additives

Only single-viscosity 'straight' oils were available, in grades from 10 SAE to 50 SAE. Usually a summer and a winter grade was specified, a typical directive being 30 SAE and 20 SAE, respectively. High-performance cars used 40 SAE oils, particularly in summer, and Castrol Grand Prix 50 SAE oil was available for racing V-twins. An alternative to this mineral-based lubricant was Castrol R, of 40 SAE, a castor-based oil giving a pungent exhaust so prevalent at race tracks such as Brooklands.

Colloidal graphite was commonly used as a petrol additive, serving as an upper cylinder lubricant and running-in compound. Other brands of UCL, such as Upperlube, Castrollo and Redex, were oils forming a wax-like film of high shear strength, fully functional at high combustion-chamber temperatures and adhering to the cylinders after the engine had cooled down.

Failure by the oil companies to adopt universally the American SAE system for grading resulted in confusion for the motorist endeavouring to trace a certain viscosity of oil to suit his car. He had, for example, to unravel the correct grade from the mystique of such brand names as Motorine C, Castrol XXL, Double Shell, Sternol WW, and so on. Only such companies as Esso and BP swept away confusion by marketing such products as Essolube 20 and Energol 30.

Chapter Five

Tuning versus transplants: engine rebuilding

Loss of power in an elderly engine is usually a symptom of excess wear. But there is always the possibility that, if correctly tuned, it will provide greatly improved performance, there being no need for a major overhaul.

A worn carburetter or distributor will frustrate accurate tuning, so these must be replaced or overhauled first. Rebushing the throttle spindle or distributor shaft is possible, but entails lathe-work, while trying to trace replacements for units made some forty years ago can be very difficult. Correcting the tappet clearances, fitting new plugs, readjusting the points, etc. could prove a morning's work very well spent. Further adjustments to the rebuilt or replacement carburetter (see Chapter 6) will then provide a little extra 'edge' on performance.

But symptoms such as low compression and an oily blue exhaust are indicative of poor overall condition. In such cases, part, or all of the engine must be stripped-down and rebuilt.

500 mpp or less?

Let us look first at excessive oil comsumption. If the exhaust is smoky and you are always having to top-up the sump, then the oil scraper rings are not doing their job or, with an ohv engine, the valve guides are badly worn and oil is being sucked into the cylinders and burnt. But should the exhaust be clean and the need for topping-up still very frequent, gasket leakage could well be the cause. To verify this, leave some sheets of newspaper under the sump overnight, having returned from a longish run. Oil drips found in the morning will help you locate that 'elusive' leak.

Excess oil entering the combustion space via worn valve guides will result in a poor oil-consumption figure such as the one above. A quick test is to leave the hot engine ticking over for a minute or two and then suddenly rev up. Clouds of blue smoke are your proof - so remove the head, drift out the old guides with a brass drift and replace with new. Worn scraper rings should be replaced, together with the top compression rings should compression be poor.

Poor compression 'in detail'

Other than worn rings, 'pocketed' or burnt valves will reduce available compression, as will gummed rings and weak valve springs. In an old engine fresh out of 'hibernation' the injection of several fluid ounces of Redex into the throat of the carburetter while revving the engine will sometimes free gummed rings and stuck valves. Examination of the condition of the valves and springs is fairly simple, of course, as it entails merely removing the cylinder head. A 'pocketed' valve cannot be reground; an insert must be fitted by a workshop and a new valve ground in. Burnt valve seats can sometimes be reground satisfactorily, and here weak springs may be the cause. One can either fit new springs or trace which springs are weak by compressing an old spring end-to-end with a new one in a vice. A weak spring will compress more than the new spring. While the head is off, one can decoke the combustion spaces, ports and piston crowns, but it is advisable to leave a thin ring of carbon around the rim of each piston, as this can act as a valuable compression seal in an old engine.

Piston ring replacement is a lengthier affair,

entailing not only the removal of the cylinder head, but also the sump and connecting rods. In some engines the pistons are withdrawn upwards, in others downwards, according to design. Worn rings are usually accompanied by worn pistons, and it is advisable to replace both if in doubt (wear in the ring grooves in excess of 0.006 in. beyond the maker's tolerance indicates replacement).

But before doing any dismantling work, perhaps the application of a compression gauge, a fairly cheap accessory (see Appendix), will indicate more clearly what needs to be done. Fitted with a rubber cone for adaptation to 14 mm or 18 mm spark-plug seatings, the conical end is pressed into the seating while the engine is revolved by the starter; but prior to this the engine must be thoroughly warmed-up to normal operating temperature, all plugs then removed and the 'SW' wire to the coil temporarily disconnected. Readings are taken with the throttle wide open, uniform readings between cylinders being most desirable rather than high compression values. Average compression values in lb/in^2 are as follows:

Compression ratio	Poor	Fair	Good
Up to 4.5:1	20-50	50-55	55-85
4.5 to 5:1	30-55	55-65	65-95
5 to 6.5:1	40-77	67-75	75 - 105
6.5 to 8:1	52-81	81-90	90-113

Variation in readings between cylinders may be due to leakage (1) past the pistons or rings, (2) past the valves, and (3) through a 'blown' cylinder-head gasket. To check between (1) or (2), pour 20 cc of engine oil carefully into the suspect cylinder avoiding letting any reach the valve seats. An immediate rise in reading now will show that the pistons or rings are at fault; the same reading as before is proof of leaking valves. Low readings between adjacent cylinders indicate a gasket leaking between the two.

Decoking aluminium heads

Extra care should be exercised with cylinder heads made of relatively soft alloys. Incorrect tightening-down by a previous owner may have resulted in distortion, and subsequent leakage at the gasket. Here the head will need reworking on a surface grinder. When decoking, avoid the use of sharp, metallic objects which may score the combustion spaces, and when drifting valve guides either in or out exercise great care to avoid distortion or 'bruising'. Tightening of cylinder-head nuts must be carried out in a methodical way, as given in the workshop manual, never just 'at random'. In general this entails tightening progressively and evenly, starting with the centre nuts and working outwards both diagonally and in a 'spiral' order.

Major engine overhaul

Complete renovation of the engine involves its removal from the chassis. Considerable economies may be effected if one removes the engine oneself, strips it down to the 'short' stage (minus all accessories, cylinder head and gearbox) and presents it to a good workshop for rebuilding. Lifting the engine from the chassis is quite easy if an inexpensive block-and-tackle is employed, hung from a stout beam (caution!) or by using a specially-designed tripod or crane (see Appendix for suppliers).

In order to restore the engine to 100% original condition, a complete top and bottom overhaul is necessary. A top overhaul involves reconditioning or replacement of the valves, valve seats, guides, springs, recontouring of the cam-followers and so on. A bottom overhaul entails reboring the cylinders, fitting new pistons, rings, gudgeon pins and bushes, regrinding the crankshaft, installing new main and big-end bearings, overhauling the oil pump, replacing the camshaft bearings and fitting a new timing chain. While the engine is out of the chassis, a new clutch can be installed and the gearbox overhauled.

To check the internal engine wear yourself, you will need an engineer's micrometer and set of feeler gauges (plus an internal micrometer or bore gauge, should you wish to check cylinder wear). The workshop manual will give outside tolerances permissible in your particular engine, i.e. the permissible wear beyond the maker's recommended working clearance. If not, a reasonably accurate average guide for the crankshaft journals is +0.003 in., the cylinder bores +0.010 in., and the piston-ring grooves +0.006 in. Wear in excess of these values indicates the need for overhaul. With the gudgeon pins and bushes there should be no vertical movement in the small-end boss and no sign of a wear ridge on the pin. Permissible wear in the piston skirt (lower sides) is +0.002 in. on the recommended clearance, measured with a feeler gauge in an unworn part of the bore, e.g. above the 'wear ridge' at the top of the cylinder. Piston-ring wear is ascertained by placing a free ring into the unworn part of the bore, squared up at 90° to the cylinder. Tolerance here is +0.010 in. per inch of bore, measured across the ring 'gap'.

Reassembly precautions

Should you do any reassembly work yourself, take great care that all grinding dust and boring swarf has been removed before installing components. Sludge in the oilways and crankcase recesses will attract this extremely harmful abrasive and ruin the rebuilt engine in a very short time.

As for torque-wrench settings, such sophistications were unknown in the Thirties. A guide is given in the table below. The use of open-ended or ring spanners and normal hand leverage is usually quite satisfactory. But avoid the extra leverages obtainable with a socket set - you are quite likely to shear a bolt if you do.

Engine component	Torque-wrench setting (lb. ft.)
Main-bearing cap studs	45 — 65
Big-end bolts	20 — 15
Cylinder-head nuts	40 — 50

These values must not be applied too literally; all engine designs vary. The above figures are based on data for the sv Hillman Minx.

Spares sources

Car Clubs often have scarce components manufactured especially for members, and specialist workshops such as the one listed in the Appendix will make up obsolete components to pattern, or from the worn part itself. Motolympia of Welshpool provide a very thorough spares service for the older car, but often request full information from the owner as to what type of wear is involved, or will ask him to trace serial numbers etc. from the worn parts so that correct replacements may be supplied - hence say, '1936 Ford' is rarely sufficient to go on! Or perhaps you may be friends with an engineer who, for a reasonable charge, will modify or make-up parts for you.

In this age of planned obsolescence, however, do not be surprised should you be met with icy indifference on approaching the staff of an engine reconditioning firm. They may well be excellent with modern engines, but have no time for (or knowledge of) those made before the war. Often it's the small workshop run by an older man which will lend a sympathetic ear. He may even have quite a stock of old engine spares tucked away on a dusty shelf, or know which set of modern pistons may be machined-down to fit. His skill and interest in old machines can sometimes surmount a problem that you were really beginning to think was impossible. And once he gets talking about 'old cars', don't be anxious to get away - it's amazing how much you can learn from a man who has been 'in the engine business' for forty years or so.

Running-in

On delivery, an engine rebuilt by a good workshop may be tight, often alarmingly so. But this is how it should be. The first short burst of power will find the engine running 'hard', and on switching-off it may well stop with a jolt. After allowing time to cool off, restart, and drive the car for a few hundred yards, then switch off, allow to cool and repeat the process. Now take the car for longer runs, avoiding low revs in high gear, and keeping below 45 mile/h for the first 500 miles. After 1000 miles, drain the sump, fit a new oil-filter cartridge and refill with fresh oil. A good quality multigrade oil is ideal.

Chapter Six

Fuel into flame: carburation and ignition systems

By 1930 lesser-known makes of carburetter such as the Smith and Claudel-Hobson were virtually obsolete, and there gradually emerged an all-powerful triumverate of SU, Solex and Zenith, the three major makes of carburetter installed in British cars throughout the 1930-39 era. Perhaps the Stromberg carburetter has best claim to fourth place.

Three patterns of carburetter

Updraught carburetters, where the incoming mixture travels upwards into the manifold, were little used by 1930. In their place sidedraught types were fitted, the mixture moving horizontally through the choke tube. By 1934 the new Zenith downdraught unit was available, mounted above the manifold; here the action of gravity assisted the downward induction of the mixture. Soon Solex and Stromberg downdraught carburettors were also in fairly wide use, particularly with 'sports' engines.

Operating principles

Zenith, Solex (and Stromberg) units all operate on the same basic principle, the fuel being metered through fixed-size jets, the 'gap' between the idling and main jets being compensated for by an intermediate jet. In contrast, the SU carburetter employs a needle moving in a jet as a metering device, the needle moving upwards as manifold vacuum acts upon a suction piston to which it is attached.

Adjustment

All SU carburetters are fitted with a throttle screw (A, Fig. 20). By this means the degree of opening of the throttle may be controlled, as when selecting a satisfactory tick-over speed. Overall mixture strength is governed by the setting of the main jet screw, B. Adjustment of B also affects tick-over. With the choke lever C disconnected, turn B clockwise to lean, or anticlockwise to richen, the mixture. Once fastest tick-over is obtained, readjust A to bring the engine speed down to about 1000 rev/min. On raising the suction piston D 1/16 in., a momentary increase of speed indicates that the mixture is correct. Should the speed increase and persist, the mixture is too rich; should it decrease and the engine stop it is too lean. With an old carburetter, always verify that the suction piston D is free to rise (and fall) freely; also remove the oil cap nut and hydraulic damper E and top-up the dash pot with thin engine oil or Redex.

Zenith and Solex carburetters are adjusted not by moving the main jet, but merely by resetting the idling mixture. Beyond this, substitution of the main and compensating jets by others of different metering values is the sole way to effect major changes to the mixture range. This procedure, however, should not be necessary to tune a 'standard' carburetter, assuming that the jets fitted are as originally specified by the manufacturer (see Part 2). Both makes are, like the SU, fitted with a throttle screw (A, Figs.21 and 22). Fastest tick-over is obtained by adjusting the idling screw B, and then brought down to a reasonable speed by

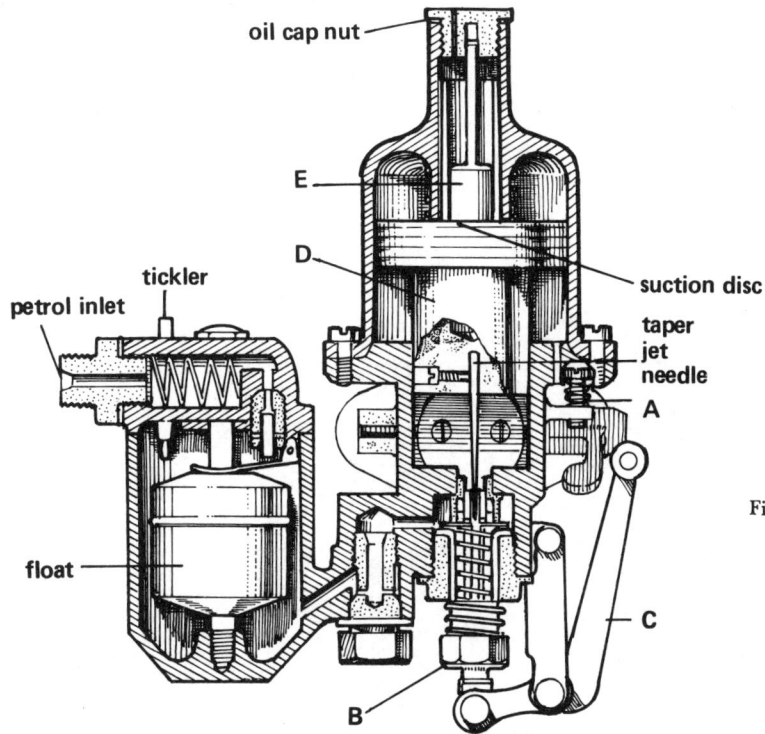

Fig 20   Sidedraught SU carburetter

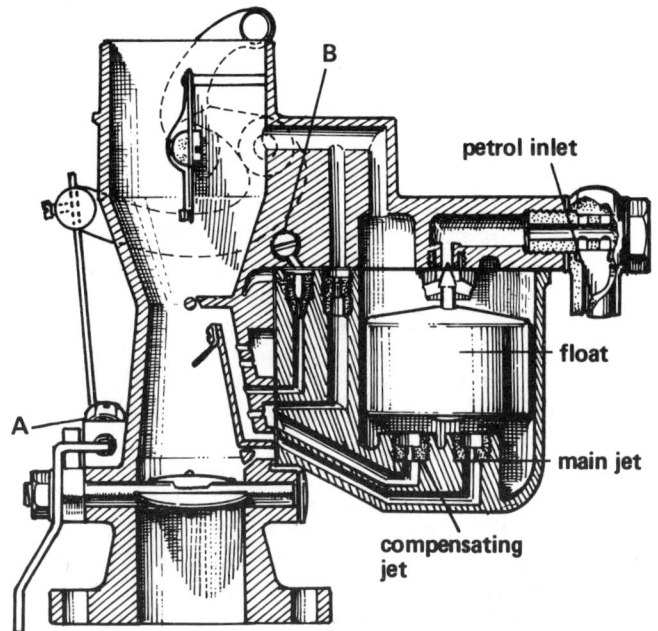

Fig 21   Downdraught Zenith carburetter

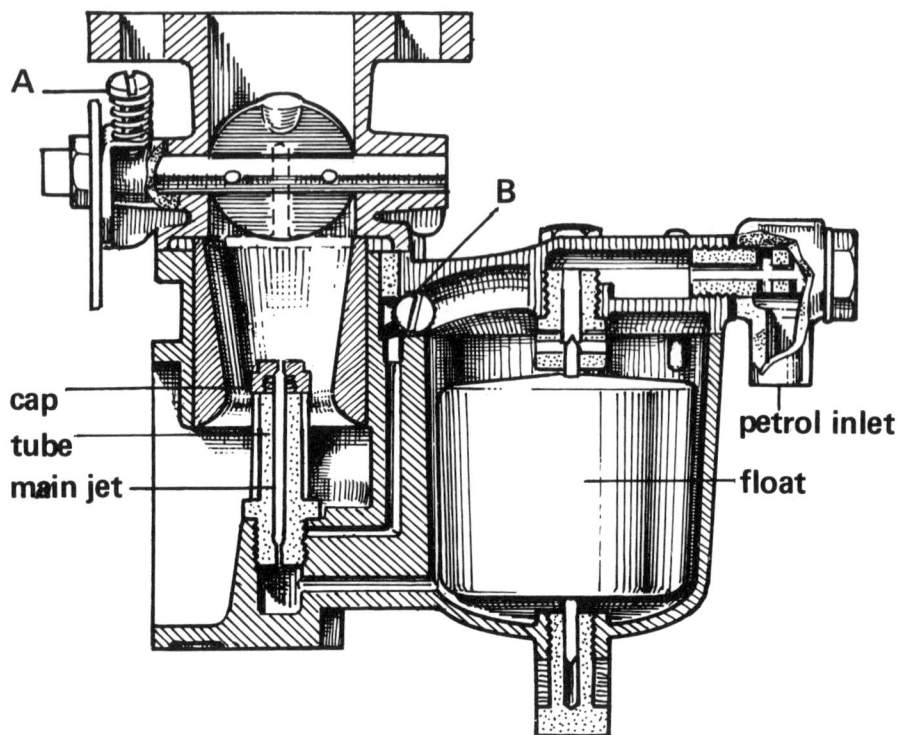

Fig 22   Updraught Solex carburettor

closing A. The screw B may be of either 'air bleed' or 'volume control type', a richer setting being, in the former case, obtained by rotating the screw clockwise, while with the latter, turning the screw anticlockwise will richen the mixture. An 'air bleed' screw is mounted, in Zenith down-draught units, near the mouth of the carburetter, 'volume control' screws being situated near to the flange.

The choke control may well be linked with the throttle-screw setting, entailing slight read-justment after tuning. But most important is to verify that the choke valve closes fully when the choke pull is operated, and, conversely, opens to the maximum when the choke is off.

It is, of course, futile to attempt fine tuning before having checked that such things as tappet clearances, contact-breaker and plug gaps are correct. Poor compression or varying values between cylinders will also render tuning in-effective.

Synchronization and tuning problems

Multi-carburetter installations must be synchronized in order to extract maximum performance and economy. Equal opening of the throttles from zero is vital - loosen the linkage, screw back the throttle screws until they just contact the stops, then relock the linkage and screw each throttle-screw in two complete turns exactly. Check that the throttles are still properly zeroed, with all stops contacting the throttle screws. Now proceed to tune the carburetters, taking care to apply exactly the same degree of correction to each carburetter in turn. If you are not very successful at first, bear in mind that synchronizing is a skill demanding quite a lot of flair, experience and 'knack'. Perhaps a Colortune plug, or a proprietary brand of 'home-tune synchronizer' designed for use with two or more carburetters may prove invaluable. Some tuners use a straw or thin tube placed in each intake to compare by ear the hiss of each carburetter at tick-over, others rely on 'feel', intuition or trial-and-error road tests.

All such skills are, however, valueless should the carburetter(s) be worn. Many tuning problems arise from the fact that old carburettors can never be finely tuned - coupled with a worn engine and sloppy ignition timing the position is often hopeless. Old carburetters need overhaul or replacement - after all, their expected life is a mere 40,000 miles. Spread over forty years, a car having covered only 1,000 miles a year will be due for a new carburetter, so your corroded 'original' unit may have provided 'posthumous' service for far too long!

Types of fuel feed

Originally, the petrol tank was mounted in the scuttle, feed to the carburetter being via gravity. In the interests of safety, the tank was later moved to the rear of the car, from whence fuel was supplied to the carburetter by some form of fuel pump. Other than using a tapping from the exhaust pipe to pressurize the tank, the Autovac pump was one of the earliest (less dangerous) devices. Shown in Fig. 23, the Autovac was mounted inside the bonnet and was actuated by inlet-manifold vacuum. The suction generated at medium speed was used to suck fuel up from the fuel tank and into a quart-capacity reservoir tank within the unit. From here, petrol flowed by means of gravity to the

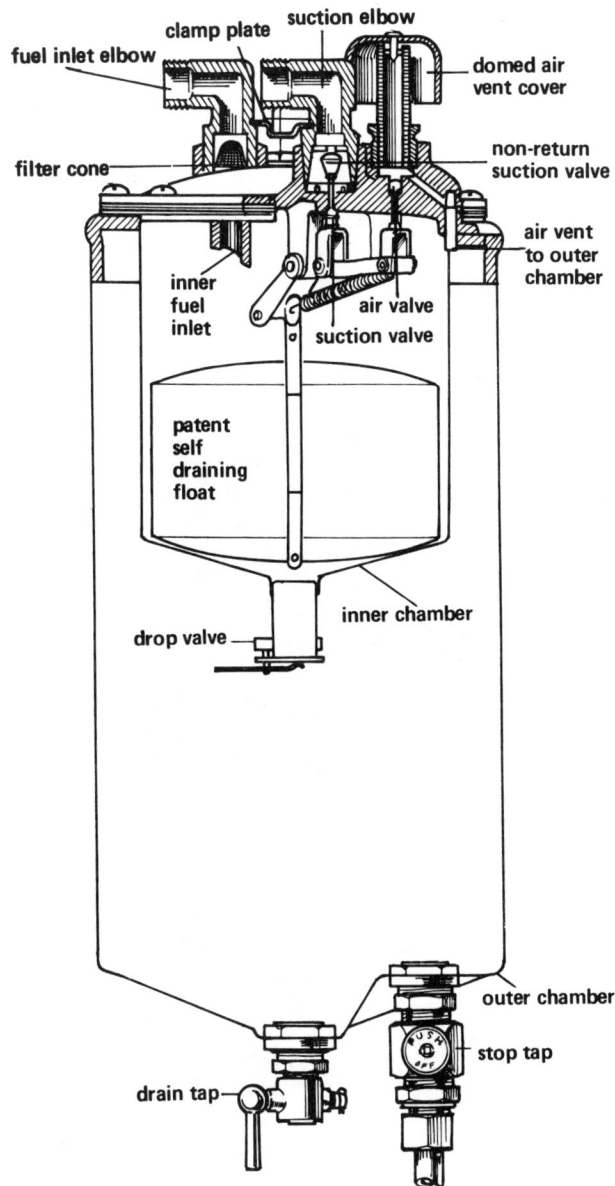

Fig 23   Autovac petrol pump

carburetter. A drain tap was provided for the weekly removal of sediment. Other than keeping all gaskets air-tight, no maintenance was necessary.

Once the practice of equipping each car with a fair-sized battery became common, electrical fuel pumps such as the Petrolift and Autopulse (Figs. 24 & 25 respectively) came into use. Here an electrically-operated solenoid actuated a simple form of diaphragm pump, a head of fuel being drawn up into a small reservoir tank, flowing by gravity to the carburetter. A float device cut off electrical flow to the solenoid once the reservoir was full.

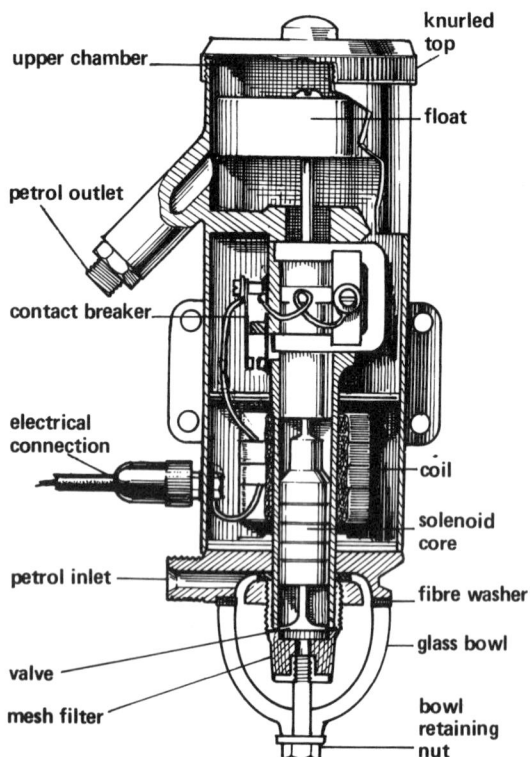

Fig 24   Petrolift electric petrol pump

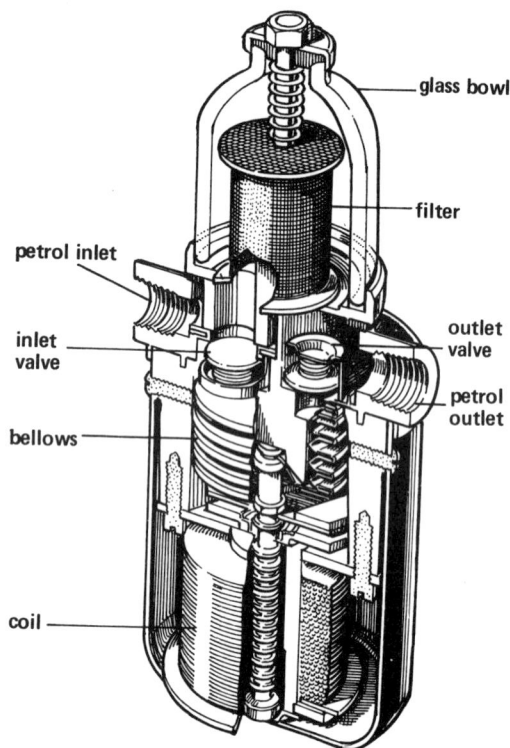

Fig 25   Autopulse electric petrol pump

Manufactured by the SU Carburetter Company, the Petrolift was the direct fore-runner of the now-common SU electric fuel pump, the design of which has changed sur-prisingly little over the years. Of far less bulk (Fig.26), the SU pump could be mounted on the firewall or more safely, under the floor of the car. Of identical operation to the Petrolift, it was in many ways simpler, and while incor-porating a horizontally-actuating solenoid, did not draw-up a reserve of fuel, but metered it spasmodically to the carburetter as conditions demanded. The sole maintenance involves cleaning the filter and polishing the contact points with carborundum paper (at very long intervals). Since fuel is supplied under definite pressure, as compared with the mere effect of gravity, special needle-valves, mounted above the float chamber of the carburetter, are demanded. Over-rich running could be due to a needle-valve in poor condition.

Also delivering fuel under pressure was the early AC mechanical fuel pump (Fig.27), which employed a diaphragm actuated by a rocker arm and eccentric cam mounted on the camshaft. Also of wide application to-day, the AC pump is nowadays of all-metal construction, the glass filter bowl having been discarded. The recipro-cating diaphragm and 'one-way' valves draw petrol from the tank and pump it to the carburetter in the same way as the modern SU device, but it operates, of course, only when the engine is running. Again maintenance is rarely needed. A blocked filter or perforated diaph-ragm are the rare causes of failure.

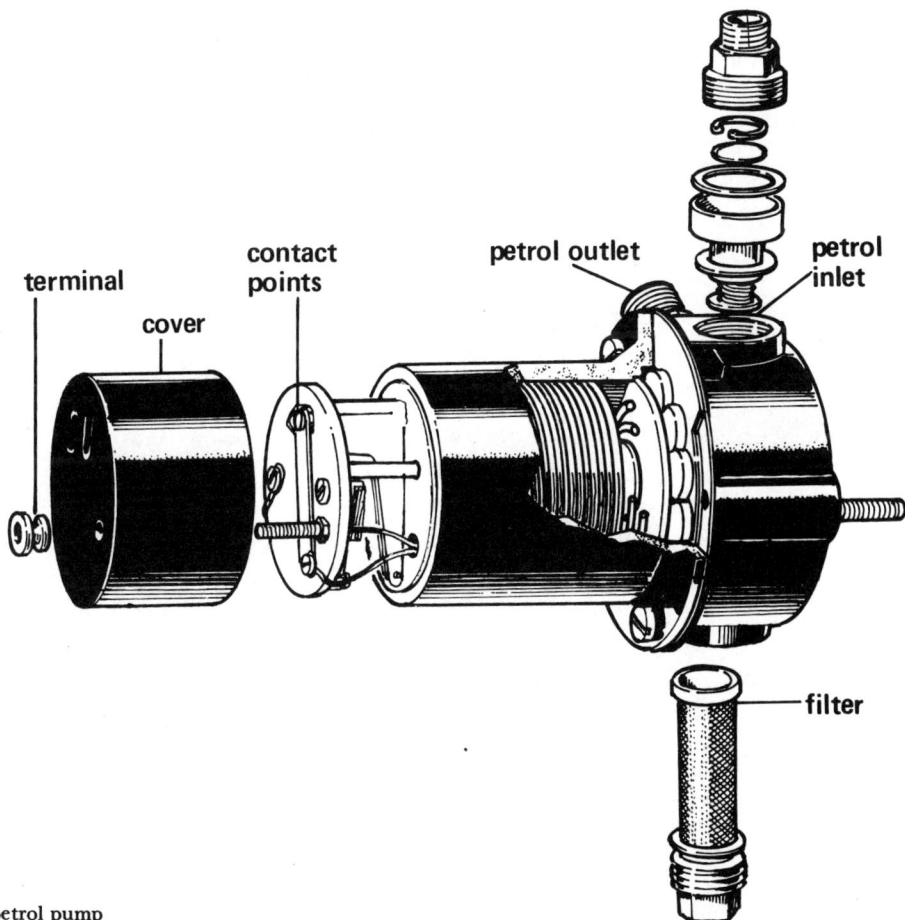

terminal   cover   contact points   petrol outlet   petrol inlet   filter

Fig 26   SU electric petrol pump

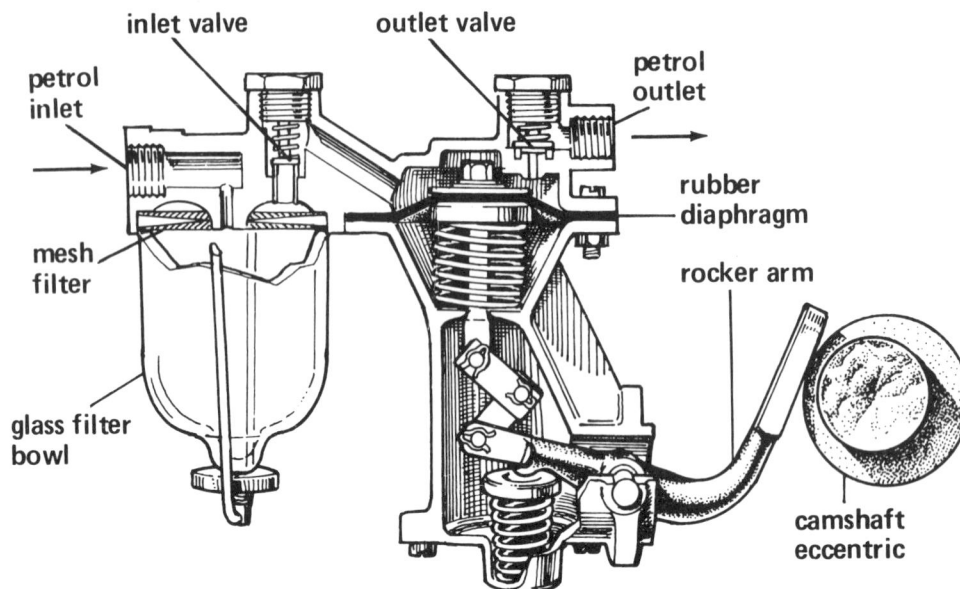

Fig 27   Early AC mechanical petrol pump

Modern fuels

The high-quality grades of petrol available to-day enable the enthusiast to retune his carburetter and sometimes effect worthwhile economy. Solex and Zenith units are simple to convert since changing the values of the jets to those of smaller fuel-flow is simply a matter of direct substitution. SU metering needles are, however, inscrutable to all but an expert, but one can try fitting a 'weak' needle (see Data pages).

Ignition systems

In 1930 a choice of ignition was available : (1) coil and distributor, (2) magneto, or (3) dual ignition.

Giving an excellent and crisp spark at high revs, the magneto fell out of favour when it came to starting on cold, damp mornings. Successful development enabled the coil system to eventually supercede the magneto and it was extensively adapted for most mass-produced cars, magneto ignition surviving only in 'fanatical' sporting and racing circles. Coil ignition proved ideal for touring and saloon cars in that the strength of its spark remained constant even at cranking speed, facilitating easy starting. Some luxury cars embodied dual ignition, the flick of a switch effecting a change from one system to the other.

Coil ignition

Still the most widespread ignition system in use to-day, it consists of an induction coil, the primary windings of which are fed with LT current from a six or twelve-volt battery. By means of a rotor within a distributor, a cam opens and closes a contact-breaker, HT current being induced into the coil's secondary windings and distributed to each cylinder in turn. A condenser connected across the points prevents burning of the contacts.

Beyond occasional cleaning, resetting or replacement of the points, very little maintenance is necessary. Sometimes a condenser will fail; very rarely, a short circuit develops in the coil. Beyond ensuring that the battery remains fully charged, the connections tight, HT leads free of dampness, and all plugs efficient and of the correct heat range, coil ignition may conveniently be 'ignored' for long intervals of time.

Magneto ignition

A relatively more complex piece of machinery, the magneto is, however, self-contained and does not rely on a battery. Moisture will, if it penetrates the internal wiring, cause failure - the cure being to remove the magneto, open the distributor cover and place the unit on a radiator to dry out. Often the magneto was timed by means of a Simms venier coupling, a rubber moulding with radial 'teeth' separating the engine drive from the magneto. Rotation of the coupling by a distance of one 'tooth' advanced or retarded the ignition by 1/380 th of a revolution.

Magneto overhaul is quite within the realm of an enthusiast, but demands delicacy of touch, some of the workings being as finely engineered as a clock. Araldite is an ideal adhesive for repairing ebonite parts that may be broken. Thorough cleaning and relubricating can often restore life to a magneto which has lain idle for a long time, but damp is the worst bogy to be overcome. Should you be unsuccessful, you can post the magneto to a specialist for repair or overhaul (see Appendix).

Contact-breaker and plug gap

With prewar coil ignition, a general guide is to set the contact-breaker points at 0.012-0.015 in. and plug gap at 0.018 - 0.022 in. In the case of a magneto, set the contact points at 0.012 - 0.015 in. and the plug gap at approximately 0.015 in. (The Vauxhall series of models of 1938-39 had 'long spark' coils, the necessary plug gap being 0.038 - 0.040 in.).

Automatic advance-and-retard

The use of bob-weights made possible the incorporation of centrifugal advance-and-retard, both in coil and magneto ignition, the distributor mechanism being modified by the manufacturers. Previous to this, manual advance-and-retard had been the only control, the distributor body being rotated by means of a long rod extending to a lever on the steering-wheel boss. By the mid-30s the inclusion of a vacuum unit connected to the inlet manifold made possible the automatic retarding of the ignition at high revs, an economy device.

Converting a magneto to coil ignition

Sufferers from an erratic or senile magneto may like to know that its distributor mechanism, if in serviceable condition, can be adapted to serve as the distributor for a coil ignition conversion. In order to reduce the load on the bearings, the faulty primary and secondary windings are first removed, and the bearings packed with grease. Next the collector brush (A, Fig. 28) is removed, its holder B sawn off flush, and the brass core drilled back as shown at C. An electrical connection D must be tapped into the core and connected to the coil HT connection. The SW terminal is connected to the unearthed pole of the battery, an 'ignition switch' being included. A suitable condenser E must be connected to the original earthing terminal F, the CB coil terminal being linked by a wire to this point also. The magneto's original earthing-wire must be discarded. Any manual adv/ret control may, of course, be retained. Set the contact-breaker points at 0.015 in.

Spark plugs

Following aero engine and motorcycle practice, the larger 18mm spark plugs gave way to the 14mm type by the mid-30s. These smaller plugs differed basically in that they were of

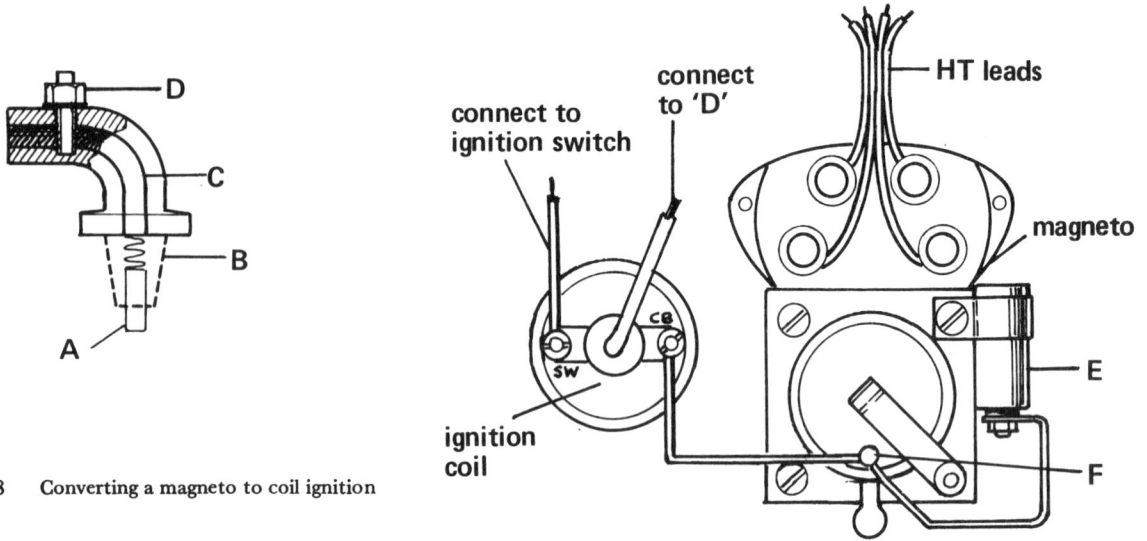

Fig 28   Converting a magneto to coil ignition

integral construction; the 18mm had been of detachable design and could be dismantled for cleaning. During the '30s, plugs with rotary or multiple electrodes were favoured as it was thought these were more reliable - nowadays one rarely sees this type.

The chart below shows common prewar plugs and their modern equivalents (if any):

18 mm types

Prewar plug		Modern equivalent	Alternative modern equivalent		
			Champion	KLG	Lodge
AC	86	C85	K-9	-	C3
	331	C83H	UK-10	M60	HV
Champion			AC	KLG	Lodge
	7	7	C85	M50	C3
	16	K-9	C82	-	-
	17	UK-10	C83H	M60	HV
KLG			AC	Champion	Lodge
	777	M50	C85	7	C3
	K1	M50	C85	7	C3
	K2	M50	C85	7	C3
	M50	M50	C85	7	C3
	M60	M60	C83H	UK-10	HV
Lodge			AC	Champion	KLG
	C3	C3	C85	7	M50
	H1	HV	C83H	UK-10	M60
	H2	HV	C83H	UK-10	M60

14 mm types

Prewar plug	Modern equivalent	Alternative modern equivalent		
AC		**Champion**	**KLG**	**Lodge**
48	48	UJ-12	FS20	BAN
Champion		**AC**	**KLG**	**Lodge**
L-10	L-10	45F	F50	CN
L-10S	L-7	43F	F70	H14
NA-8	N-5	45XL	FE70	HBLN
KLG		**AC**	**Champion**	**Lodge**
F50	F50	43FS	L-87Y	CNY
F70	F70	45XL	N-5	HBLN
TFS30	FS50	45	J-8	CAN
Lodge		**AC**	**Champion**	**KLG**
C14	C14	M45F	L-90	-
CAN	CAN	C45	J-8	FS50

Modern plug-spanner sizes

18 mm - 1 in. AF   14 mm - 13/16 in. AF

Chapter Seven

Friction, mesh and motion: clutch, gearbox and axle

The leather-faced cone clutch of the early 1920s was virtually obsolete by 1930. In its place came the dry disc clutch, friction between the flywheel, friction plate and pressure plate being varied by foot pressure acting against the clutch springs. Although most light cars employed a dry clutch by 1930, one or two models, notably the Morris Cowley of that year, retained a wet clutch, which transmitted friction through cork discs running in oil. Some luxury models were fitted with the Newton centrifugal clutch or a 'fluid flywheel', as in Daimler, Lanchester and certain BSA cars.

Clutch inspection and overhaul

Clutch renovation is possible only when the engine is out of the chassis. Symptoms of clutch malfunction are a tendency to 'snatch' due to worn friction linings, or 'slip' caused by seepage of oil. Should disengagement or engagement occur over a very short distance of pedal movement, the clutch friction-plate also needs replacing (except, perhaps, with the Austin Seven where this was normal!)

Once the engine-gearbox assembly is out of the car, the gearbox is first unbolted from the bell-housing, although with some models it is possible to leave the gearbox in the chassis and remove the engine and clutch only. Removal of the bell-housing enables inspection of the clutch and actuating mechanism. Oil which has penetrated the plates will be visible immediately, as will any broken parts. Severe wear in the friction plate is indicated when the surface of the friction material is worn level with the heads of the rivets; also any distortion in the friction plate, scoring of the flywheel surface, or wear in the ring-gear teeth will be apparent on further dismantling.

The surest means of overhaul is the fitting of new parts - attempting to reline a clutch oneself is rarely worthwhile as home workshop facilities are inadequate. But should new replacements prove unobtainable, you may have to do it yourself, purchasing suitable sheets of 'Ferodo'-type material, cutting to shape using the old linings as patterns and rivetting the new linings in place as best you can. As a rule the rivet heads should be countersunk approximately one third the thickness of the lining. The rivets must be pulled up sound and tight. Dynamic balance of the renovated assembly is checked by the manufacturer - the best you can do is to attain as exact static balance as you can by careful assembly, then spin the clutch assembly and rebalance until it comes to a stop at random, not always in one position.

It is best automatically to renew the thrust bearing. As for the ring-gear, this is removed by splitting, using a heavy hammer and cold chisel. In cases of unavailability of spares, the life of the old gear may be prolonged by expanding it slightly by heating it to 400°C using an oxy-acetylene torch, then, when it will slip, tapping it round into a new position on the flywheel rim. In this way the worn portion will no longer serve as the 'hardest worked'. The fitting of a new ring-gear is, however, best left to a workshop, as oxy-acetylene equipment is essential for preheating, and excessive heating of the gear will destroy its natural temper; the correct temperature can only be judged by an experienced operator, who at the precise moment, slips the gear over the flywheel, where it is locked in place by contraction.

Should the flywheel surface be scored, the services of a workshop must again be sought for 'skimming' and rebalancing. A faulty Newton clutch is for the expert. As for fluid flywheels, always top-up with the correct grade of transmission fluid - never engine oil. The 'Cowley' type of 'wet' clutch could be entrusted to a motorcycle workshop for renovation, as they will have had more experience with this type.

Gearbox developments

During the decade new innovations in gearbox design saw modification of the straight-cut sliding-mesh gears of Twenties 'crash' gearboxes, leading to the adoption of constant-mesh helical gears, 'silent third', and synchromesh on top, third (and later, second) gear. Manual gearboxes invariably had a floor-mounted gearchange and 'H'-pattern gate. The number of forward gears was three or four, the latter necessitating an 'up and over' branch in the gate for selecting reverse. Now of unit construction with the engine, a gearbox incorporating helical gears was much quieter in operation; and the spread of lady (and lazy) drivers soon led to the introduction of synchromesh (a General Motors innovation) for the lower gears. Preselector and automatic gearboxes formed part of the 'extra' specification of the more expensive cars.

Gearbox renovation

As stated previously, the overhaul of a faulty gearbox is best entrusted to a specialist. Should you remove the gearbox yourself, remember not to leave the transmission shaft unsupported - tie it to a chassis member so that it is not hanging from its flange. Certain minor faults can be tackled by the enthusiast, amongst these slight oil leaks, and gears sticking or 'jumping out'. Minor leakage may be due to faulty gaskets,

some of which may prove simple to renew; on the other hand, major gearbox leaks lie outside the province of the amateur, in that mainshaft oil-seals are inaccessible, often to the extent that the whole gearbox must first be stripped down. If left unattended, the leaking oil may soon find its way on to the clutch should the front seal be ineffective. With a torque tube, a rear oil-seal leak may overload the rear axle, forcing oil on to the brake linings.

A gear sticking in mesh can often be freed by removing the gearbox cover and tapping the synchomesh unit in the appropriate direction. Take care here not to lose any selector balls or springs; upon reassembly top-up the gearbox with a molybdenum disulphide additive. Weak selector springs allow gears to jump out, replacement entailing merely the removal of the gearbox cover (you can try swapping springs round first). Sometimes filing deeper knotches in the selector bars will prove an effective cure.

Stripped gear teeth, a fractured selector arm, etc. involve much deeper dismantling, and if you are new to gearbox work and yet wish to do the repairs yourself, then ensure you have exploded diagrams handy, or make careful drawings of the position of parts as you remove them and place each assembly in a labelled box.

One further word of advice - if your car has lain idle for years and, with the engine running, you find it impossible to select any gear, the trouble could well lie not in the gearbox but the clutch, the plates having become cemented together by rust (see p.41).

Rear axle and transmission-shaft maintenance

Generally of spiral-bevel pattern, the axle should be topped-up with EP 90 gear oil, a level-plug being fitted in the casing. Do not overfill, or oil could reach the brake linings. A leaky axle will need new gaskets; check also that the breather is not blocked. Stripped teeth, a broken half-shaft and so on, spell removal and dismantling; torque tubes are integral with the axle, while open transmission shafts have merely a flange-fixing incorporating Hardy-Spicer joints. Always support the shaft after axle removal. Bronze-bushed Hardy-Spicer joints are employed in torque tubes, while needle-bearing joints are found in open shafts. After removing the circlips, needle-bearing joints can usually be dismantled by tapping the casting with a copper mallet.

Vibration in the transmission may be due to a bent shaft, or decay in the fabric couplings or the rubber bushes of Layrub units; penetration by oil will also cause rotting. A slightly distorted shaft can sometimes be rebalanced with a Jubilee clip.

Needle-bearing joints need periodic lubrication, should a nipple be fitted. Sometimes SAE 140 oil is specified, not grease. In this case it is more convenient to keep a small-capacity grease gun filled with oil of the correct grade, solely for the Hardy-Spicer joints.

Never attempt to improvise when fitting new bolts in fabric or Layrub couplings. The correct type are of high-tensile steel, with castellated nuts locked by means of split pins. Ordinary 'soft' bolts will not do - should they shear or fracture it could result in a dangerous accident, particularly should the front end of the transmission shaft drop and contact the road.

As for a noisy rear axle, avoid dabbling and possibly wasting a lot of time in the process. Leave the job to an expert.

Chapter Eight

Direction plus retardation: steering and brake mechanisms

Three types of steering mechanism were in popular use during the decade: (1) worm-and-wheel or worm-and-sector, (2) worm-and-nut or screw-and-nut, and (3) cam-and-lever or cam-and-roller.

The first type relies on a worm gear mounted at the lower end of the steering shaft, which engages with a wheel fixed to the transverse steering shaft (Fig.29). This design of steering box generally has a reduction gearing of approximately 4 to 1 and hence often only part of the worm wheel, i.e. a sector, is necessary. (Should a complete wheel be fitted, however, it may later be repositioned so as to bring into use an unworn part of its circumference). When the steering shaft is turned, the rotation of the worm actuates the wheel; the shaft attached to the wheel thus describes an arc which imparts a push-or-pull movement to the front steering link. Lubrication of the moving parts is provided for by a grease nipple or oil filler-plug (SAE 140 being a suitable grade). Wear is taken up by means of an adjusting nut.

Worm-and-nut and screw-and-nut steering boxes also have a worm or screw gear, but in place of a wheel a nut is incorporated which runs up and down the screw thread (Fig. 30). The nut is of bronze, with a steel bush into which fits a ball pin attached to the rocker shaft. An adjustable ball race is fitted at the top of the steering shaft, of cup-and-cone pattern; wear may thus be compensated for. Lightness of action is a main feature of this type of steering.

Cam-and-lever and cam-and-roller steering boxes have, in place of a screw, a helical groove called the 'cam'. Sliding in this groove is a ball peg fixed to the arm of the rocker shaft. The peg may also be in the form of a roller - hence the 'lever' becomes a 'roller'. Adjustment in this type is by means of shims, placed between the steering-box lid and its seating.

The cam can be of non-constant pitch i.e. of coarse pitch for 'straight ahead' engagement, while of finer pitch near full lock to provide a lower steering ratio for easier parking. Proprietary systems of cam-and-roller steering were the Marles Weller and the Bishop. In some of these designs the cam took on more of an 'hour glass' form.

Steering geometry and toe-in

Castor angle, camber angle and king-pin inclination are all built into the car during manufacture. It is only due to crash damage, where the chassis, stub axles or steering arms are distorted, that these settings can alter. Toe-in, on the other hand, is adjustable. Measured with a tracking gauge, the correct amount of toe-in is obtained by adjusting the length of the track rod by means of threaded joints. Incorrect toe-in can rapidly shorten the life of the tyres. Toe-out is also occasionally specified.

Steering troubles

Before 'faulting' the steering mechanism, first check the condition and pressure of the tyres. Equal and correct pressures in the front tyres is vital (see the Data pages in Part 2); badly worn treads also affect the steering, but can, of

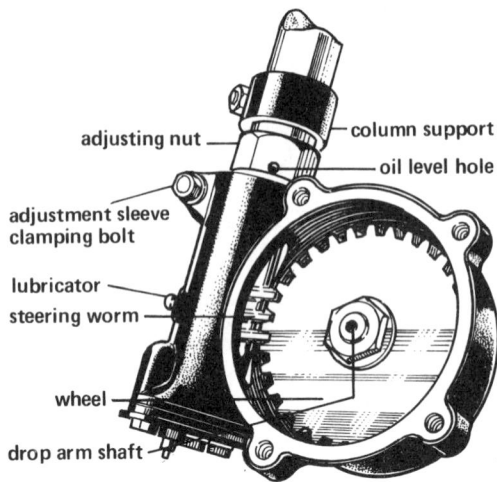

adjusting nut

column support

oil level hole

adjustment sleeve
clamping bolt

lubricator

steering worm

wheel

drop arm shaft

Fig 29   Worm-and-wheel steering box

course, be a product of incorrect tracking. Check also the balance of the wheels when fitting new tyres, as well as the adjustment of the steering box and knuckle joints, the fit of the king-pins and bushes, and the condition of the hub bearings and leaf springs, paying particular attention to side-play in the shackles. Shock-absorbers should be topped-up and checked.

These preliminaries over, and the steering still subject to wheel 'wobble', 'shimmy', 'wander' or 'tramp', the castor and camber angles and king-pin inclination should be checked. All are closely interrelated and each affects the others. In the rarer cases of models with ifs, a

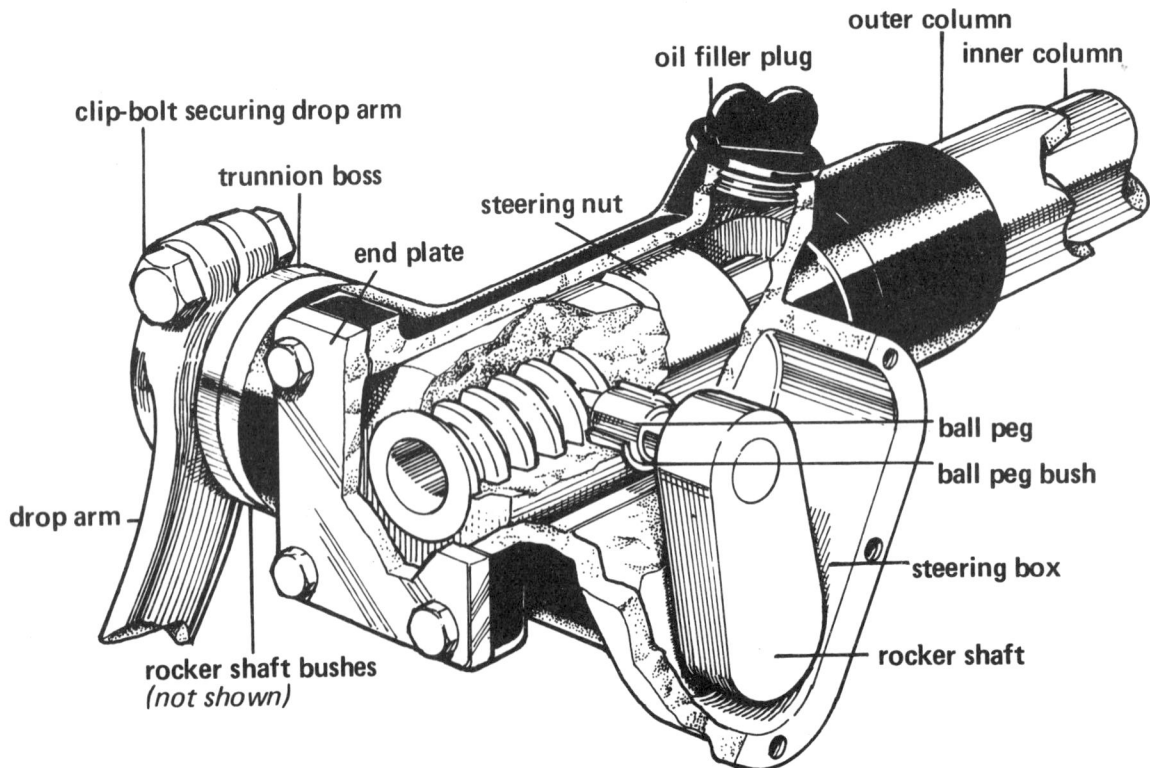

clip-bolt securing drop arm

trunnion boss

end plate

steering nut

oil filler plug

outer column

inner column

ball peg

ball peg bush

steering box

drop arm

rocker shaft bushes
(not shown)

rocker shaft

Fig 30   Screw-and-nut steering box

76

completely different geometry applies. Of whatever type, the maker's manual should be the sole source of information regarding steering geometry; carefully reasoned deduction or inspired guesswork will not do. Similarly, although rough-and-ready measures constructed with yardsticks and draughtsmen's protractors can sometimes be improvized, it is often surer and quicker to take the car to a garage which has professional equipment. A suspect front axle may, however, be removed, clamped level in a vice and its trueness checked. By means of a set-square, the enthusiast should confirm lateral and transverse levels at each end of the axle, the squareness of both mounting plates, and use a protractor head to check the king-pin inclination, a dismantled king-pin being introduced a short way into its bushing. A workshop with a forge may be able to true-up the axle.

Mechanical brakes

Many light cars of the 1930s were served purely by mechanical brakes, of Bendix-Cowdrey or Girling manufacture. Relying completely on mechanical linkages, these types of brakes were actuated by cables or rods; such systems were capable of individual or master adjustment, fully compensated, and usually embodied the 'self-wrapping' or 'two leading shoe' principle with its attendant servo effect. In general, poor mechanical brakes are due to excessive wear - locate this, remedy it, and the brakes will be 100% efficient again. But loss of efficiency may be due to incorrect adjustment at the brake shoes, or badly worn linings. All three systems are equipped with adjusters on the brake backplates, the Bendix system having three types: one rotated by means of the point of a screwdriver, another with a square-ended extension and a third having a flexible shaft and used in cases where there is little direct access. The Girling brake system, although basically similar to the Bendix-Cowdrey, incorporates 'roller and wedge' shoe-actuation giving superior leverage in the region of 6.5 to 1; adjustment is by means of a screwdriver fitting into the slotted end of a screwed steel wedge.

Routine adjustment of all types of brakes entails turning the brake adjuster until the jacked-up wheel just locks, then backing the adjuster sufficiently to allow the wheel to spin freely. Some types of adjuster turn in a series of clicks. With individually-set brakes, rod length is varied by means of wing nuts; alternatively, the length of cables is adjusted via threaded clevis fittings. Other such devices in use with compensated rod-brakes are barrel nuts or turnbuckles. All three proprietary systems mentioned above incorporate compensators, but unless these have been deliberately disturbed, no resetting is necessary. Since precise details for resetting individual designs of compensator are lengthy and complex, the reader·is advised to consult the maker's workshop manual, or the Technical Officer of his Car Club.

Relining brake shoes

In the case of a rare model, the owner may have to reline the brakes himself. Modern techniques involve bonding the lining to the shoe, but the enthusiast may have to rest content with rivets, and linings adapted to fit. Should the rivet holes not coincide, new holes should be flat-countersunk to a depth of two-thirds the thickness of the lining. Rivetting starts at the middle of the shoe, working out towards the edges to avoid buckling. The preformed head of the rivet should rest on a suitable inverted punch clamped in a vice, and each rivet be carefully pulled up sound and tight - the correct size and shape of punch being vital here. Before fitting, chamfer the leading edge of each lining at 45º. But beware wasting new linings on worn shoes with oval pivot-pins and the like.

Hydraulic brakes

Even before 1930, the inherently more efficient system of hydraulic brakes introduced in Britain by Lockheed was fitted by such makers as Morris, MG, Triumph and Wolseley. Later, Singer Motors specified hydraulic brakes for their sporting models, while die-hards like Austin and Standard postponed the fitting of hydraulics until after the war.

Ineffective hydraulic brakes, may, as with the mechanical type, require adjustment at the brake shoes or relining. Otherwise, beyond one or two small details or severe wear in the surface of the brake drums, the reason for poor brakes must lie in the hydraulic system. A 'spongy', impositive feel at the brake pedal is due to air bubbles which have entered the network of pipes. To remove air and restore correct functioning, bleeding is called for: this entails the provision of an ample supply of Lockheed hydraulic fluid (lengthy bleeding may demand the use of at least a pint), a suitable ring spanner, a two-foot length of transparent neoprene tubing to fit tightly over the bleed nipples, and a clean glass jar to collect old or aerated fluid. You will also need an assistant should you not posess a set of ABV automatic bleed valves (see Appendix for supplier): these patented valves enable you to bleed the hydraulics on your own, full instructions being supplied. Alternatively, ask your assistant to sit in the driver's seat, having pointed out the brake pedal to him, and then clamber under the car to gain access to whichever wheel is furthest from the master cylinder (usually the nearside rear). Having located the bleed nipple, slide an appropriate ring spanner over the 'flats' and attach the length of neoprene, its open end passing into the jar. Note that the neoprene will conveniently pass through the ring spanner (Fig. 31). Now open the nipple a couple of turns and ask your assistant to depress the brake pedal with three or four slow and steady strokes, holding it down after the final stroke while you tighten the nipple. Bubbles of air should be visible, passing into the jar as the old fluid is pumped out. You will now have to top-up the master cylinder reservoir with fresh fluid and repeat the pumping process - never put back aerated fluid or allow the level to fall below one inch of the bottom. Bleeding may take quite a time - repeat the process with each wheel in turn, ending up at the one nearest the master cylinder. You may well have to go round again, in the same order, loosening, bleeding and tightening the appropriate nipple before you move on to the next. The larger pockets of air must be got rid of first, your final aim being to rid the system of even the minutest bubble (the transparent neoprene is of great help here). Fully bled of air, the result should be a firm, resistant feel at the brake pedal, an aural check being a sound like crushed snow as you press the pedal, revealing that tiny air bubbles are still present in the master cylinder. Should you find the system impossible to bleed fully, dismantle the master cylinder and investigate for ruptured rubber seals, a corroded one-way valve or a worn bore.

Badly corroded Bundy tubing or frayed flexible pipes must be replaced for your own safety, and to get through the MOT test. Old fluid, too, although not aerated, will have absorbed water and may cause brake fade (check a sample for loss of colour). Leaking or inoperative wheel cylinders may be seized by corrosion or need new seals.

The handbrake, working mechanically on the rear wheels, is generally restored to full efficiency on adjusting the footbrakes. Binding may be due to rusting and lack of lubrication. Sometimes the cable is so badly stretched that all that can be done is to replace it.

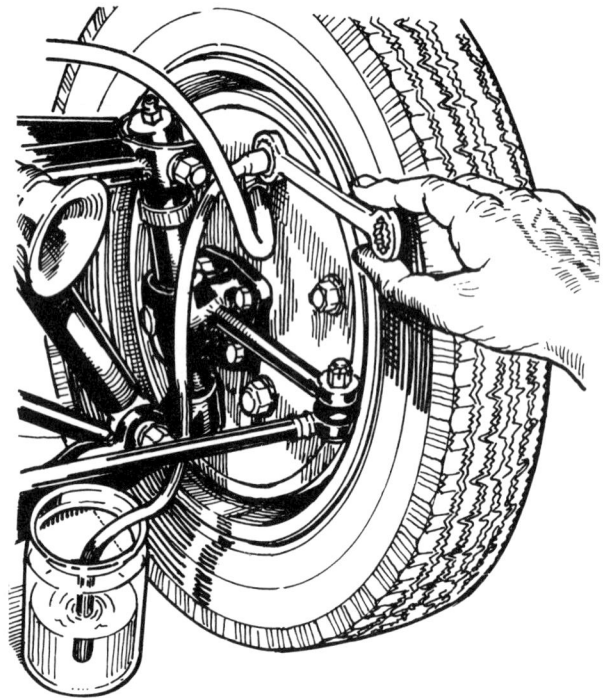

Fig 31   Bleeding hydraulic brakes

Chapter Nine

Riding into gliding: chassis and suspension systems

Virtually every British light car made between 1930 and 1938 was built on the chassis-plus-body pattern, the chassis forming a frame bearing the engine, wheels and transmission, and on to which a separate body unit was later mounted. Although certain Continental manufacturers introduced unit-construction during the early part of the decade, the legacy of the Twenties as regards basic car construction survived in Britain throughout the Thirties and here the car industry clung closely to tradition. It was not until the American-financed Vauxhall concern decided to introduce their unit-construction series of models in 1937 that a distinct departure from conformity made itself felt. Even during the early postwar period the advent of unit-construction, nowadays the norm, was slow to emerge from British car factories.

In 1930 a typical chassis consisted of a tri-angulated construction of two main down-members linked by cross-members, the frame tapering forward to accomodate the swivelling of the front wheels, while the rear widened out towards the rear wheel arches giving a large-area ground plan for the seats and floor. Frames tapering at the front were termed 'inswept', those arching over the rear axle 'upswept'; extensions to the down-members carrying the leaf-spring shackles were called the 'dumb irons'. Early chassis designs employed small-web channel-section members, and little heed was paid to flexing. Later, however, with the introduction of independently rubber-mounted engine-and-gearbox units, a stronger frame was called for. First deeper-web channel-section was used, and then an additional back plate welded across the flanges to produce an early type of box-section. Much more rigid, the box-section chassis had less tendency to flex, an important advantage as wooden-framed bodywork with an ability to 'give' was superceded by pressed-steel bodies. A later development was the introduction of cruciform bracing, yielding a frame that tended towards the ideal, its rigidity enabling advanced forms of steering geometry to be used successfully, earlier flexible frames having nullified many of the benefits. Rigidity of the chassis proved equally desirable with the application of independent front suspension.

A sound chassis vital

To the enthusiast and renovator, the soundness of a car's chassis is paramount. The modern MOT test, too, involves an inspection of the chassis, and if it is found to be unsound this can fail a car outright. A fanatically keen restorer will even go so far as to lift the entire body off the chassis and commence his renovating by checking, rebuilding and rustproofing the frame members. With the bodywork removed, ideal access to the chassis is, of course, afforded; it can be examined in great detail and repaired much more satisfactorily. Generally, prewar pressed steel bodywork was secured by nuts and bolts. But other than removing the body, one must endure long sessions of dirty and unpleasant work where much of the time is spent under the car, often groping to reach inaccessible trouble spots.

Although prewar unit-construction did employ thicker-gauge steel than we are used to to-day, corrosion in crucial areas must be looked for and assessed. Unless exceptionally sound, steer clear of this type as a renovation project.

Chassis renovation

The condition and strength of the original metal must be checked first. Where oil seeping from the sump has coated the front of the chassis, very little rusting will be found. In contrast, sections that have long been exposed to wheel spray may be badly decayed, often dangerously so. Box-sectioned areas can trap large quantities of damp mud and gravel, and this is where severe corrosion starts - add salt, lavishly applied to icy roads, and you have a highly effective corrosive mixture! Areas of decayed frame must be rebuilt, using 'patches' cut from 14 swg mild steel plate brazed to the still-sound edges. Welding is not advised due to the advanced state of decay - the thin, pitted metal will burn through easily, enlarging the problem. Fairly inexpensive DIY brazing outfits (see Appendix) are now available, operating on the electric arc principle but utilizing carbon pencils to produce an arc 'flame'. Low cost naturally means that these units are not oil-cooled, and hence they can only be used for small intervals, a somewhat annoying drawback when one wishes to 'get on and finish the job'. Nevertheless, since these arc-brazing kits plug directly into a 13-amp socket and in effect bring the technique of brazing within the reach of everyone, they are to be recommended and will be found very useful to the car enthusiast. Before brazing commences, all areas of flaking rust must be cleaned down with a stiff wire brush and electric grindstone. Next it is wisest to supplement the flux coating which surrounds the brazing rods by applying borax paste to the chassis working-area and preheating. Now clamp the steel 'patch' in place and tack it in position with a few blobs of braze. Lastly, remove the G-clamp and braze the steel plate to the chassis, running an unbroken layer of brass around the entire circumference. Tap off the cold flux before painting.

Rustproofing of the rebuilt chassis should not be overlooked; wire-brushing or grinding will remove most of the rust, after which you can apply Jenolite, Naval Jelly or a primer such as Kurust. Following this, give one or two coats of red oxide primer, then several applications of black enamel, bitumenized paint, underseal or Hammerite finish.

Leaf-springs plus beam axle

The ubiquitous leaf-spring served most commonly as a suspension device during the decade. Of either underslung semi-elliptic or reversed quarter-elliptic form, it linked the axles to the chassis, minimizing the adverse effects of rough road surfaces. Many models employed a drop-forged I-section beam axle carrying the front wheels; suspension was hence non-independent, and often relied on either two longitudinal leaf-springs or a single lateral spring e.g. in Fords and the Austin Seven. Other forms of front suspension were coil spring-and-wishbone, transverse leaf-spring and wishbone, sliding pillar, and swinging arm-plus-torsion bar.

The advent of ifs

Unlike Continental manufacturers, British car makers were slow to introduce independent front suspension. By 1939 the sole concerns who had adapted their light cars to ifs were Hillman, Humber, Standard, Vauxhall and British Salmson - though we must not overlook H.F.S. Morgan's sliding-pillar design fitted to all Morgans from 1910 onwards. Vauxhall chose the swinging-arm pattern with torsion bars, while the other concerns utilized the transverse leaf-spring-and-wishbone system, incorporating the parallel link principle.

Maintaining the suspension

Leaf-springs require periodic cleaning with a wire brush (if unprotected by gaiters) and lubricating with penetrating oil or graphite grease. Spring shackles, if of the metal-bushed type, also need lubrication; rubber Silentbloc bushes must, on the other hand, never be lubricated, or the rubber will rot. Here maintenance entails the replacement of perished rubber bushes with new. Shackles pins and bushes will, of course, wear in time. Coil springs can lose their temper after long service, giving a 'lop-sided' slant to the car, torsion bars also suffering in this way, their mountings, if rubber-bushed, again subject to decay in the rubber. Regular lubrication of the upper and lower links of an ifs system will greatly reduce wear in the swivels. Sliding-pillar ifs should also be kept well greased.

Shockabsorbers

The earliest friction types such as the Hartford (Fig. 32), resembled a caliper with its pivoting action restricted by the friction of hard-wood discs. This friction was in fact adjustable, in that the pressure between the discs could be varied by means of a dished star-shaped spring. Early in the decade new designs of shock-absorber appeared, employing the damping action provided by a fluid when forced through a small aperture. The Luvax 'vane' type (Fig. 33) incorporated an actuating arm fixed to a rotor reciprocating in a drum filled with a special fluid; restriction to fluid flow was by means of a

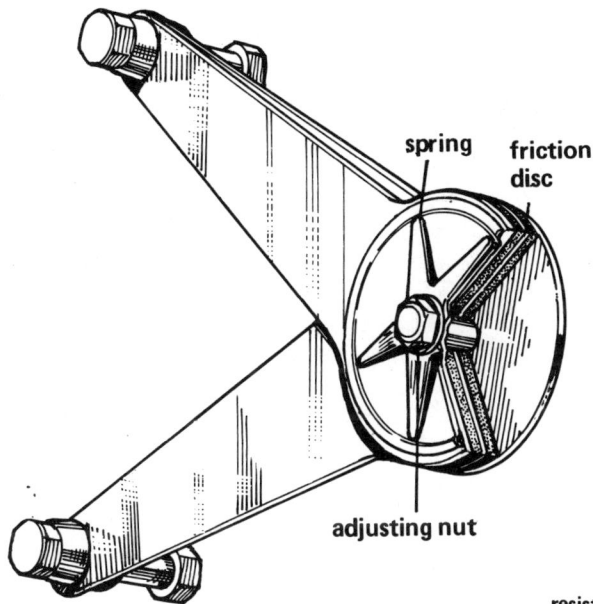

Fig 32   Hartford friction shockabsorber

spring   friction disc

adjusting nut

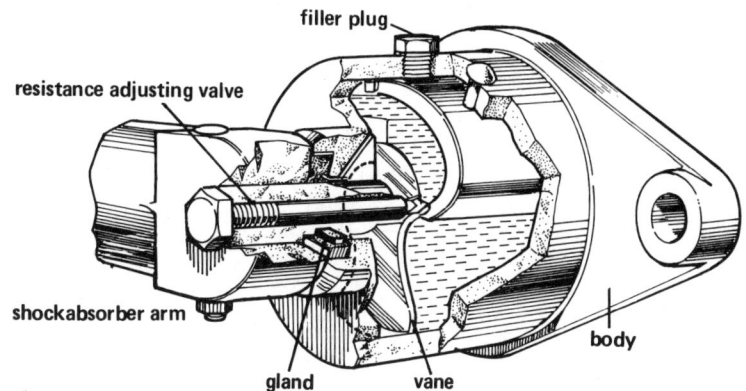

filler plug

resistance adjusting valve

shockabsorber arm

gland   vane

body

Fig 33   Luvax 'vane' hydraulic shockabsorber

spring-loaded small-bore valve. Another type, the Luvax piston shockabsorber, had, as its name implies, a piston in place of a vane; the Armstrong design, too, was of this type. Some means of adjustment was usually provided to adapt the action to city or country roads. The Andre Telecontrol shockabsorber was adjustable from the driver's seat while the car was in motion. Basically, it comprised a friction shockabsorber with its mechanical spring adjustment replaced by a rubber envelope containing fluid and connected by a pipe to a master control mounted under the dashboard.By rotating the master control knob, fluid could be injected into, or withdrawn from, the envelope, thus increasing or decreasing the pressure between the friction discs; a harder or softer damping action was thus obtained.

The maintenance of friction shockabsorbers involves occasional replacement of the discs. Hydraulic types must be topped-up with the correct shockabsorber fluid - never brake fluid. Note that Luvax vane units demand a higher-viscosity fluid. The effects of a faulty shockabsorber are at once noticeable; but don't overlook incorrect tyre pressures, which can completely upset the intended ride.

Chapter Ten

Gleam and gloss: bodywork and interior renovation

Several distinct methods of constructing bodywork existed around 1930. The first type was the fabric-covered body supported by a wooden frame, generally of ash - the bonnet and mudguards, etc. being of course, in metal. Next came bodywork of mixed fabric-and-alloy e.g. a fabric roof section allied with an aluminium-panelled body. Then, as mass-production became more widespread, the pressed-steel body appeared, needing no wooden framework to support it.

Perhaps the flexing of the types of chassis then in vogue dictated the retention of a wooden-framed body which could also flex slightly, yet with the exception of the Weymann body, a common ailment was the rapidity with which annoying squeaks and creaks developed in the joints. Perhaps the inherent lightness of wooden structures proved the greatest advantage. Also of light weight was the wooden frame panelled with aluminium, a metal highly resistant to atmospheric corrosion.

With the advent of rigid, box-section chassis frames, rigid pressed-steel bodies appeared, which while being squeak-free, were both susceptible to rusting and, to the detriment of performance, much more heavy. One has only to cite the liveliness of the fabric-bodied Riley Nine Monaco of the early '30s as compared to the sluggish pressed-steel Victor model of 1938 to show the adverse effect on performance of over-bodied designs.

Renovating wooden-framed bodywork

This is more a job for someone who enjoys carpentry. Ash, though long-lasting, will rot if persistently damp from road spray. One can renovate using ash again or one of the cheaper grades of mahogany, the rotten sections serving as patterns. The original method of construction should be carefully copied; joints were generally of a simple type, often reinforced with a waterproof glue (Araldite would prove excellent here). Weymann-type body frames were screwed together, using specially-shaped metal brackets, a small gap being deliberately left between adjacent members to eradicate the possibility of squeaks. When replacing wooden frame members it is best to weatherproof them with one or two coats of exterior-grade polyurethane varnish and, in the case of a Weymann body, to treat the brackets with an anti-rust preparation, then give two coats of a good quality enamel. Use brass screws if possible, as these will not rust, and pay particular attention to the soundness of the lower frame members, especially those which anchor the body to the chassis.

Renovating fabric body coverings

The 'fabric' used was of the Rexine type, a nitrocellulose-coated cloth. Untextured fabric served to cover the lower bodywork, while heavyweight embossed Rexine was employed for roof areas above the 'waistline'. Where a curved contour was required, the fabric was tensioned by wooden spars and a layer of wadding. In the Weymann body, expanded metal was also incorporated into the fabric support. Modern PVC-coated leathercloth or tough-quality vynide form ideal substitutes for Rexine and a wide choice of attractive colours is available. The fabric is secured by tacks driven into the frame, externally visible joins being masked by a fillet of lead or other material (Hidem binding would serve fairly well here). It must be stressed that fitting a new fabric covering demands skill, and care must be excercised in attaining suitable tensioning of the fabric.

Aluminium bodywork

Salt spray from treated roads proves the main enemy of alloy panels, and due to softness and welding complexities, repairs are best carried out with fibreglass paste. Dents in alloy tend to stretch very easily when knocked out and the temperature for 'hot shrinking' is very critical. Old cellulose may well tend to peel from alloy surfaces, the sole remedy being the use of an etching primer prior to refinishing.

Pressed-steel bodywork

Rust is, of course, the problem here. Decayed metal should be cut out ruthlessly and the remainder, should you be rebuilding in fibreglass paste, thoroughly rustproofed using Jenolite or Naval Jelly (not an anti-rust primer because then the paste cannot adhere directly to the metal). Always wire-brush or grind the pitted metal before treating, and try to rustproof both sides of a panel. This process will also be necessary after repairing by welding or brazing.

Steel bodywork repair

The practical enthusiast should find the repair of small rust holes, tears or dents fairly straightforward. Reasonably-priced sets of panelbeater's 'dollies', intended for the handyman, have recently appeared on the market, and armed with a set of these, plus a small 'home' arc-welder, a large number of minor repairs may be carried out. On the other hand, major work should be left to a professional. Panelbeating is an art, and 'invisible' repairs are the result of training, skill and experience; a set of dollies and finishing hammers are merely the tools - it is the skill of hand and eye that uses them to their best. One can only get so far on a 'hobby' basis.

The refinishing trade have always used oxy-acetylene both for cutting-out damaged metal and for welding-in new panels. At home one must be content with the sweat of a hacksaw or cold chisel and, where applicable, a low-amperage arc welder and a steady hand. Patches cut from 20 swg mild steel sheet must first be tacked in place using a good quality electrode and the welder set at 25-35 amps. A frequent problem for the beginner is the electrode sticking to the work, and this is prevented by striking the arc just as you would a match, and not jabbing. It is best to surround the edges of the working-area with quanitites of asbestos powder, made into a wet paste with water, as this prevents buckling. Once the arc is struck, move the electrode towards the earthing-clamp, keeping it inclined at 45° and the hand very steady. Proceed along the join at a slow speed to ensure a good bond, but not so slowly as to burn through the material. After cooling, the slag may lift, or must be tapped with the slag hammer to remove it. For good results, practice is essential. Refinishing may entail a lot of grinding and careful filling. Patches or tears may also be repaired by arc-brazing, as explained on p.80.

'Hot shrinking' of dents entails the use of oxy-acetylene, so should a small dent tend to stretch on beating out, it may be wisest to knock it back in and repair it by soft-solder filling. As an improvized blow torch, a Bunsen burner operating on a Calor gas cylinder is fairly adequate. Thorough cleaning and fluxing of the dented area comes first; after preheating, the dent is next tinned with tinman's solder and the depression filled with plumber's solder, a proud contour being acheived by working the semi-molten solder with a wooden paddle dipped in palm oil. Carefully filing reduces the solder to the correct contour, ready for priming and refinishing.

Fibreglass repairs

Polyester paste may prove the easiest repair method. All traces of rust must be got rid of by mechanical and chemical means, as outlined above (but do not use an anti-rust primer), and the premixed paste applied, paying particular attention to the provision of a keyed surface to which the paste can grip. Zinc or aluminium mesh or copper wool may be incorporated as a support. To speed-up the finishing, use a Surform rasp while the paste is cheese hard; final contour is effected using very fine wet-and-dry paper and soapy water. Since many brands of fibreglass paste are porous, it is most important to underseal the reverse surface of the repair - failure to do this is the reason why so many repairs rust again after a few months.

Spray-gun technique

The repaired bodywork, after degreasing, must be rendered matt at the edges of the repair using wet-and-dry paper. Cellulose putty will fill any small imperfections (allow some hours to dry) and a block, used to support the wet-and-dry paper, will ensure freedom from ripples when finishing. Before spraying warm-up the metal bodywork with fan-heaters, or choose a warm spring day. Spraying in the open air is only possible if there is no wind, or dampness in the atmosphere. If working in the garage, remember that spray vapour is both inflammable and toxic, and an extractor fan should be mounted at floor level; also it is advisable to wear a face-mask. Use a good compressor unit capable of delivering 50-60 lb/in^2 for long intervals, an efficient spray-gun, and practice on old cartons, sheets of hardboard, metal, etc. first. After masking the windows and chromework, dilute the primer 50 : 50 with a good quality thinners, hold the nozzle of the gun at six inches from the surface and spray at a good pressure, moving the gun parallel to the surface at all times, working downwards in horizontal sweeps and overlapping six inches on the return strokes. Apply two coats, leave for some hours, then rub down smooth with medium wet-and-dry paper. Give a final coat, and smooth with a fine grade of finishing paper.

The colour coats require far more care than the primer. Use a reputable brand of cellulose or synthetic enamel and make sure you have enough for the job, plus sufficient thinners, fast or slow-drying. The first colour coat is mixed 35 : 65, cellulose to thinners. After spraying, allow some minutes to dry, then apply 3-4 further coats of 50 : 50 mixture, waiting five minutes between each. Thorough hardening will take several days, then the cellulose is ready for compounding with T-cut and silicone polishing. Remember that certain pale colours will need more coats and that others demand coloured primers - your supplier will advise.

Satisfactory resprays come only after much practice; if you are hesitant about tackling it for the first time, perhaps a friend who has done some spraying may offer to supervise.

Interior renovation

Replacing the headlining and re-upholstering the seats are tasks that can be spread over many months. Once the car is running well and looks smart, work on the interior can follow when convenient. It being difficult to particularise, the soundest advice is to restore interior items by noting their construction when stripped down. Replace the headlining first, so that dust and grime falls only on to old upholstery; the headlining is generally pleated and tacked to wooden rails running across the inside of the roof. Here, too, is a chance to block-out a decrepit sunshine roof - remove the sliding portion, braze-in a metal roof panel, fill with fibreglass paste and finish with a black 'liquid vynide' spray. Recover seats in vinyl leathercloth, using the old covers as patterns. Fill pleats with fresh wadding, adding PVC foam if applicable. Doors panels are easily re-covered; use Dunlop S.708 adhesive or a close equivalent. New carpets should be cut from a modern non-fray brand such as Karvel.

Hood renovation

Torn or decaying canvas hoods, often with an opaque rear window, should be replaced so as to preserve the interior. The Car Hood Company of London W 10 offer new hoods 'off the shelf' for several popular prewar models, or will make up any hood to pattern. Alternatively, a sound but unattractive hood may be painted with Humbrol leathercloth finish and a new rear window cut from Vybak, then stitched and cemented in place. Untidy sidescreens may also be given a coat or two of Humbrol, the window sections being replaced in 1/8-inch perspex. Rustproof all hood frames and coat with enamel.

Tarnished plated parts such as chromework, whether interior or exterior, often polish up well, prewar quality being high. Replating, however, is expensive, and it may prove cheaper to seek second-hand parts in good condition.

Chapter Eleven

Postscript: electrics, instruments and controls

The six-volt battery, at one time thought the 'ideal' for light cars, yielded place to the twelve-volt towards the end of the Thirties. Some makers of mass-produced small saloons stuck rigidly to the lower-voltage system even into the early postwar period, but in general the trend throughout was towards twelve-volt electrics for all cars.

Originally of dual-pole type, circuits using the chassis as an earth-return were later developed, the single-pole circuit proving far more satisfactory as car electrics became more complex. 'Negative earth' gave way to 'positive earth' around the middle of the decade since it was found that the latter minimized corrosion of the terminals. The lead-acid battery reigned supreme over other types, and increases in amp-hour capacity were needed to run all the additional lights, accessories and even radios fitted from the mid-30s onwards (the Hillman Melody Minx being one of the first light cars where a built-in radio was standard equipment). Electric starters were the norm by 1930, and generators, originally of 'third brush' pattern, were later fitted with an automatic cut-out and compensated voltage control thus rendering obsolete the 'charge rate' switch on the dashboard. Larger junction-cum-fuse boxes were fitted and a full range of illuminated instruments, including an ammeter to check the function of the generator; Morris Motors and one or two other manufacturers installed dynamotors, i.e. a combined dynamo and starter, but Morris did not pursue the idea beyond a brief period.

Of prime importance on entering the car, the starter was energized by means of the starter 'pull' or a push button. The starter 'pull' was a mechanical device, operating the starter switch via a cable, wheras the push button connected the switch electrically. Then, as now, the choke was operated by means of a 'pull'. Switching-on did not always entail the use of an ignition key: alternatively a magneto switch was fitted, serving at the same time to stop the engine when required, by earthing the magneto. If an Autovac pump was fitted the driver had first to raise the bonnet and turn on the brass tap at the base of the unit, sometimes tickling the carburetter and thus slightly flooding it for a rich starting mixture.

Instrumentation

Petrol gauges at first worked on a hydrostatic principle where the pressure of petrol in the tank acted on an air-bell, this reaction being registered as the height of liquid in a capillary tube mounted on the dashboard. Later types were, of course, electric, a sliding resistance being actuated by a float in the tank.

Many electrical components and switches were manufactured by Lucas or Rotax, and instruments by Smiths and British Jaeger, among others. The overhaul of ammeters, oil gauges, clocks, speedometers and petrol gauges is very intricate work, more akin to that of a watch-maker, and is best entrusted to a specialist (see Appendix).

Starting routine and controls

The typical dashboard layout of an early-30s

car is shown in Fig. 34, normal starting procedure from cold being as follows: (1) check that the gearbox is in neutral and the handbrake on, (2) switch on ignition, or operate magneto switch, (3) with an Autovac, turn on petrol first and tickle the carburetter, (4) pull out the choke, (5) set the ignition lever at full retard (6) pull or press the starter, (7) once the engine is running, push-in the choke at the earliest opportunity, using the hand throttle, if fitted, to speed-up the tick-over, (8) do *not*, as many prewar manuals advise, allow the engine to tick-over slowly for several minutes before driving away, but move off at once, returning the hand throttle to zero as soon as possible. Advance the ignition on the straight, while retarding slightly on hills. For smoother pulling away in high gear, retard the ignition.

Changing gear

Once moving, use of the gears will perhaps require skill at first; a 'crash' gearbox may take a time to master, but sympathy with the speed and 'feel' of the engine is vital if gearchanges are to be perfected (and inaudible). Double-declutching, where a pause in neutral is made *en route* to the next gear, is a technique worth practising. When changing up, allow the revs to decrease during the pause in neutral, but on changing down, speed-up the revs in neutral to match the speeds of the gears about to engage. A knowledge of the different gear ratios will assist the driver to change gear smoothly, and the pause in neutral should be followed by a momentary re-engagement of the clutch before

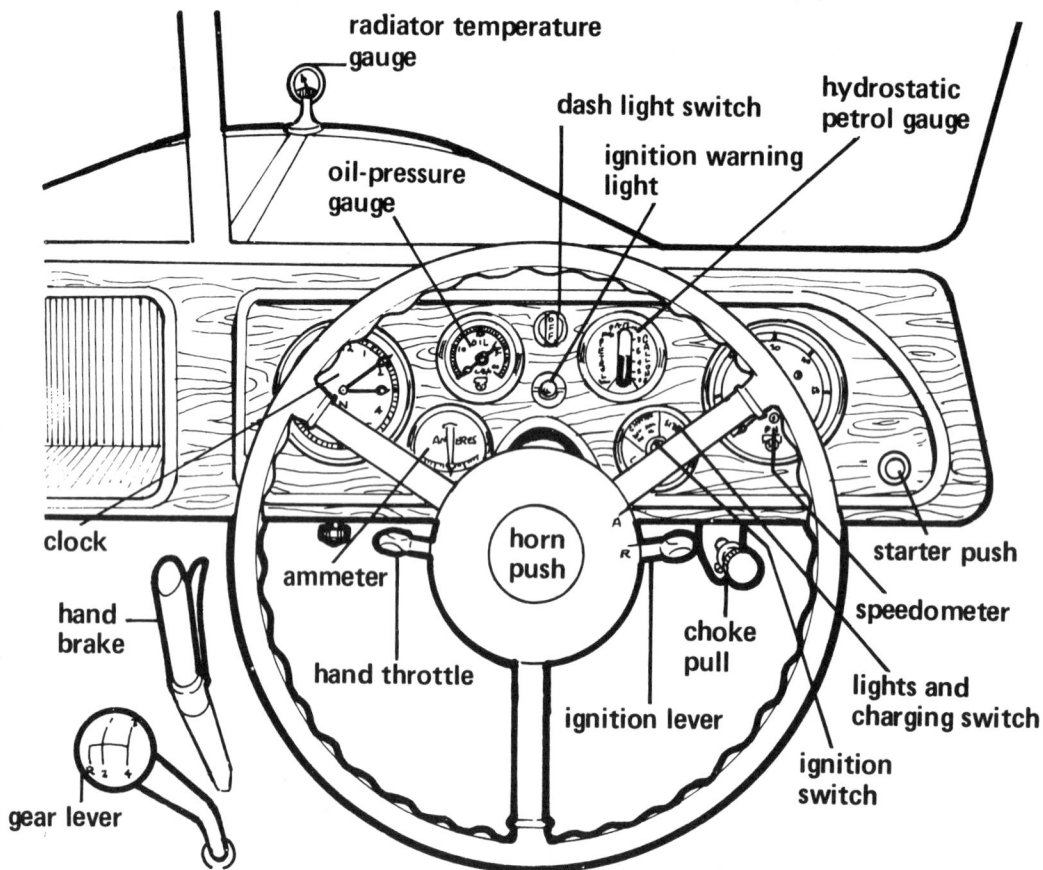

Fig 34   Typical early 1930s dashboard and controls

subsequently declutching and selecting the new gear.

Floor-change gearboxes will have an 'H' gate and a 'ball change' gear lever and, with a three-speed gearbox (as, for example, in the Ford Eight and Ten), one must be careful not to mistake reverse for 1st gear. In a four-forward speed gearbox reverse is far less 'accessible'. Preslector gearboxes are controlled via a short lever mounted below the hub of the steering wheel, a notched semi-circular plate bearing the letters 'N' for neutral and 'R' for reverse, the '1', '2', '3' and '4' positions being preselected in turn and the 'clutch' pedal depressed each time. On next touching the accelerator after preselecting, the new gear comes into operation.

A few final points

Make adjustments to your driving to accommodate mechanical brakes, anticipating their use wherever possible. As for speed, although 25 mile/h may be the best cruising speed for the condition of your particular model, remember that the sight of an old car tottering along a busy road may infuriate many drivers, who see you not as something picturesque, but as a slow-moving obstruction, to be overtaken come what may. Your very picturesque-ness may well attract more than normal attention from the police, so keep the mechanical and legal aspects of your vehicle well up to scratch.

Old cars that have lain idle for years may not conform to present-day MOT requirements regarding lights and reflectors - for example, a single tail-light, however authentic, is not considered adequate now. Also beware of relying solely on semaphore trafficators - most drivers just don't notice them! It may sound an unthinkable step, but it is far safer to fit a set of 'tasteful' flashing indicators.

Part Two

This half of the book gives a broad outline history of most models of British light car manufactured between 1930 and 1939, and the addresses of the Honorary Secretaries of all relevant Car Clubs are given in the one-make sections. Technical data for most of the models described in the text is given in the Appendix, as are sources of specialist services.

Alvis

It is indeed fortunate that our introduction to British light cars should bring us first to so illustrious a marque as the Alvis. Always beautifully engineered, superbly finished and very individual in character, Alvis cars offer an ideal, thoroughly British starting point, as well as setting an extremely high standard with which subsequent marques must bear comparison. The red triangle has found itself on the radiators of many world-renowned automobiles, all of high performance, and all tasteful yet uncompromising in style.

During the 1920s the Alvis workshops were enthusiastically involved in racing, and it was at this time that their involvement with front-wheel drive began.

Fortunately not plagued by previous US patent regulations, the Alvis Car and Engineering Company, under its chief engineer Captain G.T. Smith-Clarke and chief designer W.M. Dunn, took a clean sheet of paper and set about drawing plans for a lightweight 1½-litre fwd racer to rival J.A. Joyce's 10 cwt AC hill-climb and sprint machine. Emerging with a duralumin frame and semi-moncoque light alloy bodywork, a 'free' rear axle and reversed engine, the first sprint car had fwd, but not independent front suspension, which was to follow on later models. With a supercharged 12/50 engine delivering 100 bhp, speeds of well over 100 mile/h were attainable, but rapid acceleration and good road-holding on fast bends were the main aims. Grand Prix racers came next, built to the 1926 1½-litre international formula, but with supercharged 'straight eight' engines replacing the reworked 12/50 unit. These new engines sported high camshafts, with horizontal valves worked by short vertical rockers, the big-end bearings of the duralumin connecting-rods being unlined and running directly upon the crankshaft journals. A pressed-steel chassis and aluminium-panelled bodywork was used, and the low profile of these cars was further exaggerated by a wide, oblong radiator; a pointed rear completed the effect. Although very fast on corners, these fwd cars were often dogged by petty troubles in competitions. Undaunted, however, Alvis turned its hand to fwd sports cars, embodying ifs also. During 1928–29 four- and eight-cylinder production models were built, a supercharged four-cylinder TT version losing by only 13 seconds to Kaye Don's Lea-Francis in the 1928 TT handicap race.

8-15, 12/50 and 12/75 fwd Ulster TT models (1930)

Outside the realm of this book historically, the Alvis 'fwd story' is sufficiently revolutionary and epoch-making, that to have deleted it would have been fanatical in the extreme. To be completely accurate, only ten fwd cars were in fact built with eight-cylinder engines during 1929-30, four of which saw completion in 1930; of these, several were works cars and were never sold to the public.

According to Tony Cox, present PRO of the Alvis Owners' Club, who has made a detailed personal study of the fwd cars, none of the 8-15s now exist, although an original engine and transmission are extant. The cars are however, fascinating, and worth describing in fair detail, much of it supplied by Mr Cox. The dohc 1491 cc 'straight eight' engine, supercharged to yield 125 bhp at 6000 rev/min, was fed by a large-bore SU carburetter, ignition being via twin BTH four-cylinder magnetos. A range of compression ratios, from 6 to 8.5:1 were employed at particular times. Perfectly hemispherical combustion chambers, with inlet and exhaust valves inclined at a wide included angle made correct combustion of the mixture and free flow of the gases inherent characteristics, an eight-branch exhaust manifold providing good scavenging. A gear-driven camshaft (which could prove noisy!) was fitted, together with four separate oil pumps, of gear-type, affording more than adequate lubrication for the engine's internal workings; full roller main-bearings had been substituted, also. In overall specification similar to the 1927 Grand Prix engine units but with a slightly shorter stroke, the rest of the fwd transmission also followed earlier practice, the

1929 Alvis fwd four-cylinder FE 12/75

1930 fwd four-cylinder FD 12/75 Le
Mans Two Seater

gearbox being mounted forward of the differential. Final drive was by pot-type universal joints and shafts to the front wheels. A distinctive step was the provision of both independent front and rear-suspension, the former by means of two sets of four transverse quarter-elliptic springs upper and lower, and the latter via a single transverse semi-elliptic spring and radius arms. For 1930, ifs was by two semi-elliptic springs and two lower radius arms. Only two-seater bodies were built, these versions having a high bonnet line and well-raked steering column, a neat cockpit without doors, brief 'beetle back' and high-mounted sprint wings. A small, near-square radiator was fitted, the gearbox below being cowled-in beneath a rounded extension panel. The brakes were mounted not on the wheels, but on the engine-gearbox-axle unit. Somewhat noisy bevel gears in the four-seater works cars were to have been replaced by spiral gears in production models. Alvis guaranteed the two-seater 8-15s as 100 mile/h machines, and each was tested before sale over the flying half-mile at Brooklands; in fact their maximum speed was near 110 mile/h. Despite alloy bodywork the gross weight was close to just over a ton, so the 1½-litre car was no lightweight, but that 125 bhp made itself noticeably felt. The price of both two- and four-seater versions was £825 in 1929, rising to £975 in 1930. A short saloon (in which one wore ear-plugs!) cost £875 in 1929. By 1931 the 8-15 two-seater was listed at £955.

Production began in 1928 of the 1482 cc four-cylinder ohc-engined sports cars. In unblown form called the 12/50, (50 bhp being delivered), the supercharged versions of the engine gave 50% more output, this chassis being designated as the 12/75. In the latter case, the fitting of an Alvis-built Roots-type supercharger dictated a need to mix oil with the stipulated '50/50 Benzole Mixture' fuel to provide adequate lubrication for the supercharger rotors, etc.

In overall specification very similar to the 8-15 described above, the 12/50 and 12/75 fwd models also had both ifs and irs, and were low-slung racy-looking cars, the two-seater wearing a pointed tail and sharing a high long bonnet with the eight-cylinder cars. Two neat little doors afforded access to the cockpit, while exterior trim included elongated front cycle-wings and a radiator uncluttered by a gearbox cowling, this latter unit now being mounted behind the differential. The cars handled, of course, superbly for the late '20s; leech-like cornering, extremely smooth suspension and good acceleration made them a 'star attraction' in the contemporary motoring journals. A fabric-bodied saloon and a four-seater, both of more pedestrian aspect, were also offered by Alvis on the 12/50 or 12/75 chassis; these again were fast and very comfortable touring cars of truly thoroughbred specification. All variants had a maximum speed of 85 mile/h, the 12/75 versions posessing better acceleration and superior hill-climbing abilities. Retardation from 30 mile/h to zero took 37 ft, the Alvis-designed mechanical brakes having a fair deal of momentum to cope with. As to price, the 1928-29 two-seater cost £597, or £625 supercharged, while the saloon cost £675 or £700 supercharged. For the 1929-30 season, the unsupercharged two-seater was listed at £650 and the saloon at £750.

The Alvis FA 8-15 works team car at Brooklands c.1931, the driver being T. Dowling and the passenger E. Coleman. This eight-cylinder fwd car was driven to 7th place in the 1930 TT by Cushman, at an average speed of 67 mile/h

12/50 and 12/60 rwd models (1930—32)

Return to orthodoxy came with the new 12/50, a design based on the larger-capacity Silver Eagle range. Powered by a 1645 cc four-cylinder ohv engine delivering 50 bhp at 4250 rev/min and transmitting its power through a single dry-plate clutch, four-speed 'crash' gearbox and open propeller shaft to a conventional spiral-bevel rear axle, this new model helped to reinstate Alvis's reputation for reliable, straightforward cars that gave long periods of trouble-free service - the fwd cars had, in fact, proved somewhat erratic and troublesome to maintain. Semi-elliptic leaf-springs front and rear, an I-section 'beam' front axle and well-proven hub brakes all symbolized a return to a more normal format that the public would more readily assimilate as typically Alvis. Several versions of body were offered, among them a coachbuilt alloy-panelled saloon at £450, a high-waisted four-door four-light design with black fabric roof, large Alvis wire wheels, and the edge of the roof overhanging the long, narrow windscreen. A fabric-bodied two-seater was priced at £395. All models had tall radiators and faired-in dumb-irons, the headlamps being mounted on a horizontal bar slung between the shapely front wings.

Raising the compression ratio of the engine and fitting twin SU carburetters increased the power to 56 bhp, and the new engine was installed in a two-seater sports car called the 12/60. Here again the high Alvis bonnet fronted a model with flowing lines terminating in a pointed 'beetle back', a neat hood folding away under a lid in the tail, 'helmet' cycle-type wings closely following the circumference of the tyres, and louvred valances running the whole length of the car. A single dickey seat was mounted in the tail, again concealable beneath a flush-fitting panel. On a model with such racy lines, the running boards were dispensed with, and Alvis wire wheels, (the spare being carried on the side of the bonnet), set off the general sporting effect. A close-ratio gearbox and leaf springs modified for high-speed comfort were incorporated, as was coil ignition, in place of the 8-15 and 12/75s magnetos. Once again the gear lever was mounted on the right-hand side. The price in 1931 was £410.

1931 Alvis TL 12/60 Beetleback

1931/32 Alvis 12/50
Drophead Coupe

Firefly (1932–34)

A 12 hp high-speed tourer, the Firefly proved a short-lived return to the small car format for Alvis. Based on the Speed Twenty, power was provided by a 1496 cc four-cylinder ohv engine, developing 50 bhp at 4250 rev/min, an alternative form of gearbox, either manual four-speed or Wilson preselector, transmitting the drive via a spiral-bevel rear axle. Conventional leaf springing, front and rear, was employed, and a Marles-type steering box; overall specification was unremarkable, but sound, and finely engineered. Never intended as a sports car, the Firefly nevertheless put up a very good all-round performance as a lively, comfortable touring car.

Running an early-30s Alvis year-in, year-out, will dictate close liason with the Alvis Owners' Club, many spares being unobtainable now through other channels. Models with complex transmissions and superchargers are more a hobby for the enthusiastic engineer, overhaul possibly entailing the machining of one-off parts, demanding access to, and experience with, an engineer's lathe.

Models such as the 12/50, 12/60 and Firefly, by virtue of their relative simplicity of design, offer equal enjoyment to the more specialised racing versions, and enable the beginner to get on the road with less capital outlay, and fewer heartaches.

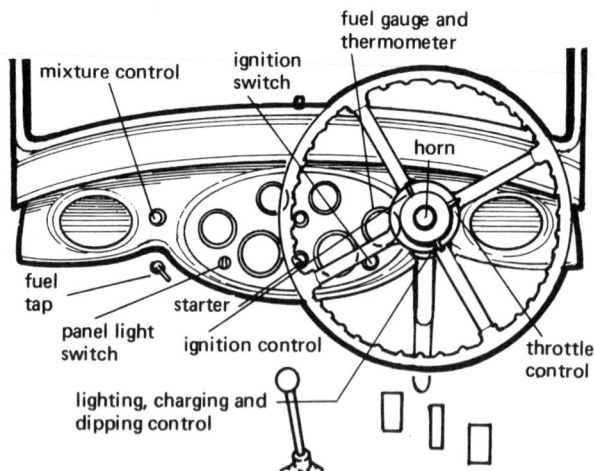

1933 Firefly Saloon

Whichever the model, the Alvis red triangle motif has always symbolized refinement in engineering, style and comfort.

Alvis Owners' Club: O. N. Trent, 'Ridgeside', Woodfield Hill, Coulsdon, Surrey. Downland 55833

Another shot of the Cross and Ellis 1932 Firefly

1932 Alvis Firefly Tourer with bodywork by Cross and Ellis,
owned by D. J. Clover

1933 Alvis Firefly Tourer. Note the extra spare wheel, a later addition

Armstrong Siddeley

To quote from the 1934 Complete Motor Show Report edition of the *Autocar*: "People who gravitate with serious intentions to the Armstrong Siddeley display are pre-eminently those who look for quality in a car yet, who, at the same time, are not by any means insensible to sound performance and attractively modern appearance. These are attributes which these cars possess in a very high degree, and throughout they are, above all, practical, sensible vehicles."

Such a statement would have rung equally true in 1924 or 1954; closely allied to the aero-engine concern, Armstrong Siddeley Motors Ltd claimed "aircraft quality and workmanship" for their cars, together with "all the most advanced features of automobile design, distinctive coachwork of the highest grade, ease of control, high point-to-point performance, and dependability and lasting qualities". One further feature was the inclusion of " the only proved self-changing gear" - the trusty Wilson preselective epicyclic gearbox, to be precise, of which they were pioneers.

The classic sphinx mascot always fronted a car of superb quality, refined style and healthy performance, six cylinders being deemed by Armstrong Siddeley to be without peer. Fleeting fashions and awkward 'modernisms' scarcely affected the classic air of their cars; throughout the Thirties an Armstrong Siddeley remained distinctive yet always instantly recognizeable as to origin. The sphinx symbolized in essence the whole rigid aesthetic which abhorred change for the sake of change.

Twelve and Twelve Plus (1930–36)

The smallest member of the family, the Twelve's mechanical specification changed little over the decade. Originally a coachbuilt four-door saloon, its long bonnet surmounted by the slanting, slatted 'V' radiator of distinctive Armstrong Siddeley design, an Economy 12 hp Saloon priced at £300 at the 1930 Motor Show forsook coachbuilding and the slanting radiator for steel or fabric bodywork, disc wheels and a flat radiator. This cheaper car did, however, retain a three-speed version of the famous self-changing gearbox and, in common with all models, featured chromium-plating throughout, automatic ignition control, twin screen-wipers, dip-switch and hydraulic shockabsorbers. In outer appearance the fabric saloon was very reminiscent of the Riley Nine Monaco. The bodywork of the coachbuilt saloon was of fine finish and graceful form, terminating in a curved back which flared out at its base. The spare wheel was carried on the nearside of the bonnet. A 12 hp 2/3-seater and four-seater open tourer were also available, with manual gearboxes, and priced alternatively at £250, or £275 plus the Wilson. Performance figures for the 12 hp Economy saloon were: maximum speed 65 mile/h; acceleration from 10-30 mile/h in 18 seconds; fuel consumption, on average, 30 mpg.

For the 1932 season, styles remained the same, but prices dropped. The Economy saloon now cost £260 and the coachbuilt saloon £295. An Economy sports saloon, a new model, was priced at £275; the two-seater, incorporating a dickey seat cost £295, as did the open tourer, and the sports saloon was listed at £315. Permanent DWS jacks were offered on all models, plus bumpers and sliding roof at £12 extra. Economy being quietly forgotten, by 1933 only the coachbuilt saloon and sports coupe were available, priced at £265. Cars for the 1934 season changed little. For 1935, the sports coupe sported a bench front seat and larger luggage compartment; it remained at £265, with the saloon at £269.

Traditionally fitted with a side-valve engine, that of a new model for 1936, the Twelve Plus, was of ohv pattern and 1666 cc capacity. This car could achieve a top speed of 66 mile/h, accelerate from 0-50 mile/h in 23.2 seconds, come to rest from a speed of 30 mile/h in 28 feet and afford 20-24 mpg. The Twelve Plus saloon de luxe cost £320, while alternatively,

An Armstrong Siddeley 12/6 of 1933

only sports coupe and sports tourer versions of the Twelve remained available, at £285 and £275 respectively.

Fourteen (1936—39)

Born directly out of the Twelve Plus, the new model was rechristened the Fourteen for the 1937 season. A single-plate clutch was added to the specification to eliminate gearbox 'hum' in neutral, and this also reduced the pressure needed to operate the gear-change pedal. Both four and six-light saloons were offered, both priced at £320, the window pillars of the former

being extremely thin and the doors specially hinged to open right back for ease of entry. Sliding rear-quarter windows were fitted on the six-light saloon. Prices remained the same for the next season, in which 'Balanced Power' was incorporated, a device whereby flywheel action was partly replaced by the momentum of the rotating parts of the preselector gearbox; new flexible mountings for the engine-gearbox unit also contributed to increased smoothness of running. Small details successfully brought the overall impression of the traditional bodywork in closer tune with the time, but such modifications were always restrained and unobtrusive. In the final prewar season, 1939, the

Fourteen continued to represent quality, dignity, good performance and comfort in the light car field, combined in a very individual way. Improved manifolding and water-jacketing contributed to the quest for more power, together with more satisfactory engine cooling. The price of the saloon in 1939 was £335.

The Armstrong Siddeley is a car for a driver who likes to combine comfort and ease of driving with a useful performance born of precision engineering. In particular, the saloon versions offer a great sense of dignity, rarely matched in cars of its class. Overhaul work will involve close liaison with the Armstrong Siddeley Owners' Club, probably the only source of spare parts there is now. Repair of the Wilson gearbox is for a specialized mechanic to tackle; alternatively, direct replacement of the complete unit may prove easiest. Ruggedness of construction should have ensured that many prewar models are nowadays still in excellent overall condition.

Armstrong Siddeley Owners' Club: J.D.Hubbuck, 90 Alumhurst Road, Bournemouth, Hants. Bournemouth 63413.

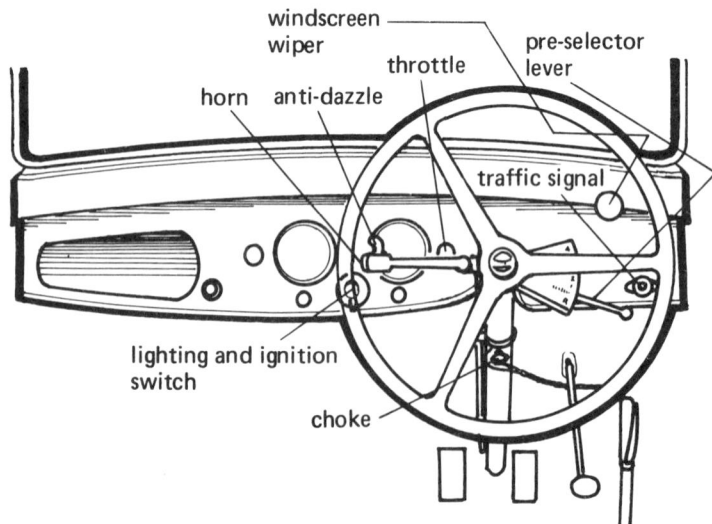

1936 Twelve Plus Saloon

Aston Martin

Named after the successes of some early cars built by Lionel Martin and Robert Bamford and entered in the Aston Clinton hill-climb before the 1914-18 war, the first 'Aston Martin' consisted of a Hispano-Suiza chassis powered by a Coventry Simplex sv engine of 1400 cc. In 1919, a 'one-off' chassis of Martin-Bamford design was equipped with the Simplex engine and this served for research purposes until 1921, when an actual prototype was completed. With the capactiy increased to 1½-litres, over 86 mile/h was achieved at Brooklands - and while Martin preferred a side-valve engine, the co-designer of the Simplex unit was later asked to design a new powerplant of ohc format and 1½-litre capacity. A single-seater Aston Martin fitted with the new engine secured many light-car records in 1922. Dohc engines followed, of sixteen-valve type i.e. two inlet and two exhaust valves per cylinder, Count Zborowski being actively involved in Bamford and Martin Ltd at this time, and racing the marque at Brooklands. Captain G.E.T. Eyston also patronized the concern, buying two ex-works racing cars in 1923, plus a sixteen-valve dohc engine with which to power one of them, entering the J.C.C. two-hundred mile event and only retiring through plug trouble after keeping in the first three for much of the race. Single overhead-camshaft 1½-litre engines were later adopted, with the conventional two valves per cylinder, and by 1926 Aston Martin Motors Ltd formed. Their chief designer, A.C. Bertelli, was responsible for the Bertelli Astons, culminating in the International of 1930, featuring dry-sump lubrication, a high compression ratio, large drum-brakes and sleek lines - in fact epitomizing all that a light sports-racing car should be.

Renowned for sporting cars possessing an indefinable air of breeding, evident in every part of their design, Aston Martin Ltd of Feltham, Middlesex maintained an excited public interest at their Motor Show stand throughout the Thirties. Offering 1½-litre high-powered sports models featuring the concern's proven ohc four-cylinder engine, the 1930 stand exhibited the 11.9 hp four-seater, an impressive open car called the International, described in outline above. Bertelli's low-slung bodywork was made feasible by virtue of the worm-driven rear axle, the underslung worm making possible a very low positioning of the transmission shaft; ground clearance, however, was still adequate. Dry-sump lubrication, a distinguishing feature of the Aston Martin, necessitated the mounting of a 2½-gallon reservoir oil tank between the front dumb irons, to gain the benefit of the cooling airstream. From this tank, cool oil was pumped to the engine bearings, a scavenging pump returning oil to the tank, where it was first cooled, then recirculated. Some 64 bhp was developed by the engine in good tune, providing a top speed of over 80 mile/h.

An interesting point was the fitting of a separate gearbox, its gear lever very short and positive in action, and located right in the middle of the cockpit, admirably accessible to the driver's left hand. Close ratios enabled really crisp use of the engine power. Very large-diameter brake drums afforded excellent deceleration, and the steering was feather-light but extremely positive and accurate. Semi-elliptic springs formed the front and rear suspension, and the large-diameter Rudge-Whitworth wire wheels gave the whole car a sporting, purposeful air, the front axle being located ahead of the radiator in the best tradition. As to the body, this was an admirably brief, but exactly correct affair, a narrow tapering bonnet widening-out to a slightly flared scuttle, the lower seating-position enabling the fitting of a brief windscreen; slightly 'cut-away' doors lead rearwards to the folded hood, astride a box-like back with curved edges, housing the fuel tank. An external exhaust and close-fitting

1929 Aston Martin Four Seater Sports at the Aston Martin Jubilee Festival held at the Crystal Palace in 1970. The car is owned by D. H. Vamplew

1932 Aston Martin Le Mans prototype at the Wiscombe Hill Climb, 1971, owned by Ian Rendall

cycle wings added a further touch of speed, and the smallish headlamps were low-mounted on brackets fixed to the dumb irons. A cast aluminium dashboard was another novel facet.

A *Motor* road test conducted on December 17th 1929 echoed all the aspirations the design provoked, indeed in full - fine handling, 'hair's breadth' steering, energetic acceleration (10-80 mile/h in 63 seconds in top gear) and a maximum speed of 81 mile/h. Acceleration in top gear from 10-30 mile/h took 11 seconds, and 10-60 mile/h 30 seconds in the same gear. These were good figures for 1929 from a 1½-litre car; we shall read later how they compare with a test on a 1935 Ulster team car. But for its time, the Aston Martin International was, as the *Motor* claimed, " an enthusiast's dream come true" adding that although it cost £598 (for the 1930 and '31 seasons also) it was "well worth it".

For the 1932 season, two-door saloon, four-door saloon and sports coupe became available, the four-door saloon and a larger four-seater being built on a longer chassis. The two-door saloon had sweeping front wings, 'helmet' rear wings and a large top-opening luggage locker at the rear, upon which the spare wheel was mounted. The International cost a mere three pounds less, and prices of the long-chassis open tourer and saloon were £630 and £745 respectively - a good sum in those days! The short-chassis sports coupe was also nòt particularly cheap, at £715, but then enthusiasts were quite prepared to pay this for a thoroughbred bearing the Aston Martin radiator badge.

The worm-driven rear axle was discarded in 1932 for a bevel final drive, the gearbox was made in unit with the engine, and a new design of cable-operated brakes was adopted. Success

Aston Martin LM 17 1½-litre team car. This car finished 7th in the 1934 TT and 22nd in the Mille Miglia of that year. The original racing body has been replaced by a MkII short-chassis 2/4 seater body. Owned by Mark Tidy

at Le Mans was followed by the marque winning the Rudge-Whitworth Cup and the appearance of a new model, the International Le Mans, a 2/4-seater with high compression ratio offering an exhilarting performance, and incorporating a five-gallon oil tank and 19-gallon 'slab' petrol tank in the rear. A remote-control gear lever was now necessary in that the gearbox was mounted further forward, the box itself being of a new type, a horizontal rod from the gear lever actuating the selector arm which picked speeds from a selection of close-ratio straight-cut gears. Other than the Le Mans, the International still represented a very healthy (but less hair-raising) sports model, the saloons and sports coupe remaining for those who enjoyed speed but not too much contact with the elements. A particularly well-balanced design, the coupe's long, amply louvred bonnet and large wire wheels were accompanied by a very neat and compact coupe roof-area, gracefully curved and evolving into a smoothly-swept tail, its double curve echoed in that of the 'helmet' rear wings. A narrow light-coloured 'flash' (as in the Talbot Scout coupe) mounted on each door, level with the waistline, added a distinctive finishing-touch. In the four-seater International Le Mans extra room for the rear seats had been secured by mounting the fuel tank externally. All models were cheaper for the 1932 season, the International costing £475 and the lwb saloon £595.

"They are few and far between, these Aston Martins", claimed a 1933 advertisement, "but they are uncommonly good cars". It listed the current models and gave maximum speeds as an incentive, together with prices. The Le Mans was good for 85-90 mile/h and cost £595, as did the 75 mile/h saloon. The tourer could also reach 75 mile/h and was priced at £550, while in Special trim another 10 mile/h was possible, the 'extras' costing an additional £75. The famed four-cylinder ohc engine of 1488 cc continued to serve its purpose admirably, delivering nearly 70 bhp, and proving capable of extensive high-performance modification, if necessary.

At the 1934 Motor Show the Mark II chassis was exhibited, upon which were erected the Le Mans 2/4 seater, the Le Mans Special open four-seater, the Le Mans sunshine-roof saloon, and a very potent newcomer, the Le Mans Ulster two-seater. Highly prized by prewar and postwar enthusiasts alike, the Ulster is often regarded as the epitome of Aston Martin achievement. Developed from the Mark II, Bertelli added a long streamlined tail to compliment the already racy lines, and the finely-tuned engine took the top speed above 100 mile/h. A *Motor Sport* test-drive in one of the team cars used in winning the Rudge-Whitworth Cup at the 1935 TT revealed, despite a rather high overall weight, just how an ex-works Ulster could move. A maximum of 105 mile/h was reached on the Home Banking at Brooklands, acceleration from 10-50 mile/h taking 12 seconds and 10-80 mile/h 32 seconds. But the car also proved flexible enough to 'potter along' at 30 mile/h, and the racing setting of the shock absorbers was far from obtrusive as regards comfort. Adding to the pleasure of such swift motoring was the sound of the exhaust, emitted through an external Brooklands-type system complete with fishtail. Maxima on the indirect gears were 77, 61 and 49 mile/h at 5000 rev/min - useful enough velocities; as to stopping power, the brakes suffered through the wear and tear of 500 miles of racing on the Ards circuit, necessitating a distance of 59 ft in stopping the car from 40 mile/h, this with both foot- and hand-brakes applied (in a standard correctly-adjusted Ulster far better braking was available, of course). Light, smooth steering was allied with extreme accuracy, bends being taken comfortably at near to ninety. A 9.5:1 compression ratio in the works car necessitated the use of 50/50 benzol mixture to obviate pinking, and special gear ratios distinguished the car from production models. A well-instrumented cockpit (but no speedo of course, just a rev-counter) was complimented by a good driving position, the rim of the large steering-wheel fitting nicely in the lap, and support for the elbows being afforded by strategically-placed padding around the cockpit edge. The car inspired confidence, had an inherent sense of 'rightness', and moved like a rocket.

Production cars for 1935 were less highly tuned, but featured counterbalanced crankshafts and new designs for their timing gears and valve rockers. An Auto-klean oil filter formed a new

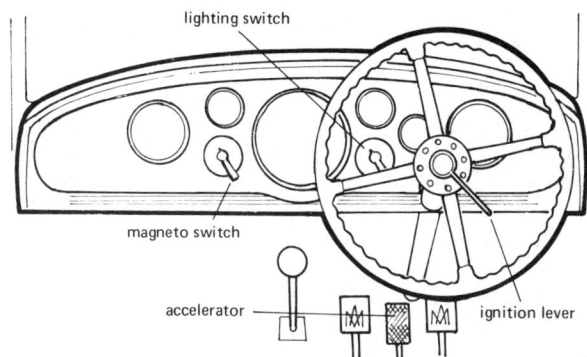

1929 11.9 hp Two Seater

seaters were also large attractions on the stand, still resplendent in their workmanlike design and air of functional performance allied to indefinably correct line and style. An *Autocar* road test on the 1936-season sports saloon recorded a maximum timed speed of 76.27 mile/h, with a best timed speed of 78.95 mile/h. Acceleration from rest to 50 mile/h took 20 seconds through the gears; 10-30 mile/h needed only 6.2 seconds in second gear, third-gear acceleration from 30-50 mile/h requiring 14.2 seconds. Rather high overall weight, much of it due to the mass of the very sturdy chassis, somewhat took the sparkle off the performance, but these figures show that even the sports saloon, with its high 1.88 lb/cc ratio, could perform very ably. Superlative engineering refinement plus great powers of stamina distinguished the Aston Martin, stamina coming from strength, which itself was often allied to lbs weight in 'traditional' prewar car design.

A rise in capacity to 2-litres for the entire range at the 1936 Show precludes further mention of such an illustrious marque in this book; needless to say it continued to go from strength to strength, an unfortunate dalliance with an ohv engine after the war being quickly forgotten through the fantastic success of the Lagonda-engined DB2.

A lusty ohc engine beneath the bonnet of a 'long-legged' sports thoroughbred is an ingredient for much pleasurable motoring to-day, albeit amid hosts of nondescript vehicles of transportation which clog our motorways. For the enthusiast who appreciates fine engineering and the handling and overhaul of finely-finished machinery, the Aston Martin offers this, over and above its exhilarating performance. Close liason with the Aston Martin Owners' Club is advised, both for spares, technical advice and above all, fanatical enthusiasm, that inexplicable 'electricity' that urges us on through periods of dark despair towards a distant gleam - a sparkle of new chrome and the satisfying roar of an invigorated engine.

Aston Martin Owners' Club: Mrs.M.Rendall, 71 Boldmere Road, Eastcote, Pinner, Middx.

facet of the dry-sump lubrication system, the periodic cleaning of which merely entailed turning a handle mounted at the top of the unit. Standard compression ratio was 7.5:1, but power output still very adequate indeed. The production Ulster had mesh stone-guards to protect the headlamps and radiator, and was finished in British racing green. The special four-seater could be had for £625, and the tourer £550.

12/70 (1935—36)

All cars exhibited at the 1935 Motor Show carried the designation 12/70, indicating their developed brake horse-power. Even the £700 sports saloon continued to display an external exhaust system with two down-pipes from the manifold passing into a parallelogram-shaped muffler box mounted just ahead of the leading edge of the near-side door. The two- and four-

The last short-chassis Aston Martin Le Mans of 1933, restored to excellent condition by its owner Ian McGregor (*Evening Echo, Hemel Hempstead*)

Austin

Sir Herbert Austin's involvement with motor-car design went back as far as 1895, when he drew the plans for the first Wolseley car, sponsored by the Wolseley Sheep-Shearing Machine Company of Birmingham.

By the early '30s large, pompous cars were not in great demand; the aftermath of the Depression saw the public wanting smaller, more economical vehicles. Hence the emergence of the Austin Motor Company of Birmingham's Light 12/4s and Light 12/6s and a general embarkation into the 8 and 10 hp field as witnessed by Austins themselves. As the Longbridge conveyor-belts began to speed up, so most of the cars rolling down from the finishing shop became more modest in porportions, powered by smaller, less thirsty engines - Austins were to symbolize the best in refined 'everyday' motoring.

Seven, Big Seven and Eight (1930—39)

First 'hatched' in 1922, Sir Herbert Austin's little baby car, the Seven, was aimed at introducing 'Motoring for the Million'. This revolutionary little car was to provide realistic transport for two adults and three small children of a type more akin to a full-size car and in direct contrast to the awkwardness and impracticability many saw in the cyclecar. The four-seater Seven of 1922, with its two-door 'bath-tub' body, large spidery spoked wheels and diminutive bonnet housing a 696 cc engine immediately endeared itself to all would-be motorists of modest income.

Centred around a very simple triangular A-plan frame, at the apex of which the radiator was mounted, the car's rear axle was supported by quarter-elliptic springs jutting from the stub ends of the rearward side-members. A single transverse semi-elliptic spring provided the front suspension. Steering was by worm and sector: transmission via a torque tube. Failure to provide Panhard rods to steady the front or rear axles, or adequate brakes (a *Motor* road test of 1932 evidencing that 30-0 mile/h took a whole 56 feet to accomplish!) spoiled the car as regards handling. A three-speed gearbox was provided.

The engine, enlarged to 747.5 cc for 1923 production models, was a simple two-bearing design, roller- and ball- races replacing the usual white metal. It in fact was rated at 7.8 i.e. 8 hp, but was of appropriate bore and stroke to be elligible for international Class H competition, even after rebores. The engine originally developed 10.5 bhp at 2,400 rev/min to give a top speed in 1923 of 38 mile/h, a later 1933 test on the four-seater Seven claiming a maximum speed of 50 mile/h, 0-50 mile/h taking over 34 seconds. Originally the ignition was by magneto, a Zenith updraught carburetter being fed by gravity from a scuttle tank holding four gallons of fuel. Later developments resulted in a change-over to coil ignition and a sidedraught Zenith plus rear tank. Manifold design was rudimentary, the exhaust manifold discharging forward to bring the exhaust pipe clear of the firewall. Instrumentation was minimal.

Originally in four-seater Chummy form, the 1922 price of £225 dropped to £165 for 1923 and £155 for 1924. Certain coachbuilding firms such as Mulliners brought out special bodies on the Seven chassis, but most noticeable were the £180 Swallow Sevens originating at William Lyons' Swallow Coachbuilding works, fully-wrought designs which brought a suave, modern air to the still 'cranky' look of the ex-works Seven saloons.

With the advent of the Thirties, modifications begin to mount up. The tendency for the crank-shaft to whip made a thicker shaft inevitable; a centre-bearing, bowever, did not appear until 1937. A ball-change gear lever came in 1930, four-speeds being offered in 1933, and synchromesh on third and top in 1934, covering second gear by 1936.

Dry weight was up to 11 cwt by 1934, 'modernization' of shape coming in the form of the 1935 Ruby saloon and Pearl cabriolet at £120 and £128 respectively. In order to harmonize with the current range of Austin saloons, the Seven radiator, once stove-

1931 Austin 12/6 Harley Saloon owned
by T. S. J. Cooper

1932/33 Austin Seven Saloon

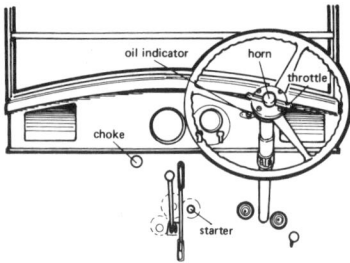

1929 Seven Tourer

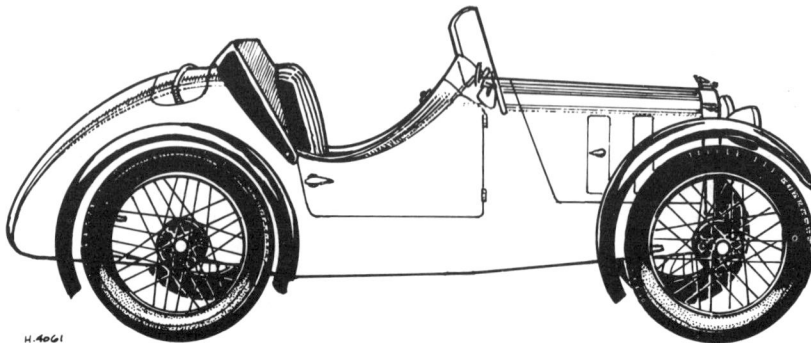

1935 Austin Seven Speedy Competition
Two Seater

108

enamelled in black, then chromium plated, was finally cowled-in behind an oval chromed grille. As for the bodywork, the rear of the Ruby was flared out. Continual development had, however, up-rated the power from 10.5 bhp to 13.5, and now to 17 bhp at 3,800 rev/min - more power was there, and better Girling-type brakes. The general handling, too, had improved, as is witnessed in an *Autocar* road test of 8th March 1935. Here the stronger and lengthened chassis was noted, as was the roomier body and lower seating position. On 'a calm day at Brooklands' a top speed of just over 50 mile/h was recorded, 10-30 mile/h taking 17.2 seconds and retardation of 30-0 mile/h, on a damp surface, 41 feet. Average fuel consumption was 45 mpg which, in the light of the fact that the dry weight was now over 12 cwt, was a good figure. Apart from a certain tendency for fore-and-aft pitching due to the short wheelbase and soft springing, the Ruby came out of test well.

Other than the Pearl cabriolet, a two-seater Seven was available at £102-10s, a de luxe saloon at £125, a fixed-head coupe at £118 and an Open Road Tourer at £112. By 1937 typical performance figures for the Seven were: maximum speed 55 mile/h, 0-50 mile/h in 31 seconds, 30 mile/h to zero in 37 ft (82% efficiency), and 38 mpg. These were creditable figures, proving how the little car's 'teething troubles', long-term though they may have been, were over.

The 1938 season brought forth the 8 hp Big Seven, a more spacious extrapolation of the basic theme. A six-light four-door saloon, its 900 cc sv engine developed 25 bhp at 4000 rev/min. The Seven's 'big brother' was aimed at attracting a wider public. A top speed of 60 mile/h, front air cushions and other trimmings, plus spoked disc wheels, completed the transformation. The Forlite saloon cost £139.

The Eight of 1939 used the Big Seven engine in a completely new body of 'air flow' line but greater total weight. It proved a thoroughly serviceable, reliable and economical 60 mile/h car, production continuing after the war.

1935/36 Austin Seven Ruby Saloon

BRITISH LIGHT CARS

Seven Ulster, 65, Nippy, Speedy, and racing models (1930–37)

Close rivalry existed between Sir William Morris's MG concern and the Austin works in the '30s. Determined not to be out-done by the racy little Midgets, Austins introduced their Seven Ulster model, a supercharged sports-racer born out of successful research into supercharging a reworked Seven engine started in 1928. Using a stiffer crankshaft and Cozette blower, sports versions of the Seven capable of 70-80 mile/h became available in 1929, remarkable for their fast lines, swept windscreens, external exhaust systems, pointed tails and lack of doors. These were later developed into the true Ulster, a formidable car with carefully balanced supercharged engine featuring ultra-light reciprocating parts and a specially-designed cylinder head. Improved engine lubrication was included, plus rugged clutch and gearbox assemblies, the front of the chassis differing from the normal Seven in its downswept front axle and inverted transverse leaf spring.

Far less hair-raising than the Ulster were the 65, Nippy and Speedy - small 'fun' cars with only medium performance. Semi-streamlined competition models with small two-seater cockpits, brief windscreens, cycle wings and the like, the Nippy and Speedy had three-bearing crankshafts, special cylinder heads and downdraught carburetters, the Nippy engine developing 21 hp at 4400 rev/min. Large, 3.50 x 19 in. wheels were fitted, and a six-gallon tank. For the 1937 season the Nippy was priced at £142, or £130 with the standard power unit.

Murray Jamieson's brilliant developmental work on the little 747.5 cc engine led ultimately to some fine Class H racing cars. At Montlhery in 1933, with himself as driver, a white streamlined racing type achieved several international records - the 5-mile at a speed of 119.38 mile/h, 10 km at 119.39 mile/h and the 10-mile at 119.18 mile/h, all consistent enough figures. Of side-valve layout, with dry-sump lubrication, the engine was supercharged via a Roots-type unit. In 1934, Pat Driscoll, driving at Southport Sands and rivalling the MG-held 128.62 mile/h record, in fact came away with

the national Class H flying kilometre record of 122.74 mile/h. At Shelsley Walsh in May '35, Driscoll did the fastest 750 cc climb in a mere 43.4 seconds, Sir Herbert Austin being in attendance.

In 1936, Murray Jamieson produced his *piece de resistance* - a dohc engine based fairly broadly on the Seven. Of 744 cc capacity and developing 80 bhp at 12,000 rev/min, the new engine was mounted in six Mighty Atom racing cars specially designed for the 1936 season as answers to the MG Q and R - types. Near-perfect in concept, these miniature Austin racers vied continually with the MG stable for first place in competitions, albeit not always successfully; however, they served to keep the Austin Motor Company in the limelight and boost sales of their more orthodox cars.

Ten (1932–39)

Introduced in 1932 as an answer, together with the Light 12, to the public's need for smaller and more economical cars, the 10/4 was powered by an economical 1125 cc four-cylinder sv engine. In harmony with the exterior appearance of the rest of its Austin contemporaries, the 10/4 sported a chromed radiator, squared bonnet, curving saloon body and rounded back, upon which the spare wheel was mounted. A four-speed gearbox, mechanical brakes and other conventional fittings ensured that the Ten typified a good, solid, orthodox light saloon. Priced at £152 to £215 according to specification, the 1933 de luxe saloon worked out at £172-10s. By 1935, and re-christened the Lichfield saloon or Colwyn cabriolet, the model's new cowled radiator treatment was in evidence together with more smoothness of line. The Open Road Tourer and Clifton two-seater (a handsome car), supplemented the existing range for 1936, together with a lively newcomer, the £215 Ripley Sports, its modified engine giving 30 bhp at 3800 rev/min. The Ten saloon was renamed the Cambridge a year later and was further changed in body style, its six-light coachwork echoing the trend towards greater streamlining. In sliding-head saloon form the Cambridge sold for £178, the Clifton and Colwyn of 1937

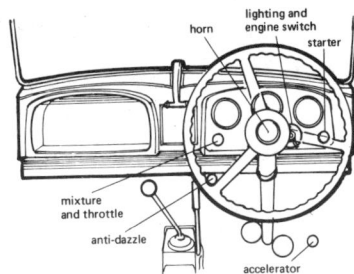

1935 7hp Ruby Saloon

1933/34 Austin 10/4 Cabriolet

1933 Austin 10/4 Cabriolet

costing £160 and £170 respectively. The Open Road Tourer and Clifton were dropped for 1938, and by 1939 the series made way for a new, more striking Ten with new frontal treatment incorporating 'alligator' bonnet opening, an up-to-date radiator grille and headlamp mountings on the bonnet nose.

Twelve (1931—39)

The impressive but ponderous Heavy Twelve yielded place to both four- and six-cylinder Light Twelves by 1931. The 13.9 hp 12/6, with 1496 cc engine was at once faster, and cheaper to run, the six cylinders affording smoothness and improving acceleration. The 12/6 Harley saloon at £225 was of 'de luxe' six-light specification with a comfortable four-seater interior and a folding luggage grid mounted at the rear. Also available at £198 were a two-seater tourer and four-door saloon. Of similar overall line, the 12/4 of 1932 offered four-cylinder motivation. Both chassis were of rugged down-to-earth design, free of momentary novelties. The 1932 12/4 saloon cost £178.

H.4063

1939 Austin 12 Ascot Saloon

Cruciform chassis-bracing was added for 1935, the bodywork tailored to blend with the unified appearance of the entire range, and the 12/4 and 12/6 renamed the Ascot, a 15.9 hp engine being available at the same price - £235 for the de luxe saloon. An Open Road Tourer version of the Ascot appeared in 1936, together with a smart Eton two-seater and a 12/6 Kempton Sports Saloon with modified engine, as paralleled in the 10 hp Ripley Sports. Prices of the 12/4 ranged from £188 to £208, and of the 12/6 from £205, to £295 for the Kempton. In 1937 all prices were increased by £2 and styles followed the unified trend towards a smoother line and roomier bodywork. The six-cylinder engine was withdrawn, the Twelve range being represented by an Ascot saloon, fixed-head saloon, and cabriolet, priced from £220 to £237. Doggedly traditional still in specification, the Ascot 12 hp range continued for 1939, the cabriolet costing £252 and a £272 shooting-brake variant being added.

Still, surely, one of the most popular and numerous of all prewar small cars, the Seven is sufficiently well-known not to need recommendation.

The Ten and Twelve are not so immediately endearing, but are in fact more realistic vehicles for everyday use, once fully renovated. The Clifton and Eton two-seaters are very distinctive cars with long curving backs and, like the Open Road Tourer versions, offer open-motoring - a marvellous bonus for the warmer weather. The saloons, on the other hand, can be fun in their way and are far more suited to all-season driving.

The Prewar Austin Seven Club: J.Tantum, 142 Cuzon Street, Long Eaton, Nottingham.

Austin Seven Owners' Club (London): Howard Annett, 8 Champney Close, Cheam, Surrey. 01-642-9106.

North-East Club for Prewar Austins: A.Pelton, 10 Ribbledale Gardens, Newcastle-upon-Tyne 7.

*For details of many other Austin Seven clubs, consult the Veteran and Vintage Directory see p.328.

British Salmson

Built by British Salmson Aero Engines Ltd, of Raynes Park, London SW 20, these powerful light cars are rare to-day, a brief span of roughly three years' manufacture representing an all too short lease of life. Closely allied with the French Salmson concern, their rapid demise witnessed an attempt by the French branch to keep the London firm alive by substituting two models made in France for the smaller-hp British cars, limiting production in England to the larger 20/90 model only. The cars did not reappear after the war, however.

To quote from a description of the marque written in 1937 by the staff of the *Motor*, and outlined in enthusiastic terms: "Quality is the distinguishing characteristic of all British Salmson cars. Their unsurpassed efficiency is the result of quality alike in design, construction and materials. They are hand-made by craftsmen accustomed to working to the fine limits imposed in the making of aeroplane engines, ensuring a standard of quality unusual in the manufacture of cars".

With radial engines becoming obsolete in aeronautics towards the mid-decade, a new venture into car manufacture could have resulted in the firm's rejuvenation, and as makers of printing-presses and cyclemotors in the 1940s and '50s, the company did carry on for a while after the war. But like the Squire car, the British Salmson product may have been 'too good', quality *per se* not always proving marketable. Their hand-build specialist cars somehow failed to find the right market during the troubled second half of the 1930s.

12 hp S4C (1934–37)

A newcomer to the Olympia Motor Show, the 1934 British Salmson stand displayed five new models that year. Two were open four-seater versions, partnered by two saloons and a drophead coupe; all embodied the 1½-litre dohc four-cylinder engine of 1470 cc, and carried certificated claims as to both top speed and length of trouble-free service. Powered by a standard 55 bhp engine, the 12/55 chassis later served as the basis of three 70 mile/h saloons, two coupes and a medium-performance four-seater tourer; in contrast, a modified and slightly higher-compression engine powered the 12/70 four-seater sports, providing a sparkling performance, the car being guaranteed to top 80 mile/h. All models were further guaranteed for two years, the cylinder bores themselves providing 40,000 miles of running before regrinding was necessary.

Finer points of detail regarding the engine were the meticulous care with which it was hand-assembled, and the patented valve-gear. This, as well as including the inclination of the valves at 45° to the vertical (and working in hemispherical combustion spaces), incorporated valve actuation via piston-form tappets sliding in cylindrical spring-covers, each tappet being cushioned by an aluminium plug mounted beneath the tappet plate and expanding on contact with hot oil as the engine warmed up. The crankcase and sump were in aluminium, and the special-alloy cylinder block was detachable. An extremely sturdy crankshaft, balanced both statically and dynamically, was equipped with large balance weights and sizeable main bearings and big-end journals. Shaft-driven via skew gears, the twin overhead camshafts were fed with oil through the shaft's being hollow, by which means lubricant reached the cam boxes under pressure from the gear-type oil pump. A thermostat coupled with an oil pressure control actuated the hinged radiator shutters, the latter immediately closing upon stopping the engine, thereby conserving heat. On restarting, the shutters were automatically reopened by the oil-pressure control. A single Solex carburetter was matched by twin Solex or SU units in sports versions, a Scintilla Vertex magneto being an alternative form of ignition for the 12/70 engine; a dynamotor provided electric starting and the engine was five-point rubber mounted.

1934 British Salmson S4C
Victoria Saloon

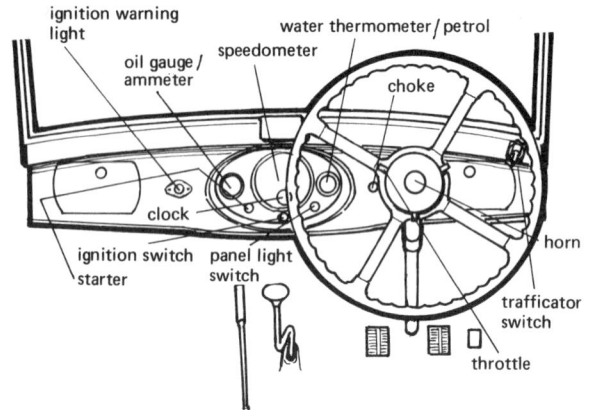

12 hp Saloon

ignition warning light · oil gauge / ammeter · speedometer · water thermometer / petrol · choke · clock · ignition switch · starter · panel light switch · throttle · horn · trafficator switch

British Salmson 12/70 chassis. A
fine example of the care and skill
needed to restore a chassis to a
condition equal, if not surpassing
the original

1935 British Salmson S4C 12/70
Works Special

A recently restored British Salmson 12/70 rolling chassis. Full renovation of the chassis frame is only possible with the entire bodywork removed

The imposing 'front end' of a 1935 British Salmson S4C 12/70 Works Special. Note the closed radiator slats, which open automatically immediately the engine is started, and the dynamotor mounted on the nose of the crankshaft

Another view of this finely restored Works Special

Transmission was through a single dry-plate clutch to a four-speed gearbox featuring synchromesh on third and top, but retaining straight-cut gears - noisy when 'elderly'. A torque tube conveyed power to the spiral-bevel rear axle. The sturdy chassis frame was not cruciform-braced, but very adequate rigidity was engendered by four crossmembers, that spanning the chassis adjacent to the rear quarter-elliptic spring mountings being fabricated from channel-sectioned components to give an amply-proportioned hollow I-sectioned member of great stiffness. Silentbloc rubber spring-bushes were used all round, the front suspension being by semi-elliptics acting upon a 'beam' front axle, and Hartford friction shockabsorbers served all four wheels. Steering was of Marles Weller pattern and brakes of Bendix 'duo servo' type. DWS jacks were standard fitting.

The close-coupled and lwb saloons were priced at £395, while the 12/70 four-seater cost £445. The latter was akin to the 12 hp Riley Lynx in overall 'feel', also featuring a swept tail, whereas the later two-seater 12/70 had a beetle back and flared scuttle. An attractive car of tasteful proportions, the close-coupled saloon was almost a precursor of the 1937 Riley New Monaco in the arched curve of its boot-line and overall gracefulness. Wire wheels were a standard fitting for all Twelves from 1934 to 1937.

An *Autocar* road test on a £325 '12/55' four-seater of 1936 echoed in full the manufacturers' claims as to quality of workmanship, the accompanying performance being revealed in a 0-50 mile/h acceleration which took only 17 seconds. An average top speed over the quarter-mile was 73.92 mile/h, and a best timed speed 75.63 mile/h. Other acceleration times recorded were 10-30 mile/h in 5.7 seconds using second gear, 30-50 mile/h taking 10.5 seconds in third. A stopping distance of 29 feet from 30 mile/h evidenced the efficiency of the brakes, in the same way as 30 mpg revealed that the engine, although powerful and not designed for cheap running, could also offer worthwhile economy.

At the 1936 Motor Show a 12 hp drop-head coupe finished in cream and green was exhibited, fitted with a three-position hood and priced at £345, as was the 12 hp saloon. The style of the 1937 saloon was again reminiscent of a Riley model - in this instance the trend-setting Kestrel - a 'fast' back and coupe-style rear roof-quarter being included in the S4C. The contemporary coupe shared much in common with the saloon as regards body shape below the waistline; above this was found a conventional fabric top, complete with chromed hood-irons. In 1938 the entire 12 and 14 hp range was replaced by a single 14 hp French Salmson model.

14 hp S4D (1936–38)

The Fourteen's chassis incorporated several new features such as independent front suspension, hydraulic brakes, and a box-section frame with a tubular crossmember carrying the front suspension; power was provided by a 1596 cc version of the four-cylinder dohc engine. The S4D chassis was available as a two- or four- door saloon, or as a drop-head coupe. Displayed at the 1936 Motor Show were a coachbuilt two-door saloon finished in red, and a coupe in blue and cream, both priced at £395. A top speed of 70 mile/h and two years' perfect service were guaranteed, as was the longevity of the cylinder bores. The 1937-season four-door four-light saloon featured sweeping lines reaching back from a long, straight bonnet. Two darker-coloured flashes ran along either side of the bonnet, widening-out in a gracefully descending curve to touch the crests of the rear wings. A sharply sloping back panel was surmounted by the curved rear of a coupe-type roof, and three diagonal banks of bonnet louvres completed the tastefully sporting effect.

In tune with a contemporary phase in styling, the 1938-season 14 hp saloon was now of four-door six-light layout, the traditional bonnet fronting a 'fast back' body of rugged proportions with a downward-curving waistline. Spoked disc Jordan wheels were featured, retained by metric-thread 'knock-on' hubs, and added a more powerful air to the overall strength of line. In contrast, the drop-head coupe retained an earlier, more graceful style, its sizeable hood with long hood-irons giving a less 'modern' outline. Jackall permanent hydraulic jacks formed part of the standard equipment of

British Salmson S4C Drophead Coupe owned by Dr. Ralph Canter. The car is used daily

1935 British Salmson S4C 12/70 Four Seater Tourer

1936/37 British Salmson S4D Drophead Coupe

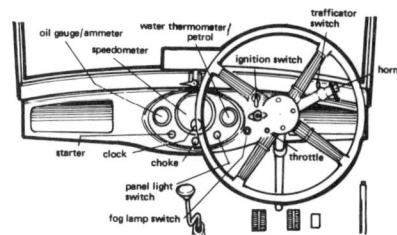

14 hp Saloon

the S4D chassis. The sum of £395 continued to secure either 14 hp version until the French-built two-door sports saloon replaced them at the 1938 Motor Show. The French car was of discernible Continental styling throughout, a 1730cc dohc engine giving a top speed in excess of 75 mile/h; a £495 18 hp French Salmson car with a 2300cc dohc engine, capable of over 85 mile/h, partnered the 14 hp model.

Although technically outside the scope of this volume, some mention should be made of the British Salmson 20/90, a powerful luxury saloon with six-cylinder 2596cc dohc engine priced at £695, and capable of 90 mile/h. In final 1938-39 guise it bore outwardly a striking resemblance to the Talbot Ten, albeit scaled-up, and was fronted by an imposing long bonnet. A highly potent £645 two-seater sports version was also built.

The small, but fanatically keen British Salmson Owners' Club offers a sole haven for the new owner with technical problems, or who would welcome the companionship of other British Salmson owners. The mechanical excellence of the marque makes it attractive to those appreciative of the finer points of automobile engineering. Despite the close liaison with French Salmson, this latter make is catered for by a separate register, given below.

The British Salmson Club is ever eager to swell its membership beyond a present 50-odd; perhaps more examples of this rare make will soon emerge from 'anonymity' to double this number. In the meantime it's worth keeping a look-out for that distinctive 'winged radial engine' radiator badge - at times looking more like a blowfly with a propeller on its nose - being thankful that at least somewhere the remaining examples are being preserved from extinction and kept in their accustomed fine condition.

The author is grateful to Keith Taylor for his help in compiling this section.

British Salmson Club: P. Perry, 14 Rowhill Crescent, Aldershot, Hants. Aldershot 23499.
French Salmson Register: G. Weightman and B. Fordham, Apple Tree Cottage, Rectory Close, Ashtead, Surrey.

1938 British Salmson 'fastback' 14 hp Saloon as depicted on a contemporary cigarette card

PLAYER'S CIGARETTES

BRITISH SALMSON 14 H.P. SALOON

BSA

The illustrious three-wheeler Morgan had one important rival during the 1930s. It was the BSA, a sophisticated design incorporating both front-wheel drive and independent front suspension. Although never as fast as the racing Morgans, the Blue Star versions were definitely high-performance models with excellent road-holding capabilities. Graduating from twin-cylinder air-cooled form to a four-cylinder water-cooled engine, the Scout later acquired four wheels, continuing in production until the war. BSA may rightly claim to be the only British car manufacturer to have featured front-wheel drive throughout the Thirties, Alvis having dabbled with it from 1927 to 1930. Certain Continental makers employed 'traction avant' at this time, of course, as did the 129, 810 and 812 Cord models manufactured in the USA.

The close connection between BSA and Daimler-Lanchester resulted, during the mid-30s, in the emergence of two conventional rear-wheel drive models, utilizing the Daimler 'fluid fly-wheel' as part of the transmission. Body styles were fairly close to those of the smaller Lanchesters.

Near the end of the decade a rationalization of output occurred, the sole remaining BSA model being the four-wheel fwd Scout of 10 hp, Series 4, 5 and 6. BSA cars did not, regrettably, re-appear after the war.

9 hp two-cylinder Scout (1930–36)

A three-wheeler, with air-cooled V-twin engine, the nine horse-power Scout first appeared in 1929. Its engine, of 1021cc capacity and low compression ratio, was a flexible unit closely following motorcycle practice but for the transmission, where a worm- driven spur differential drove the two front axles via fabric couplings at the near ends and enclosed Hookes joints at their extremities. Independent front suspension, a natural by-product of this layout,

was by two sets of four quarter-elliptic springs, each set controlling the travel of its appropriate front wheel. The rear suspension, acting on a single cantilever arm bearing the rear wheel, was by means of another quarter-elliptic spring, a felt-lined steel slipper forming an extension and riding against the inside of the main tubular 'backbone' frame-member. The felt lining was impregnated with grease to minimize friction.

As for the frame itself, the central 'king-post' tubular member was complemented by two channel-section side-members running parallel to it at the front and tapering to meet it at the rear. This very sturdy form of construction provided an ample foundation for the styles of bodywork fitted: the Standard model furnished with a fabric body on a wooden frame, the fabric being replaced by aluminium panelling in the De Luxe model. Finished in black fabric, the Standard version had red wheels, a folding hood with sidescreens and a safety-glass rectangular windscreen. The lighting set was black enamelled, while the interior fittings were finished in chromium plate; the two seats were of pneumatic 'air cushion' type. A luggage locker at the rear was concealed under a hinged lid, and when a wheel change proved necessary, a quickly detachable guard was provided to gain access to the rear wheel. The front wings of all models were finished in black, and the dummy radiator, fitted to all models, was chromium-plated - unlike the faster Morgans, the fascination of whirring machinery was very effectively hidden out of sight. Wire wheels were standard, front-wheel braking taking the form of a single drum brake fixed to the differential.

A choice of colour was offered for the aluminium-panelled De Luxe bodywork: lavender and grey, two-tone grey and black with ivory, blue, red or green. The Family De Luxe model was a '2+2' layout, access to the two childrens' seats being gained by tilting the front passenger's seat forward; black with blue was an extra colour scheme here.

A Blue Star special sports model with chromed headlamps and side-lights, aluminium bodywork and an engine with higher compression ratio, could also be obtained, offering an exhilarating performance coupled with smooth riding and good road-holding, particularly on fast corners.

A steady price of £100 secured the Standard model during its production years. By 1931 the Special Sports model cost £105, rising to £115 in 1935. De Luxe versions were a few pounds extra, the price of the two-seater being £108 in 1935, while that of the Family De Luxe was £110.

The BSA two-cylinder models themselves had three-wheeler rivals - the Coventry Victor, the JMB and the Raleigh, all rather short-lived, however. The former, of 1933-34 era, was an attractive machine with an 850cc sv or 499cc ohv flat twin engine. The larger engine powered a £99-15s Family Model, while the smaller was used in the 500 Model two-seater. A Luxury Sports streamlined model, on very attractive lines, and with a striking two-colour finish, was powered by a tuned version of the 850cc flat twin, its chassis closely resembling the BSA's structure. In contrast, the sub-frame of the JMB three-wheeler, supporting the engine, gearbox and rear wheels as a unit, was detachable from the body's ash frame, ifs being afforded by means of two transverse leaf springs at the front, and rear suspension being via leaf springs, also. A Standard Model at £75-10s and one of De Luxe specification at £83-10s were offered, both powered by a 497 cc JAP single-cylinder sv engine, a side-mounted kick start pedal, three-wheel brakes and chain-geared steering being common to both types. The Raleigh 7/17 chassis, with motorcycle-type front wheel forks and single wheel, (two wheels being provided at the rear), rivalled the BSA models in its Safety Seven open or saloon versions, a transmission shaft and rear axle akin to light car practice making them distinct from the general run of cyclecars. Complete with dummy radiator and bonnet, and rows of louvres along the bonnet sides and bottom valance, adequate cooling was afforded the air-cooled 742cc sv V-twin engine of Raleigh manufacture; sufficient power was developed for the provision of four full-sized seats in both versions, which were produced at £99-15s and £110 for the open and saloon models, respectively.

Price-for-price, and in the light of their individually attractive variations in design, these three competitive makes kept BSA on their toes, although it must be realized that the life of the three-wheeler in general was rapidly ebbing by the middle of the decade.

9 and 10 hp four-cylinder Scout (1933—39)

Perhaps having got wind of Morgans' plans for increasing the number of cylinders and providing a light-car engine to power some of their models, BSA themselves brought out 9 hp four-cylinder Scout versions in 1933. Using a BSA side-valve engine of 1075cc and 6:1 compression ratio, the fwd transmission and overall specification remained the same, an increased power output, however, making possible a livelier performance. A chromium-plated radiator provided cooling for the engine's water jacket; ball-and-roller bearings, as in the V-twin (and, incidentally, the Austin Seven) served to support the crankshaft, and a scuttle-mounted fuel tank supplied the Solex horizontal carburetter by gravity. Apart from the single rear wheel, everything to do with the mechanical specification closely followed light-car practice. Outwardly, the two- and four-cylinder models were very alike, the bodywork of the latter models being in aluminium only. A De Luxe two-seater model featured a distinctive two-tone colour scheme in black and ivory, dual grey, or lavender and grey, the upper contrasting colour widening out from a point at the front of the bonnet and sweeping down in a curve past the cockpit to envelop the rear section. Some models had a two-piece windscreen, curved at the edges, as in the MG M-type.

Capable of 60 mile/h and 40 mpg, the four-cylinder Scout made a good match for the Ford-engined Morgan, its added adhesion on corners and independent front suspension tipping the scales in its favour for some. Priced at £125 in Standard trim and £128 in De Luxe form when first introduced, these figures remained constant for several years.

Three-wheeler production at BSA terminated in 1936 with the announcement of a new model for the 1937 season - a four-cylinder, four-wheeler Scout of 10 hp, retaining both fwd and ifs, and replacing all other BSA models.

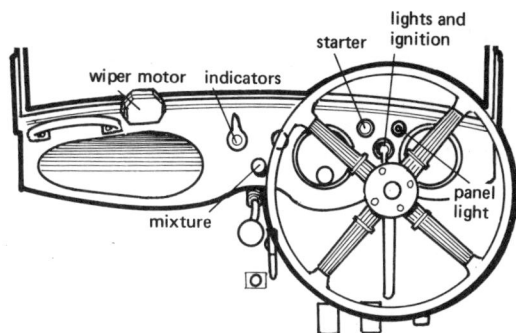

1939 10hp Scout Four Seater Tourer

1934 BSA rwd four wheeler model, equipped with Daimler 'fluid flywheel' drive and self-changing gearbox. Bearing a close affinity with the contemporary Lanchester saloons, the BSA was likewise available in 10hp and Light Six forms. This particular model is owned by Miss M. D. Bailey

1936 BSA three-wheeler 9hp Scout. This model has a four-cylinder engine

1937 BSA four-wheeler 10hp Scout Two Seater at the starting line in a prewar Welsh Rally

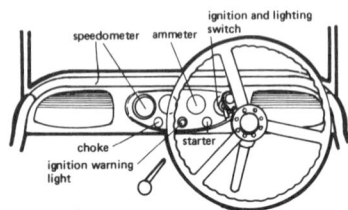

1933 three-wheeler water-cooled model

1937 BSA Scout photographed during the progress of the Welsh Rally

Using a larger sv engine of 1203cc, a choice of twin carburetters was available, and the Scout 10 was offered in two-seater form at £159-10s, a two-seater 'de luxe' costing £166-10s, a four-seater 'de luxe' £176-10s and coupe 'de luxe' £189. With a single carburetter, 23 bhp at 4000 rev/min was developed, whilst in twin-carburetter form the 26 bhp produced ensured a lively performance, the two-seater version weighing a mere 12½ cwt. The 'free' tubular rear axle was located by leaf springs and damped by hydraulic shock absorbers, drum brakes being provided on all four wheels, of Bendix mechanical actuation. Friction shockabsorbers served the front suspension.

Now a fully-fledged light car, the Scout, particularly in its two-seater form, was aimed at attracting new customers looking for a light four-wheeler sports car that handled well and looked the part - which the new Scout certainly did. Small details like a fold-flat windscreen, cut-away doors, well-louvred bonnet and so on, certainly indicated that this new enterprise had been given its fourth wheel for a purpose. A novel and distinctive feature that the new driver had to accustom himself to was the dashboard-mounted gear lever, operated in a 'pull, twist and push' movement.

At the 1937 Motor Show a longer and wider chassis was announced as the basis for the new Series 5 range, the shorter chassis serving the Series 4 models. The larger chassis made possible the addition of roomier bodywork with increased luggage space; the Series 4 two-seaters were down £10 in price, as was the 'de luxe' coupe, a very attractive little car indeed and described by the *Autocar* as "undoubtedly among the best-looking small cars in existence". The Series 4 four-seater cost £159-10s, and in 'de luxe' form, £7 more; the Series 5 range comprised two-seater, four-seater and coupe versions at £162, £172, and £182 respectively.

The Series 6 cars appeared at the 1938 Show with a new three-bearing engine giving 32 bhp and a top speed of 70 mile/h, a Solex down-draught carburetter significantly improving the carburation. The standard three-speed gearbox and 'wet' cork-disc clutch were retained, as were all other distinctive mechanical features. A new 2/3 seater at £168, a four-seater at £176, and a

new two-door saloon at £196 appeared on the stand; as fate would have it, these 1939-season cars were BSA's last. Other than a short-lived Alvis prototype of 1955, we had to await the BMC Mini before fwd became widely seen again in a British car.

Ten and Light Six (1933—36)

A close connection with the Lanchester Motor Company involved BSA in marketing two rear-wheel-drive models, a four-cylinder 10 hp Ten and a six-cylinder 12 hp Light Six, each model bearing close affinities with the contemporary Lanchester Ten and Light Six cars. Introduced for the 1934 season, the Ten Saloon cost £230, and offered high-quality interior finish coupled with a coachbuilt body; transmission was via a Daimler 'fluid flywheel' and self-changing gearbox. Overall chassis specification of both the Ten and £275 Light Six saloon of 1935 may be paralleled with those of the equivalent Lanchester models (see Lanchester section). Both models were available also in sports saloon versions, 'de luxe' and fixed-head coupe companion models being built on the Ten chassis.

A prewar front-wheel drive car is a rarity nowadays and will incite interest, plus not a little admiration, among the technically-minded devotees of 'old car' matters. If you are prepared to weather the Scout's unorthodox unit-construction gearbox-cum-fwd differential when it comes to overhaul or rebuilding, then in return you will have a distinctive 'curve-hugging' little car very rarely seen to-day. Should you like lots of 'bits and pieces' under the bonnet, then the air-cooled V-twin engine is for you.

BSA Front Wheel Drive Club (includes three-wheelers): P. D. Kine, 5 Mervyn Road, West Ealing, London W 13. 01-567-7232.

BSA Daimler-Lanchester Owners Club: H. D. Saunders, Eastgate House, Top Street, Appleby Magna, Nr. Burton-on-Trent, Staffs. Measham 70253.

Crossley

Famous for their RFC staff car of the 1914-18 war, Crossley Motors Ltd of Gorton, Manchester, retained an interest in commercial vehicles throughout their car-manufacturing days, returning to heavy vehicle manufacture in 1938.

The concern's 12/70 model, guaranteed to top 75 mile/h, was a noteworthy sporting machine of the 1920s and built in the tradition of the great vintage sports cars. Crossley Motors were also concerned with the later production of the Crossley-Burney Streamline, a revolutionary 'fastback' rear-engined car initially designed by Sir Dennistoun Burney. Featuring both ifs and irs - a very novel specification for the time - the car was later powered by a six-cylinder engine of 1990cc, developed from that used in the Crossley Shelsley model of the late '20s. Not many Streamlines were sold, however, although the original 4.4-litre version was still listed by the SMMT in 1936.

Crossley Motors tried desperately to keep their motor-car interests alive towards the end of the Thirties by introducing a variety of new models and body styles. Their failure to keep this side of the business viable was perhaps a direct result of an overall surfeit of manufacturers, each vying with the other for the public's favour, survival depending on a very sure financial footing and a policy more and more directed towards mass-production. The passing of both the Crossley saloons' quiet dignity and the verve of their open cars is to be mourned, even to-day. It cites yet another example of the rapid march of standardization that began at the end of the Thirties decade, spread further after the war, and which looms ever larger.

Ten (1931–37)

A 1122cc ioe Coventry Climax engine was chosen to power the new 10 hp chassis introduced at the 1931 Olympia Motor Show.

Styles and prices ranged from the fabric-topped Family Saloon at £265, the de-luxe Semi-sports Saloon and Family Saloon at £228 and the £295 four-seater Sports Tourer, to the Semi-sports Coupe at £310. The three-bearing Climax engine employed a Whatmough-Hewitt cylinder-head incorporating overhead inlet- and side exhaust-valves with 'mushroom' tappets, full-pressure lubrication, coil ignition, duplex-chain drive for the camshaft and generator, and a downdraught SU carburetter.

The channel-section chassis, upswept at the rear, featured an I-section 'beam' front axle forged oval at each end, with Magna wire wheels swivelled by means of a worm-and-nut steering box; suspension was via semi-selliptic leaf springs all round. The Ten's transmission embodied a single dry-plate clutch and 'silent third' four-speed gearbox, linked to the spiral-bevel rear axle by means of an open propellor shaft. Mechanically-operated brakes were fitted, the handbrake being of the externally-contracting type and acting on the transmission shaft. A high standard of coachwork coupled with an established ruggedness and durability made the new smaller Crossleys very attractive vehicles, destined, it appeared, to go from strength to strength.

The model name Quicksilver was introduced in April 1932, first of the breed being the new £325 Torquay saloon, so called because of its success in winning the *Autocar* Trophy at the Torquay Rally. A de-luxe version of the Ten, the Torquay featured a chromed mesh stoneguard in front of the radiator and an improved wing shape. The price of the Torquay fitted with a preselector gearbox is given above; the conventional-gearbox version cost twenty pounds less.

A spirited return to the sporting aspect of motoring was evidenced in the 10 hp Super Sports model first displayed at the 1932 Motor Show, a rapid two-seater with low bodywork on a dropped cruciform frame underslung at the rear, powered by a special 1097 cc Climax engine featuring two inlet valves per cylinder and fed by twin RAG carburetters. The model's aluminium-panelled body was set

1931 Crossley Ten Family Saloon. This car is most probably the prototype displayed at the 1931 Olympia Motor Show

1934 Crossley Regis 10hp Saloon. Note the absence of bumpers in this original publicity photograph

off by 'helmet' wings and wire wheels, its frontal aspect being especially rugged-looking due to a shortened radiator, the black honeycombing of which contrasted effectively with two chromed bars mounted in a 'V' formation, each linking a corner of the grille to a central point at the radiator's base. A choice of a standard or pre-selector gearbox was offered, operated through a central remote gear-change mechanism, the two higher ratios being desirably close.

In 1933 Crossley were proudly advertising the fact that a stock-standard Ten had been the only car to finish the Australia 24-hour Trial without losing a single mark, and this for the second year running. Such dependability was to continue as an essential Crossley virtue throughout the Thirties. At the 1933 Motor Show another Quicksilver model was announced, the aluminium-panelled Buxton saloon, priced at £298 with preselector gearbox. Its prototype had in fact been awarded the Buxton Town Trophy for putting up the best performance of any car starting the RAC 1000-mile Rally from Buxton itself. In essence the Buxton was a six-light variant of the standard Ten saloon.

By August 1934 the 10 hp Regis designed by C.F. Beauvais was announced, its graceful body-work being mounted on the little-modified Quicksilver chassis. A longer bonnet and angled radiator, automatic clutch, preselector gearbox, hydraulic shockabsorbers and sliding roof as standard fitting were the model's main distinguishing features. The 10 hp Regis was priced at £325 in saloon form or at £310 for an attractive four-seater Sports Tourer with airstream wings.

A year later the price of the Regis had risen to £335, and at the last Motor Show at which Crossley Motors exhibited, that of 1936, their stand revealed certain stylistic changes, the fitting of Ace disc covers to the wheels of their cars contributing to an almost Continental air overall, an impression closely echoed in the smaller-hp Citroen saloons of the era. For the 1937 and last season, a square-meshed radiator grille now fronted the bonnet, the sides of which now sported hinged louvres, locked by chromed handles. Plenty of headroom for the passengers was matched by a sizeable boot, and all fittings and details were of a high quality. An *Autocar*

road test on the 1935 Regis saloon recorded a maximum timed speed of 59.4 mile/h, 0-50 mile/h acceleration occupying 34.1 seconds; some 28-30 mpg were afforded. It is perhaps notable that the model's 2.29 lb/cc weight: capacity ratio was the highest of all the cars tested by that magazine during the 1935 season. In those days strength was often still equatable with mass.

1½-litre (1934–35)

A 1½-litre Regis saloon was exhibited at the 1934 Olympia Motor Show. An ioe power unit of 1476 cc provided additional power to propel the £355 Sports Saloon, its design incorporating such typical features as a preselector gearbox, centrifugal clutch, four-point rubber engine mountings, servo-shoe brakes and a low-swept frame.

Twelve Six (1936–37)

A new radiator and grille for the Regis series of 1936 coincided with an increase in price to £365 for the Twelve, which used an identical body to the Ten but sported a larger 1640 cc six-cylinder four-bearing engine. This unit included the provision of centrifugally-cast renewable valve guide inserts. The Regis Six was a quality car with good handling characteristics and smooth performance, an *Autocar* test finding it capable of 64 mile/h, 22.4 seconds being taken to accelerate from 0-50 mile/h through the gears. Affording a satisfactory weight:capacity ratio of 1.88 lb/cc, the car could return some 25 mpg.

Geoff Lee, present secretary of the Crossley Register, always welcomes new members. The club caters for all Crossley cars, and there is a large library of works' records and other information, from which much of the above outline history was drawn. The Register's efforts ensure that an ever-increasing number of these distinctive cars are traced, and by virtue of the spares offered, kept in good running condition. By taking out membership the Crossley owner not only shares the camaraderie of the club but also helps the cause, ensuring the marque's Maltese Cross radiator badge is regularly seen throughout the U.K. and in other countries.

Crossley Register: G. Lee, 'Arlyn', 4 Brickwall Lane, Ruislip, Middx. HA4 8JX.
Ruislip 36757.

Ford

The gift of being able to sugar the 'pill' of utility with an attractive coating has always been a notable facet of the Ford Motor Company. Basic, functional and 'everyday' the prewar cars may have seemed, yet their great popularity stemmed from the fact that Ford could make a utility car still look like a 'car', low purchase price often being accompanied by a lively performance and good fuel economy.

From the Model T, on to the Model A, Fords had, up until 1932, only offered cars of fairly large engine capacity - the Tudor saloons - the A and AB models of 1928-31 having 3¼-litre engines, their contemporaries the AF and ABF being powered by engines of two litres. Despite constant modifications and improvements these larger models did not sell well. The Great Depression finally convinced Fords that as regards the British market, a venture into the light-car field would seem opportune. Thus in 1932, at the independent 'Ford Show' held in the Albert Hall, the new 19Y model appeared, a small 8 hp car later to be called the Popular - a name that proved fully justified.

Popular, Eight and Anglia (1932–39)

The 19Y, priced in May 1932 at £120, represented tremendous value for money. Yes, the 1931 Morris Minor had been offered at a flat £100, but then for so little one got very little - an overall lack of power, comfort and instrumentation. In the new 8 hp Ford things were different. For one thing, the car was well-equipped and comfortable; no wood-and-fabric 'mock-up', the rotund bodywork was in pressed steel, and despite this the total dry weight was a mere 14 cwt. The rugged 933 cc sv engine, developing 22 bhp, also moved the car along at a top speed of 62 mile/h, giving 35-40 mpg and a decent enough 0-50 mile/h figure of 34 seconds. A full four-seater saloon, the 19Y's three-speed constant-mesh gearbox was fitted with synchromesh on second and top gear, and full interior

equipment including dip-switch, ammeter, keyed ignition switch, vacuum-operated windscreen wipers and a central winder to open the front windscreen panel. The 1933 Ford Show (again in the Albert Hall) was reported upon by the *Autocar* staff, relating that new refinements in the Y included "better mudguards and improved radiator shell, much improved headlamps, a redesigned steering-wheel, better upholstery, improved bumpers, a new design of dashboard, better brakes and considerably more accomodation in the bodywork". The price was £115; a de-luxe four-door saloon was also available. Notable too were one or two special two-seater bodies on the 8 hp chassis, the £162-10s Mistral, the Kerry Sports at £185, the Kerry Cairn at £192-10s and an Alpine tourer, attractively painted in cream and green, built by W.J. Reynolds Ltd. Obviously the little 933 cc engine could give good account of itself.

Called the Popular by Fords in 1935, the sale price had been wheedled down from £110 in September to the record sum of £100 by October - a direct product of well-organized mass-production methods, unequalled elsewhere. As it happened, this could not be continued for more than a season or so; nevertheless the point had been made. Production continued until 1937, when the new Ford Eight was first introduced, using the same engine in a larger, more modern style of body. The car was one hundredweight heavier, performance suffered, and the top speed fell to 57 mile/h. But the interior was more roomy and the whole car more solid-looking and refined, the two-door saloon selling for £117-10s, while the de-luxe version cost £127 - 10s. Acceleration from 0-50 mile/h was certainly not staggering at 40.5 seconds, but the 35-40 mpg was still attractive. Pressed-steel spoked wheels completed the transformation, and by 1939 the Anglia made its bow, powered by the same 'old faithful' engine of seven years' proven reliability. A new radiator-grille treatment fronted a flowing, but matter-of-fact body line. Here then, was Fords' oft-repeated 'service with a smile' - comfort, economy, and functional performance all for £120, or 'de luxe' at £10 extra. It is interesting (and staggering) to look at total production figures: 19Y Popular - 157,668; Eight and Anglia - 65,098.

1930/31 Ford Model A. Out of touch with the British public's need for a smaller, more economical car, the A series yielded its place to the very successful 8hp 19Y of 1932

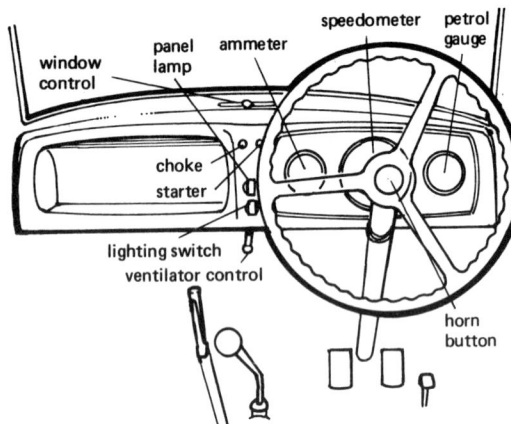

1936 8hp Popular

1932 Ford 8hp 19Y Saloon

De Luxe, Ten and Prefect (1934—39)

Ford Facts, a bulletin published by the Public Affairs staff at Brentwood echoes the justifiable pride that Fords experienced on reading the *Autocar* road test of the newly-introduced Ford CX De Luxe - "outstanding...0-50 mile/h in 18.2 seconds... maximum speed 70 mile/h... 35-40 mpg in normal driving". A more powerful, roomier and better-equipped version of the 19Y, the new 10 hp De Luxe got off to an excellent start, encouraged by such enthusiastic test reports. Powered by a 1172 cc sv engine of straight-forward design, developing 30.1 bhp at 4300 rev/min, the De Luxe saloon was a slightly enlarged version of the 19Y, but with a choice of two or four doors, and despite the extra 1-cwt payload resulting from the roomier body fitted, the CX was a far cry from being a sluggard. Externally bearing a distinct 'Transalantic' flavour akin to the 2½- and 3½-litre Ford V8

1935 Ford 10hp CX De Luxe Saloon

1938 Ford 10hp Prefect Saloon

series, the CX was a likeable little car combining a utility cost-price with very good performance, passenger comfort, and what must be called a definite 'character', endearing itself immediately to the British public - who bought 96,553 CXs in the three years of its manufacture (1934-37). It definitely looked more 'fun', at £135 for the Tudor model and £145 for the Fordor, than the 1937 Ten which superceded it. Powered once again by the 1172 cc sv engine the Ten's larger bodywork, though more streamlined, added further to the original load imposed by the CX, top speed falling to 67 mile/h, 0-50 mile/h taking 24.7 seconds and 33-35 mpg being afforded. So very reminiscent of the postwar Prefect saloon (into which the Ten evolved, in 1939), the Ten could look very smart, its modernized frontal treatment and six-light two- or four-door bodywork being tasteful and unobstrusive. Spoked disc wheels replaced the wire wheels of the CX, and a 'fast' back with flush boot lid completed what was a very apt transformation from a mid-30s style into one more suited to the 1940s

(and 1950s as it happened). Priced at £143 and £155 in 1937 for the Tudor and Fordor versions respectively, by 1938 the sole two-door saloon cost £145. In January 1940 came an increase of £3, the model being somewhat remarkable in that at £193, it remained on sale until July 1941, well into the second full year of war.

'A Ford is a Ford is a Ford' perhaps - but the period flavour of the 1932 19Y and the 1935 CX is certainly attractive. One thing is certain: the straightforward Ford design makes restoration far more simple. In return one gets a serviceable, 'unfussy', small prewar car, both practical and economical to run. An open tourer version of the 1938—39 Prefect is worth seeking out, too.

Model 'A' Ford Club of America, Rose of England Chapter (for 'Y' owners): Mrs B.W.Belcher, 'The Cottage', Rickinghall, Diss, Norfolk. Botesdale 258.

1939 Ford 8hp Anglia Saloon

Frazer Nash

A nick-name as evocative as the 'chain gang' is guaranteed to raise the eyebrows of any fast-car enthusiast not too conversant with the intimacies of the prewar Frazer Nash. Chains there were - four of them in fact - transmitting the drive from the gearbox bevel shaft to four sprockets mounted on a solid rear axle. Why chains? Well, one clue lies in the cipher 'GN', makers of very fast cyclecars which held many hill-climb records during the Twenties. GN stood for Godfrey and Nash - H.R. Godfrey and Archie Frazer-Nash to be explicit - co-designers of these 8¼ cwt twin-cylinder, 'four-wheeler motorcycles plus'. Post-1914 GNs had swopped belt for chain drive, and this mode of transmission was faithfully retained until 1922, experiments with four-cylinder engines and shaft-drive proving unsatisfactory and prompting Captain Frazer-Nash to quit the firm. One can quickly gather how faithful 'N' was in the Renolds chain, for on forming AFN Ltd, the new concern producing Frazer Nash cars, chaindrive was stipulated in all designs, and featured unswervingly until the end of the Thirties. The first Frazer Nash was freely based upon the last production GN model which had been fitted with a four-cylinder 1500 cc Anzani engine, the drive embodying four trusty chains.

Four-cylinder series (1930–39)

Four-cylinder engines rated at twelve RAC horse-power served as the most common power-units for Frazer Nash cars. Taken over by H.J. Aldington in 1929, AFN Ltd moved to new premises - Falcon Works, Isleworth, - early in 1930. Rejecting the Anzani, Aldington chose the 1½-litre Meadows 4ED engine as a substitute; of four-cylinder ohv layout and respectable power output (55 bhp at 4500 rev/min, unmodified), the 4ED was selected by many such sporting concerns as the motive force for their cars, just as the manufacturers of fast cyclecars had chosen engines made by JAP, Anzani and Blackburne in the Twenties. Chain-drive, of course, was the norm, and the Meadows engine was mated to the standard chassis. Perhaps poor results, arising from much mechanical trouble with an Anzani-engined TT model, convinced AFN that it would be a wise move, although a Meadows-engined car itself failed to finish in the 1931 Tourist Trophy race. Better performances were witnessed in the '32 and '34 TTs, however, and anyway the entry of the 1931 car had justified the use of the name TT Replica, a new model offered to the public in 1932.

Of classic appearance, with a long, well-louvred bonnet, shorter nickel-silver radiator, cycle wings, large wire wheels, external chromed siamesed exhaust pipes jutting out of the bonnet, exterior-mounted brake-and gear-levers, trim two-seater cockpit with folding screen,and a characteristically rotund 'bath tub' rear atop a 'slab' fuel tank with its quick-release cap mounted on an extension filler-tube, the Replica was startling to the uninitiated. Priced at £445 in return for a maximum speed of 90 mile/h and an acceleration from zero to 50 mile/h in 10 seconds, it was money well spent to the professional racer or wealthier young man of the time. Its aluminium-panelled bodywork complemented the Boulogne II fabric-bodied models, which were of similar specification.

During 1932 the attributes of these racy, hand-built cars spread far and wide, their individual style of roadholding proving very effective, once fully mastered - fast bends being taken more by sliding round than steering! As was the practice in those days, the channel-section frame, of extremely simple form, was allowed to flex with the movement of the car; two side-members of 3½-inch depth channel-section carried the main weight of the car, while a bolted-on extension supported the fuel tank, of 12-gallon capacity. Necessary extensions to the frame in order to accomodate the six-cylinder engine fitted to some models from 1933, led first to this longer chassis being used in the four-cylinder cars, and eventually to an underslung design with one-piece side-members. A slightly-curved, tubular front axle was sprung by quarter-elliptic leaf springs, as was the solid

1934 Frazer Nash TT Replica

1934 Frazer Nash at a VSCC
meeting at Prescott in 1970.
Driven by I. G. Teacher, the
car is seen passing the
Marshall's Post above Pardon

rear axle, Hartford friction shockabsorbers acting as radius arms at the front end. Alford and Alder 12 in. cable-operated drum brakes provided retardation, alloy finned drums soon replacing the inefficient pressed-steel type originally fitted. Rack-and-pinion steering, of extremely positive action, made general handling a pleasure, the total reduction ratio being a mere 4:1, full lock from side to side being attained in under one turn of the steering wheel.

Gear-changing, involving operation of the sweet-actioned, though 'heavy-pedalled' clutch, was by means of bell cranks, actuating sliding dog-clutches which engaged the required primary drive sprockets on the bevel shaft. Almost instantaneous changes were possible, irrespective of road or engine speed. The chains were protected from road grit and kept well-lubricated by the provision of an undertray and a handpump ejecting oil on to the chains when actuated from the cockpit.

To extract more power from the 4ED engine, Albert Gough, designer with the firm, invented his 'deflector head' which prompted turbulence in the combustion spaces. The inclusion of larger valves, a 10:1 compression ratio and magneto ignition pushed the power up to 62 bhp at 4500 rev/min, a notable enough increase, and one which led Frazer Nash to fit a 14:1 cylinder head in a Replica driven by Roy Eccles, capable of regularly exceeding 100 mile/h. Supercharging the Meadows came next, but it was not reliable at high pressures, a disappointing fact that had to be faced, despite speeds of 113 mile/h at Brooklands and the ascent of Shelsley Walsh in less than 50 seconds. To acheive these results the Meadows engine was forced into delivering some 120 bhp, and the crankcase and crankshaft were not up to it.

Albert Gough was subsequently called-in again, but this time given 'carte blanche' instructions to design a new Frazer Nash engine. This appeared in 1934, an ohc four-cylinder unit of identical bore and stroke to the Meadows, but with a 'deflector head', a massive nitrarded crankshaft, sturdy aluminium crankcase and water-cooled main bearings. But insufficient development time for ironing-out certain casting-porosity problems resulted in another erratic engine. Called the 'Gough' engine by Frazer Nash devotees, it performed well enough in supercharged form, but in unblown tune was too heavy for the power developed.

Supercharged Meadows engines were fitted to the Nurburg models, a mere 25 Gough engines going into TT Replicas from 1935 onwards.

The TT Replica, while not outstanding in major international races, did well in the Alpine Trials of 1932 and 1934, two cars being entered in the 1932 event, seven in that of 1933, and six in the Alpine Trial in 1934. No points were lost by either car in 1932, but 92 points were docked when a team car slid off the road in 1933. The 1934 event saw four cars finish without losing a point. Other records were attained at the 1932 Brighton speed trials and over the flying kilometre at Southport. Very often H.J. and D.A.Aldington drove the team cars themselves. To the public, the TT Replica and Boulogne II four-cylinder models, though not cheap, offered excellent all-round performance and a genuine taste of the excitement of speed allied to positive handling, the firm springing contributing to this.

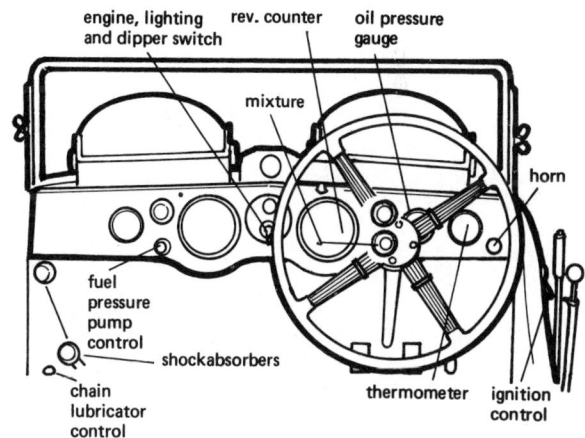

1933 TT Replica Two Seater

1934/35 Frazer Nash Colmore

1931 six-cylinder Frazer Nash at a VSCC meeting held at Castle Combe. The driver is Freddy Giles

Prices for the 1935 season were £475 for the Boulogne II, a specialist Shelsley model with twin superchargers and straight front axle selling for £850. By 1936 the TT Replica cost £650, the Shelsley's price remaining the same, as did the price of both cars for 1937 (in this year A.F.P. Fane took the Shelsley record in a *mono-posto* version). In 1939 the Boulogne's price had dropped to £425 (metal panelling having replaced the fabric body by 1934) while the TT Replica stood at £625 and the Shelsley at £750. Despite its straight front axle, cantilever semi-elliptic springing and 14 in. drum brakes, the change-over to a Bishop cam steering-box in the Shelsley was a retrograde step in the eyes of many.

Six-cylinder series (1933—39)

A dohc version of the six-cylinder 1667 cc Blackburne proprietary engine was fitted to certain TT Replicas from 1933 to 1935. Unfortunately the power : weight ratio was somewhat low and it could often be outpointed by the Meadows-engined cars. But it ran more smoothly on five crankshaft bearings, and gave an air of sophistication to the Replicas and a new model, the Colmore, produced from 1935 to 1939. An August 1937 *Autocar* road test on a Blackburne-engined short-chassis Replica revealed, despite a gross weight of nearly a ton (compared to 16½ cwt in the four-cylinder car) a maximum speed of 87 mile/h, 0-50 mile/h being accomplished in a mere 9.8 seconds. Increased engine weight had effectively limited the performance of the six-cylinder car to little better than one equipped with a four-cylinder 4ED. Nonetheless, the performance as such was still excellent. Production Colmores were priced, in 1936, at £550.

Six-cylinder 1498 cc versions of the Blackburne found themselves under the bonnets of the Byfleet I and Byfleet II models (named after the Byfleet Banking at Brooklands, and having wider TT bodies) and the Ulster 100 model of 1937-39. The Byfleet I, at £595 for the 1935 season, sported a 2/3-seater body, the TT-bodied Byfleet II costing £570; the four-cylinder Gough engine was also fitted to this latter model. As for the Ulster 100, this was a two-seater conforming to A.I. regulations, twin Amal carburetters, each with double float-chambers, providing carburation for the 1498 cc dohc engine; it was priced, in 1936, at £700, dropping to £650 by 1939.

For the final 1939 season a six-cylinder ohv engine was mounted in the new Falcon, priced at £425; most expensive of all was the mono-posto Shelsley version at £1050, a single-seater racer, retaining the ohc four-cylinder engine and twin 'Centric' superchargers.

Everyone enjoys startling acceleration and an exhilarating top speed, but for some an open cockpit and very firm springing lacks appeal - all this, of course, being relevant to whether one can afford a good-condition prewar Frazer Nash at to-day's climbing prices.

For the fanatic, however, the Frazer Nash has everything, symbolizing a past era of 'real' sports cars - small details like broken chains or perpetual colds in the head will never cool his ardour!

Frazer Nash Section of the V.S.C.C. : M.T.Joseland, 65 Coventry Street, Kidderminster, Worcs. 0562 4211.

Hillman

The Thirties were difficult times for the 'independent' car manufacturers. Liquidations and take-overs were rife - if your profits were not continually expanding, or if your cars happened just not to catch the public's eye (and purse) you went to the wall. Hillman were by this time absorbed into the expanding Rootes combine which we have seen, in recent years, itself absorbed into the Chrysler Corporation under the name of Chrysler UK.

Building cars then of large as well as small horse-power, Hillman of Coventry introduced their new light car, the Minx, in 1931. So successful was it that it survived into the 1960s, albeit with myriad modifications. The Minx also served as a basis for the Talbot Ten which was to develop into the very successful postwar Sunbeam-Talbot 90 Mks I and II.

Minx (1931—39)

Intended as a small, reliable family saloon which was both comfortable and capable of a fair turn of speed, the Minx models were all powered by 1185 cc sv engines fitted with flat-base tappets and delivering a useful 27 bhp. The Family Saloon, with pressed-steel bodywork affording a comfortable interior with plenty of room, was equipped with a pair of bucket seats at the front, direction indicators, Triplex safety glass, chromium-plated interior fittings, pile carpets, interior roof-light, rear-window blind, door pockets and a rear-view mirror. For £179 this was good value - no evidence of 'scrimping' on equipment in order to whittle-down the retail price. In appearance the Minx was fashionably smart, its vertical honeycombed radiator fronting a squared-up bonnet and six-light two-door saloon body with open wings, rounded high back plus spare-wheel mounting, and wire wheels with fairly large chromed nave-plates. A maximum speed of nearly 60 mile/h was attainable in the 1933 model, a three-speed gearbox with suitably-chosen ratios making driving easy and relaxing. Mechanical 'Bendix duo-servo' brakes were another feature of this well-equipped little saloon, steering being of worm-and-nut pattern, and a comfortable high-speed ride the result of Hillman 'Vari-load' semi-elliptic leaf springs coupled with Luvax hydraulic shock-absorbers of 'vane' actuation. The Minx was economical too; the driver could expect well over 30 mpg in normal driving.

The De Luxe Saloon, with more lavish interior appointments, incorporated a system of draughtless ventilation, ashtrays, a sliding 'sunshine roof', an interior sun visor, two-blade windscreen wiper, hide upholstery, rope pulls and a clock on the dashboard. A 'de luxe' four-light saloon looked distinctive in that the rear area of the roof wore chromed 'dummy' hood irons; a recess inside the roof interior housed a vanity case and newspaper rack.

By the 1934 season the Family Saloon was down to £159, featuring a new slatted 'V' radiator, a very attractive four-door body with sporting lines and finished in beige and crimson being offered on the Minx chassis at £195 and called the Club Saloon. The two-seater Minx was another well-proportioned 'sporting' car, the usual Minx front end evolving into a smart, compact open body with a graceful downward sweep at the rear, the hood folding away flush with the tops of the seats, 'cut away' doors completing the overall effect. It cost £185.

For the 1935 season the chassis frame was lowered to provide easier access and the engine quietened by fitting a larger air-intake silencer. But perhaps the most important innovation, as far as the driver was concerned, was the fitting as standard of a four-speed gearbox with synchromesh on all gears. The two-seater was withdrawn, so as not to 'overlap' with the Aero Minx and three saloon versions were offered: 'standard', at £159, 'de luxe' at £179, and a good-looking four-door sports saloon in two-tone finish at £225.

Slightly modernized in outward appearance for the 1936 season, the Minx basic saloon remained at £159, its overall specification being unchanged. At the 1936 Motor Show the new pressed-steel 'spoked' wheels were included; by mounting the steering-box forward of the front axle a good angle of rake was now obtained at the steering column. Box-girder construction was also applied to the chassis in the interest of rigidity. The Safety Saloon (Triplex glass all-

1931 Hillman Minx Saloon

round) was priced now at £163, with the De Luxe Saloon at £175. Other variants were a tourer at £175, a tourer 'de luxe' at £195 and a foursome drop-head coupe at £215, with 'three position' folding hood.

The 1937 Show revealed a new radiator treatment - a rounded split-grille design of two long oval panels fitted with short horizontal bars. The boot lid was now flush with the graceful concave sweep of the rear, and the whole six-light body expressed a degree of unity very concordant with the spirit of design then prevailing. The roof was now in one piece and minus provision for a sliding panel, while the interior, still large, offered wide seats; a novel feature was the windscreen wiper motor's relocation under the bonnet, and the way the wiper blades folded in a concealed position below the edge of the windscreen. Maximum speed was now 61 mile/h and power output 33 bhp at 4100 rev/min, coupled with 30-34 mpg. Prices of the models were £169 for the Safety Saloon, £184 for the 'de luxe' and £215 for the coupe.

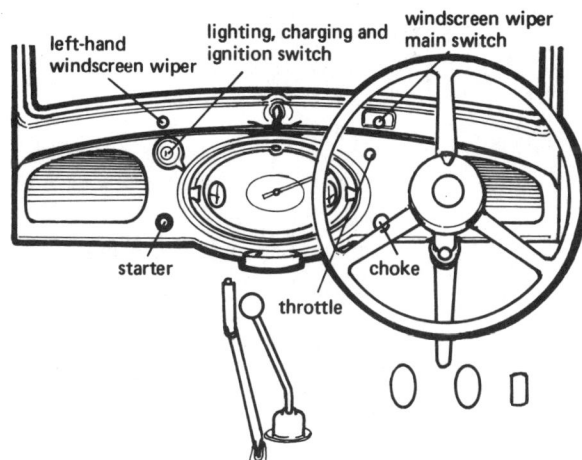

1937 Minx Saloon

The 1939 season saw the appearance of a touring Minx, plus sunshine roof once more. Further economy of fuel was acheived by fitting a Solex downdraught carburetter and, on Vauxhall lines, using a 'long spark' ignition coil, the wide gaps permissible at the spark plug points enabling the engine to 'coast' on a far leaner mixture; also to this end, a vacuum unit was added to the distributor's centrifugal advance-and-retard mechanism. The four-speed gearbox now had synchromesh on the upper three ratios only but was quieter-running, a very robust mainshaft being incorporated. Smoothness of ride was supplemented by new piston-type shockabsorbers, the driver finding also that the forward repositioning of the gear lever gave more foot-room. Reflecting modern technological trends, a Bakelite dashboard and window surrounds were featured. For 1939 the Safety Saloon cost £163, the Saloon De Luxe £175 and the Touring Saloon £166. A drop-head coupe remained available at £210.

The Medody Minx, introduced for the 1936 season, included a six-valve battery-operated Philco radio set as standard equipment. In essence a 'de luxe' Minx saloon, the Melody Minx's radio was tuned from a dashboard control; a harp emblem distinguished it from the De Luxe.

Aero Minx (1933–35)

The aeroplane made a tremendous impact during the '30s, and it was natural for manufacturers to call their sports versions 'aero' models. The Aero Minx, companion to the basic Minx series, was introduced in 1933.

A car designed to offer a higher performance, the Aero Minx was equipped with a modified engine, a higher compression (6.3 to 1) cylinder head, better manifolding and Stromberg downdraught carburetter, increasing the power output noticeably and generally livening-up the performance. Built around a shorter-wheelbase chassis,

Two models of the Hillman Aero Minx. On the left is a 1933 March Special, with bodywork designed by the contemporary exponent of motor racing, the Earl of March; on the right, a standard Sports Tourer of 1934. (*Aero Minx Register*)

1934 Hillman Aero Minx Tourer

The Hillman Aero Minx team which gained a Team Prize and a Gold Medal each in the 1934 Welsh Rally. The drivers are, from left to right: B. K. Biscombe, M. Biscombe and W. P. Uglow (*Aero Minx Register*)

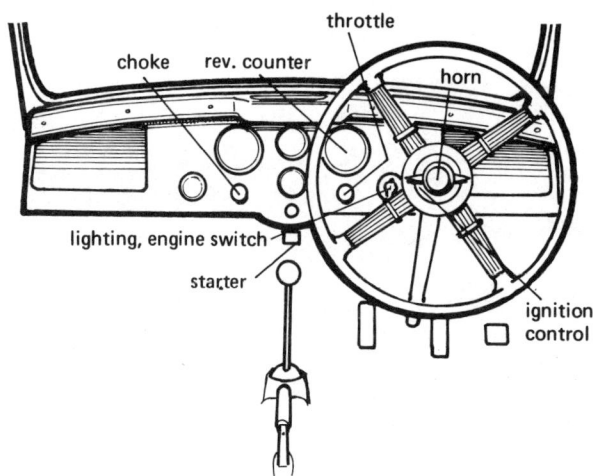

1934 Aero Minx Foursome Coupe

ground clearance was less, enabling lower, more rakish sports bodywork to be fitted. Hillman's own open bodywork for the Aero was of attractive, though conventionally-styled, four-seater tourer type with the favoured long tapering bonnet, long sweeping front wings, 'cut away' doors and squared-off rear, the hood folding away very neatly, level with the top line of the doors. Rudge Whitworth 'knock on' wire wheels added that extra dash of 'sporting flavour', and the finely-meshed radiator grille was given a tasteful outward curve at the base. Louvres, of course, were plentiful, appearing not only in the sides but in the roof of the bonnet, also. The finely-proportioned scuttle was flared upwards into two individual 'cockpit' fronts, arranged behind a brief, squared-cornered windscreen. The Aero Minx certainly looked the part, and performed well, (attaining 72 mile/h), but never startlingly - fun coupled with reliability was its main aim. At £225 for the 1934 tourer version, and £255 for a foursome coupe model, the 'Minx Plus' proved very popular. Other than the above-mentioned modifications, the Aero models were of very similar specification to the ordinary Minx.

Several coachbuilders offered pleasingly-styled bodywork on the Aero Minx chassis, among the designs an outstanding March Special two-seater, superfluous louvres being wisely removed and the neatly-curved open cockpit evolving towards the rear into a 'duck's back' tail, a concealed hatch housing the folded hood and spare wheel.

For the 1935 season the Aero Minx Cresta saloon was introduced, combining, at £265, the comfort of a 'de luxe' body and interior with the zest of the Aero Minx engine. In this season, when the two-seater was priced still at £225, production came to a close.

The dignity of the mid-30s Minx and the masculine, almost military aura of the 1938 version are attractive attributes. Always lively yet economical, these Hillman Tens should give both pleasure in ownership and represent thoroughly satisfactory day-to-day transport. For that extra charm and gusto, the Aero models offer a satisfactory solution, the standard ex-works body having immediate sporting appeal, while a coachbuilt two-seater such as the March Special symbolizes the ultimate in finesse.

Hillman Register: D.S.Johnson, 14 Queensway, Bletchley, Bucks.

Hillman Aero Minx Register: A.B. Demaus, Cadmore Close, St. Michael's, Tenbury, Worcs. Tenbury Wells 377.

1938 Hillman Minx Saloon

HRG

While the trend in sports motoring seemed to some by the end of the decade to be towards softer-sprung, well upholstered, 'flabby' sports machines, a certain small concern, HRG, decided to reverse things and swim against the current. Building firm-sprung, purposeful open cars with a '1920s' flavour, HRG equipped their models with positive leech-like steering and startling acceleration, gaining many successes in competitions during the short four-year span between their introduction and the advent of war. Fortunately the firm were able to resume production in 1946 and despite financial hardships continued in business for another ten years.

1½-litre (1935—39)

Upon dissolving the GN cyclecar enterprise in 1925, 'N' - Captain Archie Frazer-Nash - went on to found his own Frazer Nash concern; as for 'G' - H. R. Godfrey - it was not until November, 1935 that the first announcement of a new company under his aegis was made to the press. Now in partnership with E.A.Halford and Guy H.Robins, 'H.R.' had taken a light, albeit flexible, yet sturdy 'ladder' frame, utilizing deep-section side members and tubular cross-members, and married to it a rigid tubular front axle sprung by quarter-elliptics, a light ash-framed alloy body and a Meadows 4ED 1½-litre engine. Carburation being by twin SUs and a magneto providing the ignition, the developed power (58 bhp at 4100 rev/min) propelled the 14 cwt projectile from 0-30 mile/h in 4 seconds, 0-50 mile/h in 9.8 seconds, and up to a maximum speed of over 85 mile/h. A Moss gearbox and ENV rear axle were complemented by a Marles-pattern steering box and 11 in. drum brakes, adding up to an exciting specification. Owing to the need for two years' prior registration with the SMMT before one could exhibit at the Motor Show, HRG had to rest content with the publicity afforded by participation in

competitions and the occasional press notice or national advertisement. At the end of 1936, five 1½-litres had been built and were offered for sale at £395, the factory being sited at Tolworth, near Kingston-upon-Thames. Competition successes, such as gaining second place in the 1½-litre class of the 1937 Le Mans, together with regular victories on British circuits, did more than any advertisement could in spreading the HRG gospel.

Twenty-five 1½-litre models were completed before the outbreak of war, all powered by the Meadows 4ED engine, which by 1938 was virtually obsolete. As a substitute, HRG and Singer Motors collaborated in constructing a modified version of the ohc Singer 12 engine with its three-bearing crankshaft, one production model fitted with this engine being finished by September 1939.

The 1937 HRGs were given wider bodies on a wider chassis and 1938 proved to be an important year in that the first of the 1100 cc cars were constructed. Unfortunately, a special 1½-litre Le Mans model, completed in June 1937, and of distinct potential, did not reach the starting-gate, although it did take second place in its class in 1938 and won the class in 1939. This Le Mans HRG sported cycle-type wings, and had an extended tail concealing twin spare wheels, a neater cockpit and folding windscreen. The single completed Le Mans Replica was offered for sale in 1939 at £495.

Of great interest, but regrettably a nonstarter, was the two-seater coupe designed by E. A. Halford and powered by a Triumph 1½-litre engine. The functional severity of the HRG front end, wedded to a compact little 'fast back' coupe body was eye-catching; a sliding roof was incorporated, together with a windscreen which could be wound open at the bottom by means of a handle on the dashboard. In overall effect reminiscent of the early MG Magna and SS II two-door coupes, but with a superlative performance, it would have sold well. In the 1938 Motor Show editions of the *Autocar* the coupe

The early 1½-litre Meadows-engined HRG proved a formidable competition car right from its inception. This is E. J. Newton competing in a Prescott Hill Climb

1937/38 HRG 1½-litre Two Seater at a Lawrence Cup Trial

1937/38 HRG 1½-litre Two Seater hugging a bend during a 1930s event

was listed at £475, an extra £10 securing the fitment of a sliding roof.

In 1939 the basic 1½-litre two-seater was offered at £424-12s-6d.

1100 cc models (1938–39)

Liason with Singer Motors also engendered the 1100 models, their Singer 9 ohc engine of 1074 cc, duly modified, being used to power them. Very similar in overall external detail and appearance to the 1½-litre cars, a bonnet 3 inches shorter distinguished the 1100s. Producing 40 bhp at 5200 rev/min, good performance was extracted from the engine-chassis combination, the road-holding abilities of the smaller-engined cars if anything excelling those of the 1½-litres. Eight 1100s were built between 1938 and 1939, and were offered at £275, rising to £295 in 1939. A Singer synchromesh gearbox forming part of the specification, though not an ideal unit for competition work, did in fact make the 1100 easier to drive.

To enthusiasts of the marque, the HRG is more a way of life than a mere car. The rarity of the prewar models makes them legendary - no owner in his right mind is ever going to part with one!

HRG Association: I.Dussek, 'Hustyn', Packhorse Road, Bessels Green, Sevenoaks, Kent.

Humber

Humber Ltd of Coventry were an old-established firm dating back to the 1890s. Although better known for building large cars, the concern did, as a member of the Rootes combine, produce some smaller-capacity vehicles in the light car field. These were the Humber Twelve series of cars which, throughout the Thirties, ran parallel with the Hillman range. The Twelve offered a more luxurious overall finish than, for example, the Hillman Minx, and was intended more as a prestige car.

This section covers a period from 1932 to 1937 only. After this time, all Humber cars were of a capacity greater than 1700 cc - an arbitrary but necessary dividing line separating, for the purposes of this book, light cars from their heavier larger-capacity counterparts.

Twelve (1932–37)

Conspicuous as a newcomer at the 1932 Olympia Motor Show, this 'small Humber' was well received by the public. Typically a Humber as regards appearance and refinement, its engine was a 1669 cc sv in-line four rated at 12 hp, other mechanical chassis specifications being the fitting of a four-speed gearbox in unit with the engine, a single dry-plate clutch, spiral bevel rear axle, semi-elliptic springing all round and cable-operated brakes. At £265, the Twelve represented a useful smaller edition from the impressive Humber stable, which included the 16-18 hp Snipe and the seven-seater Pullman limousine of 23.8 hp. Scaled-down elements of Humber styling marked the Twelve immediately as to origin - the characteristic heavily-chromed slatted radiator, for example, with its impressive breadth of shoulder, setting-off a finely-proportioned bonnet - but something 'extra' was called for to make more of a mark in the public's esteem.

The 'something extra' was to appear a year later at the 1933 Motor Show, in the form of a completely new stylistic venture, the Humber Vogue saloon. Designed in collaboration with Captain Molyneux, whose fashion designs were renowned both in London and Paris, this new car offered three distinct departures from the 'run-of-the-mill' saloons as regards body styling. Firstly, the Vogue, although a full four-seater, was entered via one single large door on either side, encompassing the entire width from a line parallel with the windscreen to just forward of the rear wing. Secondly, the area of glass spanning the side windows was unbroken by door pillars or any other impedimenta; a single broad window afforded an untrammelled side view for the rear passengers, and this was made feasible by overlapping the glass panes of the doors and 'quarter lights'. A third very fashionable inclusion was a Continental-type luggage trunk, mounted distinctly separate from the curved rear of the car. Priced at £335, this new Twelve was at once aimed at the driver who was looking for a 'different' smaller car, styled on Continental lines, but with the more accustomed British mechanical specification. Extra smartness came with the fitting of black-cellulosed wheel discs, entirely concealing the spokes, coupled with large chromium-plated nave plates. A constrasting two-colour scheme of black for the roof, bonnet and wings, with a very pale colour for the main bodywork further added to the overall fine appearance. Companions to the Vogue, a standard 12 hp saloon and an open sports four-seater of pleasing lines, were also offered.

Few stylistic changes were deemed necessary for the 1934 season, barring a new V-type radiator, which still carried a glittering plated mascot on its prow though not now mounted on the filler cap, which was concealed below the bonnet. Servo-shoe brakes were a further welcome inclusion as regards stopping-power, as was the application of the box-girder principle to the chassis, making it far stronger and more resistant to flexing. The engine mountings were now of the flexible rubber type, and it was positioned further forward in the frame, increasing body space relative to the same body dimensions. 'Multi-rate' springs, with reinforced short bottom leaves, gave extra riding comfort, and synchromesh on all four speeds made

starter throttle horn twin screenwiper choke lighting anti-dazzle

1935 Twelve Six-Light Saloon

1933 Humber Twelve Saloon climbing the Hardknott Pass. This is the standard Six-Light saloon version

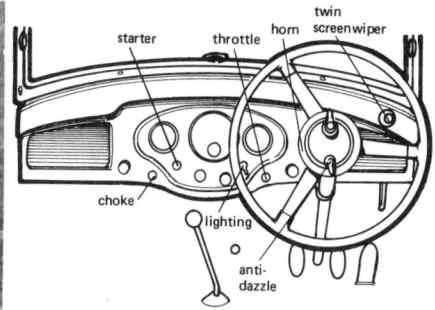

1935 12hp Humber Vogue Saloon

driving easier. To achieve greater quietness a large air-intake muffler and more effective silencer were fitted, and the carburetter was better insulated against heat conduction through the inlet manifold. The standard saloon remained at £285, the Vogue's price being unaltered.

A reduction in the area of a chromium-plate for the radiator came for the next season; although still very impressive and tall, the sides and shoulders were now cellulosed and blended into the bonnet lines, the bright V-form slatting forming part of a grille fixed in a sloping position at the front of the bonnet. A foursome coupe, priced at £325, was introduced, while the standard saloon and Vogue continued at 1934 prices. An *Autocar* road test on the standard six-light saloon of 1935 found a car of high-quality finish, smooth-running and handling well. It was well anchored too - stopping in 31 feet from a speed of 30 mile/h - and the best timed speed was 68.18 mile/h. A fairly heavy car, weighing 25 cwt, the Twelve's acceleration was not very vivid, 24.6 seconds being needed to achieve a speed of 50 mile/h from rest; however, useful third-gear acceleration of 9 seconds for 10-30 mile/h and 9.8 seconds for 20-40 mile/h was some compensation. A good driving position and front visibility made the driver feel relaxed and confident, the well-silenced engine proceeding with little more than a whisper and giving an impression of smoothness usually engendered by an engine with more than four cylinders. A realistic 25 mpg could be returned in give-and-take motoring. Very comprehensive equipment was supplemented by the fitting of permanent jacks of DWS manufacture. Interior features were first-quality hide upholstery, a rear seat with centre folding arm-rest, two folding sun vizors, and a centre-locked sliding roof, cubby holes, door pockets, a horn switch in the form of a ring circumscribing the steering wheel hub, and comprehensive instrumentation including a radiator temperature gauge and a clock, together with an electric cigarette lighter. Exterior fittings of note were a twin-blade screen wiper and flush-fitting, self-cancelling trafficator signals. In sum the Humber Twelve lived up to the Humber traditions of comfort,

finish and ease of driving, despite its smaller size.

By 1937 decreases in price were in evidence, the Vogue now costing £298, the six-light saloon £258 and the Foursome Coupe £298. For this, the final season of the 12 hp Humbers, the Vogue remained little changed from 1933 but for the single-colour decor, newer radiator and smaller, lower-positioned headlamps. Gone, too, were the row of five louvred panels fitted along either side of the bonnet and the chromed sidelights, now replaced by a streamlined 'modernistic' variety. But the long side windows, that original distinctive feature of the model, remained to the end. The car was aptly named - it set the vogue for several 'long-windowed' saloons appearing throughout the mid-30s.

Mechanical orthodoxy makes the prewar Humber an attractive proposition, overhaul proving free of tricky problems and oddities. Always an imposing car, a small Humber combines dignity with smaller petrol bills, while affording the fairly luxurious specification for which the marque was well known. As for a finely-restored Vogue, this could well prove a 'show stopper' at any rally, particularly in the *concours* event.

Jowett

There is something very distinctive about the sound of a flat twin - a blend of a rather 'lumpy' rumbling exhaust note with a rhythmic clicking from the tappets - it's really a sound that seems unrelated to car engines and more associated with the rough-and-tumble cyclecar or motorcycle world. Few people realise that the 1948-54 Jowett Bradford van with its characteristic flat-twin sound, many of which could be seen on the roads in the 1960s, represented the last direct historical link with the flat-twin Jowett engine of 1910, an engine which, with few modifications, served to power all 7 hp Jowett cars from that year onwards up until 1939. Still little modified, this same engine drove the Bradford 'utility' from the early postwar days to the liquidation of Jowett Cars in 1954.

Formed by two Yorkshire brothers, William and Benjamin, Jowett Cars Ltd remained insistent that the horizontally-opposed cylinder arrangement was the ideal form for small motorcar engines. The motto "Balanced Power" - inherent due to the fact that the reciprocating parts were unaffected by the force of gravity since their motion was along a horizontal axis - was emblazoned all over their publicity material. Their archetypal flat twin soldiered on through the 1920s and '30s, to be joined in 1936 by a 'flat four' which powered the Jason saloon and formed the basis for the postwar Javelin saloons and Jupiter sports models.

7 hp models (1930–36)

Firmly established at Idle, near Bradford, Jowetts' programme for 1930 was a direct continuation of what had gone before - to provide hard-working small saloons giving reliable service rather than erratic, spectacular performance. Over the years the well-tried 907 cc flat twin had proved to have powers of longevity, giving a serviceable bhp output without fuss, coupled with a useful torque figure, making the tourers ideal in certain hill-climb events. Of

7.04 rated horse-power in 1930, the sv engine developed 16 bhp at 3000 rev/min; compared to the Austin Seven of the same year, whose 747 cc engine produced 10 bhp at 2400 rev/min, this was a fairly creditable figure - but considering that the ohc Morris Minor engine of 747 cc developed 20 bhp one can appreciate that the Jowett twin was merely of average performance, capable only of powering a car with comparatively light bodywork.

Two chassis types were available, the lwb and the swb. Up until the mid-30s the Jowett chassis was of a simple 'ladder' type, employing channel-section members and offering very little resistance to flexing. Inswept at the front and upswept at the rear, the front and rear extensions to the frame carried the mountings for the semi-elliptic springs, friction shockabsorbers giving way to the Luvax 'vane' hydraulic type by 1934. For the 1935 season the frame was stiffened by the addition of cruciform centre-bracing and lowered, so as to make possible the addition of more fashionable low-slung bodywork. With the up-rating of the Seven to 8 hp and the addition of the 10 hp 'flat four' few modifications were deemed necessary to the basic chassis, which served as a foundation for both models.

The late-20s models, bearing a certain outward frontal resemblance to the 'bull nose' Morris Cowley, were simple, functional vehicles, cheap to run but far from exhilarating. By 1932 new styles of steel bodywork were introduced on the short and long chassis and picturesque names were chosen by the Jowett brothers. For example the lwb saloon of 1932 was given the name Blackbird to replace its former title the Long Saloon; later the name Kingfisher was given to a Long Saloon bearing blue paintwork, the final prewar name being the Falcon. A lively little twin-cylinder two-seater on the long chassis rejoiced in the name of the Flying Fox while the Long Four's title became the Weasel. Other ornithological touches came with the Kestrel (the Long Saloon 'de luxe'), and the 8 hp Plover. A last prewar fling into the realms of classic mythology resulted in such names for the flat four 10 hp models as the Jason and Jupiter. We might also note here that Motor Show publicity

1933 Jowett 7hp Kestrel Saloon, owned by Dennis Mitchell

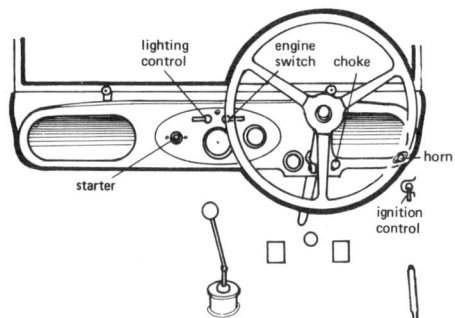

1929 Black Prince Fabric Saloon

Another view of Mr. Mitchell's Kestrel

material appearing in such journals as the *Autocar* was occasionally humorously angled at the 'ee bah gum' image - a definite air of Yorkshire pride coming through between the giggles. And yet a rapid glance at the standard of their manuals and technical literature could quickly reveal conclusive evidence of hard-headed expertise coupled with precision in every facet of their products - those Yorkshire lads knew exactly what they were doing, of course.

The low-speed torque of the Jowett twin engendered a noticeable degree of vibration, particularly on tick-over. Rubber flexible mountings gave way in 1937 to an unusual hydraulic device, a pair of which provided the front mounting. Needing topping up with oil each month, each unit worked in the same way as a piston-type shockabsorber (but these were found unnecessary on the 10 hp four-cylinder engines). Among other interesting mechanical points was the use of a bonded die-pressed asbestos friction plate in the clutch from 1930-32, which in 1933 was duplicated to give a 3-plate 'sandwich', the centre plate being of steel and bearing slots to provide added friction. In 1934 a Cardan shaft of Laycock manufacture was incorporated, flexible Layrub couplings proving another anti-vibration device. Eccentric-bush steering proved standard until the advent of the new Ten heralded the change-over to Marles Weller. As for the gearbox, this remained of 'semi-crash' constant-mesh pattern, a helical-cut 'silent third' gear and single-plate clutch being added in 1935, a freewheel having been standard equipment up until then. Following this, Jowetts, proving reluctant to rework their gearbox, added in 1937 a 'synchronizer' which coupled the benefits of a freewheel with pseudo-synchronized gear changes. This took the form of a dog-clutch controlled by the freewheel and synchronizing the speeds of the propeller shaft and gearbox tail-shaft.

By virtue of the flat-twin engine the Jowett bonnet as such was largely empty, but for some years Jowetts stuck to tradition, their early-30s models closely resembling those produced by other 'family saloon' manufacturers. The Kestrel of 1934, for example, closely resembled the yet-unborn Morris Eight saloon, retaining a high square bonnet and full-size vertical chromed shell for the radiator. And yet the thought of that empty bonnet rankled until, at the 1935 Olympia Motor Show, Jowetts took the courageous (but unwise) step of sharply angling the 10 hp radiator and sloping the top of the bonnet, both steps in the interests of logic and visibility, but steps that needed to be re-traced somewhat before the 1937 models were displayed at the 1936 Show. The 1934 models comprised a two-seater and tourer, both priced at £150, a Short Saloon at £151, a 4-door Long Saloon at £160, and the Kestrel Sports Saloon at £175. The two-seater, an angular design akin to the Morris Minor, sported a long rounded back resembling a drophead coupe and had a dickey-seat in the rear. The saloons were again somewhat unremarkable in shape but were very roomy, the long chassis being even larger than that of the Standard Nine - their very 'roominess' and size implying a certain amount of surplus weight for the little 7 hp engine. In 1935 a four-seater sports tourer at £158 seemed to precedent the Morris Eight open tourer in overall line, whilst the 'de luxe' saloon, by chance reminiscent of the Wolseley Nine and priced at £185, had the first vestige of a boot, called a 'locker', which also housed the spare wheel.

8 and 10 hp models (1936–39)

With the 1936 Motor Show came Sankey pressed-steel 'easy clean' wheels and a larger capacity for the twin of 946 cc, giving a new rating of 7.35 hp. The *Autocar* of October 16th voiced the opinion that notwithstanding the traditional roominess and reliability of the Jowett models "to-day one finds these qualities allied with a grace of outward appearance not previously attained". Outwardly there was indeed every sign of their following fashion, from the pressed-steel semi-streamlined bodies with close 'helmet' wings, to the smaller diameter wheels, large section tyres and gracefully flowing tail with concealed boot lid *a la* Hillman Minx. As for the new four, this was now modified to employ a single carburetter, delivering 31 bhp at 4000 rev/min, a favourable enough figure for a

lighting and ignition switch

clock

screen wiper motor

headlamp dipping control on steering column

screen opener

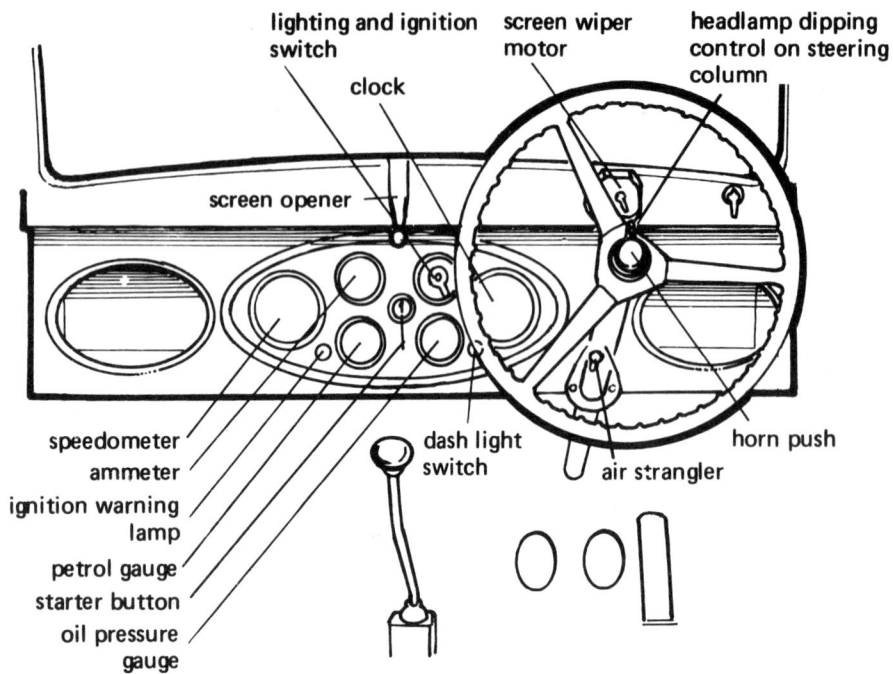

1937 Eight Saloon

speedometer
ammeter
ignition warning lamp
petrol gauge
starter button
oil pressure gauge

dash light switch

air strangler

horn push

1934 Jowett 7hp Kestrel Saloon, owned by Dr. O. J. Follows

ANU 796

1166 cc sv engine of the time. In comparison the twin delivered only half of this output, yet the nominal 8 hp unit was employed in a body as large as the Ten - a high cruising speed was certainly not envisaged. The price of the '7G' 8 hp saloon was £158 or in 'de luxe' form £168, while the '7J' 10 hp cars cost £189 for the standard saloon and £195 for the 'de luxe'.

By 1937 the gently-sloping radiator grille had evolved a more rounded curve; prices were roughly £5 up on the previous year. In the 1938 season a new one-piece front bumper replaced the divided type, but all remained very little changed - a drop in prices for the 1939 season resulted in the 8 hp saloons selling for £159-10s in standard form and £169-10s 'de luxe' (including adjustable steering wheel and sliding roof), the 10 hp versions being priced at £186

standard and £195 'de luxe'.

If you can tolerate that idiosyncratic exhaust note and transmission judder, the Jowett flat twin offers something 'different' plus the bonus of economical running (40-45 mpg). Alternatively, the flat four, kept in good tune, can offer a smoothness of power transfer very close to that of an electric car. With the power unit low-down in the depths of the bonnet, well silenced and correctly gapped at the tappets, one almost forgets that one is being moved by an internal combustion engine. "Balanced power" indeed!

Jowett Car Club: A.A.R.Pluckrose, 'The Briars', Casteldon Road, Downham, Billericay, Essex.

1937 Jowett Eight Saloon ripe for restoration. This car has recently been acquired by a member of the Jowett Car Club in York

Lagonda and Rapier

Famous for their larger sporting cars of several litres capacity, Lagonda Ltd, of Staines, reverted to a small version with their 1104 cc dohc Rapier. Designed by Tim Ashcroft, the prototype first exhibited at the 1933 Motor Show was slightly different from the production models available by mid-1934. Such modifications as were necessary to convert the body from a two- to a four-seater did not, however, affect the basic concept of the little car as an energetic and refined 'small Lagonda'. In appearance reminiscent of a scaled-down two-litre, the Abbot-built tourer bodywork gave the Rapier a purposeful air, and although of somewhat low power : weight ratio, the car performed well.

After only a year of manufacture, the Lagonda Company sold out all rights and stock-piled mechanical parts to the designer, who set up Rapier Cars Ltd, their workshops being situated at 195 Hammersmith Road, W6. Called the Rapier Ten, the engine capacity was reduced to 1087 cc so that the car could be entered in 1100 cc-class competitions - an idea that Lagonda had deliberately 'scotched' by fixing the original capacity above 1100 cc.

By 1939 economic difficulties forced Ashcroft to wind up the firm, but not before several hundred Rapiers had been built, many of which still exist, in good condition, to-day.

Lagonda Rapier (1934–35)

Constructed on a sturdy channel-section chassis frame with tubular crossmembers, the Rapier's engine also afforded additional bracing.

Of 1104 cc capacity, the engine's double overhead camshafts were driven from a fibre half-timing gear by chains, an 'ideal' hemispherical form being given to the combustion chambers. A cross-flow cylinder head afforded untrammeled flow for the inspired charge and exhaust gases, a compression ratio of 7.5:1 was employed, and 45 bhp at 4500 rev/min claimed by the manufacturers, although the revs could be taken nearer to 5500 rev/min if desired. A cast iron block and cylinder-head were complemented by an aluminium sump pan, for more efficient oil cooling. Ignition was by BTH magneto. It is rumoured that perhaps all the Rapier engines were built in 1934 as part of a batch of 400 contracted out to the Coventry Engine Company; this too may apply to the ENV 75 preselector gearboxes and other components, many of which bear the date-stamp '34'.

As for the transmission, a single dry-plate clutch was mounted between the engine and the ENV gearbox, the latter being chosen to afford extremely crisp gear changes and extract the maximum acceleration from the diminutive power unit. Four forward speeds were available via a right-handed gear lever, with a higher axle ratio for the open cars. A Bishop cam-and-roller steering box connected with front stub axles pivoting at the extremities of an I-section forged 'beam' axle; the rear axle, of ENV manufacture, was, like that at the front, fitted with 'knock-on' wire wheels. Semi-elliptic springing was used front and rear, and braking was via a rod-operated Girling system, fully compensated and embodying 13 in. brake drums. In all, it was an impressive enough specification, the engine being its salient point, if anything. A gross dry weight of 17 cwt somewhat took the edge off the accelerative properties of the tourer versions, but the inherent robustness of the engine has enabled very profitable modification in the hands of present Rapier Club members, a 10:1 compression ratio, special camshafts, and even two-stage supercharging at 20 lb/in^2, extracting valuable extra power in several instances.

How did contemporary motoring journals receive the Rapier? An *Autocar* road test of July 20th 1934 called it "a thoroughly worthwhile newcomer among small sports-type cars" - and figures of 0-50 mile/h in 15.6 seconds with a

1933 Lagonda Rapier, one of the two prototypes with bodywork designed by the Earl of March. Owned by Peter Whitman

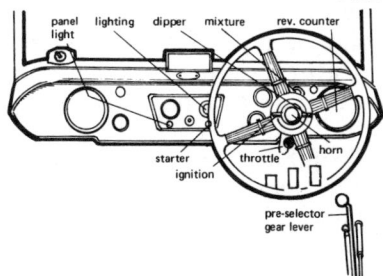

1934 Rapier Four Seater Tourer

1934 Abbott-bodied Lagonda Rapier Four Seater Tourer. The owner is Muir Laidlaw

maximum timed speed of 74.07 mile/h 'two up' speak of the thrilling aspect of driving this plucky little Lagonda. Remarkably stable and safe feeling, the car handled like a larger model and the Girling brakes proved very effective at all speeds, a figure of 26 feet being measured in stopping from 30 mile/h, for example. Fairly firm springing was, of course, an inherent factor in stability but did not obtrude more than was normal. An experimental run with the windscreen folded flat achieved 77.59 mile/h, with 61 mile/h attainable in third gear. Revs near to 5500 were observed at this latter speed, but over 6000 rev/min could be used for short intervals without concern for the engine bearings. A two-stage clutch pedal action freed the clutch first, then engaged the preselector gear - a very apt device for the sporting driver, producing really swift gear changes. The driving position and overall comfort were found to be good. The new Rapier had made a very favourable impression.

The four-seater tourer version tested had bodywork coachbuilt by Abbott, the most common makers of bodies for the Rapier, and its price was £368. Other Abbot models were a fixed-head coupe, drop-head coupe and a very rare four-light saloon, only five of which were built. Aluminium panels on an ash frame were used in their construction, whereas steel wings, with a fine swept line for the front pair, were incorporated in the interests of strength and resistance to minor crash impact. Details that immediately distinguish the Abbott bodies from others are the twenty-five louvres down each side of the bonnet and to a lesser extent the flat-topped scuttle. The spare wheel was mounted on the sloping tail, without a cover. Abbott fixed-head coupes had a line moulded along the top of both bonnet sides, coinciding with a corresponding moulded line across each door. The weight of the doors eventually caused hinge and door-pillar trouble, unfortunately. The hardtop was of leathercloth or aluminium, the former being contoured by wadding supported on expanded metal. Only one aluminium-topped Abbott fixed-head coupe now exists. Dummy hood irons, mounted to the rear of the side windows, set off the effect (and was the accepted fashion of those days). As for the drop-head coupe, this had a folding hood

capable of being fixed in the halfway 'de ville' position with the front seats open to the sky while the rear seats remained covered. About eleven of these now remain. Only five four-light saloons were made and these all during 1935; none now exist. A total of about 250 Abbott-bodied Rapiers were manufactured altogether. A note of interest to the postwar-car enthusiast is that Abbotts built bodies for some of the early Healey cars.

Next in importance are the Rapiers with Ranalah bodywork, another set of distinctive designs and ardently championed by those owners who prefer them to the Abbott bodies! The four-seater tourer, again aluminium-panelled plus steel wings, was wider than the Abbott and in overall style more 'suave', stressing a more curved line throughout. The front wings were less open, having side valances, and an 'aero' cockpit with two rounded 'humps' in the scuttle made a further distinguishing point from the Abbott, together with the twenty-one Ranalah bonnet louvres on either side. The spare wheel was concealed behind a moulded metal wheel cover, and other features were an aluminium apron under the dumb irons and vertical radiator slats. There were no 'aero' cockpits in the thirteen Ranalah drop-head coupes, however, and of the three four-light saloons built, none now exist. This latter design was not very 'happy' in appearance due to the short wheelbase; up to the windscreen it was identical to the drop-head coupe, but rearwards of this point evolved into a small saloon body of ungainly proportions, with two heavy doors.

Lord de Clifford's specially prepared Rapier secured fifteenth place in the Le Mans twenty-four hour race in 1934. Subsequently, Ranalah were contracted to produce bodies for the de Clifford Special, a Rapier with a two-seater body sporting a fin on the tail and bearing the de Clifford badge on the radiator. No running boards or 'aero' cockpit was included. The degree of tune of the engine is now uncertain; of the three built, two remain, one of which is in excellent condition.

Other 'one off' coachbuilt Rapier bodies came from Corinthian (a tourer version), Eagle (a two-seater and four-door pillarless saloon) and Maltby (a drophead coupe model).

1935 Lagonda Rapier Drophead Coupe
with bodywork by Abbott. Owned by
Dennis Waddams

1935 de Clifford Special Two Seater
version of the Lagonda Rapier. This
car is one of the two still extant

1936 Rapier Ten Four Seater with
bodywork by Ranalah. Owned by
Donald Curren

Rapier Ten (1936—39)

As stated above, Tim Ashcroft's new enterprise, Rapier Cars Ltd, reduced the bore of the Rapier engine by 0.5 mm to bring the capacity down to 1087 cc and thus make the car eligible for 1100 cc-class competition. Some later Tens were supercharged at 7lb/in ^{2}. For the 1936 season three four-seater models were offered, a tourer, drophead coupe and saloon, priced at £375, £410 and £415, respectively; for the most part, bodywork was by Ranalah. By 1938, prices for the final season had not changed, although the provision of a supercharger cost an extra £60. Some forty-five Ranalah-bodied Rapiers were built altogether from 1934-39, and this includes models from both 'stables'. Rapier Cars Ltd closed down prior to the war.

The author is indebted to Tony Wood, Honorary Registrar of the Rapier Register and editor of their monthly news magazine, for much of the above information and for supplying photographs with which this section is illustrated. The Rapier Register is a very friendly club catering for all owners of Rapier, whether of Lagonda origin or built by Rapier Cars Ltd. As for the Rapier itself, the little car needs no recommendation - it is virtually faultless and its very robust engine makes it ideal for modern motoring and VSCC racing.

Small details which may occasionally cause engine breakdown are faults in the camshaft driving-chain and spring tensioner in the un-supercharged cars, failure of the latter resulting in stripping of the fibre timing-gear teeth. Of late, oil pump drive failures have been complained of - but considering that their gear and pinion mechanisms are some thirty-five years old, Rapier enthusiasts have certainly had excellent service from them! All spares for the above are, of course, available through the Register, as are parts for all models; it is a lively little club and well worth joining, if only to keep in touch with the latest news. Remarkably, of the 350-400 Rapiers built, the club has traced 313 still in existence.

Rapier Register: A.J.Wood, 128 Hazelhurst Road, King's Heath, Birmingham B14 6AG.

Lanchester

The name of F.W.Lanchester is always associated with that spirit of 'fresh thinking' which brought revolutionary solutions to the problems of the early motor car. The first British four-wheeled car, Lanchester's two-seater phaeton was built in 1897, fitted with a two-cylinder air-cooled engine driving the rear wheels by means of a shaft and worm gearing; it was the first car to be fully silenced and the first with magneto ignition. It also employed a Lanchester 'wick' vaporizer - a simple precursor to the jet carburetter - in which the inspired charge was drawn through a container inside which fabric wicks were suspended, dipping into a reservoir of petrol; in this way the incoming volume of air was saturated in petrol vapour before it entered the cylinders. An epicyclic gear was incorporated.

By 1913, the Lanchester car had reached the peak of its pioneering achievements, F.W. Lanchester having invented the disc brake in 1904, and added further individual concepts to his cars over the years. Orthodoxy had, however, because of commercial considerations, become Lanchester policy by 1920. Amalgamation with the Daimler Motor Company and BSA was in force by 1930.

Ten (1932–36)

First introduced in June 1932, this new Lanchester was unique among 10 hp cars in that it embodied both a Daimler fluid flywheel and a preselector gearbox; worm gearing, an early feature of the marque, was retained for the final drive in the interests of silent running. Powered by a forward-mounted four-cylinder engine of 1203 cc capacity, the chassis frame was of low braced type, enabling a body with a low floor level to be constructed on it. Underslung at the rear, the channel-section frame was of cruciform pattern further braced by tubular crossmembers, a design affording valuable rigidity; the side-members were hardly upswept at all at the front. Semi-elliptic leaf springs provided the suspension both front and rear, and efficient brakes were part of the specification also. Despite a return to the more orthodox, one can readily appreciate that Lanchesters chose wisely from the better trends of current automobile practice.

The preselector gearbox was operated via a short lever, mounted on a quadrant below the hub of the steering wheel. Gear changing entailed moving the lever to the gear-position required and pressing the foot-operated gear-change pedal. Upon releasing the pedal, the required gear came into action. As for the fluid flywheel, this was in effect two turbines facing each other, one connected to the crankshaft and the other to the gearbox shaft. Separated by a chamber full of transmission fluid, the rotation of the turbine on the engine side set in motion the fluid in the flywheel housing, this in turn rotating the driving turbine, once initial 'slip' had been overcome. This inherent 'slip' of the fluid made possible very smooth pulling-away from a standstill. Fully automatic, no clutch pedal was necessary.

Offered in several styles, all models were coachbuilt. The six-light saloon, with a rounded back, externally mounted spare wheel, tapering bonnet - in fact a design typical of smaller saloons of the period - was built by Arthur Mulliner Ltd and priced at £315. Also by Mulliner was a very attractive two-seater version in cherry red, with red upholstery - a particularly smart, low-built sports car with a high prow, flared scuttle and low driving position enabling the fitting of a very brief fold-flat windscreen. The sports saloon version was by Carbodies and priced at £335.

In a road test conducted by the *Autocar* in July 1932, the Ten saloon was found to be very roomy, rear-seat comfort in particular being indistinguishable from that of the front seats. Flexible, yet smooth springing made travel on all types of road surface very agreeable and free of jerking, pitching or rolling, and the low-slung frame added to the road-holding stability. Due to flexible engine mountings, a general absence of transmission vibration was noticed. As for hard-and-fast test figures, a maximum speed timed over a flying quarter-mile of 61.64 mile/h was recorded, acceleration from 0-30 mile/h taking 16.2 seconds in top gear, 10 seconds in third and 9.2 in second gear. Sixteen seconds were needed in accelerating from 20-40 mile/h in

1934 Lanchester Ten Saloon

1932 10hp Saloon

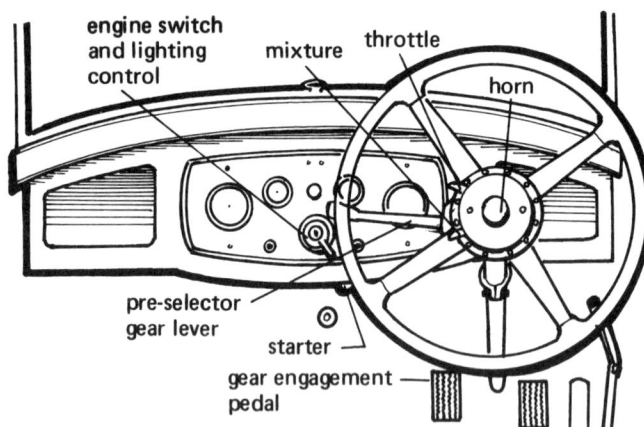

engine switch
and lighting
control

mixture

throttle

horn

pre-selector
gear lever

starter

gear engagement
pedal

1934 Lanchester 10hp Special Sports Tourer with bodywork by Abbott

top and 12.2 seconds in third; 30-50 mile/h took 21.2 seconds in top gear. The distance required for bringing the car to a standstill from 30 mile/h was 33 feet, this in a car weighing over 21 cwt. An average of 33 mpg was afforded, speaking well for the engine's powers of economy. One is left with a final impression that the Lanchester Ten accomplished exactly what its designers set out to do - to provide a smooth-running, comfortable car, very well appointed, of adequate performance and very easy to drive.

Few modifications were necessary in subsequent seasons; by 1934 the saloon cost £20 more, while for 1936 a new range of models was introduced, powered by 1444 cc engines. An increase of power, brought about also by better valve cooling and a higher compression ratio, resulted in the new engine developing 38 bhp, improving the range's acceleration. The wider cylinder bore made the engine eligible for the 11 hp class, and the model was referred to as the Eleven by 1937.

Six versions of the 1936 Ten were offered: a saloon at £298, a sports saloon, Streamlined Saloon and fixed-head coupe at £308, and drop-head coupes at £325 standard, or £375 for the two-door Salmons Tickford model. Close adherence to traditional Lanchester 'reserve' was only slightly relaxed even in their Streamlined Saloon. All Lanchesters continued to offer a form. of 'small Daimler' specification, stressing silence and comfort rather than out-and-out performance, and as interior appointments became more lavish so any new power was in part absorbed by the car's added weight. But smoothness of ride can only be achieved in a car that has a certain mass, lightweight cars proving too much a victim of their own lack of inertia on undulating or rough road surfaces.

Besides the coachbuilt bodywork, executed with much care as to detail, the interiors of Lanchester cars were also of a high order, 'de luxe' trim representing upholstery of highest-grade hide and the provision of several ash trays, a cigar lighter, door pockets, silk door pulls, a driver-controlled rear blind, etc., the fixed-head coupe even being provided with a locker under the rear seats to house golf clubs. The Ten models continued as the Eleven range for the 1937 season.

Eleven (1936–39)

Powered by the larger 1444 cc ohv four-cylinder engine the Ten in 10.8 hp guise continued to retain in essence the prewar tradition of a silent, unfussy, comfortable, quality light car, effortless to drive and dignified in appearance.

The cost price for the saloon of £298 for the 1937 season dropped to £275 for 1938, with the introduction of a sports saloon version at £290; wider doors, a folding centre arm-rest and a new range of colours were added attractions on both models. Metal panelling replaced fabric for the roofs of the Elevens by 1939, the price of the saloon being £295 and that of the sports saloon £298.

Light Six (1933–36)

A six-cylinder engine, derived by scaling-down that of the Lanchester Eighteen, powered the 1378 cc model. Incorporating an integral block and cylinder-head, as did the 18 hp engine, Lanchesters claimed that this design prevented barrel distortion, reduced wear on the bores and pistons, gave less valve trouble, saved weight, provided better cooling and prolonged the intervals between decarbonising. A model parallel with the BSA Light Six, both marques' ranges of models closely resembled each other, in the same way that Morris and Wolseley cars of the late '30s were 'mirror images' but for their radiator grilles and small details. Offered in saloon, sports saloon, drop-head coupe, fixed-head coupe and Streamlined Saloon variants, prices for the 1935 season ranged from £365 to £390, the Streamlined Saloon costing £375. Rearwards of the bonnet, the streamlined Light Six saloon (and its BSA counterpart) was given gracefully sweeping lines, the waistline's descending curve being accentuated in the boundaries of the dual colour-scheme. This downward sweep was complemented by the curve of the roof which terminated in a long sloping tail. A flush-fitting boot lid enhanced the effect, and two half-panes made up the divided semi-oval rear window. Otherwise, the rest of

1934 Lanchester 10hp Abbott-bodied Drophead Coupe

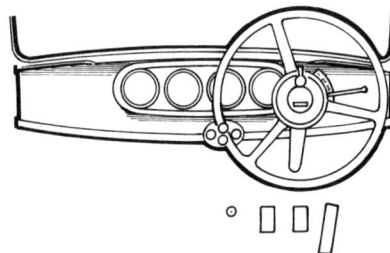

1936 Light Six saloon

1938 Lanchester 14hp Roadrider De Luxe Drophead Foursome Coupe with bodywork by Abbott

the Light Six range were conservative, tasteful light cars, well centred in the Lanchester tradition. A different radiator grille comprised the main distinguishing feature of the BSA Light Six range - without doubt the same overall dimensions and patterns were used for both. For the 1936 season, prices varied from £340 to £365 for the standard versions. A 'de luxe' series using bodywork identical to the contemporary Daimler Fifteen, was in a higher £375-£495 price range, a Tickford four-door cabriolet representing an 'extra de luxe' version, priced at £545. The 'de luxe' cars featured a new style of radiator with longer slats and briefer chromed surround, contrasting with the well-established 'portico' design, its triangular top bearing the name Lanchester in bright plating against a black background.

Roadrider (1936—38)

With the discontinuation of the Light Six, a new 13.4 hp model called the Fourteen Roadrider, appeared, to bridge the gap between the Lanchester Eleven and Eighteen. Equipped with a 1527 cc six-cylinder ohv engine developing 40 bhp, the Roadrider was the lowest-priced six in the Lanchester range. Sporting the new design of radiator and a longer bonnet, the frontal aspect was more imposing than hitherto; nevertheless, the traditional fluid flywheel and preselector gearbox were retained, as was the underslung worm-driven rear axle. The radiator and front wings were rubber-mounted via a cross-beam to a crossmember of the chassis, any small flexing of the frame having hence no effect on the front bonnet assembly; a wider scuttle and windscreen improved the driver's forward view, and a large rear window permitted good rear visibility. Generous head-room and comfortable seating were complemented by grouped controls on the dashboard, designed for ease of reading. Two large circular dials, one on either side of the steering head, encompassed all the instruments, which were clearly visible through the spokes of the steering-wheel. A coachbuilt saloon, sports saloon and coupe were available, the saloon and coupe costing £330 and the

sports saloon £10 more; a fabric-topped saloon was offered at £325. Magna hub-bolted wire wheels were fitted throughout the range, the coupe being a smart smooth-lined car with a curved boot, the lid of which supported the external spare wheel, neatly concealed beneath a circular cover. The sports saloon, in contrast, forsook flowing lines for a 'razor edge' style, the rear section in its almost 'geometric' variation of streamlining, having curved surfaces butt-jointed at sharp, crisp boundaries. A large rear compartment formed an added attraction.

An integral cylinder head, large-clearance silent cams, a hot-spot manifold and an aluminium crankcase made up the salient features of the ohv Fourteen engine, together with an extra-stiff crankshaft and longer pistons. The chassis frame, too, was different, in that box- and lattice-section frame members afforded extra rigidity, the strengthened cruciform centre-section forming a tunnel through which passed the open propeller-shaft. Long semi-elliptic springs formed both the front and rear suspension, allied with large Luvax hydraulic shockabsorbers; Girling mechanical brakes supplied stopping-power. A good performance coupled with ease of handling hall-marked this new Lanchester.

There is something very attractive about a machine that performs well, but silently - a mysterious 'presence' seems to emanate from it, at once efficient and fascinating. Such silky, silent performance is an inherent part of the Lanchester ideal, and should it appeal, then one of the light cars described above will, if put into good order, continue to exert that indefinable attraction wherever the car is driven.

Spare parts for Lanchesters are best sought through the Daimler-Lanchester-BSA Owners' Club. Brian Smith, who is both its president and historian, and who has recently written a very thorough and detailed history of the Lanchester's sister marque, entitled *The Daimler Tradition*, can supply members with information from a wealth of Lanchester reference material.

B.S.A.-Daimler-Lanchester Owners' Club: H.D.Saunders, Eastgate House, Top Street, Appleby Magna, Nr. Burton-on-Trent, Staffs. Measham 70253.

Lea-Francis

Originally manufacturers of 3½ hp V-twin motorcycles, Lea-Francis Ltd, of Coventry, launched into making cars in 1922. Like many other firms who did not build their own engine, Lea-Francis had to resort to fitting a proprietary power unit, and like their non-selfsufficient contemporaries, they chose engines manufactured by Coventry Climax Engines Ltd and Henry Meadows Ltd of Wolverhampton. Meadows engines came with the D-type, which employed an ohv 4EB unit, and proved itself very capable in trials events. Types E to H had Meadows 4EB engines also, and either three-or four-speed gearboxes, the latter of Lea-Francis manufacture. A new engine, the 4EC, powered the J-type, which was designated as the 12/22 in the light of the increased power (from the 4EB's 19 bhp to the 4EC's 22 bhp).

But of far more obvious potential and higher performance was the 4ED power unit, delivering 37.5 bhp at 4000 rev/min in standard form and powering the sports L-type of 1925, legitimately described as a 12/40. Coachbuilt by Cross and Ellis, these first sports cars were capable of 70 mile/h. Following after came the N and O-types, the former in tourer guise; with the advent of the P and S-types we reach the peak of Lea-Francis' sporting achievements - a modified Hyper-Sports S winning the Ulster TT of 1928 at the hands of Kaye Don.

10 hp H-type (1930)

First offered in 1926, and still on sale in 1930, the very sedate 1247 cc Lea-Francis Ten combined an 8 ft wheelbase, as in the G-type, with a four-speed gearbox. Of ohv layout, but with primitive lubrication and cast iron pistons, the Ten's Meadows 4EB engine could deliver only a modest 19 bhp at 2000 rev/min.

Maximum speed was around 45 mile/h. In appearance, the Ten was an upright, large-windowed affair, rather top-heavy overall. Wide gear ratios and inadequate power dictated a very pedestrian performance.

12/22 (1930)

Parallel with the H-type, the U-type 12/22 was built from 1927 to 1930, its chassis being of the design used in the first 12/40 cars, and power supplied not by a 4ED engine, but by the less powerful Meadows 4EC unit. Of 1496 cc, the 4EC engine was virtually a larger-bore 4EB, giving 3 bhp more; it was still far removed from the concept of a 'performance' design. A leather-faced cone clutch and four-speed Lea-Francis gearbox connected with an open propeller shaft and spiral bevel axle made up the transmission, while mechanical brakes and semi-elliptic springs, front and rear, comprised the braking specification and suspension.

12/40 (1930–32)

All 12/40 models had the Meadows 4ED engine in standard form, delivering just under 40 bhp at 4000 rev/min. Alloy pistons, a three-bearing crankshaft and full-pressure lubrication marked it at once as an engine capable of further tuning and modification, if required.

Types P, V and W were of tourer, sports foursome coupe and four-door fabric saloon form (called the Francis saloon), respectively. All used a lower, wider-track channel-section chassis with semi-elliptic leaf springing front and rear, mechanical brakes (some of Dewandre servo-type) and a four-speed gearbox. At first of cone pattern, the majority of models were fitted with dry-plate clutches. Gravity feed, from a tank in the P-type's scuttle, was modified to an Autovac fuel pump and rear tank in the V, W, and late P-types.

The most obvious distinguishing factor externally was the slope of majestic Lea-Francis radiator. In the P-type it was vertically mounted, whereas that of the V-type was inclined at 15°

1928 Lea-Francis P-type Four Seater

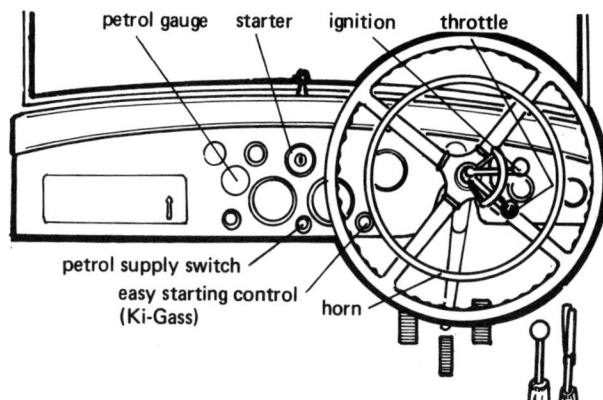

petrol gauge   starter   ignition   throttle

petrol supply switch

easy starting control
(Ki-Gass)

horn

1929 Hyper-Sports Fabric Saloon

1932 Lea-Francis 1½-litre S-type Hyper-Sports Four Seater Tourer

1932 Lea-Francis S-type Hyper-Sports Two Seater. Note the well-angled radiator and overall rakish lines

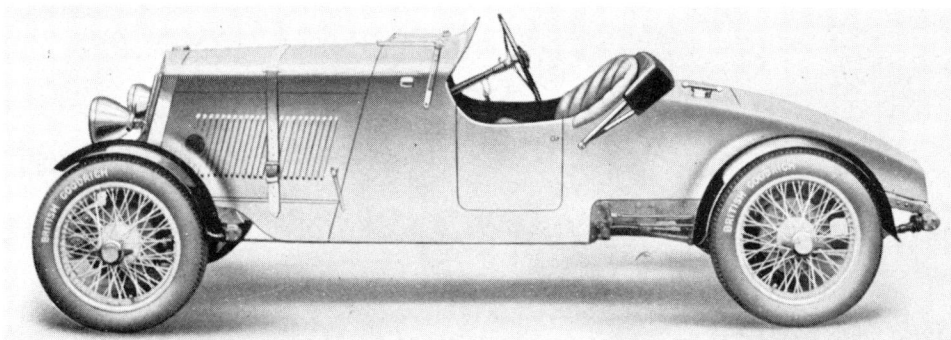

1932 Lea-Francis S-type Hyper-Sports Lea-Fabric Saloon

1932 Lea-Francis 12/40
P-type Four Seater De Luxe Tourer

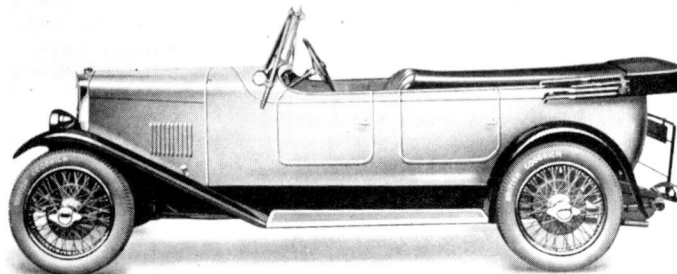

1932 Lea-Francis 12/40 V-type Fixed Head Coupe

1932 Lea-Francis 12/40 P-type Two Seater

and that of the W-type at 10°. The P-type was a large four-seater tourer with full-length hood reaching from the windscreen to the 'bath tub' back, while the V-type had only two large doors and occasional seating for two other passengers. The Francis four-door fabric saloon was a roomy car of distinctive appearance, selling for £375; the P-type cost £325 in 1930, and the V-type coupe £420. By 1932 the open cars were listed at £295. A maximum speed of over 60 mile/h could be expected from all versions, all of which sported louvred fairings over the dumb irons, centre-lock wire wheels, and a right-hand gear change.

12/50 (1930)

The Lea-Francis O-type was a true sports car, powered by a modified version of the 4ED called the 'Brooklands' engine. Developing 52 bhp at 4500 rev/min, this unit was a highly modified type with special cylinder head, racing valves and twin carburetters. A vertical radiator (unlike the Hyper-Sports) was fitted and four-seater coachbuilt sports bodywork.

12/60 (1930—32)

Extra power for the Hyper-Sports Type S was extracted from the Meadows by supercharging, a No. 8 Cozette unit delivering 7 lb/in² pressure being fitted to production models: the carburetter too, was of Cozette manufacture. Quoted as developing 61 bhp at 4100 rev/min, the engine's extra power yielded a startlingly better performance over that of the 12/40 models but remained nearer to the O-type than that of the works racing versions, the engines of which released 88 bhp at 4750 rev/min by virtue of their more drastic modification and Berk superchargers. These latter non-production racers were of the form which gained victory at the 1928 TT.

Nevertheless, the production S-types were definitely fast and sufficiently 'athletic' to keep the *Autocar* tester on his toes while driving a 1929 Hyper-Sports close-coupled coupe version,

with Weymann fabric bodywork. A maximum speed in top gear of 80-85 mile/h was recorded, acceleration from 10-30 mile/h in this gear taking 14 seconds, or 8 and 5 seconds in third and second gear respectively. Maximum speed in third gear was 68 mile/h, and 50 mile/h in second. Nice close ratios of 8.47, 5.56 and 4.27 for the top three gears made 'sporting' driving a pleasure and very exhilarating, but in contrast, the very flexible engine would potter along at 8-10 mile/h in top gear, and the car could be driven as if it were a saloon. Hill-climbing was taken completely in the Hyper's stride; a gradient of 1 in 6½ could be climbed at 32 mile/h in third, or at over 40 mile/h in second.

Easy starting from cold was achieved via the Ki-Gass injector fitted, squirting a shot of petrol mist into the manifold - this, coupled with full choke, resulting in an instant start. Very comprehensive instrumentation included a clock, ammeter, petrol gauge, rev counter, speedometer, oil-pressure gauge, temperature gauge and supercharger-pressure indicator. Both the gear lever and hand brake were on the driver's right-hand side, but practice was needed to extract silky changing from the 'crash' gearbox. A noticable lack of castor action made the steering feel 'different', soon becoming a happily acquired taste, but definite faults lay in the noisy bevel-gear drive to the supercharger and in the Dewandre vacuum-servo brakes, which were very effective at high speeds but faded off as speed lessened - a distance of 85 feet being needed to slow from 40 mile/h to zero!

In all, however, the Hyper-Sports proved a true thoroughbred, the standard tourer being priced at £495, while a two-seater 12/75 competition version could be had for £550. For the 1930 season, the close-coupled standard coupe was listed at £525.

Regrettably, an official receiver was called-in in 1931, the Lea-Francis concern run down, and the cars sold off, even up to 1935. Two years later however a new enterprise, Lea-Francis Engineering (1937) Ltd, recommenced production, which continued after the war into the 1950s.

1932 Lea-Francis 12/40 P-type Four Seater Tourer

1932 Lea-Francis 12/40 W-type De Luxe Saloon

Twelve (1937–39)

Now under completely new management, Lea-Francis manufactured their own engines, ohv 'high camshaft' units (like the Riley engines) with short pushrods and hence valve gear of low reciprocating weight. Of 1496 cc capacity, the 1½-litre engine had, in common with the 14 hp engine, hemispherical combustion chambers together with inclined valves, and a high performance. Although still available, the Meadows 4ED engine was virtually obsolete by the mid-30s.

Generally referred to as the Twelve, the 1½-litre chassis was available with bodywork in several versions; a four- or six-light saloon, a drophead coupe, a four-light sports saloon or a 2/4-seater sports model were available, this latter called the 1½-litre Super Sports. Of conventional form, the chassis was strong and rigid, relying on semi-elliptic springs all round and Girling mechanical brakes. Only vaguely reminiscent of its 'former glory', the new radiator was of slatted type, heavily chromium-plated and tapering inwards slightly from the top to the base. Large chromed headlamps were carried high on a cross-bar, and the bodywork was acceptably conformist in style. Always considered a 'quality' motor car, the new models were in the medium price-range; both saloons cost £395, the coupe £410 and the Super Sports £475. The specification of the last-mentioned version included a higher-compression ratio engine with twin SU carburetters and larger-capacity sump, plus a top gear of extra-high ratio.

Fourteen (1937—39)

Offered at the same prices as the 12 hp models, the Fourteen range was powered by a 1629 cc four-cylinder ohv engine of identical overall design to the smaller units. In a 1938 *Autocar* road test, the Fourteen saloon performed well, particularly as regards handling. Maximum speed recorded was 75.63 mile/h, 0-50 mile/h taking only 18.1 seconds, and 0-30 mile/h 17.7 seconds. Hence acceleration was brisk - recorded times for 10-30 mile/h in third and second gear being 8.2 and 5.9 seconds - and decelarative qualities good, too, 29.5 feet being covered in slowing from 30 mile/h to zero. A fuel consumption figure of 23-38 mpg was attained.

Seating comfort and roominess were among the interior's virtues, absence of back footwells proving that the space was quite genuine and not contrived. Light, positive steering with decisive castor action made the taking of fast bends easy, rather firm springing contributing to the lack of 'roll' on corners and engendering smoothness at high speeds. A four-speed synchromech gearbox gave quiet, direct changes, and a typical 'all-day' cruising speed was 60 mile/h on main roads.

One can appreciate that the Lea-Francis had come a long way since the fabric saloons of the late '20s. Whether the cars were the same as the old-style models in feeling, is debateable; nevertheless in 1938 the public expected a certain breed of car to perform a certain duty, effortlessly and at the touch of a pedal. This the new cars could certainly do.

Not exactly a 'chalk or cheese' decision, one's preferences for an 'early' or 'late' model depend on what one expects from it. Postwar sophistication is already there in the late-30s Lea-Francis, but should one be looking for that extra, indefinable degree of old-world charm, the fabric models with their trusty Meadows engines offer all this and more.

Old, high-performance sports models are without doubt exciting, but as mentioned in other sections of this book, maintaining them in a good condition must be a labour of love.

Should you settle for a prewar 'Leaf', keep in close contact with the Lea-Francis Owners Club for technical advice, a sympathetic ear and details of spares - Peter Pringle, chairman of the club (and supplier of much of this section's technical information and illustrative material) would like to hear from you.

Lea-Francis Owners' Club: D.Purdy, 54 Gresham Way, Shefford, Beds. Eagle 5203.

1938/39 Lea-Francis 1½-litre Super Sports 2/4 Seater

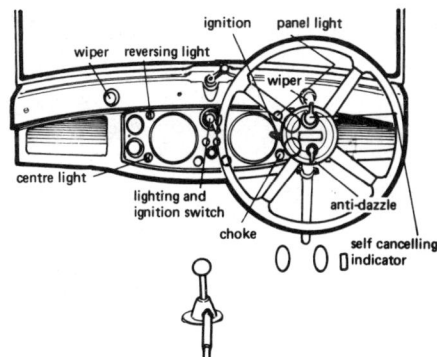

1938 Fourteen Saloon

1938/39 Lea-Francis 12hp Four Seater Tourer

1938/39 Lea-Francis 12hp Drophead Coupe

1938/39 Lea-Francis 14hp Four-Light Saloon De Luxe

1938/39 Lea-Francis 14hp Six-Light Saloon

MG

A 'souped-up' Morris is hardly likely to raise many eyebrows nowadays. But the first of the illustrious MG cars were initially nursed in the Morris cradle and in fact at one time during the '30s saved the Nuffield colossus from toppling. Significantly, 1927 proved an eventful year for Morris and MG in that the shaky Wolseley concern was taken over by William Morris and 'amalgamated' as Wolseley Motors (1927) Ltd. Before their *debacle*, Wolseley had been modifying their ohc Ten engine in order to produce an 8 hp version to power a Wolseley rival for the Austin Seven. Suddenly this 'little gem' of an engine was the rightful property of the Morris organization, and ripe for application in the ultra-light car field. Cecil Kimber saw in the little ohc engine the basis of a whole range of 'Minor' MGs, to be called the Midget series. The Wolseley Hornet six-cylinder ohc engine, evolved logically by adding two extra cylinders to the Minor unit, formed the original basis for the MG Magnas and other ohc 'sixes'.

Midget series (1930–39)

Quick on the heels of the ohc Morris Minor came the MG Midget M-type of 1928, a new product to be built in a new factory, this time under the title aquired in 1930 of the MG Car Company, Pavlova Works, Abingdon-on-Thames. Designated as the '8/33', and of 847 cc engine capacity, the M-type was available in two versions: the two-seater and Sportsman's Coupe, both on a fairly standard Minor chassis with few modifications, the two models having light bodywork constructed by covering a plywood-panelled wooden frame with fabric. The engine's actual output was 20 bhp, but with a dry weight of 10 cwt there was plenty of power for a lively performance. In appearance the M-type two-seater combined a Minor front end (plus a scaled-down MG Six radiator) with a diminutive

body terminating in a boat tail, the lid of which concealed a small locker with the spare wheel mounted on the floor. Cycle-type mudguards, a 'V' screen and 'pram'-type hood (barely adequate, giving little headroom and minus side-screens) completed the overall effect - one of cheeky liveliness.

One unusual engine feature was the adaptation of the vertically-mounted dynamo shaft to drive the overhead camshaft, this device being also employed in the early 'sixes' and the engine of the Wolseley Hornet - more positive and direct than chain-drive, perhaps - but a definite pest when the fabric coupling needed renewing! And as for the brakes of the early 1928-29 M-types, they were in fact far from good. By 1930, re-designed brakes had made respectable retardation a possibility. Road tests conducted in 1929 and 1930 were full of praise, the *Motor* for example, stating in their 30th July 1929 issue that the Midget was an exceptionally attractive little vehicle with its maximum speed of 61 mile/h (0-50 mile/h being accomplished in 25 seconds), and finding the early-type brakes "quite good". A year later a test conducted by *Light Car* found the brakes greatly improved; also 10-40 mile/h could be achieved in 11 seconds and an average fuel consumption of 36 mpg obtained; a cruising speed of 52 mile/h "could be maintained indefinitely on good roads". The little car, priced in 1930 at £185 for the two-seater and £245 for the Sportsman's Coupe, went from strength to strength. Following the triumphs of the 1930 JCC Double Twelve Replica came on the market, 10th May, where of six Midgets entered, five finished 3rd, 4th, 5th and 7th in their class, a Double Twleve Replica came on the market, designated as the '8/45' and selling at £245. A new 'overlap' camshaft, used so successfully in the above race, became a standard fitment for the M before the end of 1930.

During 1931 the C-type or Montlhery Midget appeared, a racing model with supercharger (see below), and the D-type four-seater with under-slung chassis, its 'M' three-speed gearbox now fitted with a handy remote-control lever and its engine delivering 27 bhp, giving a healthy top speed. Priced at £210, it was again excellent value; the M-type, still with fabric body, remained at £185.

1930 MG M-type Midget

1930 MG Double Twelve Replica M-type Midget

The J-type was announced in 1932, erected on the underslung D-type chassis but with a new 'opposed-port' cylinder head fitted atop the 'M' engine and a remote-controlled four-speed gearbox. The J1 was available in both tourer and Salonette versions, the later priced at £255. Also in the same year, its cousin, the J2 was born, a rakish little two-seater at once recognizable as being free of all Morris Minor undertones - a 'pure' MG at last. A longer bonnet, an Ulster body with slab tank mounted visibly at the rear beneath the spare wheel, sweeping cycle-type wings etc. were all hall-marks of things to come. Beneath the bonnet was a twin-carburetter engine now delivering 36 bhp at 5,500 rev/min, the *Light Car* testing a 'hack' J2 in 1933 and finding even then a top speed of 77 mile/h. Still on sale until the end of '32, the faithful M-type, now with metal-panelled body and folding hood, could be purchased for £185, the price of the J2 being £199-10s.

For the 1934 season the new PA Midget was announced in two-seater, tourer and Airline Coupe variants. The two-seater PA symbolized finally the layman's concept of the classic open

MG with its long bonnet, flared scuttle, distinctive MG radiator set back behind sweeping and open front wings, Rudge Whitworth wire wheels, 'chopped-off' sloping rear-end plus spare wheel, cut-away doors and close-fitting cockpit. Retaining the underslung chassis, a new three-bearing engine of equivalent power to the J2 was fitted, the top speed recorded in a 1934 test by *Light Car* being 76.27 mile/h; they also added that "the P-type MG is a car for the man who enjoys driving for driving's own sweet sake" - third gear was there to be used. The standing quarter-mile was accomplished in 24.4 seconds. Twelve-inch brake drums gave a silky, smooth action but were very effective and free from judder or squeal. The instruments, too, were well placed, the driving position excellent, and the hearty 'dark brown' exhaust note typically thoroughbred. For the 1935 season the PA four-seater version was priced at £240, the Airline Coupe selling for £290; by 1936 the PA cost £199-10s in two-seater form, the coupe's price remaining unchanged. The year 1935 saw the appearance of the new PB with 939 cc ohc engine, similar in overall shape and specification to the PA but recognizable by its slatted radiator bars. Ideal for trials and an ideal rival to the Singer Le Mans in such events, the PB was to prove the last of the overhead-camshaft Midgets, its engine with that 'dark brown' exhaust note yielding place to a more placid-sounding but nonetheless very lively ohv unit powering the TA.

Why the change to ohv was deemed necessary is uncertain; the pundits of course, deplored it, but early suspicions were allayed when the TA's performance figures were released. Increased in capacity to 1292 cc, the new ohv power unit, featuring a 'wet' clutch, was charged with propelling a larger body (the redesigned chassis being fitted with hydraulic brakes, and still underslung at the rear) "but," said the *Light Car*, "it is almost certainly the fastest light car MG has ever produced (racing models excepted, of course)". In appearance like a slightly scaled-up PA, the TA could exceed 80 mile/h, the standing quarter-mile taking a mere 21.6 seconds. The engine was also much more flexible than the ohc units. *Practical Motorist* found, in a test on 26th

December 1936, that the new Lockheed brakes could stop the TA from 30 mile/h in 29 feet on a wet road, while 28 mpg was an average figure. The TA was 'different' but still delightful. Manufactured from 1936 to the outbreak of war, some 3000 TAs were built, the price of the two-seater being £222 in 1939. A Tickford-bodied drophead coupe, the TB, powered by a 1250 cc ohv engine, appeared later in that year, its power unit proving even more powerful than the TA's and taking its top speed well above 80 mile/h.

Not to be overlooked is the VA, a 1½-litre series of 1937-39, a comfortable VA four-seater saloon capable of 85 mile/h delighting a member of the *Light Car* staff who 'caned' it from London to Scotland without mishap.

Supercharged Midget racing models (1931—35)

In order to conform with international 750 cc Class H racing, the stroke of the Midget engine was reduced by 10 mm to bring the capacity down to 746 cc. The C-type Montlhery Midget, named after the French racetrack at which it performed, capturing several international-class records at over 100 mile/h, was in the form of a stripped down M-type fitted with a brief, pointed-tail body. The smaller engine, in finest tune, was of 9:1 compression ratio, a more massive crankshaft being fitted, 'semi-dry sump' lubrication regulated by a float, and the unit supercharged by means of a No. 7 'Powerplus' blower working at 12-14 lb/in^2, the engine producing 62.5 bhp at 6.500 rev/min; carburation was via a 1¼ in. SU carburetter mounted on the atmospheric side of the blower. Forty-five C-types were built altogether.

Available during 1932-33, the J3 Midget was a supercharged version of the J2 fitted with a No. 6A 'Powerplus' working at 8-10 lb/in^2. A two-seater, like the J3, the J4 of 1933 featured a carefully-balanced crankshaft, opposed-port cylinder head fitted with near-horizontal 14 mm plugs, a 'twin top' close-ratio gearbox and was supercharged by a No. 7 or No. 8 'Powerplus' blower working at 12 lb/in^2 or 14 lb/in^2 respectively. Average power output was 72.3

bhp at 6000 rev/min. A mere nine J4s were built and twenty-two J3s. Prices for the C and J4 were £345 and £575 in supercharged form, both being capable of attaining 105-110 mile/h.

First displayed at the 1934 Motor Show, the two-seater Q-type Midget was a racer *par excellence* with a maximum speed of 120 mile/h. Priced moderately at £550, the Q-type's 746 cc engine, equipped with a Zoller Q4 supercharger blowing at 28 lb/in^2, could be coaxed into producing 113 bhp at 7200 rev/min. A pre-selector gearbox was fitted. Only eight Qs were built, but they gained many successes in competitions.

A companion to the Q, the R-type of 1935 was a *monoposto* version fitted with torsion-bar ifs and irs; using a Zoller R4 blower, its engine delivered a similar bhp figure to the Q-type, giving a similar top speed. Unlike the Q, the R-type failed to gain many successes or attract much public attention. Only ten were built.

Although not a Midget, the K3 racer finds a place here. Built in 1933-34, the K3 was a Magnette road-racing version conforming to AIACR regulations, the power if its 1086 cc engine (120 bhp at 6500 rev/min by virtue of high compression and a Powerplus No. 9 or Marshall supercharger working at 14 lb/in^2) making possible a top speed of well over 110 mile/h. In shape very like the Q-type, a Wilson preselector close-ratio gearbox was also fitted to the K3. Altogether thirty-three were produced. Prices for the 1934 season were : in standard trim £475 (Ulster body), supercharged £575, or with AIACR body, £595.

Many standard MGs were, of course, also available in supercharged form; also not to be overlooked is the 1100 cc MG record-breaking streamliner, driven by Major A.T.G.Gardiner at speeds of over 200 mile/h at Dessau in June, 1939.

Magna series (1931—35)

Using the Wolseley Hornet six-cylinder engine of 1271 cc, the F1 Magna was brought out in 1931, the long bonnet of its foursome-coupe body set off by a slightly sloping radiator. Embodying a four-speed gearbox with comfort-ably-placed 'remote' gear lever, underslung frame with grouped-nipple lubrication, light positive steering and efficient brakes, the first Magna was, down to its Rudge-Whitworth wire wheels, a fine start to a new series. The price at the 1931 Motor Show was £289. The F2 and F3 were re-shuffled variants of the F1, the former, while fitted with 12 in. drum brakes, sharing the FI chassis with a body similar to the J2, while the latter combined the F2's better-anchored chassis with F1-type bodywork. The L1 and L2 Magnas of 1933-34 had smaller 1086 cc engines, fitted to the later F2 and F3 chassis, the power units embodying opposed-port cylinder heads as in the J- and P-types. For £285 one could purchase a highly potent L2 12/70 (mile/h, not bhp) two-seater, or an L1 tourer and saloon at £299 and £345, the Continental Coupe, a round-backed version with large luggage trunk being priced at £350. The Magna series terminated in the 1935 season.

Magnette series (1932—36)

Originating in 1932, the K1 and later K2 at first employed a 1086 cc engine fitted with three SU carburetters plus magneto ignition, or alternatively two SUs and coil ignition, the K2 two-seater resembling the Magna two-seater. A luxury car, with engine designed also for super-charging, the frame was underslung and fitted with powerful 13 in. drum brakes, plus grouped lubrication. A special central gear lever was fitted to the Wilson preselector gearbox, which was modified to provide stronger brake-band grip when driving and less on the over-run. The luxury pillarless saloon was tested by *Light Car* in 1933; although lively, 0-50 mile/h took 28 seconds, general driving entailing rather too much constant gear-shifting. In order to propel the later KD saloons more rapidly at 80 mile/h, a 1286 cc engine appeared, which also powered the NA, ND and KN - the NA being a two-seater replacement for the Magna open cars, the ND a four-seater and the KN a rapid 75 mile/h pillar-less saloon. Priced at £305, £335 and £399 respectively, the 1935 Magnette range was impressive and powerful, some 56 bhp being available, and speeds of over 80 mile/h proving

1931/33 MG F-type Magna
Salonette

1932/33 MG K Magnette

The road-racing 750cc MG Q-type

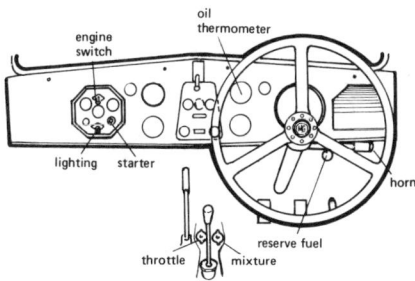

oil
thermometer

engine
switch

lighting   starter

horn

throttle   mixture

reserve fuel

1935 Magnette KN Saloon

1933/34 MG L-type Magna
Salonette

1936 MG PB, last in-line of ohc MGs

1936 MG TA owned by Miss Georgina
Tree. This type was the first MG to have
an ohv engine

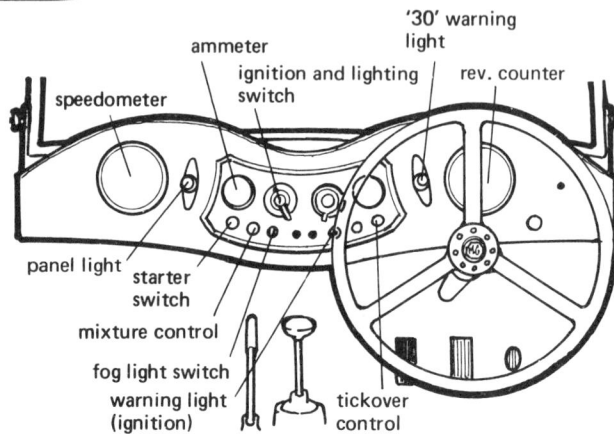

speedometer
ammeter
ignition and lighting switch
'30' warning light
rev. counter
panel light
starter switch
mixture control
fog light switch
warning light (ignition)
tickover control

1936 TA Two Seater

174

attainable in the NA. The chassis frame was new, fitted with flexible body mountings and sported 12 in. brake drums. In a *Light Car* NA road test of 22nd March 1935, the magazine stated: "The time recorded for the standing-start quarter mile - 23.4 seconds - is one of the best that has ever appeared in the 'Light Car' road-test series". Top speed was 83.33 mile/h, 0-50 mile/h taking 18.4 seconds. In the KN there was no synchromesh, the gearbox being of 'silent third' constant-mesh pattern, a lower top-gear ratio being fitted; the elongated chassis enabled a comfortable, well-appointed body to be fitted to a chassis endowed with such paramount qualities as ease-of-handling, stability, excellent performance and positive braking. Slatted radiators distinguished the Magnette N series for their last season. A TT two-seater NE version with high compression engine was offered during 1934.

To the enthusiast, all prewar MGs are fascinating and equally desirable. But should a choice have to be made, then perhaps the cars of the 1930-34 era have just that extra 'something'.

MG Car Club Triple-M Register: C.G.Butchers, 21 Hill Farm Way, Southwick, Sussex. BN4 4YJ.

MG Car Club 'T' Register: B.Lacey-Malvern, 7 Truro Drive, Exeter EX4 2DY.

Another view of Miss Tree's MG TA

Morgan

A leather helmet, goggles, silk scarf and flying jacket comprised, in 1930, ideal wear for the local flying school - or for driving a Morgan Aero cyclecar. Snug in the open cockpit, with the wind licking your face and pulling at your scarf, you gazed ahead over the stubby bonnet to where the air-cooled cylinders crackled out their lust for life, the exposed valve rockers a mere blur, their rhythm blending with the swish of the tyres and throb of the exhaust. And could it be that the unwinding highway was like some endless runway, slowly receding, dropping away ...?

By the start of the Thirties the Morgan Car Company of Malvern Link, Worcestershire, had already been in the business for twenty years, founded by H.F.S.Morgan. Production of three-wheelers began in 1910. Brilliantly conceived, the basic simplicity of H.F.S.'s frame, consisting of three long tubes braced by crossmembers supporting a motorcycle-type V-twin engine, plus two wheels at the front with a single chain-driven wheel at the back, was startlingly apt and supremely functional. The larger 'king-post' tube not only formed a rigid backbone for the frame, but housed the propeller shaft, which ran through it, linking the engine with the two-speed bevel-box; from here the final drive was by chain and sprocket. The two lower tubes were linked at the front by 'X-plan' tubular bracing and at the rear by a cross-tube, upon which the bevel-box was mounted. Such was H.F.S. Morgan's gift for functional economy, that we find the lower frame tubes serving as integral exhaust pipes, an expansion chamber being mounted at the front end of each! Very direct steering, i.e. with never more than a 2 to 1 reduction gear, was part of the Morgan aesthetic. Also not to be overlooked was the sliding-pillar ifs, another product of the inventor's basic directness, resolving the problem by means of coil springs and double-duty steering pivots-cum-suspension slides. This suspension design was incorporated, unaltered, in all the Morgan three-wheeler models and in the four-wheeled cars from 1936 onwards.

Offered in Standard, Family and De Luxe specification, other 1920s variants included the faster Grand Prix and Aero models fitted with more powerful engines, often in racing tune. Harold Beart's racing Morgan with 1096 cc water-cooled ohv Blackburne engine, considerably modified, took the Class H2 records for the flying-kilometre and flying-mile at 103.37 mile/h and 102.65 mile/h respectively, in 1925. Not only were Morgans fun, they could be very fast!

Record-breaking continued unabated throughout the '20s, culminating in the efforts of Gwenda Stewart and her mechanic Douglas Hawkes at Montlhery in 1929-30. Here Mrs Stewart took the five-kilometre and five-mile records at over 103 mile/h in a Super Sports JAP-engined 'projectile'. Final glory came in 1930 with officially-timed runs at 110.69 mile/h over five miles, 113.52 mile/h being reached at one time - the highest speed to be officially recorded by a 1920's Morgan.

Three-wheeler models (1930–39)

The year 1930 was the last in which the two-speed bevel-box formed part of the specification. The Aero had supplanted the Grand Prix in 1924 and was now offered at £110, the Super Sports model costing £145. Alternatively, for those less speed-conscious, the 55 mile/h Standard and Family saloons were offered at £87-10s. These models all had the 1910-type chassis, two driving-chains, leather-faced cone clutch, external-contracting brake on the rear hub and a dry weight of about 5½ cwt. With the Super Sports engine developing over 40 bhp, one can appreciate that a very healthy power-to-weight ratio made good acceleration and high top speed readily attainable. All engines were of twin-cylinder 'V' formation, and either air- or water-cooled; use of the racing Blackburne and Anzani V-twins in sports Morgans did not continue beyond the '20s, JAP and Matchless powerplants being the sole alternatives.

Detail improvements were perhaps due after twenty years, and in 1931 the new M-type chassis was evolved with a three-speed gear and

1933 Morgan F Super

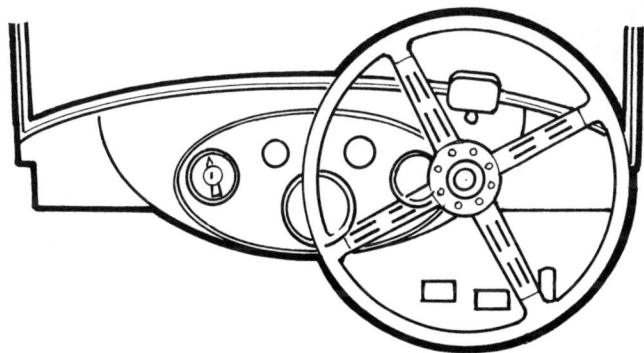

1934 three-wheeler De Luxe Family Model

1931 Morgan three-wheeler Super Sports fitted with a JAP 1000cc V twin air-cooled engine, three-speed gearbox and constructed on the M-type chassis

1933 Morgan three-wheeler Four Seater Family Model

single driving-chain, underslung rear suspension and knock-out rear spindle. An electric starter replaced the side-mounted handle, a gear-driven generator feeding the battery now stowed in the tail. A lower centre of gravity also made the little three-wheeler more stable.

Fully-enclosed valve gear became standard wear for the JAP engines in 1931, the Aero model being given a two panel V-screen in place of the twin aero-screens featured up until this time, but remaining an extremely distinctive sporting machine. Very individual, perhaps a specialized taste more suited to the athletic, outdoor-type, the open Morgan was for the purist, the ex-motorcyclist who wanted rather more comfort but no less thrill nor less direct contact with the 'naked' machinery. A top speed of over 80 mile/h in a tuned Super Sports Morgan gave all this.

The 1933 models included a Family version

with a longer bonnet and dummy radiator grille, somewhat concealing the whirring 'bits and pieces' from the wife and children! Three-wheel brakes became standard, the wheels now being of quickly-detachable hub-bolted type with chromed nave-plates. A water-cooled sv Matchless V-twin provided the power, mission being via a single dry-plate clutch and three-speed-plus-reverse gearbox. A dashlight and needle-type speedometer were provided, with electric lighting an optional extra. Cycletype front mudguards were complemented by a fully cowled-in rear wheel, the spare being mounted on the angled rear quarter of the body. A tall square-cornered windscreen provided ample windproofing and a fold-away hood, stowed beneath a 'Rexine' cover, made provision for bad weather. With electric lighting, the 1933 Family model cost £105. As for the speed range, this now included a Super-Sports Special with a forked connecting-rod, water-cooled ohv Matchless V-twin engine. Of 990 cc capacity, the engine was guaranteed to give 40 bhp. Chromium-plated wheels and nave-plates, three-speed-and-reverse gearbox, three-wheel brakes, a spring steering wheel and superlative finish made up the specification, high-level chromed exhaust pipes running the length of the body and the spare wheel now concealed in a recess in the rounded tail. A mere £150 bought all this. But the 'surprise' on the Morgan stand at the 1933 Motor Cycle Show was a brand-new Model F with four-cylinder sv Ford Eight engine and channel Z-section outer chassis, the Family model being priced, with electric lighting, at £120. A long bonnet with chromed radiator fronted the bodywork, overall specification embracing all the season's innovations listed above; but repair work was made easier in that the front axle and engine-cum-gearbox assemblies could each be removed as a unit.

The 1934 Motor Cycle Show revealed that only Matchless engines would be used as V-twin powerplants in the future Family and Super Sports models, their cylinders being set at 50° and coil ignition standardized. The price of the V-twin Family model, with electric lighting, remained unchanged; the specification of the Super Sports model now included drilled and chromed engine-plates, and a plated luggage grid mounted on top of the rear body section. In sv water-cooled trim the price was £110; the ohv air-cooled version cost £115, with water-cooling an extra £5; additional electric lighting came for another £17-10s. The Model F continued also to be available at 1933 prices, a 'de luxe' edition, featuring a two-tone colour scheme, chromed windscreen surround, electric wiper and alloy spare-wheel cover, being displayed. Roomy rear seats were extra features of both four-cylinder models.

By 1936 both 8- and 10-hp engines had become available in two- and four-seater versions, and a twin-cylinder Sports two-seater at a modest price of £101-17s. The V-twin Family four-seater carried on, as did the ever-popular Super Sports models; the price of the Ford Eight-engined Model F was £115-10s. Work on a 1933 prototype, in which the front

of the F model was married to the rear section of the Super Sports culminated in the F Super model of 1172 cc, employing a sv Ford Ten engine. Erected on a shortened version of the 'F' chassis, the Super represented a Super Sports version of the four-cylinder range and could attain 70 mile/h; compensated Girling wedge-and-roller brakes acted on all three wheels. Throughout 1937-39 the more comprehensive Morgan range continued to be available, the last twin-cylinder models being exported just after the war and the F4 and 'F Super' three-wheelers continuing in production until 1950.

4/4 (1936-39)

Four cylinders were complemented by four wheels in the 4/4 model displayed at the 1936 Motor Show. Ford-engined, and with chain drive replaced by a conventional rear axle, the first two-seater had visible affinities with the front of the 'F' models, but for the cycle wings, which were replaced by the larger, sweeping variety extending to the front edges of the rear wings. The headlamps were now mounted on a bar, but the ifs mechanism was still very exposed to the vagaries of country gravel roads. Beneath the well-louvred bonnet was later to reside a 1122 cc Coventry Climax ioe (inlet over exhaust valve) engine, affording an even better power-to-weight ratio. At the rear, a sloping back supported the twin spare-wheel mounting, and wide enveloping wings, flared-out at their extremities, further neatened the effect. Z-section steel channel continued to form the main sidemembers of the low frame, which was further stiffened by the thick plywood floorboards. Vibration from the engine was alleviated by rubber mountings. A worm-and-nut steering box was incorporated, the lower-geared steering remaining extremely positive, as was gear-changing via the stubby, remote gear lever. There was a choice of three colours, and the price for the 1937 season was £194-5s.

During 1937, competition 1100cc-class versions were built, the capacity of their Coventry Climax engines reduced to 1098 cc and embodying balanced crankshafts, magneto

1937 Morgan 4/4 Two Seater. A competitor in a prewar RAC Rally, note the car's twin spare wheels, a standard Morgan fitting at the time

1936 10hp 4/4 Two Seater

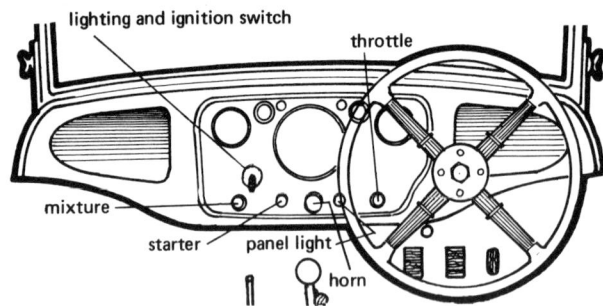

lighting and ignition switch

throttle

mixture

starter

panel light

horn

Morgan 4/4 Two Seater. Probably a works publicity photograph of the time

ignition, downdraught carburetters and four-branch manifolds plus externally-mounted exhaust systems. Of these TT Replicas, with their 42 bhp engines, one was entered in the 1938 Le Mans race and came away with the Biennial Cup. At the 1937 Show the standard two-seater with 1122 cc engine was priced at £210, a four-seater costing £225.

By the late '30s other users of the Coventry Climax engine, such as Triumph, had found alternatives; Morgans wanted a proprietary mass-produced engine like the Ford unit but one with more sparkle. This they found, thanks to a very satisfactory liason with the Standard Motor Company. After experimenting with Ford's V-8 22 hp engine and finding the gross weight (and 90 mile/h top speed!) rather 'extravagant', and having dabbled with a supercharged version of the sv Standard Ten unit, Sir John Black, of Standards, offered H.F.S. Morgan am ohv version of the Ten engine. This was found to 'fill the bill' nicely, and, coupled with a gearbox and 5 : 1 rear axle, both of Moss manufacture, the Standard-engined 4/4 became the last prewar version, available throughout the 1939 season. At £199-10s, the two-seater offered twin spare wheels, pneumatic cushions and rear space for luggage, the windscreen capable of being folded flat and side-screens forming a standard part of the equipment. The four-seater version, at £215-5s, had only one spare wheel, the fuel tank being mounted below the rear seats. A two-seater drophead-coupe model, offered at £236-5s, was equipped with Silentbloc spring-bushes, large luggage platforms and removable window frames.

The Morgan three-wheeler 'magic', combining a firm ride, much fresh air and an exhilarating sensation of speed with the fascination of exposed machinery, has much to recommend it. Unfortunately, very few three-wheeler Morgans appear for sale nowadays, and when they do, the high price asked reflects both the rarity and the demand for them among enthusiasts. Surely a scarlet Aero or Super Sports with an air-cooled JAP engine must rate as to-day's most 'way out' mode of transport for the '1930s-conscious' younger generation.

As for the 4/4, here we have a more con-ventional but still entirely distinctive small sports car, combining lively performance with the atmosphere of more golden days. Again, one gets a firm ride but extremely positive handling is the result, allied with a satisfying sensation of being 'at one' with both the machine and its progress along the open road.

In whatever guise, be it the crackle of a V-twin at full throttle, or the more sophisticated sound of the 4/4, a Morgan's exhaust note is pure music!

Morgan Three-Wheeler Club: N.H.Lear, 'Banyan House', 191 Wells Road, Glastonbury, Somerset.

Morgan Sports Car Club (for '4/4' owners): C.J.Smith, 23 Seymour Avenue, Worcester. Worcester 52995.

Morris

Sir William Morris's take-over of Wolseley Motors in 1927 bore fruit immediately in the acquisition by Morris Motors of a prototype 8-hp ohc Wolseley engine which served both as the initial powerplant for the Morris Minor and also, more importantly, gave birth to the long line of MG Midgets. The new Minor, although never a serious rival to the Austin Seven, did help for a time to stem the tide of Morris' financial difficulties, Cowley sales dropping noticeably during the Depression. Only with the advent of the Morris Ten and later the Eight of 1935 did Morris Motors get back on a surer footing.

Minor, Eight and Series E (1930–39)

Introduced in 1928, the ohc Minor with its light weight and better brakes offered a far superior performance to its hitherto un-challanged rival, the Austin Seven. The energetic little 847 cc power unit could yield some 20 bhp as compared with the 10.5 bhp of the 747.5 cc sv Austin Seven. But for some reason the Minor did not catch on with the public; perhaps added complexity of maintenance seemed hardly worth it to them, a runabout being a runabout, and the less attention it needed, the better. Sir William Morris, too, had a inherent aversion to 'fiddly' overhead valve-mechanisms and as the Minor was not selling too well, disposed of the ohc ex-Wolseley engine to Cecil Kimber of MG and set about planning a sv Minor to sell at a lower figure, one open version perhaps dropping to the legendary target of £100 'all-in'. The ohc Minor's last season was that of 1930; it shared with the Cowley a flat-faced radiator, and had a wooden-framed body with metal panelling. Mechanical brakes were fitted, and a gearbox with only three forward speeds retained. Performance, however, particularly in two-seater form, was good - the 20 bhp made possible a top speed of 55.2 mile/h, and over 45 mpg were attainable, although the brakes needed 44 feet

to stop the car from 30 mile/h. In 1931 the new sv Minor appeared, the two-seater tourer version indeed selling for a mere £100, but offering in exchange no choice of colour, poor instrumentation, and an overall air of 'economy *ad absurdum'*. Peformance as compared with the ohc version, was poor, power output being little more than that of the Austin Seven, the saloons proving even less 'athletic'. Hence the new Minor range was no more of a success, although production staggered on until 1934, by which time hydraulic brakes, a four-speed syncromesh gearbox and Bishop Cam steering had been added. In its final season the sv Minor's variants were priced at £127 for the two-door saloon, £120 for the tourer, £150 for the four-door lwb Family saloon and £110 for the two-seater. The days of Morris's '£100 car' were long since over.

At the 1934 Motor Show a desperate attempt to produce an answer to several very successful rival 8- and 10-hp mass-produced light cars saw visible form in the new Morris Eight. Here at last was a small car at once up-to-date, 'ordinary' in the best sense, serviceable, practical and well-priced. Its 918 cc engine could produce 23.5 bhp, well up to the old ohc unit, and was mounted in a far more rigid box-section frame fitted with such 'mod cons' as Bishop Cam steering, hydraulic brakes (that few rivals could boast), hydraulic shockabsorbers, electric petrol pump and Magna wire wheels. The body was also larger and wider overall than the Minor. Now entirely of pressed steel, both open and saloon bodies were offered, the two-seater being partnered by a four-seater tourer. If the open cars were faintly reminiscent of 'utility MGs' the saloon was certainly more akin in appearance to one of its close rivals, the Ford 19Y. Fairly thorough instrumentation, a fool-proof three-speed gearbox, and horn button, dip and trafficator switches on an elongated stalk at right angles to the steering-column, were details that appealed to the new breed of novice motorists, as did the prices - £118 for the two-seater, £120 for the tourer, and £132-10s for the sliding-head two-door saloon. A fixed-head four-door saloon cost £130.

The Eight's performance was examined in a *Practical Motorist* road test, maximum speed

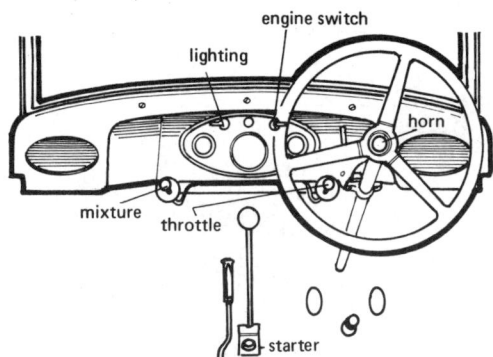

1930 8hp Minor Two Seater

1932 Morris Minor sv McEvoy Special and two 1934 Two Seaters

1931 Morris sv Minor Two Seater Tourer. Although it was Britain's first £100 car, it was not a commercial success, and the laurels finally went to the £100 8hp Ford Popular Saloon of 1935

1933 Morris Minor Four Door Saloon

1933 Morris Minor Two Seater. Note the revised rear treatment

1935 Morris Eight Series I Saloon alongside a 1937 Ford 8hp Popular Saloon owned by Don Windibank. Mrs. G. Harris' Morris reveals the similarity in style between the two cars

1937 Morris Eight Four Seater Tourer

1937 Morris Eight Two Seater

1938 Morris Eight Two Door Saloon

attained being 58.06 mile/h, 10-30 mile/h taking 8.8 seconds in the saloon version. It is interesting to compare these figures with those of the 8 hp Ford Popular (as the 19Y was later called) - here maximum speed was 58.44 mile/h, 10-30 mile/h taking 7.6 seconds. Both cars could return, on average, 40 mpg.

As Series I and Series II versions, the Morris Eight remained very little altered. 'Pre-Series' models had a comma-like metal motif on the radiator cap, while that of the Series models bore a figure '8' on a red enamelled background, the actual radiator emblem bearing the word 'Eight' and not a numeral. To the collector or enthusiast the few differences in the Series models were the inclusion of Hardy-Spicer joints on the transmission shaft, a hand throttle, flexible-spoked steering wheel and trafficators mounted to the rear of the doors. By 1937 spoked disc wheels had become standard, and by 1938 cellulosed radiator cowls i.e. not chromium-plated as in earlier Eights.

For the 1938 and final season, prices were £126 for the two-seater, £128 for the tourer and two-door fixed-head saloon, and £139 for the sliding-head and fixed-head saloons.

In 1938 the new Series E 8 hp model was announced, its reworked engine now delivering 29.5 bhp and powering a brand-new concept in body design - one minus running boards, and featuring a sloping and curved radiator grille, headlamps integral with the front wings and overall mild 'streamlining' throughout. A four-speed gearbox meant that 0-50 mile/h took only 33.2 seconds; maximum speed was well up in the sixties. The E handled well, and was a vigorous enough performer for its 918 cc. Pre-war prices of the E series were the same as the Series II models of 1938. No two-seaters were built, but the four-seater tourer, with its chubby front, and 'fast' back incorporating a circular spare-wheel cowl, was particularly attractive.

10/4 (1933–39) and 10/6 (1933–35)

The 10 hp Ten-Four model of 1933 represented for Morris an inroad into a new size of vehicle, sales of the Cowley having severely fallen off and a replacement for it being only in the prototype stage. The Ten-Four's steel body, with rounded back and luggage grid astern, shared with many cars of the period a long tapering bonnet and tall upright chromium-plated radiator. Its design was deliberately 'middle of the road', a four-cylinder in-line sv engine of 1292 cc being in unit with a four-speed gearbox, open transmission shaft and spiral-bevel rear axle - but for the 'wet' clutch, as in the Cowley. Suspension, front and rear, was by semi-elliptic leaf springs coupled with friction shockabsorbers. Prices for the 1934 season were £165 for the two-seater, and £169 for the tourer and four-door saloon. The Ten-Four offered comfort, economy and a serviceable enough overall performance. By 1936, 'modernization' having been applied to the entire Morris range, the Ten could attain 66 mile/h, 0-50 mile/h taking 40 seconds and 32 mpg being afforded; prices ranged from £172-10s for the fixed-head saloon to £215 for a Special Coupe, the same for the Series II models of the 1937 season. A 1140 cc ohv engine became standard on 1938 Series III models, prices rising slightly, ranging from £185 to £220. More obvious streamlining and the fitting of spoked disc wheels were in evidence. In 1939 unit construction, in the form of the Series M model, was introduced.

The mid-30s Ten-Six models had slightly longer bonnets to accommodate their 1378 cc sv six-cylinder in-line engines. While offered in six-light saloon and Special Coupe form, most distinctive on the Morris stand at the 1934 Motor Show was a scarlet sports tourer, its high, square bonnet-line leading rearwards to a very short but wide folding screen, and two aero-type cockpit mouldings. Two brief 'cut away' doors and a flat back were complemented by large stone guards on the rear wings, 'Magna' wheels with simulated 'knock-off' hubs moulded in the nave plates, and long rows of louvres running along the bonnet sides and the length of the valances. Its twin-carburetter engine provided a sports performance, and the price was £230; the Special Coupe version cost £215, but had the standard six-cylinder engine. Production of the Ten-Six series terminated in 1935.

1932 Morris Ten Special Coupe

1933 Morris Ten Saloon. Very distinctive trafficators have been fitted

1933 Morris Ten-Six Sports Special Coupe. Very dashing for Morris; note the simulation 'knock off' hub knave plates on Magna wire wheels

1933 Morris Ten-Six Four Seater Tourer

1938 Morris Ten-Four Series M Saloon

1938 Morris Ten Series III Saloon

1937 Morris Ten Series III Coupe

1937 Morris Ten Saloon

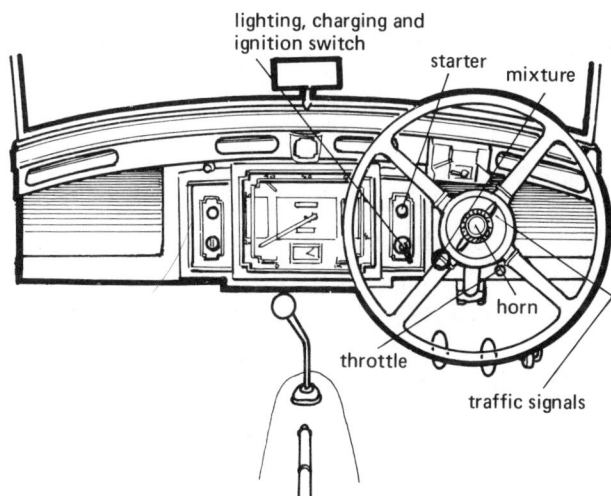

1937 10 and 12hp Sliding-head Saloon

Cowley (1930—34) and Twelve (1935—39)

Losing its 'bull nose' to adopt a flat radiator in 1927, the Cowley continued in production well into the 1930s as a bigger version of the Minor. Its 1550 cc four-cylinder sv engine developed 28 bhp, the 1932 saloon achieving a maximum speed of 55.6 mile/h, acceleration from 10-30 mile/h taking 15.6 seconds. It was never a lively car, and its appeal lessened after 1927; it offered, however, reliable transport at a fair price (£185 in 1930, rising to £195 in 1934).

The 12/4 replaced the Cowley in 1935, representing a car far more in tune with public demand. A later 1938 Series III saloon version with ohv engine and four-speed gearbox could reach 68 mile/h, 10-30 mile/h in third and top gear taking 11.9 and 16.5 seconds, respectively. Like the Ten, an in-built permanent 'Jackall' system of hydraulic jacks was included, but unit construction was not used in the Twelve before the war. Prices of the fixed-head saloon ranged from £195 in 1935 to £205 in 1939, the sliding-head saloon costing £187-10s in 1936 and £215 in 1939.

The Minor and Cowley have both period charm and rarity-value, an ohc Minor having the edge over the sv versions, being a sought-after little vehicle nowadays. The Eight, too, has quite a following now, open versions being very popular and almost accepted as 'sports cars'. The rare Series E tourer is well worth seeking out, and the Ten-Six models, especially the sports tourer, are distinctive, but also rare. Like the Series E saloon, the Series III Ten and Twelve models are rather too 'bland' for our taste at present but must in time take their place in the halls of nostalgia.

Morris Register: Miss B.D.M.Hicks, 'White House', The Heath, East Malling, Kent.

1937 Morris Ten Series II Saloon

1937 Morris Twelve Saloon

1939 Morris Twelve Series III Saloon

Riley

The Riley Nine engine of 1926, with its hemispherical combustion chambers, and overhead valves inclined at ninety degrees and operated by short pushrods from a pair of high camshafts, was revolutionary in its way. Inherently efficient, and perfectly suited for intensive tuning, the Nine's 1087 cc engine powered not only a whole range of 9 hp Riley cars, from standard saloons to high-performance sports models, but also inspired the subsequent introduction of 1½- and 2½-litre versions.

Throughout the 1930s the Riley diamond was proudly displayed to the world as a symbol of fine design. Unfortunately, by 1938, the financial affairs of the firm were none too sound, and in 1939 they were absorbed into the Nuffield Organization. Worst still, the Blitz on Coventry virtually destroyed the entire Riley factory, many valuable prototype projects and most of the firm's technical records being lost for ever. Many competition successes and fond memories of prewar motoring in Rileys have kept the flame bright, however, mere bombs having failed to eradicate a memorable history or dim the brightness of the legend.

Nine (1930–38)

Right from its introduction the Riley Nine was a trend-setter. If Percy Riley had been responsible for much of the engine's design, it was Stanley Riley's flair for body design which presented it in such an attractive package. The Monaco four-seater saloon of 1927, a close-coupled low-slung fabric saloon with high waist-line, immediately caught on with the public at the expense of the earlier tourer. Very modern for its time, not only were the seating and interior more advanced (and more comfortable), but the outward panache of the Monaco was lived up to in its 60 mile/h top speed - a remarkable figure for a 9 hp car of the time. The Nine's good roadholding and steering qualities,

together with such unexpected 'verve' hall-marked the Riley concern as innovators worthy of note, and from the late '20s onwards the Coventry firm became more and more renowned for building very individual fast touring and sports cars.

As mentioned above, motive power was provided by a very modern design of ohv engine of 1087 cc capacity, with hemispherical combustion spaces and valves inclined at an included angle of 90° and operated by short pushrods from two high camshafts, driven from the crankshaft by an intermediary idler-gear. Cylinder-block and crankcase were integral and of cast iron, the cylinder-head and sump being detachable. A sturdy four-throw crankshaft was supported by two white metal-lined bronze bushes, white-metal being used for the big-end bearings also. Lubrication was via a unique 'double plunger' oil-pump where two long pistons, operated by crank-rods from an eccentrically-mounted drive-wheel, alternately drew-in oil through the sump filter and pumped it to the bearings, 'splash' aiding the lubricant in reaching certain other components. Ignition was originally by magneto mounted vertically at the front of the crankcase and driven by means of a skew gear from the gearwheel of the 'inlet' camshaft, and the dynamo was mounted on the nose of the crankshaft. From 1933 the magneto was replaced by a coil distributor. Good for some 30 bhp in standard form in 1930, by the turn of the decade the engine's original horizontal Zenith carburetter had been complemented by a Solex or SU instrument. The stamina of the basic engine design is reflected in the manufacturer's claim of 50,000 miles between overhauls - many contemporary engines needing stripping-down after covering less than half this mileage. Flexible rubber trunnion engine - mountings reduced vibration considerably, and were another advanced feature in the days of solid mounting direct to the chassis.

By 1930 the Plus series of 9 hp models had been in production for six months, the substitution of a single dry-plate clutch for the earlier type, together with modifications to the brakes, silencer and suspension, being taken further in other modifications. A rear fuel tank plus Autovac to supply the carburetter, together with centralized chassis lubrication and Silent-bloc spring-bushes were introduced, with smaller-diameter wheels. Models available at the time were the Monaco four-door four-seater saloon in a Weymann fabric version, and the Brook-lands, a racing two-seater, which was available also in road trim. The price of the Monaco remained constant, at £298, from 1927 to 1938. Also listed at £298 was the 1930 open tourer, and the Biarritz half-panelled saloon, priced at £325.

Performance-wise, the Monaco saloon in light, fabric-bodied form, could exceed 60 mile/h, acceleration from 10-30 mile/h in 'silent third' gear being accomplished in a mere 12 seconds, five more seconds being needed in top. The gear-box was, in fact, capable of fast, quiet changes, and was there to be used if full benefit was to be taken of the engine's torque curve. Coupled with such liveliness was a fuel consumption figure of some 33-40 mpg. A Special Series higher-performance engine, embodying high-compression pistons, twin carburetters, racing valve springs etc., was capable of developing 35-40 bhp and this could be had at an extra charge of £17, fitted into any tourer or saloon model. Here, acceleration and top speed were considerably improved, of course. Racing versions of the Nine engine were good for some 50 bhp or more.

The 1931 Motor Show revealed that for a blanket price of £298 one could choose from the Weymann or half-panelled Weymann-bodied Monaco, a full-panelled two-seater coupe, and the new Gamecock sports two-seater. The Biarritz remained at £325, while an Army-type high ground-clearance four-seater tourer was offered at £310, rejoicing in its coat of War Office green paint. All these cars were of the 1931-32 Plus Ultra specification, with chassis lowered by six inches, affording greater interior

A 1931 Riley Nine Monaco on the right. A 1929 Morris Six Coupe is pulling out behind

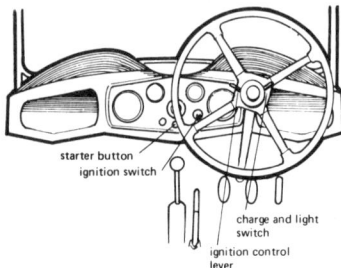

1933 9hp Lynx Two Seater

starter button
ignition switch

charge and light switch

ignition control lever

1932 Riley Brooklands Nine, originally owned by the legendary racing driver Freddie Dixon

1934 Riley 9hp Lynx Four Seater Tourer

1933 Riley 9hp March Special 2/4 Seater Tourer

1934 Riley-engined ERA racing car R1A. This is in fact the first ERA, and Tony Merrick is seen at the wheel

1934 Riley 9hp Imp Two Seater, owned by Frank Hawke

191

space and ease of entry. By the 1932 Show a stiffer chassis offered more rigid construction (the Weymann body had been chosen for its specially designed flexing abilities) and improved stability on fast corners. The whole of the Monaco's roof structure had been moved back, thus angling the windscreen more, bringing it nearer the steering wheel and giving more headroom for the rear passengers. The new Lynx tourer, a close-coupled four-seater version of the Gamecock, was partnered by the Lincock coupe, the Falcon saloon and the sporting March Special four-seater at £335. The Falcon had the patented Riley 'Roofdoors', small hinged panels in the roof lifting, via a linkage, with the doors and making disembarking far easier (and more graceful for the ladies). As for the March Special this came from the Kevill-Davies and March Ltd stable, a specialized coachbuilding firm constructing racy-looking bodywork on proprietary chassis, designed by the famous contemporary exponent of motor racing, the Earl of March. Salient features were the March Special's swept front wings, well-louvred bonnet, flared scuttle, folding windscreen, very brief 'cut away' doors, flush-folding hood, twin tank-filler caps, and twin spare wheels. The Lincock coupe had seating for two persons, its rounded roof-area dropping away to a prolonged arched back of pleasing proportions. Its two large doors provided excellent access and much luggage capacity was another feature. A further newly-introduced model was the Trinity Special - intended to be three cars in one, but proving a poor seller, in actual fact. The Trinity was capable of conversion into a two-seater, open four-seater or four-seater coupe by virtue of a swivelling panel at the rear of the two front seats. If desired as a two-seater the panel was swivelled upwards to blend-in with the back panel; turning the panel towards the rear of the car revealed a further bench seat, an upholstered underside to the panel forming the back rest. A third variation was the erection of the concealed hood, converting the car to a four-seater coupe.

The price of the Trinity was £325; still offered, from 1931 to the end of 1932, was the Ascot drop-head coupe with external dickey-seat, at £298.

The 1933 Show saw the introduction of the sports Imp and Ulster Imp on a shortened chassis, the former an open two-seater with sharply flared wings and radiator set well back, the latter a highly-tuned version incorporating a high-compression cylinder-head and special crankshaft, modifications which gave a top speed of over 90 mile/h. Also in manufacture during 1933 was the 9 hp version of the Kestrel four-door saloon, an early essay in 'fast back' styling, the steep angle of the back panel being uninterrupted due to flush mounting of the recessed spare wheel. At this time the Riley diamond motif was to find echoes both in the outlines of the windows and in the overall boundaries of the bonnet louvres. The 1933 Monaco panelled saloon was typical in both these respects, while the Kestrel, for example, had diamond-boundaried louvres but side-windows of less obvious geometric plan. Should one have wished to purchase a Kestrel or Monaco for 1934, the price remained static at £298, while the Imp two-seater was priced at £325; the March Special was no longer offered. Fairly lightweight construction at this time made the Nine still an energetic performer, and competitive in the 9 hp 'middle price' range. The Lynx four-seater tourer was another sporting version made between 1933 and 1935, its 'double front' humped scuttle and other expected 'sports' features making it an attractive and lively car that many a prospective purchaser would have weighed carefully in the balance against such alternatives as the smaller tourers manufactured by Crossley, Lagonda, Lea-Francis, MG, Rover, S.S. and Triumph.

In tune with a passing trend, Riley added the choice of their 'Preselectagear' plus an automatic clutch or a synchromesh gearbox with freewheel for the 1933-35 season series of Nines (and 12 hp models). The preselector gearbox was of Wilson design. By 1935 box-section chassis sidemembers afforded extra rigidity, Luvax hydraulic shockabsorbers improving the riding qualities and Enots' one-shot chassis lubrication simplifying maintenance (unless a pipeline became blocked); there was no extra charge for the preselector in the latter course of its 'reign'. The Falcon chassis was equipped with

Another ERA Riley-based special, R9B.
Martin Morris is the driver

1934 Riley MPH Two Seater. A particularly good-looking prewar sports model, akin to the smaller Imp

1935 Riley TT Sprite Two Seater.
Originally Bob Gerard's car, it now belongs to Colin Ready

1935 Riley Nine Imp Two Seater

D W S permanent jacks, the 'Roofdoors' being fitted only to certain bodies. The passage of a year saw the evolution of the Nine saloon body into an all-steel version called the Merlin, in shape close to the Kestrel and sporting a similar 'fast' back with slightly-protruding circular wheel cover. The Monaco was temporarily withdrawn, and at £269 it was hoped that the Merlin would prove its natural successor. The public, however, deplored the Monaco's disappearance and an all-steel heavier version reappeared at the 1936 Motor Show, back at its old price of £298, which included the Special Series 40 bhp engine as a standard fitting. The Merlin had Girling rod-operated brakes, replacing the Riley cable type. A 6.6:1 compression-ratio engine in the standard Merlin could be substituted by the Special Series twin-carburetter unit at £10 extra. With this latter engine, the 9 hp Kestrel cost £295.

Overall mass was, of course, increasing in the Nine saloons, hence any extra power delivered by the tuned Special Series engine was regretably absorbed in propelling this extra payload. As a result the Nine's performance remained static, or if anything became inferior to that put up by its early-30s ancestors. In consequence the later cars were not particularly competitive in the 'amoral' market, already brim-full of clamouring rivals eager to outdo each other and secure more sales. Take-over by the Nuffield combine in 1938 coincided with a single-season run of the new 9 hp Victor all-steel saloon, a body design again based on the Kestrel but with evident new, but subtle, trends linking the overall style of the car with the postwar 1½-litre RMA. Of four-door four-light format, the Victor's design incorporated a slightly longer bonnet, the engine being moved further forward and a heat-insulating bulkhead added. A 'fast back' still served as a mounting for the covered spare wheel, while the interior underwent certain changes, deep foot-wells being built in, to afford extra leg-room; pneumatic air cushions for the rear seats were aimed at aiding the springing. At £299, the Victor proved a rather over-bodied saloon for its power output, and one that did little to reflect the glory of former small Rileys. Production of the Nine ceased at the end of 1938, the 'high camshaft' engine design fortunately living-on in postwar 1½-litre and 2½-litre form.

Twelve and 1½-litre (1932–39)

The progress of the 12 hp and 1½-litre cars ran parallel with that of the Nine, the six-cylinder 1458 cc engine delivering some 45 bhp, while the later four-cylinder engine of 1496 cc developed 54 bhp in standard tune or 61-65 bhp in twin-carburetter form.

Introduced at the 1932 Motor Show, the Six-Twelve chassis formed the basis of such models as the Mentone and Kestrel four-door 12 hp saloons, the Gamecock two-seater tourer, the Grebe three-carburetter two-seater sports, and the 12 hp Lincock coupe. These 1932 and 1933 models, higher-powered than the Nines, were capable of putting-up a commendable road performance, equal to that of the less highly-tuned MGs; it is notable that the ERA racing car's engine of 1934 was basically a six-cylinder 1½-litre Riley unit.

In 1934 an exceptionally apt sports-racer design, the MPH, a long-bonneted, beetle-backed two-seater with high, flared front wings, was produced for a single season. Alternative power units were available, of either 12 or 14 hp, both engines being fitted with three carburetters; their performance was like their appearance, startling, that of the larger-engined version being, of course, superior.

The 1935-season 12 hp range included the Kestrel at £345, the Lynx four-seater tourer at £360 and Falcon saloon at £335. For this season the four-cylinder 1½-litre engine was introduced, superceding the 'six'. In 1½-litre guise the Lynx was offered for £335. An *Autocar* road test on a 1935 1½-litre Special Series Kestrel saloon found it "an outstanding car, to arouse enthusiasm in seasoned drivers" - accuracy of control, good road-holding, a sweet-running yet powerful engine, favourable power:weight ratio and a high degree of comfort at all speeds were all facets of the new car. A mean maximum speed over a quarter-mile was recorded at 80.36 mile/h, the best timed speed being nearer to 82 mile/h. Time for accelerating from 0-50 mile/h through the gears was 14.2 seconds, 10-30 mile/h, 20-40 mile/h and 30-50 mile/h taking

engine switch · mixture · throttle · ignition · traffic signal

starter · horn · lighting and anti-dazzle · pre-selector

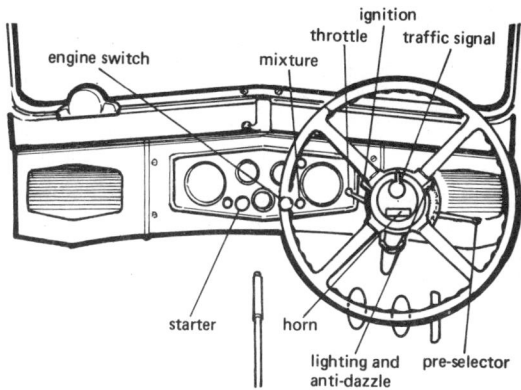

1935 1½-litre Special Series Kestrel Saloon

1936 Riley 12/4 Adelphi Saloon

1936 Riley Sprite Two Seater owned by Gordon Middleton, slipping past an Aston Martin at a Silverstone meeting. It is now registered ELM 516

1936 Riley Sprite Two Seater owned by Gordon Middleton. Originally the factory demonstrator, this fine car is now re-registered and wears the number plate it had in 1936

1937 Riley 1½-litre Continental Sprite Saloon once owned by David G. Styles, the photographer responsible for all the photographs in the Riley section of this book

11.6, 11.2 and 13 seconds respectively in top gear. Times for the same accelerations in third gear were 8.2, 8 and 9.6 seconds. The 'Pre-selectagear' gear, a Wilson preselector unit, made gear-changes crisp and fast, enabling excellent through-gear acceleration, as is evidenced in the 0-50 mile/h time given above. A stopping distance of 27 feet from a speed of 30 mile/h was proof of good brakes, the pedal pressure needed to actuate them was light and they were effective also at high speeds. For a gross weight of 23 cwt, a top speed of 80 mile/h and 25 mpg average fuel consumption were fine qualities in a 1½-litre car costing £372. This figure included a system of permanent jacks, pneumatic upholstery throughout, a centre-winding windscreen, twin windscreen wipers and other special points of equipment.

A 1½-litre four-cylinder version of the all-steel Merlin saloon appeared at the 1935 Motor Show priced at £308 in standard trim, or £335 with Special Series engine, both models being constructed on the swb chassis. On the longer-wheelbase chassis were erected the 1½-litre Falcon saloon at £335, the Lynx open tourer at £10 more and the Adelphi and Kestrel six-light saloons at £350 each. Special Series versions of these cars cost £27 extra. Most interesting of all were the new Sprite series, the modified twin-carburetter Sprite engine being fitted in a £425 open two-seater with flared front wings, and a Kestrel Sprite saloon and Lynx Sprite tourer both listed at £450. The preselector gearbox, which formed part of the standard Sprite specification, afforded once more the fullest opportunity of extracting snappy gear-changes and hence maximum acceleration. The two-seater was based on contemporary Riley racing-car practice.

Modifications to the 1½-litre engine for the 1937 season included the provision of a water pump and fan, a mechanical petrol pump, four-nut fixing for the rocker covers and a neat conduit for the HT leads. All the 1935 models were continued, the Falcon standard and Special Series versions being reduced in price by £20, and the Kestrel Sprite and Lynx Sprite now listed at £398. Rileys were offering a very large number of models and variants at this time - a factor which later may have had some bearing on their critical financial position. Some rethinking of their future policy was needed at this stage, their adoption of heavy pressed-steel bodywork outpacing the capabilities of the old-established high-camshaft series of engines, but no new 'breath of fresh air' seemed to come.

By 1938, the year of the take-over, the number of models had been cut back, the 1½-litre Victor being relied on to save the day, priced very close to the new Monaco, at £299. It featured 'dual overdrive', a special gearbox giving five forward speeds from only three gear-lever positions, a box-section chassis and, like the 9 hp version, an all-steel body. The torque-tube transmission was by then firmly withdrawn, economic pressures indicating the adoption of a conventional open propeller shaft from 1936. Girling rod-operated brakes had also superceded the Riley cable type which had, however, afforded 'master' adjustment from the driver's seat. The disappearance of these smaller Riley niceties augured a lack of flair and loss of earlier 'colour' and distinctiveness. A touring-saloon version of the Victor was offered at £345 (a large luggage locker being incorporated), while the old die-hards, the Kestrel and Adelphi saloons, remained listed at £385 and £375, respectively.

The last prewar season saw the removal of all 'early Riley' nostalgia, the evocative model names vanishing and a bald 'Twelve' label sufficing. The sum of £310 bought the saloon, or £335 the drop-head touring saloon; tuned engines could be fitted for another £25. A new style of radiator marked the Nuffield aegis.

14 hp models (1932–35)

A six-cylinder, 1633 cc engine was fitted in the Stelvio five-seater saloon and as an alternative to the 12 hp engine in the MPH sports two-seater. Virtually a 'bored-out' version of the Six-Twelve engine, some 50 bhp was afforded. An lwb saloon in appearance akin to the Alpine, the Stelvio was longer and wider-tracked, giving far more passenger space and a more comfortable ride.

In contrast, the MPH two-seater epitomized the public's concept of a mid-30s open sports car from its very flared front wings and long, louvred bonnet to its cowled-in spare wheel beneath a 'beetle back' and exhaust pipe terminating in a Brooklands fishtail.

The 'clan Riley' is numerous - the pre-1938 Riley Register now numbering some 1100 members. All Rileys are interesting, the earlier models particularly so. As regards the engine, the unique Riley 'double plunger' oil pump represents one of the more unorthodox features, and if good pressure is to be maintained, with attendant long life for the white-metal bearings, this unit must be correctly overhauled. Otherwise, the well-engineered power unit is a pleasure to work on, contrasting strongly with present-day 'anonymities' of casting and overall finish. Fabric-covered or aluminium-panelled bodies, constructed on an ash frame, must be checked for soundness in this latter area, the re-covering of bodies (in 'Rexine') being skilled work, rarely successful in the hands of an amateur. Box-section chassis members entrap moisture and can prove severly weakened by contact with salt or as victim of electrolytic corrosion, as can aluminium panelling when in 'sacrificial' decay when joined to ferrous metals.

But certain Riley models are definitely not unique in their troubles - all 'old cars' fall victim to such vagaries of weather and time. To split the Riley motto, their individualistic roots were 'as old as the industry'; the enthusiast must strive to keep the condition of his prized car 'as modern as the hour'.

Riley Register: A.P.Dunn, 162 Leicester Road, Glenhills, Leicester LE2 9HH.

Rover

An early seed in the form of a motorized **bath-chair** built in 1899 with a De Dion-Bouton-type rear axle and rear tandem driver's seat, led, for the Rover Company, to a series of voiturettes made from 1905 to 1912. Of advanced design for the time, these single-cylinder runabouts formed an important link between the voiturette and the light car.

In 1924 the 998 cc Rover Eight was introduced, a neat little four-wheeled vehicle with an air-cooled 'flat twin' engine, a three-speed-and-reverse gearbox and a live rear axle driven by an open propeller shaft. The body-work was fronted by a conventional bonnet with a 'dummy' radiator, had compact open two-seater accomodation, and rode upon large-diameter disc wheels. The Eight however, could not, even then, be described as a fully-fledged light car.

A direct link with their early roots, Rover's **post-Depression** 'economy runabout' of 1931 was short-lived and its failure so sudden that a year later no trace of it remained. Virtually anticipating the 500 cc Fiat four-wheeler of 1936, the Rover 'beetle' (described below) became extinct almost at birth.

Heavier vehicles followed, more comprehensive in specification, and from their light cars Rover developed a parallel series of models with larger engines, silky performance and more lavish bodywork.

7 hp Scarab (1931–32)

The cheapest car at the 1931 Motor Show, and priced at £89, the Scarab was a four-wheeled four-seater with a rear-mounted air-cooled V-twin ohv engine of 839 cc. Independent suspension on all four wheels was a marked feature, the transmission consisting of a single dry-plate clutch, three-speed gearbox and spiral-bevel rear axle all in unit. A special oil pump supplied lubricant to the engine bearings,

gearbox and axle. Four-wheel brakes were fitted, an aspect of the design distinguishing it from the run of cyclecars then available; top speed was 50 mile/h.

In appearance there were similarities to the 1924 Eight, right down to the Scarab's black disc wheels. The rear of the car, however, was a type of 'beetle' back, but more steeply arched, the central panel being heavily louvred to provide sufficient ventilation for the engine; a short transverse-mounted 'stub' exhaust (like that of the modern Hillman Imp) conveyed away engine fumes. Rigid side-screens formed part of the weather equipment, complemented by a folding hood resting on the crest of the rear panel. Two brief doors provided access to the diminutive seating arrangements. Obviously devised as a viable commercial enterprise, a great deal was made of the Scarab at its first showing. The *Autocar* in its Show Report Number for 1931 ventured: "It will be interesting to see if the little vehicle meets with success". We must assume it did not, for the 1932 Motor Show stand gave no indication that the little 'curiosity' had ever existed. Rover's concentration on cars of larger capacity was soon to flower as a range of models of from 10 to 20 hp renowned for their quality and performance.

Ten (1930–39)

Introduced before 1930, the 10/25's re-appearance at the Motor Show of that year concurred with an evident redesigning of its entire bodywork - although to modern eyes the car still epitomized the small medium-priced saloon of the era. A 1185 cc four-cylinder ohv engine in unit with the gearbox powered an all-steel saloon version with a long, straight bonnet, rounded back plus spare-wheel mounting, and close-fitting wings connected by alloy-panelled running boards. A purposeful look emanating from the long, louvred bonnet and high 'divided' radiator made the Rover range attractive cars, as did their good finish, silent performance and overall sturdy construction. A freewheel device was favoured by Rover for many years. During

1931 Rover 10/25 Four Seater Tourer

the early '30s it was controlled via a big hand-wheel mounted on the right-hand side of the dashboard; with the freewheel in action gear-changing was rendered foolproof and silent.

A coachbuilt saloon version of the Ten was listed in 1930 at £189, while a fabric-bodied Weymann saloon cost £212; the steel saloon was equipped with a three-speed gearbox while the Weymann body's gearbox had four speeds. By 1931 Magna-type wire wheels were fitted, and a choice of colour-scheme became available; a distinctive touch was that of painting the radiator slats to match.

By the time of the 1932 Motor Show flexible engine mountings had been adopted for the 10/25 Family model, an early example of this anti-vibration device. A new model, the Ten Special, also appeared at the Show, incorporating flexible mountings for the engine,

together with a four-speed constant mesh gear-box (giving silent running in top, third and second gear), freewheel, semi-elliptic springing all round, hydraulic brakes, hide upholstery and a Lucas Startix automatic restarting mechanism for the engine. Priced at £228, the Ten Special was derived from the new 12 hp Pilot Six saloon.

A new radiator treatment, where the Rover badge was mounted on the front of the shell, gave the frontal aspect an individual and more powerful aura. The centrally-divided V-angled slatting was surmounted by wider radiator shoulders, their radiused corners blending into the centre-line. This Rover 'hall-mark' was to survive, little altered, until the late 1940s.

Cars for the 1935 season embodied an overall styling treatment that also was to survive in essence until after the war: the long Rover

1934 Rover Ten Saloon

1937 Rover Ten Saloon

bonnet and radiator fronting a series of semi-streamlined, semi-angular body styles on longer wheelbases, each with an air of indefinable ruggedness. Coming from the New Meteor Works at Coventry, the Ten shared, with the rest of the 1935 Rover range, this new-found sense of 'rightness', its bodywork acquiring more dignity by virtue of a lower-slung chassis and hence low floor level. A larger, 1389 cc engine, rated at 10.8 hp, provided extra power, the flexible mounting and fairly high top-gear ratio yielding fast yet quiet cruising speeds. A novel harmonic stabilizer fitted to the front axle helped 'iron out' jolting on uneven road surfaces; automatic chassis lubrication and the fitting of a thermostat in the cooling system were other salient technical features. High standards of coachwork in the larger-capacity bodies went hand-in-hand with a commendable performance - a road test carried out on the 1935 Ten revealed a 0-50 mile/h acceleration occupying 19.4 seconds, a maximum speed of 66.7 mile/h,

1939 Rover Ten Coupe

and a stopping distance of 25 feet from 30 mile/h by means of its Girling rod-operated brakes.

Little change was evident in the appearance of the Ten from 1935 to 1938, its price also remaining constant at £248.

The Earls Court Motor Show of 1937 witnessed certain adaptations in styling however, most typical being the squarish 'box boot' which was to survive well after 1945.

The last prewar Motor Show of 1938 saw downdraught carburation standardized, together with Girling brakes and Luvax-Bijour centralized lubrication. Higher efficiency was extracted from all the engine units, a counterbalanced crankshaft being installed, and the water jacketing redesigned to direct coolant on to the valves and spark-plug seats. A smoother ride was afforded by the fitting of Luvax piston-type shockabsorbers, and a new clutch design gave a sweeter action. The saloon and coupe cost respectively £275 and £285.

Twelve (1931–39)

First introduced in six-cylinder ohv guise, the 12 hp Pilot saloon of 1931 employed the same body as the Ten. Of 1410 cc capacity, the engine was flexibly mounted, afforded smooth and silent running and was fitted with a large four-bearing crankshaft, supported by an extra-rigid crankcase. Out-and-out speed not being the prime objective, the Pilot performed easily and without fuss, the engine power being transmitted smoothly over a wide range of speeds, enabling the car to be driven at walking pace in top gear and then pull-away from this speed. An efficient hot-spot and the provision of a thermostat ensured quick warming-up from cold. Light steering, comfortable springing and easy gear changing were virtues that attracted attention to the new model, the reasonable price of £225 for the all-steel saloon representing good value for money - the six-cylinder engine and smooth transmission being

1936 Rover
Twelve Open
Four Seater

matched by a high degree of finish in the body-work and leather upholstery of the interior. A £230 fabric-covered Weymann saloon, by virtue of its inherent lightness, afforded more lively acceleration, the special jointing of its wooden frame ensuring squeak-free travel, the body being free to flex on corners and when the car was traversing rough roads. Both versions of the Pilot had four-speed gearboxes with a 'silent third' gear. A sliding roof was standard.

No 12 hp model was marketed for the 1932 season, probably because of Rover's decision to install a 14 hp six-cylinder engine in the Pilot, a scheme which made snappier acceleration at once attainable, together with more reserve of power to haul the none-too-light steel body.

A four-cylinder engine became, in 1933, standard fitting for the 1934 season 12 hp range, coinciding with the introduction of the new-style radiator and lower, longer-wheelbase chassis for all models. The new powerplant was of 1496 cc and ohv layout with a three-bearing counterbalanced crankshaft. Retention of the Rover freewheel ensured effortless driving. Marles Weller steering, and Girling compensated brakes were proprietary systems in the Twelve, to which Lucas Startix automatic engine restarting was added, for convenience, together with Rover's own harmonic stabilizer. Zinc interleaves between the leaf-spring layers were allied with the damping effect of hydraulic shockabsorbers. A £278 saloon and £288 coupe were listed, the sports saloon version at £298 coinciding exactly in price with the Riley Nine

range and representing a serious rival in the light of its advanced features, quality finish and lavish fittings.

A stringent *Autocar* road test at Brooklands on a 1935 Twelve saloon registered a maximum speed of 69.77 mile/h, acceleration from 0-50 mile/h taking 18.4 seconds while its powers of retardation were reflected in the mere 23 feet needed to bring the car to a halt from 30 mile/h. In essence, the Twelve was a quality, medium-priced car of good performance, comfortable, modern in design and attractive in a restrained way.

A four seater tourer version of 1936, selling at £288, was a particularly well-found machine where the 'quiet' frontal Rover styling and long wheelbase formed distinctive features and provided an apt basis for the well-proportioned 'beetle back' body.

The Rover Company's ability to somehow combine restrained streamlining with an overall near-geometric line at once gave their products the stamp of individuality, appealing to the more subtle sensibilities; a brilliant balance was struck, neither too flambouyant nor too utilitarian.

A coupe-type rounded roof surmounted all the closed versions of 12 hp from 1934 to 1939. Bonnet louvres were eliminated from late - 1937; Luvax-Bijour chassis lubrication, downdraught carburation and piston-type hydraulic shock-absorbers were standard fitting in 1939, by which year the saloon cost £300 and the sports saloon £310.

Fourteen (1932–38)

As mentioned above, a 14 hp edition of the Pilot Six was introduced in 1932, its 1577 cc engine powering a coachbuilt body of merely 10 hp-saloon dimensions and giving a top speed of over 60 mile/h. Top-gear acceleration from 10-30, 20-40 and 30-50 mile/h occupied 13.4, 16.6 and 20.4 seconds, respectively; the car could be arrested from 30 mile/h in a distance of 32 feet, and the engine gave 25-28 mpg. Overall smoothness, comfort and ease of operation were the model's salient virtues.

While the progress of the standard 14 hp cars kept pace with the general trends of other models, perhaps the Speed Fourteen chassis, introduced in 1933, is most worthy of more detailed examination. Designed to provide sports car performance, the open four-seater works entry in the RAC 1000 Miles Rally was awarded highest marks in its class for the acceleration tests as well as gaining the Buxton Town Trophy for the best performance of any car starting from that point. The admirably-proportioned tourer body was served by a power output of 54 bhp at 4,800 rev/min, the six-cylinder 1577 cc Fourteen engine being fitted with a four-bearing crankshaft, three semi-downdraught carburetters, flowed ports and a high-compression cylinder head. General specification was otherwise similar to that outlined for the Ten and Twelve of the era. The sum of £395 purchased the Speed Fourteen sports four-seater and Hastings coupe during the 1934 season, the

1933 Rover 14hp Pilot Coachbuilt Saloon

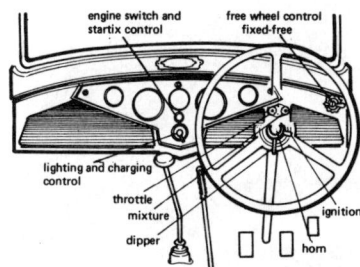

1932 Pilot Saloon

203

1934 Rover Fourteen Saloon

1934 Rover Speed Fourteen Sports Four Seater

1934 Rover Speed Fourteen Hastings Coupe

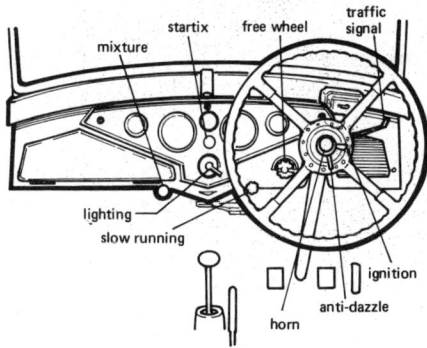

1935 Speed Fourteen Streamline Coupe

1936 Rover Fourteen Streamline Saloon

standard tourer costing £308 and the saloon £288. By 1935 a handsome Speed Fourteen streamline coupe was being offered at £415, a lively 'fast back' version combining the best elements of contemporary advances in engineering and styling. The *Autocar* staff were quick to appraise its overall excellence, its accelerative abilities, for example, being vividly evidenced in a 0-50 mile/h figure of only 14.4 seconds, through the gears. A top speed of 81.45 mile/h and best timed speed nearer to 83 mile/h were also proof of the extra power realised through the engine modifications. Docility and tractability went hand-in-hand with this rapid pace, as did passenger comfort, silence of operation and finger-light steering. Hydraulic brakes stopped the car in a distance of 26 feet from 30 mile/h; swift, 'sports' gearchanging could be enjoyed with the freewheel locked out of action, or clutchless, silent changes obtained with it in operation.

For the 1936 season the streamline coupe on the Speed Fourteen chassis was listed still at £415; other 14 hp standard versions were the saloon at £298, sports saloon at £318, and streamline coupe and saloon both priced at £348

- this was also the last season for the **Speed Fourteen**. The Rover 'boxed' rear and round spare-wheel cover replaced the 'streamline' slant, and for the 1937-39 period the Fourteen fell into line with a uniform styling concept which involved the entire Rover range. A 1937 price of £305 for the saloon and £10 extra for the sports saloon increased in 1938 to £320 and £350; for the 1939 season the engine capacity was increased to 1901 cc.

The 'long legged' Rovers of 1934 onwards have carved an individualistic niche in the annals of British car design. Their very length, allied with low-positioned bodywork has a distinct attractiveness, its design all the more noteworthy in the restrained balance between the worse excesses of 'modernity' and the more tasteful elements of the coachbuilder's art. Advanced engineering features and an overall sense of 'quality' throughout make the prewar Rover a car to cherish.

Rover Sports Register: T.L.J.Bentley, 11 Woodhall Drive, Pinner, Middx. HA5 4TG.

Singer

Developed from their Junior model's power unit, the Singer and Companys 9 hp ohc engine, used first in their Nine saloon of 1932, formed an ideal basis for later models such as the Nine Sports and Nine Le Mans. The Nine Sports immediately began to rival the MG entries at trials events, often sweeping the board. A standard model then took 13th place in the 1933 Le Mans, and engendered the two-seater Le Mans version, again so successful in competitions that MG introduced their PB-type as an attempted answer to it. Soon to follow were the 1½-litre Le Mans cars, but mechanical disaster at the 1935 TT persuaded the concern to withdraw from racing and they thenceforth concentrated their efforts on 9, 11 and 12 hp light cars, retaining their ohc engine layout right up to 1939, long after MG had adopted the ohv format. The illustrious HRG also owes Singer Motors a debt in that Singer-HRG engines became the mainstay of its design by 1938. Full absorption of the Singer Company into the Rootes combine took place in 1936.

8 hp Junior (1930–32)

In 1930 this 848 cc car underwent many detail improvements. Repositioning of the tank at the rear and the fitting of a four-speed gearbox in place of the three speeds of the earlier unit was matched by the fitting of a larger sump; a new design of radiator, with corrugated mouldings at the head and base of the radiator shell, appeared also. Typical features such as the unit mounting of the gearbox, single dry-plate clutch, spiral-bevel rear axle and semi-elliptic springing all round were embodied. By 1931 pressure-feed lubrication was accompanied by added power, better brakes, a lighter clutch, dropped frame and extra leg-room - at £150 the Junior was very good value. A unique type of body was used on the Junior Special, a four-seater special with a larger 972 cc ohc engine, priced at £185.

Nine (1932–39)

The Junior Special engine found itself powering a brand-new chassis which owed little to the Junior. An aluminium-panelled coachbuilt body of larger dimensions was erected on the new Nine chassis, equipped with extensive interior fittings and high-quality appointments. The 972 cc engine approached the 'ideal' configuration in its overhead camshaft, hemispherical combustion spaces and inclined valves; two large bearings supported a robust crankshaft, carrying steel connecting rods and aluminium slotted-skirt pistons. Full pressure lubrication was included, a hot-spot manifold and flexible mounting. Simple but effective clutch and gearbox designs further enhanced the £159 saloon.

By 1934 the two-seater, tourer and saloon versions of the Nine were all listed at £162, a 'de luxe' tourer and saloon also being offered in cream and black. As for the 1935 season the Nine Le Mans chassis sported two-seater, four-seater and coupe bodywork, a Special Speed model costing £225, ten pounds more than the two-seater and coupe. Lively performers, the Le Mans series could attain 70 mile/h, or in Special Speed trim 80 mile/h, or as a £525 Le Mans Replica 90 mile/h. A fifteen-gallon tank formed part of the latter car's specification, and all Singer sports models had hydraulic brakes. The trusty 972 cc ohc engine propelled all these worthy sports cars. For an extra ten pounds the Singer 'Fluidrive' fluid flywheel could be had in the closed 9 hp cars, plus ifs on the £199 'de luxe' saloon and £230 drop-head coupe.

A new policy led to withdrawal from sports car manufacture late in 1937, perhaps influenced by the controlling interest of the Rootes Group. The Nine became the Bantam, a small saloon closely resembling the Morris Eight, the Popular Saloon version selling for £135 in 1936, rising to £139-10s in 1938. The Bantam could attain 57 mile/h, 0-50 mile/h acceleration through the gears taking 33.6 seconds; 33-38 mpg could be obtained. The 1938-season Bantam had a new 1074 cc three-bearing engine, and a year later a redesigned bonnet and radiator were added, the out-moded curved back being

1934 Singer 9hp Le Mans Two Seater competing in the Lawrence Cup Trial of 1934. A. T. K. Debenham is the driver

1935 Singer 1½-litre Le Mans Speed Model

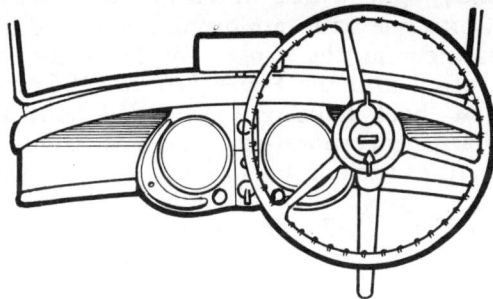

1936 Super Nine Saloon

1935 Singer 9hp Le Mans Two Seater at Brooklands for a competition event. J. L. Chappell sprints to the cockpit in an engine starting test

retained. At £149-10s the Bantam was the only ohc-engined small, cheap saloon on the market in 1939.

Ten (1930–32 and 1937–39)

Fitted with a 1261 cc engine, the £225 Singer Ten of 1930 closely followed the specification of the Junior outlined above. By 1931 improvements were made to the clutch, generator mounting, transmission, carburation and brakes. The four-door saloon was withdrawn a year later.

Reappearing under the Rootes aegis for the 1938 season, both Popular Saloon and Super Saloon versions, at £169-10s and £189 respectively, were offered, powered by a 1185 cc 35 bhp ohc engine. Subtle streamlining of the body, spoked disc wheels and the like, brought it into line with fashionable trends and its larger partners in the range. By 1939 the car had evolved into the Super Ten at £195, its flared 'fast' back housing a concealed boot and the chassis incorporating many desirable modern features such as a four-speed synchromesh gearbox, double-action shockabsorbers and Lockheed hydraulic brakes.

Eleven (1934–36)

The Singer Co made much of the fact that their 11 hp Airstream model was the first mass-produced 'all-streamline' car. Close in outer appearance to the Chrysler Airflow of the same era, with a curvy, flowing body devoid of running boards and fronted by a 'waterfull' radiator grille, the Airstream could be purchased for £300. Outward novelty failed, however, to sustain sales for more than a brief period and it was withdrawn at the end of 1935.

In contrast, the conventional Eleven saloon body housed, as well as the 1384 cc ohc engine, independent front suspension and Fluidrive transmission. A thoroughly businesslike model with well-louvred bonnet, 'hare-lipped' radiator shell, and bodywork akin to the Wolseley Nine, the Eleven saloon cost £245 or £50 more in sports saloon guise. A constant-mesh gearbox and hydraulic brakes were other features. A Popular Saloon and De Luxe Saloon were listed in 1936 at £215 and £230 respectively.

Twelve (1932–34 and 1936–39)

The early Twelve was arrived at by installing a four-cylinder 1441 cc engine in the chassis of the six-cylinder Fourteen. At £199, it was felt the car's ruggedness would have particular appeal to the overseas market.

The £225 Twelve of 1936 was a five-seater saloon with wide doors and dual cloth-and-leather upholstery, of contemporary design. An attractive four-seater drop-head coupe version sold originally at £265, continuing in production for the 1938 season at £279; a standard saloon and Super Saloon were also offered. By 1939 the Super Twelve saloon, at £249, embodied a curved radiator grille, flared 'fast' back, Vaumol hide upholstery, a Bluemel telescopic steering column, full interior equipment and 'windtone' horns. The engine developed a useful 43 bhp and combined the flexibility of a 'six' with the economy of a 'four'.

1½-litre (1934–36)

An October 1934 *Motor* road test on a £375 Le Mans two-seater recorded a best timed speed of 84 mile/h. The three-carburetter six-cylinder 1493 cc engine was found quiet and tractable, yet could accelerate the car from a standstill to 70 mile/h in 30 seconds. Bodied in the popular and conventional open sports form with sweeping front wings, 'cut away' doors, folding screen and twin spare wheels, the 1½-litre Le Mans offered exciting performance coupled with flexibility and ease of control. Its hydraulic brakes could bring it to a halt from 30 mile/h in 30 feet, and an unladen weight of 19 cwt gave, when driven hard, a fuel consumption of 21.8 mpg.

Overhead-camshaft engines of any vintage are worthy of respect, and those powering the Singer range represent a batch of high-efficiency

1934 Singer 11hp Airstream Saloon.
The bandleader Jack Payne bought
fourteen Airstreams, all finished in the
same colour, for the members of his band

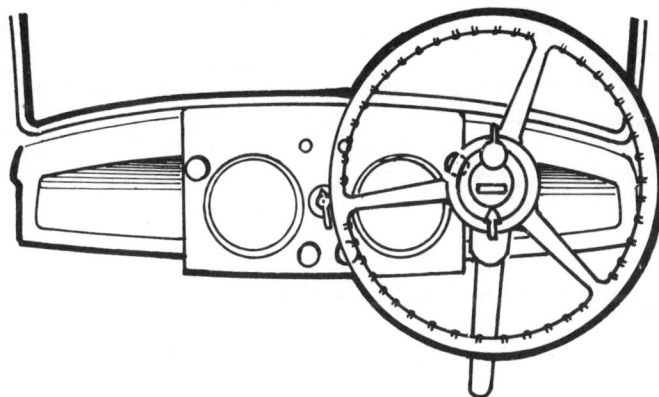

1938 Ten Saloon

designs. Hydraulic brakes on many of the models afford extra safety and the ifs systems on some versions contribute greatly to a more comfortable ride than is experienced in many prewar light cars. The Le Mans cars are, of course, out-and-out sports machines, and enviable acquistions.

Singer Owners' Club: D.C.Freeth, 31 Rivershill, Watton-at-Stone, Hertford, Herts. Watton-at-Stone 517.

Squire

A schoolboy design for a 'dream car', a hasty but brilliant apprenticeship with Bentley and MG, a cottage workshop and carbuilding enterprise founded on a mere £6000 capital, the construction of seven *creme de la creme* sports cars priced at over £1000, a brief flash of publicity at Brooklands, rapid liquidation, and the early and tragic death of the designer-romantic in the Blitz - such are the ingredients of the legendary Squire saga.

1½-litre (1934–36)

Even as a boy, Adrian Morgan Squire's obsession with his concept of 'the perfect sports car' proved so dominant that he was able, at 16, to draw up plans for the projected car to such a degree of accuracy that his early vision crystallized nine years later in virtually identical form to the brittle, pencil outlines of his youthful sketches. As early, then, as 1926 the Squire 1½-litre was fully conceived both in outward guise and in the more intimate details of its mechanical specification. Minutiae such as the engine capacity of 1496 cc and the provision of a dynamotor for starting, were ultimately to be found in the finished *beau ideal* - the Squire engine was in fact of 1496 cc and equipped with a Rotax dynamotor, impressively mounted on the nose of the crankshaft.

Such clarity of vision in one so young is evidence of A.M.Squire's colossal inherent gift for car design - down virtually to the last detail, the finished prototype was an exact realization of the young boy's inspired, and somewhat romantic, 'dream'. Yet in the hard-headed world of business, particularly the business of selling specialized cars, romanticism tempered by a degree of realism was called-for in the unstable material climate of the mid-30s. Squire had relied on the premise that top-quality merchandise, instantly recognizable as such, would naturally sell, no matter at how high a price. This fallacy unfortunately led to the collapse of his magnificent yet still-born 'miniature revolution'. Even HRG, founded about the same time, faced huge odds in getting underway; with far more experience and much more capital it remained 'hard going' for them, ultimate liquidation being postponed as late as 1956. It appeared that one could be 'too good'.

Squire moved to a cottage in Remenham Hill, Henley-on-Thames, in 1931. Behind him lay brief spells at Faraday House as an electrical engineering student, at Bentleys, and with the MG Car Company; his obvious restlessness with marking time coming to a head in the opening of Squire Motors Ltd, with a workshop behind the cottage and showrooms at 52 Bell Street, Henley. G.F.A. Manby-Colgrave, an old schoolboy chum, later to prove himself as a capable racing driver, and Reginald Slay were the other two co-directors; with Squire at 21, Manby-Colgrave aged 20 and Slay an 'elderly' 26, the Squire Motors 'board' must have been one of the most youthful ever. Slay acted as salesman, while a newcomer, Percy Kemish (an ex-Bentley man) was enlisted as foreman for the Remenham Hill works. By the spring of 1934 the prototype Squire, built by the new Squire Car Manufacturing Company, was being road-tested around Henley wearing untidy temporary bodywork and its very imposing and characteristic Maserati-styled radiator hidden from public gaze by sticky tape. The basic chassis, at once impressive in its strength and excellence of specification, was displayed during the summer of the same year at the Bell Street showrooms, and orders invited.

For one's £1220, what did one get in return? On the swb or lwb chassis was erected a Vanden Plas two- or four-seater body of superlative quality and workmanship. The extremely rugged cruciform-braced chassis formed the mounting for a 1½-litre R1 Anzani high-performance engine of four-cylinder dohc type, supercharged at 10 lb/in^2. Ignition was by coil, and carburation via a large-bore SU unit. A clutchless Wilson preselector gearbox plus ENV rear axle provided the transmission, a choice of ratios being available; Rudge Whitworth wire wheels were swivelled at the front by a Marles Weller steering-box and equipped all round with massive 15 1/8 in.-diameter brake drums, the brakes being of Lockheed hydraulic actuation. Surmounting the finely-engineered engine was the sloping wide-sided Squire radiator, heavily chromed and slatted and of 'V' configuration. Below it jutted the dynamotor, providing silky starting, and adjacent to it huge Marchal chromed headlamps. Suspension was by conventional leaf springs coupled with Houdaille hydraulic shockabsorbers, thermostatically controlled.

Early in 1935 the first coachbuilt two-seater body was married to the prototype chassis. It was finished in light blue with silver upholstery, the latter distinguishing colour being echoed in the gleaming metal dashboard burnished in circular patterns. From the neat cockpit, fully instrumented and dominated by a large-diameter Bluemel steering wheel, one gazed out along the lengthy tapering bonnet to the glistening radiator and its Squire-built quick-release filler cap, partnered at either side by large sweeping wings protruding an apt distance ahead of the radiator slats and headlamps. A folding windscreen, heavily chromium-plated, formed a frame for this attractive picture. To the rear of the brief rear-hinged doors lay a beautifully

proportioned sloping back, curving gracefully down to the trailing edges of the close-fitting rear wings, capaciously faired-in at the stern. Without interrupting the downwards rear sweep, two hinged panels concealed stowage for the hood and a fairly large boot. Bumpers were noticeably absent.

Few though they were, prospective customers saw, on lifting the well-louvred bonnet, an impressive and powerful engine, its inlet manifold and crankcase breather caps bearing the Squire 'S' motif. The name Anzani was never included in publicity literature, but in fact Squire did not design the engine himself. Slight modifications were, however, carried out under his direction; the fitting of roller tappets, and adaptations to the cylinder-head gasket and mounting-bolts were found necessary, the latter due to the higher stress set up by supercharging. Twin water pumps, but no fan, provided cooling - the engine was known to boil at low road speeds.

The train of gears driving the camshafts, wide tappet clearances, plus the whine of the Roots-type David Brown supercharger, all made for a noisy engine. But to compensate, this '12/110' power unit released some 110 bhp at 5000 rev/

1935 Squire 1½-litre with Vanden Plas bodywork, chassis No. X103

min. Since each Squire was sold with a BARC 100 mile/h certificate, top speed must have been nearer the 110 mile/h mark. Acceleration from 0-70 mile/h took merely 15 seconds, and Squire's self-designed brakes could bring the car from 30 mile/h to a halt in a distance of only 23 feet! Low slung, and with excellent adhesion on corners taken even at 70 mile/h, the Squire 1½-litre was all-in-all just about the last word in fast touring cars of the era.

But it just did not sell. In order to attract publicity, Squire decided to equip their fourth chassis with a high-compression engine and single-seater body, and entered some events held at Brooklands in 1935. Driven by Luis Fontes, the *monoposto* Squire racing car unfortunately broke its crankshaft during the British Empire Trophy Race held on July 6th, after completing only nine laps. Then, in September, the car had to retire from the BRDC's 500-mile race with a fractured chassis and fuel tank, although at the instant the failure occurred Fontes was leading his class. In October, Fontes, in the Squire, was placed third in a Second Mountain Handicap race, having averaged 70.8 mile/h. But the Squire concern never went racing again.

By fitting briefer bodywork made by Markham, the price of the swb two-seater was brought down to £995 late in 1935. More luxurious Ranalah bodywork was also offered, however, a four-seater being planned on the lwb chassis. Customers were to be tempted by the services of a Squire mechanic who, free of charge, would call every three months and retune and service their cars.

But by July 1936 the critical financial position made a creditor's meeting inevitable; seven cars had been built and only five sold over a two-year span. Upon liquidation, even some alloy castings for Squire's own six-cylinder 1½-litre engine were sold off for a few shillings, as were complete wheel assemblies. It was a bitter finale.

Despite the fact that the owner of a lwb Squire bought up the remaining chassis and components and kept production going for a brief spell, these Corsica-bodied cars being completed by late 1939, the original Squire 'flame' had flickered and died - also the grace of the earlier cars had vanished.

After returning as a member of W.O.Bentley's design team at Lagonda, Squire joined the Bristol Aeroplane Company, keeping in touch with the old Henley staff and planning a new

1934 Squire 1½-litre rolling chassis as displayed at the Bell Street, Henley showrooms during the summer of that year

Another view of the 1935 Vanden Plas-bodied Squire

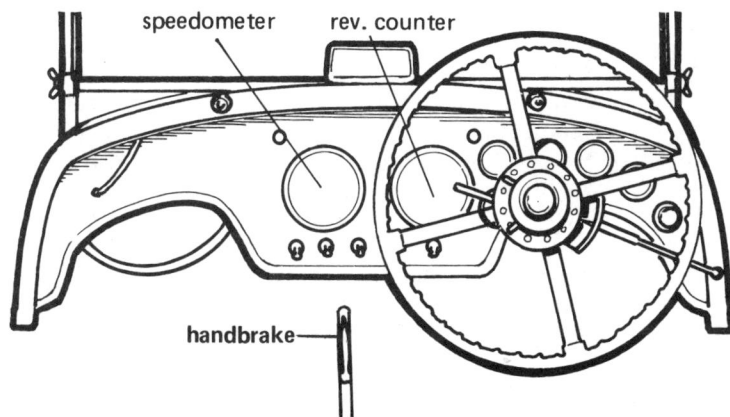

speedometer   rev. counter

handbrake

1936 1½-litre Markham-bodied Four seater Tourer

postwar enterprise. He was tragically killed in an air-raid on Bristol on 20th September 1940. At thirty, A.M.Squire was ready to put his 'teething troubles' as a businessman behind him and, as a designer, potentially destined to become a leader in postwar motoring development; as fate would have it, that was not to be.

The photographs illustrating this section are of the first production model, chassis number X103, first owned by G.F.A.Manby-Colegrave and registered as JB 5568. It is now in America, as are two other cars; two remain in Britain and one is in South Africa. The Luis Fontes single-seater was dismantled. As the epitome of sporting cars of the era, the Squire was more a symbol of one man's ideal than a viable proposition, even among the wealthier sections of the motoring public. It was an inspiration rather than an investment then; today it is both.

S.S.

Comparing a humble motorcycle sidecar with the latest Jaguar XJ-12 would seem like a comparison between a rowing-boat and the QE2, but in actual fact, if we look back through the history of the coachbuilder's art we find that it was just such a 'small acorn' as building sidecars that eventually could yield such a 'great oak' as Jaguar Cars Ltd. Back in the Twenties, William Lyons was running a small workshop in Blackpool called Swallow Sidecars, hand-building smart, tasteful 'chairs' for the motorcycle fraternity. Such experience naturally led on to the fabrication of special coachbuilt car bodies to suit the basic chassis that were at that time freely offered by the motor manufacturers. As luck would have it, the new Swallow saloon constructed on the Austin Seven chassis proved extremely popular - by this time the firm, now called the Swallow Coachbuilding Company, had moved to fresh pastures at Foleshill in Coventry, and orders for the Austin Swallow were coming thick and fast. The models of 1930 and 1931 were at once distinctive in their tastefulness of style; the smoothness of line, from the slightly-angled cowled radiator through the well-proportioned two-tone saloon body to the individual rounded back, was something new in coachbuilding. More than just another 'special' body, the Swallow, barely recognizable as an Austin, symbolized the emergence of a new and very imaginative designer, one who would not be content for long merely to drape his ideas around the limitations of a seven horse-power 'letter-A' frame.

S.S. II 10 and 12 (1932–36)

Inevitably, in 1932, 'the buds blossomed' in the form of a brand new enterprise, a sports car of purely 'Swallow' concept. Immediately a sensation, the first model, the S.S.1, bore to stunning effect the individual stamp of genius. By arrangement Swallow were supplied with engines and chassis units by the Standard Motor company, and the very long tapering bonnet of the S.S. 1 concealed a powerful reworked six-cylinder engine of alternatively 16 or 20 hp supported by a rugged cruciform-pattern chassis underslung at the rear. The occasional-four body, with its high waistline, long flowing wings, large wire wheels and very neat rear trunk was dominated at the front by a characteristically suave V-angled radiator set well back behind the leading edges of the front wings and complemented by huge Lucas P170 headlamps. The S.S. magic was born.

By 1933 a smaller-engined counterpart, the S.S. II, was exhibited, virtually a scaled-down version of the S.S. 1 but retaining in essence all that characterized its big brother. It was powered by a tuned version of the Standard Little Nine engine fitted with aluminium pistons, duralumin con-rods, a special cylinder head and downdraught carburetter. Like the S.S. 1, the driving position and visibility of the S.S.II were excellent, its occasional-four body having a somewhat shorter bonnet. Decked in such colours as Nile blue, carnation red, apple green or primrose complemented by black wings and roof, the new 'pint-sized' S.S. was offered at the extremely attractive price of £210. A well-furnished leather interior, highly accurate steering, powerful brakes and a maximum speed of 60 mile/h made the 9 hp version eminently desirable to the sporty young men of 1933, for it could also offer 31 mpg.

S.S. Cars Ltd, (Standard Swallow or Swallow Sports - it remains a debateable point even today) was formed in 1934. By this time the factory had been enlarged by 300 per cent so as to attempt to cope with the number of orders that were flooding in. The S.S.II of 9 hp was superceded by two new models, the Ten and the Twelve, the original engine capacity rising from 1005 cc to 1343 or 1608 cc, flexible engine mountings being provided and RAG downdraught carburetters standardized. But most important, the somewhat primitive and not very rigid Standard Nine chassis frame was given cruciform centre-bracing and underslung at the rear, the front and rear track also being widened. To complement the new engines, both saloon, coupe, and later, open four-seater versions of the

1935 S.S. II 12hp Saloon. The 10hp version employed the same body

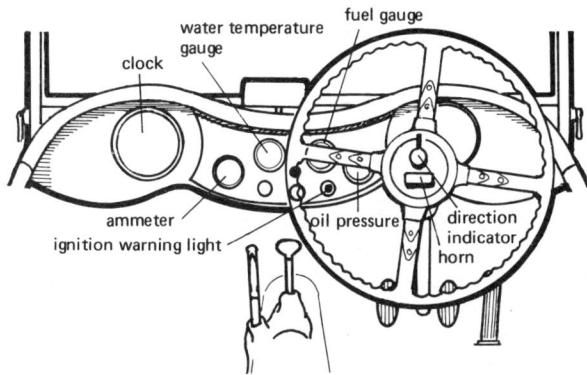

1935 S.S. II Open Four Seater

Ten and Twelve were available, the 10 hp saloon being priced at £265 and the 12 hp saloon at £270, the coupe versions being £5 cheaper in each case.

The open versions were particularly handsome and beautifully-proportioned in the classic 'British' format of longish tapering bonnet, open front wings, a neat functional two-seater cockpit and graceful tail (upon which the angled spare wheel was mounted). Coupled with a fold-flat windscreen, wire wheels and a hood folding flush with the top line of the body, the S.S.II 10 and S.S.II 12 two-seater epitomized the best in tasteful sporting light cars. There was also a distinct sense of 'rightness' about the saloons, their graceful body shape being married to well-appointed comfortable interiors. A new radiator with high shoulders and tapering sides fronted an engine compartment housing power units with 6.2 to 1 compression 1-1 ratio cylinder heads, free-flow manifolding and polished combustion chambers and ports. The worm-and-nut steering

box gave way to one of Marles Weller cam-and-lever pattern and synchromesh was provided on second, third and top gear, a nicely placed remote gear lever fitting snugly into the palm of the driver's hand. Powerful Bendix duo-servo brakes were retained, retardation from 30 mile/h to zero being accomplished in 27 feet; as for attainable speeds, in a *Light Car* test an S.S.II 10 saloon took 27.4 seconds to travel a standing quarter-mile, achieving a speed of 61.23 mile/h, petrol consumption being 27 mpg.

'No change' was S.S. policy for the 1936 season excepting an Airline saloon on the S.S.1 chassis. The coupe versions of the Ten and Twelve were dropped, however, alternative versions being the four-light saloon and open sports four-seater, prices remaining unchanged. The frames were further stiffened and better shockabsorbers fitted. Twin SU carburetters and a compression ratio of 7.1 uprated the power by 2 bhp; a thermostat was also included to prevent over-cooling.

SS 1½-litre Jaguar (1936–37)

The name 'Jaguar' now enters the picture in that for the 1936 season a new series of SS Jaguar models was introduced, the smallest of which was the 1½-litre, a scaled-down version of the 2½-litre model. Attempts to modernize the S.S. image resulted in a more flowing line, echoed again as late as the postwar Mk V saloon.

The imposingly long, straight-tapered bonnet and high waistline of the S.S. 1 and II models was modified in the Jaguar saloons; less angularity and greater homogeneity of form was apparent. The classic tall radiator, too, was simplified; the 'helmet' wings, though still bulbous were more close fitting, and the whole of the four-light bodywork was smoothened and blended. Only in the open four-seater of 2½-litres were traces of the S.S.1 still discernible. Interior finish was of course, still superlative, the facia being of French walnut, upholstery in Vaumol hide and a good driving position offered, allied with much comfort for the driver and his passengers. Unlike the ohv 2½-litre, the four-door 1½-litre Jaguar saloon had to make do with side-valves, the S.S.II 10 and 12 models continuing in production unchanged as two-door saloons, and the 1½-litre and Twelve sharing the same engine. At £285, the 1½-litre car could, given time, reach 70 mile/h, the *Motor* test team finding that 0-40 mile/h took 13 seconds in third gear, while the standing quarter-mile took 24 seconds. Perhaps it was the massive cross-braced underslung frame and the voluminous pressed-steel body increasing the total weight of the car to 21 cwt, which overloaded the somewhat inadequate side-valve engine. Now fitted with a Solex carburetter, it could deliver 50 bhp at 4000 rev/min, but the time of 33 seconds taken for 0-60 mile/h through the gears indicates clearly enough just how over-bodied the car was. Compared, in fact, to the SS 100 and the 2½-litre series, the smaller sv cars were, from here on, always unspectacular and left in the shade - an ohv head and briefer body could have transformed the performance of the 1½-litre. Reversion to worm-and-nut steering was, however, accompanied by the fitting of Girling brakes, their highly efficient roller-and-wedge action

being coupled with 12 in. internal-diameter finned alloy brake drums, giving a Tapley meter reading of 96% from 20 mile/h and 86% from 40 mile/h, the corresponding stopping distance from 20-0 mile/h being 14 ft - an excellent figure. Synchromesh on second, third and top meant effortless gear-changing, and if you were prepared to wait, a cruising speed of 60 mile/h could, once reached, be held indefinitely, the engine proving very quiet in operation and also flexible at low speeds. Luvax hydraulic shock-absorbers contributed greatly to the overall comfort of the ride.

For the 1937 season the Ten and Twelve saloons were withdrawn, the 1½-litre representing the smaller-capacity range at £295. Perhaps the firmly established following for the MG Midgets and other 1½-litre open sports cars dissuaded S.S. from developing this field further themselves. As it was, they tended to concentrate more on large cars, the SS 100 open two-seater with a top speed of nearly 100 mile/h offering ample evidence that technical means was there, if not applied to the smaller engines. The transition from light cars to those of larger size

The impressive radiator view of the SS Jaguar

and higher engine-capacity began to take shape in the 1938 season with the introduction of a 3½-litre SS Jaguar model. At this time the 1½-litre saloon cost £298 or £318 in drop-head coupe form. In order to extract more power, however, the nominally 1½-litre engine was re-designed in 1775 cc ohv form, developing 70 bhp. A more massive box-section frame now formed the foundation of these two models, neither of which could be described as light cars.

In sum, the early S.S.II cars represent the peak of achievement in the light-car field by Swallow Coachbuilding, later S.S. Cars Ltd. Although scaled-down versions of the S.S.1, the

available power from their finely-tuned side-valve engines could impart a lively performance due to the lighter weight of bodywork - the S.S.II 12 open four-seater perhaps representing the most desirable model. Although much more comfortable, the later over-bodied 1½-litre saloons lacked the flair and sparkle of the early years and were eclipsed by their more powerful brothers, which, going from strength to strength, culminated in Sir William Lyons' masterpiece, the XK120 of 1948.

S.S. Register: Mrs P.A. Mayfield, 138 Kingsway, West Wickham, Kent. 01-462-7572.

1937 SS Jaguar 1½-litre Saloon owned by Tony Lake

1937 SS Jaguar 1½-litre Saloon taking part in a prewar Welsh Rally

Standard

The Standard Motor Company of Canley, Coventry, earned a reputation with their Flying Standard series for building modern streamlined cars offering a good performance at a fair price. Prior to this, the Standard range had always stood for dependability; but livlier performance went hand-in-hand with their technical research throughout the decade. Sir John Black instigated useful liasons with new enterprises such as S.S. cars, as well as offering power units to old-established concerns such as the Morgan Motor Company. Like Vauxhall, Standards proved themselves adept at pioneering new techniques and new technologies, making considerable advances. Mass-production, of course, was inevitable and very necessary if cars were ever to come within the financial reach of the ordinary man; yet Standards could always be relied on also to offer something 'extra' with the package. 'Fast' backs and 'waterfall' grilles apart, a deal of very up-to-date engineering and design lay beneath the cellulose of many a trendy Flying Standard saloon.

Little Nine (1931–33), Nine (1934–36), Flying Nine (1937–39) and Eight (1939)

The Little Nine, introduced at the 1931 Motor Show, was a partner for the Standard Big Nine, a pre-1930 model with 1287 cc engine. Of 1005 cc sv four-cylinder form, the engine of the Little Nine could propel the car's 13 cwt at speeds of up to 57 mile/h. Excellent suspension, too, made the ride of the little six-light four-door saloon distinct from many of its small-capacity contemporaries, and this, coupled with very serviceable acceleration, was further allied to light and positive steering. A really hard push on the brake pedal could easily lock the wheels - a 1931 *Autocar* road test recording a stopping distance of only 29 feet from a speed of 30 mile/h. Acceleration from 10-30 mile/h in second gear took 7.4 seconds; there was a three-speed gearbox sporting a 'silent second' - unknown until then. That the Little Nine was

lively is evidenced when we compare the above figures with those of the 9 hp SS II, which shared the same engine. Intended as a sporting car, top speed of the SS II coupe was only a few mile/h more, nearer to 60 mile/h, in fact.

The Little Nine was easy to drive, automatic ignition advance-and-retard demanding no skill from an inexperienced driver, who might, in other similar small saloons, be expected to select the ignition advance 'by ear' for best hill-climbing and acceleration. The body was well finished, well furnished and roomy, particularly in the rear seats. In all, for the moderate price of £155 the 1931 Little Nine was excellent value, a well-propertioned small saloon that in overall effect belied its diminutive size. A two-tone colour scheme, light-coloured wire wheels and bright nave plates added further charm to the car's classic rounded back, upright tapering bonnet, and black wings linked by miniature running boards. An attractive double-bar bumper made, at the front, a distinctive accent below the high radiator, divided down its centre by a thin chromed strip. Parallel with the bumper, a curved bar linking the inside faces of the front wings bore the headlamps and an electric horn with brightly-plated grille. Besides a coupe priced at £175, a special saloon, at £169, offered such extras as hide upholstery, safety glass and special fittings. The *Autocar* described the Little Nine as " one of the outstanding cars" of the 1931 Olympia Motor Show.

By 1934 several new Standard models had been added to the range, and a single Nine model of 1052 cc introduced, the Big Nine evolving into the 1343 cc Standard Ten. Under a slogan "Built to Public Demand", typical advertisements listed sixteen new features on all models, among them roomier bodywork without foot wells, flexible engine mountings, better brakes, synchromesh on second, third and top gears combined with controlled free-wheeling, Startix automatic restarting, cross-braced frames, compensated voltage control, illuminated direction indicators that were self-cancelling, rubber Silentbloc spring-shackle bushes, and a concealed spare wheel and luggage grid. The standard saloon cost £135, whilst the

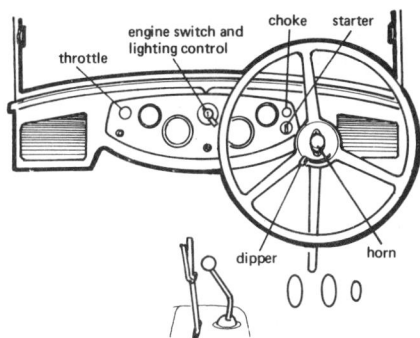

1931 Little Nine Saloon

1933 Standard Little Nine Saloon

1938 Standard Flying Eight Open Tourer

1939/40 Standard Flying Eight Saloon

Saloon de Luxe was listed at £152, the same figure purchasing the Tourer de Luxe.

For the 1935 season the Nine remained in four-door saloon form, varying in price from £165 to £185, according to specification, and for 1936 adopted the four-light format and £135 to £169 price range, the latter sum purchasing a four-door six-light Saloon de Luxe on the long-wheelbase chassis. A slightly sloping radiator with black slats and chromed rim made the Standards distinctive, as did groups of fine horizontal louvres along the bonnet sides; otherwise the Nine bore a certain coincidental resemblance to the Wolseley Nine, introduced in 1934, but for its rounded spare-wheel cover.

The first of the streamlined Flying Standards were introduced at the 1935 Motor Show, and a Flying Nine appeared for the 1937 season, the all-steel saloon offering added room, comfort and ease of entry coupled with higher power, this from a modified engine with an aluminium cylinder-head. A four-speed synchromesh gearbox, 'buoyant power' flexible engine mounting, forward weight distribution, seating within the wheelbase and Bendix-type brakes all made for a

good specification, and with the Flying Nine priced at £145 for the saloon or £10 more for the 'de luxe' version it was an attractive proposition. A new all-steel 'waterfall' type of radiator grille was innovated for 1938; the sum of £152-10s would have bought the saloon, and £10 more its 'de luxe' version. Independent front suspension was added in 1938 to certain models, among which was the new Eight, a tourer version selling for only £125. A transverse front spring and piston-type shockabsorbers gave a very smooth ride to this chubby little car, 45-48 mpg being claimed for it. A three-speed gearbox afforded the tourer a maximum speed of 63.5 mile/h, acceleration from 0-50 mile/h taking 28 seconds, and 10-30 mile/h 11.8 seconds in top and 7.3 seconds in second gear. A speed of over 60 mile/h, more than forty miles to the gallon and independent front suspension, all for just under £130, was exceptional value for the time. The £129 saloon was partnered by a 'de luxe' saloon at £139; also available was a Flying Nine saloon priced at £149 to £165, with a four-speed gearbox and capable of 62 mile/h plus 40 mpg.

Big Nine (1930–33), Ten (1934–36) and Flying Ten (1937–39)

Similar in overall appearance to the Little Nine, the narrow bore and long stroke (63.5 x 102 mm) of the Big Nine's engine enabled it to be taxed at 9 hp despite a total capacity of 1287 cc. Inherently good low-speed pulling power also proved a useful asset. The divided radiator was new in 1930, and symbolized a host of detail improvements. The Popular four-seater fabric saloon was offered at £195, while a coachbuilt saloon cost £225. Alternatively there were the Special models, combining the provision of a 'twin top' four-speed gearbox with hide upholstery and safety glass, and priced at £245. The Big Nine was a fairly sizeable car of six-light four-door layout, and remained in production until 1933, the 1932 season bringing a rear fuel tank, improved springing, better steering, quieter gears and more powerful brakes. The 1932 saloon cost £205, a special saloon being priced at £255 and a close-coupled coupe by Mulliners costing £245. A preselector gearbox could be fitted to the saloon for £25. Two- or four-seater tourer versions were priced at £195. Metal panelling was standardized.

The 1343 cc sv Ten for the 1934 season included all the new features described for the Nine. A year later, the 10-12 hp Speed Saloon and streamlined Speed Saloon became available, built on the Ten chassis. The latter, called the Speedline Saloon, was a gracefully styled 'airstream' model distinctive in its 'nose up' attitude and sweeping lines terminating in a sharply-angled 'fast' back. Offered at £250, it had a 12 hp 1609 cc engine with an aluminium cylinderhead, higher compression ratio, twin carburetters and higher rear-axle ratio. This and the Speed Saloon were claimed to attain 70 mile/h and accelerate from a standstill to 50 mile/h in 16 seconds - a commendable enough performance. The Speed Saloon was externally indistinguishable from an ordinary Ten and cost £245. In 1936 the sole 10 hp Saloon de Luxe cost £189.

For the 1937 season the Ten became a Flying Standard model and in 1938 an all-steel grille distinguished these from the earlier models.

1929/30 Standard 10hp Teignmouth Saloon with metal-panelled body

Little Twelve (1932–34) Big Twelve (1932–34)

A pair of six-cylinder 12 hp models, of 1337 cc, were introduced in 1932 to span the range between the Big Nine and the 2054 cc Sixteen. Smoother running was afforded, the Little Twelve sharing the same body as the Nine, whereas the Big Twelve was larger and could even be equipped, at £240, with a preselector gearbox. Prices of the Little Twelve ranged from £189 for tourer or saloon versions, up to a Special Saloon at £204 or a coachbuilt Mulliner-bodied close-coupled saloon at £215. By 1932 all Standard chassis had a wider track, a grouped lubrication panel under the bonnet, and could support roomier bodies; trap-doors in the rear floor-boards opened to reveal useful stowage space. The Big Twelve saloon and tourer both cost £215.

Both a four- and six-cylinder Twelve were available for the 1934 season, the latter of 14 hp and priced at from £225 to £255, giving a more vivid performance. With the spread in popularity of radio in cars, 1935 witnessed the advent of the Twelve Radio Model, which at £285 incorporated a dashboard-controlled Philco five-valve superhet radio set. In 1936 a rechristening took place: there was to be both a Light Twelve and Twelve, as well as the new 'fast'-back Flying Twelve - the forerunner of a whole series of Flying Standard models. The original 1936-season price of the Flying Twelve saloon was £259, but this was to drop some fifty pounds by 1939. A typical member of the Flying Standard range, the Flying Twelve embodied all the innovations described for the Flying Nine, plus the distinction of a curved 'fast' back, which gave the bigger-hp Flying models a unique and instantly recognisable appearance. A divided rear window composed of two half-oval panes further typified the Standard streamline aesthetic (and disregard for the benefits of an unrestricted rear view!)

An *Autocar* road test on a 1938-season Flying Twelve saloon, priced at £205, found the car "an excellent example" of the forward-looking trends reflected in the Flying series. Its acceleration and hill-climbing abilities were found " surprising" and the Twelve was "a pleasing car to drive slowly or quite fast, and one that can put up a decidedly useful average speed". An average cruising speed was found to be 50-55 mile/h, top speed being 68.7 mile/h. A mere 20.9 seconds was needed in accelerating from rest to 50 mile/h; a useful piece of performance was the acceleration from 20-40 mile/h - 9.3 seconds in third gear. As for the Bendix-Cowdrey brakes, these could stop the 20 cwt car from 30 mile/h in 35 feet on wet concrete, full pedal pressure not being required to achieve this result. A slick gearbox, light, accurate steering and firm roadholding made the Flying Twelve a pleasant car to drive, the suspension representing a successful compromise between sufficient firmness for stability and the degree of softness needed for rough surfaces. Other than the rear view, overall visibility was good, the driving position comfortable and the interior's leather trim pleasingly executed. In all, the new Twelve was lively, easy to drive and comfortable and at just over £200, good value.

The final season's price of the saloon remained unchanged, while the Saloon de Luxe cost £225 and a new drophead coupe £245. All these cars incorporated ifs and Luvax-Bijour chassis lubrication.

All prewar Standards are interesting, the older models naturally having the edge on charm and a pleasant degree of 'quaintness', as do all early-30s cars. The Flying Standards were revolutionary cars at the time, the rear aspect in particular stamping them as individualistic and finding an echo in the postwar Jowett Javelin (the latter albeit sired by Lincoln Zephyr out of Lancia Aprilia).

Perhaps the reader will be good enough to overlook the pun when asked, if enthusiastic for the marque, to 'keep the Standard flying'!

Standard Register: B. Blackwell, 11 Springfield Court, Linslade, Beds. Leighton Buzzard 4448.

1934 Standard Twelve Saloon

1937 Flying Standard Saloon De Luxe

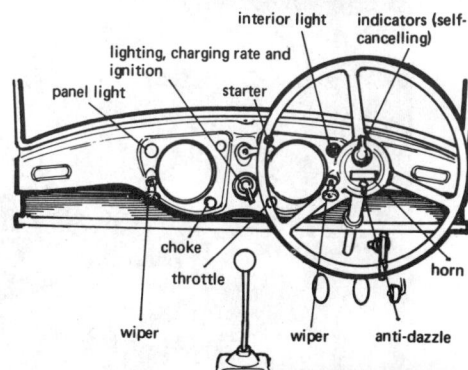

1936 Standard Flying Ten Saloon. The Flying Light Twelve shared the same bodywork

1939 Standard Flying Twelve Saloon

Sunbeam Talbot

As members of the Sunbeam-Talbot-Darracq combine in the Twenties, Sunbeam and Talbot have been lumped together here firstly because their close association was to result in the Sunbeam-Talbot merger of 1939, and secondly because the small number of light cars each produced does not warrant separate sections. The above amalgamation's decline at the close of the Twenties was reversed by the appointment of Georges Roesch as chief engineer; the result was some superlative Talbot models, among them the 65, a small sporting car which was later to be replaced by the Talbot 10. From the Sunbeam stable came the 12.8 hp Dawn, a luxury light car manufactured from 1933 to 1935.

Sunbeam Dawn (1933–35)

First displayed at the Motor Show of 1933, the Dawn saloon, priced at £485, was a logical extension of the Sunbeam luxury-car policy into the light car field. Coachbuilt bodywork, a very well-appointed interior and rugged chassis frame were prominent Sunbeam features; cruciform bracing, grouped chassis lubrication and ifs were added to the specification of the Dawn, as was a preselector gearbox.

The engine, of 4-cylinder ohv pattern, was of 1627 cc capacity and constructed largely of alloy. Flexible mountings prevented vibration from being transmitted to the chassis. A good performance was provided, despite the rather high gross weight, a top speed of over 60 mile/h being comfortably achieved, effective retardation being the product of hydraulic brakes.

By 1934 a choice of bodies - a four-light or six-light saloon - was available, the six-light version being of traditional concept with a rounded back, while the four-light saloon proved more distinctive in the prolonged downward sweep of its rear panel, a concealed lid to the luggage locker forming the spare wheel mounting. Both saloons were typical in most respects of the style of the era, a large well-slatted high 'V' radiator, heavily chromium-plated, fronting a long bonnet with well-louvred side panels, the large headlamps carried high upon a horizontal mounting-bar, all in heavy chrome. Wide sweeping wings, running-boards and wire wheels formed the lower complement to a high-waisted body, giving a wide narrow windscreen.

At the 1934 Show a manually-operated four-speed synchromesh gearbox was standardized, its remote gear lever in the centre of the floor being conveniently placed for the driver; both saloon versions were offered at £425.

Talbot 14/45 (1930–32)

Called the Scout, and in close-coupled four-seater sunshine saloon and Long Saloon versions, the Talbot 14/45 offered, at its original price of £395, a combination of Roesch's lively 1666 cc 6-cylinder ohv engine with light bodywork, giving a top speed of 65 mile/h. The Scout was an attractive car, high-waisted as was the fashion, its compact two-door body graced by capacious open mudguards and large-diameter wire wheels, the spare wheel being carried on the offside bonnet panel. This made possible the inclusion of a smooth, neat back blending well with the four-light window scheme, the roof rising from the waistline in a form not unreminiscent of the coupe.

Efficient brakes with large-diameter drums, and easy, accurate steering with a good lock, made manoeuvring in town very simple. A four-speed gearbox, operated by a right-hand gear lever, was fitted. Leather upholstery, wooden trim, and attention to every detail made the interior finish of high quality. The Long Saloon, on an lwb chassis, had coachbuilt bodywork.

Talbot 65 (1932–35)

The Rootes Group took over the London

1934 Talbot 65 Special Saloon

1935 Talbot 65 Four Light Saloon De Luxe

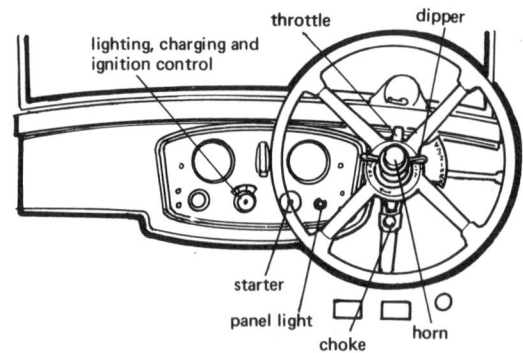

division of the Clement Talbot Company in 1935. From 1932 until that year, the British faction of Talbots continued to manufacture the 65 model, an engine similar to that of the 14/45 being fitted into a nicely-proportioned small saloon and coupe at the same price as the 14/45 - £395. A special saloon was offered in 1934 at £425, and a four-light or six-light Saloon De Luxe at £460. These two latter models incorporated the Talbot 'Traffic Clutch', a form of centrifugal clutch embodying a flywheel hollowed into a drum and within which two Ferodo-faced driving shoes were flung outwards, as crankshaft speed increased, by centrifugal force. The increasing friction between the shoes and the inside of the drum took up the drive, making starting fully automatic, without re-

course to a conventional clutch pedal. The Roesch-designed gearbox, also forming part of the transmission, was of a novel type, changing upwards automatically; only when a lower gear was needed did the selector lever have to be touched. A reversed freewheel maintained a positive engine connection on the over-run.

Like the Sunbeam, a high well-slatted radiator formed part of the Talbot image, with large chromed headlamps held close to it, mounted on a horizontal bar; wire wheels and a general 'sporting' air made Roesch's models attractive and distinctive, as well as good performers. A top speed of 68 mile/h was attainable in the 65 Saloon de Luxe, 0-50 mile/h taking 31 seconds, and 22 mpg being afforded. On a dry surface the car could come to a halt from 30 mile/h in 33 feet.

Talbot and Sunbeam-Talbot 10 (1936—39)

With the temporary disappearance of the Sunbeam concern, the Talbot design team, in close liason with the Rootes Group, launched a new model, the BE 10, a development of the well-received, but discontinued, Hillman Aero Minx. A modified version of the Minx's 1185 cc sv engine, with higher compression ratio and Zenith downdraught carburetter, was fitted into a small, neat pressed-steel Sports Saloon, combining something of the 'Minx-to-be' with a frontal treatment synthesized from scaled-down elements of both the Talbot and the Sunbeam. A pillarless design, the Sports Saloon's side windows, while dividing at the door posts, in fact butt-jointed on closing into a continuous piece giving one long uninterrupted oval window, very like that of the Humber 'Vogue' saloon of 1934-37. Now far closer to the Rootes' concept, a more orthodox chassis with

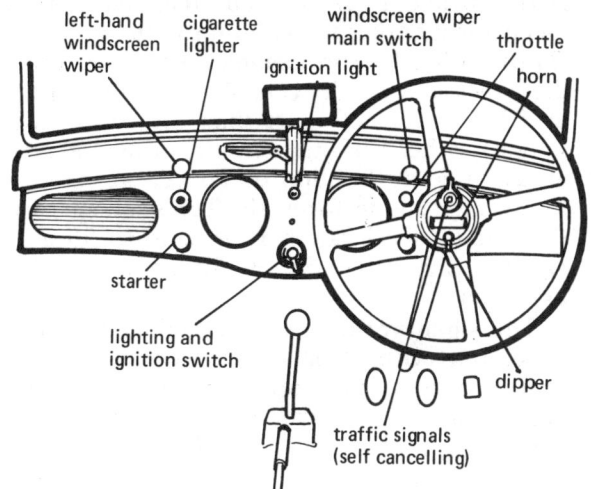

1937 Ten Sports Saloon

1935 Talbot Ten Saloon, outside Bush House in London

leaf springing front and rear and Bendix mechanical brakes served to unite the design; the 'Traffic Clutch', for example, was fitted only in the larger six-cylinder cars. Priced in saloon form at £265 (only £20 more than the 'Minx' sports saloon), other variants were the drophead coupe at £295 and the Sports Tourer at £260. In four-seater coupe form, the Ten's top speed was 68 mile/h, acceleration from zero to 50 mile/h taking 23 seconds; 28-30 mpg could be expected.

The open versions were certainly dashing in style, but with their rather workaday engines could never put up a really exhilarating performance - this was to come after the war, when bigger ohv units of really healthy power output were somehow squeezed into bodies little larger than the Ten!

Heralding new trends, the cars on the Talbot stand at the 1936 Show augured a more colourful 1937 with the introduction of their 'jewelessence' finishes - early types of metallic cellulose with evocative names like 'steel dust' and 'gun-metal'. The Sports Saloon and four-seater Sports Tourer were now £248, the drophead coupe costing another £30. The characteristic 'Talbot boot' made its appearance at this time - a rear end that can only be likened to a parallelogram-box shape with smoothened edges and corners; this was, however, not part of every design. In an *Autocar* road test of September 17th, 1937, the Sports Saloon was found to be a brisk performer, able to cruise indefinitely at 50 mile/h. Maximum speed was 68 mile/h (equal to the earlier 65, a heavier car with a larger ohv engine), and coupled with 30 - 33 mpg, the Ten was both lively and economical. From a standstill a speed of 50 mile/h through the gears could be reached in 22 seconds, while the car could be brought to a halt from 30 mile/h in 32 ft.

'No change' was the theme for the 1938 season, the Sports Saloon being described by the *Autocar* as "unquestionably one of the best-looking small cars in existence" - as indeed it was, wearing its newly-acquired wheel covers, and retaining that long side-window. The Sports Tourer, too, now had covered wheels, seating four and incorporating excellent all-weather equipment all for £248, seven pounds less than the foursome drophead-coupe.

The last prewar Motor Show, of 1938, hearalded the formation of the Sunbeam-Talbot enterprise and saw its first light car, the Sunbeam-Talbot Ten, as virtually a continuation of Talbot practice. By this time the name Sunbeam, as symbolizing a separate entity within the Rootes Group, was no more. The Ten's open versions remained little changed, while the Sports Saloon lost its long window at

1937 Talbot Ten Sports Tourer

the side and went into four-door six-light form. Engine modifications helped the power, but cruciform chassis-bracing was not included as in the 3-litre cars. A new 'Cellustra' instrument panel, with instruments marked both in metric and English figures, added a brighter touch to the interior, as did 'jewelessence' colours to the bodywork.

For the final season the price of the Sports Tourer was increased by a mere £2; the Sports Saloon could be purchased for £265 and the drop-head coupe for £285.

Roesch's cars are prized nowadays (there is a 1934 105 Sports Saloon at Beaulieu), and light versions such as the 14/45 and 65 will also be small enough for a really detailed restoration. As for the Talbot Ten, here again this represents a compact little car of economical type, its simpler sv engine proving quieter and less fussy to the relative novice, overhaul of its orthodox clutch and gearbox proving straightforward. As with most 'old cars', the soundness of the relatively 'ancient' chassis is of paramount importance.

Sunbeam Talbot Darracq Register:
F. Gray, 27 Mowat Court, Hightown, Liversedge, Yorks.
Sunbeam Talbot Alpine Register (1935 on): D.J.Elsbury, 12 Everest Road, Fishponds, Bristol.

1939 Sunbeam-Talbot Ten Saloon

Triumph

"Expensive large cars in miniature" is how a 1930 *Autocar* magazine article described the Triumph range for 1931. Most noticeable was the high-revving engine of the 7 hp Super Seven, a lively unit employed to advantage in the Gnat sports two-seater; a pillarless four-door 12 hp saloon on the six-cylinder Scorpion chassis was extremely well appointed and finely finished.

By 1933 the Triumph Motor Company Ltd of Priory Street, Coventry had expanded their range, using Coventry Climax four- and six-cylinder ioe engines, and these power units were the motive force for such famous models as the Southern Cross and Gloria Monte Carlo.

A return to ohv format came in 1937 with the Dolomite and Vitesse series of fast tourers and roadsters, always well-finished and offering comfortable, spacious accommodation. By the end of the decade the hp-range of the Triumph stable had widened considerably, the smaller capacities having been discarded in favour of large engines capable of comfortably propelling the weightier payload of lavishly-equipped pressed-steel bodies and reinforced chassis.

Super series (1930–34)

First manufactured in 1927, the diminutive Super Seven, with its 832 cc four-cylinder sv engine lent itself to 'sports' modification, either in normal-capacity form plus Cozette super-charger or in supercharged 747 cc guise for international Class H competition. The standard coachbuilt saloon presented an attractive enough appearance, the 1930 model sporting distinctive ribbed radiator cappings and resting daintily on wire wheels. A four-seater tourer, a £167-10s two-seater, a £185 fabric saloon and Tickford saloon at £198 were also available - as was the Gnat beetle-backed two-seater sports, its very tall radiator and high prow contrasting with rather small wheels. Its price was £185.

Tested by the *Autocar* on January 24th 1930,

the Super Seven saloon was found to be "a very efficient car which gives the impression that it is well up to its work". Peak engine rev/min in the 5000-6000 range was at once noticeable but not obtrusive, a high cruising speed and smooth acceleration being attainable, even in top gear from a slow crawl. A maximum timed speed over the quarter-mile of 52.94 mile/h was obtained - a highly commendable figure for a 1930 8 hp car - the speedometer showing 57 mile/h on longer stretches. Good handling with light, positive steering was evidenced, the hydraulic brakes stopping the car in 32 feet from 30 mile/h. Instrumentation included a clock but not a fuel gauge. Pneumatic upholstery, a comfortably-furnished interior, fully-opening windscreen and other details made the Super Seven good value for money, the 35-40 mpg afforded proving an economical aspect of the engine's efficiency. The thin-shell radiator's ungainliness was remarked on, perhaps prompting the blanking-out of part of the core in 1931-season models.

A three-bearing ioe engine plus worm final drive was found in the 62 mile/h Super Nine of 1931, a capacity of 1018 cc being employed. Available as a four-door six-light saloon, this model was again finely fitted and well equipped. At the 1932 Motor Show the sv Super Eight appeared, an 832 cc model supplanting the Super Seven and offering a larger, wider chassis and improved suspension. Pillarless in layout, the interior was more roomy; there were Leveroll adjustable seats, a winding mechanism to work the sliding roof, an interior light and a rear tank feeding the carburetter via an Autovac. Saloon, two-seater and tourer versions cost £155. Also on the Triumph stand was the year-old Super Nine, a fully-equipped car offered in £189 saloon and black-and-green two-seater form. The four-door six-light saloon was capacious, the underslung worm drive enabling a low floor level to be used.

The year 1933 saw the birth of the Popular and De Luxe Ten, a 1122 cc ioe Coventry Climax engine supplying the power; a reduction of 1 mm in the bore gave, in 1934, a 1087 cc version rated at 9.5 hp and used to power open and closed models ranging from £198 to £225, all 'luxury cars in miniature'.

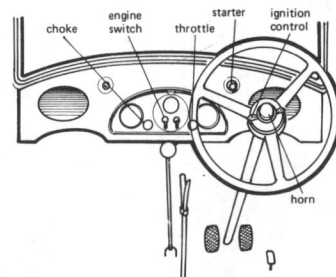

1930 Super Seven Saloon

1930 Triumph Super Seven Saloon
owned by E. H. Bavenstock

Scorpion (1930—33)

A 12/6 of 1202 cc capacity, this model featured a coachbuilt saloon body of two-door, or pillarless four-door design, again fully equipped in every detail. The main bearings of the six-cylinder sv engine were housed in a particularly robust ribbed casting. Very distinctive two-colour decor gave the Scorpion a smart appearance, the window frames being relief-painted and hence made to look larger, and a curved dark stripe, descending from the roof sides, gave a graceful *trompe l'oeil* effect against the rather hunch-backed rear outline. The sum of £237-10s purchased either saloon in 1930; at the 1931 Motor Show the Twelve Six family saloon was introduced also on the Scorpion chassis, more spacious coachwork being a new facet of each. The £210 Scorpion

de-luxe saloon now offered a four-speed gearbox, semi-elliptic rear springs and a rear tank, to which was added the standard fitting of hydraulic brakes and silent-running worm final drive. The Twelve Six saloon cost £198 in 1932, the body dimensions of the Super Nine being similar.

10 hp Southern Cross (1932—34)

A high-prow, low-slung four-seater sports car fitted with a four-cylinder ioe 1122 cc Climax engine, the Southern Cross proved immediately popular, and successful in competitive events including the Monte Carlo Rally. Again beautifully finished both inside and out, the bodywork shared, in common with several other small sports cars of the time, certain styling

1933 Triumph Southern Cross Open Four Seater owned by R. J. Broad

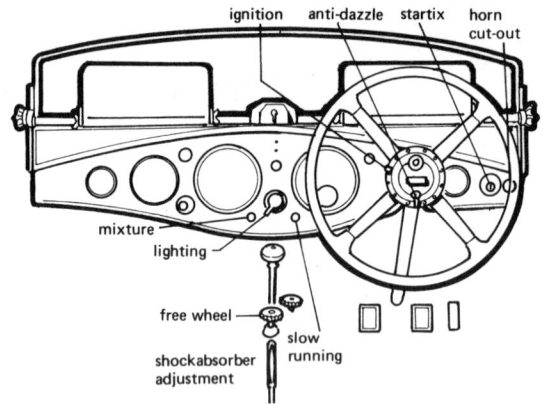

1935 Southern Cross Two Seater

features perhaps epitomized best in the Swallow bodies erected on the Wolseley Hornet Special chassis. The Southern Cross's high bonnet, head-lamps mounted on a curved cross-bar, sweeping front wings, fully-louvred valances, 'helmet' rear wings and so on, echoed in full the functional exuberance of the medium-priced small open cars designed at this time for semi-professional competition work. A handsome instrument panel bore large-diameter speedometer and rev-counter dials. At £225, the open four-seater was an attractive proposition. A green sports coupe version could be had for £260.

In 1934 the engine-capacity was reduced to 1087 cc - the car being then eligible for 1100 cc-class events.

Gloria series (1933–39)

"Triumph introduces Gloria - on stand 106", said advance Triumph publicity before the 1933 Olympia Motor Show. Not, in fact, merely a 1930s pin-up girl, 'Gloria' turned out to be a new range of cars with ioe Climax engines, smooth-running, powerfully braked, more beautiful in line, and all equipped with the then-fashionable freewheel, permitting a form of clutchless gear-preselection. Ten, twelve and fourteen horse-power versions, of 1087, 1232 and 1476 cc capacity respectively were offered, the last-mentioned a six-cylinder model in fact rated at 12.9 hp. All engines had a 90 mm stroke and varying bore. Considerable sophistication of line marked the Glorias as cars for the individualist, their flowing style and the 'rightness' of proportion of the Vitesse range with tuned engines making an excellent impression on the motoring scene. At first called a Speed Model, the name of the 12 hp Gloria Vitesse tourer was changed in mid-1934 to the Gloria Monte Carlo, the car incorporating special equipment, extreme gracefulness of line and twin spare wheels. Two Gloria Southern Cross models became available in 1934, also sporting machines, one with a 1232 cc power unit. Spiral-bevel final drive now formed part of the Gloria specification, as did semi-elliptic springing all round and the omnipresent hydraulic brakes. Prices for the 1934 season ranged from £285 for the saloon and Speed Model to £340 for a six-cylinder Special Saloon of 2-litre capacity. (Impressive though the Glorias were, the limelight was stolen at the 1934 Show by the 100 mile/h eight-cylinder dohc supercharged 2-litre Dolomite, an attractive two-seater super-sports machine priced at £1225.)

In October 1935 proof of the Gloria's reliability was shown in a 1700-mile endurance test. A 2-litre car, running non-stop for two twelve-hour periods averaged 70.1 mile/h over 1000 miles and 70.93 mile/h over 1500 miles. The 1936 Show included the exhibition of the Triumph Vitesse and Dolomite models as well as listing six cars in the Gloria 12 hp range, priced at from £268 to the £315 Special Foursome Coupe. The 1937-season Southern Cross cost £278.

By 1937 the Gloria range was cut back to a sole representative, the 1½-litre with 1496 cc ohv engine, this size of power unit also powering a few 1½-litre Dolomite versions, although in general the smaller Dolomite was of 1767 cc. In 1939 the 1496 cc New Twelve was introduced for 1939-40. Heavy bombing by the Luftwaffe reduced the Triumph works to mere rubble during the war, all plans and records being destroyed. Amalgamation with the Standard Motor Company came in 1946.

1934 Triumph 10hp Monte Carlo Sports Tourer owned by G. Binns

1939 Triumph Dolomite 14/60 Saloon. This model had the 1767cc engine

Triumph

The pre-1940 Triumph Owners' Club is a lively and enthusiastic organization and many of its members are at present very busy renovating their prized cars. From the diminutive Super Seven and finely-finished Scorpion and Southern Cross through to the late-30s Glorias the final span of 'real Triumph' development engendered a batch of fine light cars, each hall-marked with the Coventry firm's unique flair for combining engineering excellence with attractive styling.

Despite the fact that all works records were lost the club has amassed a large quantity of technical information and offers help with spares as well as organizing club meetings, rallies, etc. So should you be struggling with that Climax engine rebuild, or perhaps ready for your first *concours*, write off for a membership form straight away!

Pre-1940 Triumph Owners' Club: C.Watson, 14 Castlefields Drive, Charlton Kings, Cheltenham, Glos.

Vauxhall

Already under American control by the early Thirties, Vauxhall Motors brought out their Light Six in June, 1933. The 2-litre Cadet had proved too large to weather the aftermath of the Depression and it was felt that a smaller, more lively car, still with a six-cylinder engine, would find more success. Vauxhall were right - by the time the Light Six's official debut took place at the 1933 Motor Show, many thousands had already been sold, and the new model continued to sell well. Independent front suspension and a choice of 12 or 14 hp engine came in 1935. Then, for the 1938 season the new unit-construction Ten with ifs and a four-cylinder engine arrived, to be partnered in 1939 by a four-cylinder Twelve, also of unit construction, both cars having a fine performance and offering a high degree of comfort as well as economy of operation. Always pioneers in the latest technology, Vauxhall Motors were often in the forefront of new ideas in motoring and much of their awareness is reflected in the specifications of the cars described below.

Ten (1937—39)

Unit construction, a logical development in motor-car assembly at the end of the 1930s, was born out of the need to balance the increasing payload of more spacious bodywork with the necessity of maintaining a respectable power:weight ratio. Since the fitting of larger engines would have reduced the economic virtues of running a light car, the only alternative was to reduce overall weight to a minimum by eliminating the traditional chassis frame and using the pressed-steel body of the car as a unifying structure. Continental manufacturers had been quick to realise this, and put the principle to good effect; Britain, on the other hand, lagged behind, and car designers here were hesitant at introducing a car that could prove merely a 'seven-day wonder'.

Tradition was paramount; novelty for those foolish enough to gamble with the public's fickle tastes. Vauxhall, however, secure and fully backed by tremendous resources, found that the public were completely ready to accept unit construction, and none too bothered to enquire as to its lasting qualities. By the time the first bad winters had come to test the corrosion - resistance of the Ten's floor pan, war was upon us, petrol rationing in force, and most cars in mothballs. Notwithstanding, unit construction was universally adopted after 1955.

The new 1937 Vauxhall Ten saloon was a sophisticated-looking car, its integral structure embodying many fashionable contemporary trends emanating from across the Atlantic, suitably scaled-down. A new type of slatted 'waterfall' radiator grille was set between chromium-plated headlamps mounted on either side of the bonnet, the smooth line of which was echoed in the characteristic chromium 'flutes' running along either side, as in all Vauxhall cars of the period. The four-door four-light body was fronted by a slanting one-piece windscreen and terminated in a steeply sloping 'fast' back; neat, rounded wings cowled over spoked disc wheels with large chromed hub caps. Comfortable seating was allied to a well-appointed interior, set off by a distinctive instrument panel where three main circular dials placed centrally were linked by a wide striped chromium-plated band; beneath this all other switches and panel lights were arranged in another line, linked by a narrower chromed band. A trafficator switch was mounted on an arm extending at right angles to the steering column, and gear selection was by means of an elongated, centrally-placed gear lever. Power was conveyed via a three-speed synchromesh gearbox to a conventional propeller shaft and rear axle, whereas at the front, the then-uncommon principle of independent front suspension was applied, operating by means of torsion bars. Under the bonnet was a very neat and clean-cut 1203 cc ohv engine with flat-topped pistons, its big-ends split diagonally and keyed by deep serrations. Developing 31.5 bhp at 3600 rev/min, a lively performance went hand-in-hand with economy

1931 Vauxhall Cadet Saloon, a large 2-litre six-cylinder car whose diminished sales paved the way for the very popular 12hp Light Six

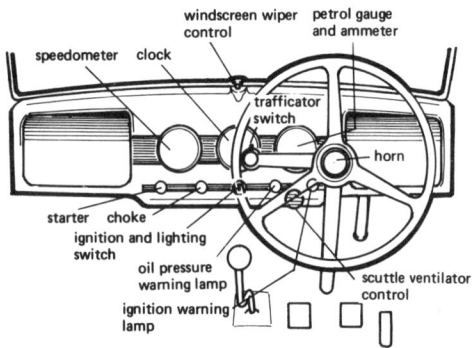

speedometer   clock   windscreen wiper control   petrol gauge and ammeter   trafficator switch   horn   starter   choke   ignition and lighting switch   oil pressure warning lamp   ignition warning lamp   scuttle ventilator control

1938 Ten and Twelve Saloon

1936 Vauxhall Ten Saloon, a sectioned vehicle for display purposes

1936 Vauxhall Ten-Four Saloon

by virtue of a downdraught carburetter which, while fitted with a pump device for sudden acceleration, had small-bore jets affording a 30 per 1·1 cent leaner mixture than normal while cruising on half throttle, smoothness being achieved by means of very wide spark-plug gaps and a 'long spark' coil. A top speed of 60-65 mile/h in the Ten was matched by 40 mpg. Acceleration from 10-30 mile/h in top gear took 11.8 seconds, or in second gear, 7.6 seconds, and a speed from rest of 50 mile/h could be achieved in 25 seconds. For the 1938-39 season the Ten saloon was priced at £168, a 'de luxe' version costing £182; in 1939 a coupe model was added, at £188.

Light Six (1933—38) and Twelve (1939)

Immediately successful right from its inception in June 1933, 25,000 Light Sixes had been sold before the 1934 Motor Show. Its bonnet bearing the characteristic Vauxhall 'flutes', a finely-meshed chromed radiator and plated headlamps formed the focal point for the Light Six's sweeping body lines, a dignified yet dashing essay in mid-30s styling, and one that in many ways remains more basically likeable than the late-30s Vauxhalls. Smallish wire wheels and low-mounted enveloping wings gave the car a slightly rakish air and this, coupled with the glistening brightwork of the radiator mesh and headlamps seemed to strike just the right note -

tasteful, yet trend-conscious. A true chassis frame formed the foundation for the bodywork and transmission. Offered first only in 12 hp form, a 1531 cc ohv six-cylinder in-line engine was fitted, developing 32 bhp. Front and rear suspension by means of leaf springs was used, and a centrally-mounted four-speed gearbox, semi-servo mechanical brakes and worm-and-sector steering were other conventional features of the early models.

For the 1935 season, several important innovations were announced: independent front suspension, higher compression ratio with more power, forward mounting of the engine, cruciform chassis-bracing and lower-positioned bodywork. The ifs mechanism consisted of a fixed tubular front axle with pivoting extension arms to which the stub axles were attached. A coil spring working horizontally in a cylinder of oil provided the suspension medium for each wheel. Four-point flexible engine mounting made necessary the fitting of a cable clutch-linkage.

Little change in style was in evidence for the 1936 season, but alternative power units became available, of 12 or 14 hp. So too did a 'de luxe' saloon version, which the *Autocar* tested in March 1936. This was of 12 hp, and priced at £225, compared to the standard saloon at £205. The car was found to be comfortable over bad road surfaces with little tendency 'roll' on corners; steering, too, was positive-

237

1935 Vauxhall Light Six saloon

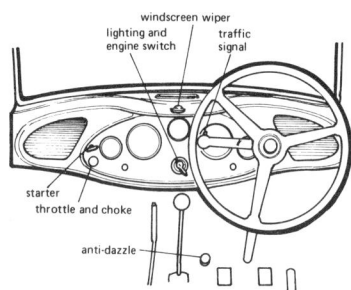

windscreen wiper
lighting and
engine switch
traffic
signal
starter
throttle and choke
anti-dazzle

1936 Light Six De Luxe Saloon

1936 Vauxhall saloons. On the left the Vauxhall Fourteen and on the right the Vauxhall Ten

in fact it was a good 'all-rounder'. Maximum speed was 67 mile/h, and acceleration was good, 27.6 seconds being needed to attain 50 mile/h from a standing start. In top gear 10-30 mile/h took 13 seconds, while 20-40 mile/h needed 15 seconds and 30-50 mile/h 20.4 seconds. Fuel consumption worked out at 26.28 mpg and the brakes were efficient, the car coming to rest from 30 mile/h over a distance of 29 feet. In all, the Light Six was very good value for money - a comfortable, smooth-riding car with a good overall finish. A lack of castor action was, however, noticed.

This point was remedied in the 1937 car, the castor action being increased, resulting in lighter steering. The brakes and clutch were further improved and a drive taken from the camshaft to operate the now mechanical windscreen wiper; the faster one travelled, the more rapid the sweep of the blades. As for appearances, a curved 'V' radiator grille (as in the Ten) was adopted and an easy-to-read instrument panel fitted. A reduction in price of £10 on all models brought the price of the 'de luxe' saloon down to £215, and that of the coupe to £235, while the standard saloon was replaced by a touring saloon at £220 which incorporated a luggage boot at the rear, access to it being by means of a lid hinging open at the top. The spare wheel was carried beneath a rounded cover and mounted upon the projecting boot. By 1938 prices were lower still, the sole saloon version cost £215 - a very reasonable figure for a six-cylinder light car with ifs; the coupe was priced at £245.

Finally, in 1939, the six-cylinder engine was regretably dispensed with and the model became a 12/4, of unit construction. Much attention was paid to sound-proofing, and a high top-gear ratio afforded smooth, economical cruising, a maximum speed of 65-68 mile/h being attainable. Acceleration from 10-30 mile/h took 11.4 seconds in top gear and 6.9 seconds in second gear, while through the gears it took 22 seconds to reach a speed of 50 mile/h from a standing start. Unlike the Ten, the piston crowns in the new Twelve engine were of an assymetric domed form, one side being steeply sloped, while the other, both longer and shallower in slope, incorporated a hollow pocket. Upon the piston reaching tdc, the compressed mixture was thus concentrated within a narrow confine between the cylinder head and the piston-crown pocket, the location of which coincided with the spark 1-1 plug recess; thus very complete combustion was achieved. Realising 35 bhp at 3600 rev/min, the 1442 cc Twelve engine also afforded useful economy due to its novel combination of a lean cruising mixture and wide-gapped spark plugs, as in the Ten.

Early versions of the Light Six are attractive, serviceable cars and if sound in structure, well worth restoring to former glory. As for the unit-construction models, view these with extreme caution. Nearly forty years have passed since they were new, and probably very few remain; with those that do, one is faced with the (now common) paradox of excellent mechanics housed in a 'limited longevity' body structure. Should you feel fitted for a battle with prewar 'planned obselescence' or its equivalent, then you will become the new owner of a Vauxhall model rarely seen nowadays.

At the time of writing there is no specialist club for the post - 1930 Vauxhall owner.

Wolseley

The ohc engines which were part of the Wolseley legacy on being taken-over by Morris Motors, formed, of course, the basis for a long line of MGs, the ohc Morris Minor, and the Wolseley Hornet and Hornet Special.

Dating back to the 10 hp Wolseley Stellite tourer and the fast single-seater Moth, which broke many records at Brooklands, the ohc concept was next adapted to a 7 hp design of engine, but a project for a small Wolseley saloon aimed at catching the public's eye - and purse - was never realized. Taken as it was, the four-cylinder 847 cc engine went into the Morris Minor and MG M-type; by adding two more cylinders, the 1271 cc 'six' proved ideal for powering the Wolseley Hornet.

Lord Nuffield conceived the later Wolseleys as 'de luxe' versions of the Morris.

Hornet (1930–36) and Hornet Special (1932–36)

Morris components featured significantly in the early Hornets. A lengthened Minor chassis, body, wheels and wings were used in the first version, which as an 8 hp car with a 12 hp engine, naturally performed well. The smooth six-cylinder ohc power unit possessed plenty of low-speed torque and top gear could be used even when starting from a standstill. Acceleration from 0-40 mile/h, solely in top gear, took 24 seconds; through the gears 0-60 mile/h took 30.2 seconds. A cruising speed of 50 mile/h and maximum of over 60 mile/h were commendable figures for a £175-185 12 hp car of 1930. Perhaps 33 mpg was somewhat on the debit side, but irrespective of this the new Hornet was a sensation, even when new owners found that the brakes were far from 'fantastic', needing a distance of 69 ft to stop the car from 40 mile/h - obviously Minor brake drums would not do for long.

The engine's overhead-camshaft was, as in the Minor, driven off the vertically-mounted generator via a fabric coupling, this device being later modified to chain-drive in order to condense the layout. Slightly inclined valves, a four-bearing crankshaft, coil ignition and SU carburation were matched by very 'utility' manifolding. A single dry-plate clutch, three-speed gearbox, semi-elliptic springing and hydraulic brakes formed the specification for the rather flexible chassis. Wire wheels set off the diminutive little body with its long bonnet, the radiator barely disguised as to its Cowley origins by affixing the oval Wolseley badge at its apex. For the 1931 season a £187-10s fabric or £195 coachbuilt saloon were available.

A 'real Wolseley' radiator, mounted ahead of the axle on the 1932 Hornet, signalled more forward location of the power unit, plus adaptation of the camshaft drive to double-chain pattern, thus shortening the engine. More room for the passengers was thus provided, the driver's bonus being a four-speed 'silent third' gearbox and a better clutch. The price of the coachbuilt saloon was little changed, while a £245 four-seater coupe, with built-in luggage box, was a new addition. The earlier two-door saloon, now with plated radiator shutters and Magna wheels, was sold off at £180. Little outward change came at the 1932 Motor Show. Mechanical improvements, however, included cast-iron cylinder liners, a stronger rear axle and 'Startix' automatic engine restarting. From this season on, the oval Wolseley badge was illuminated on all models. Coachbuilders had been glad to use the £145 Hornet chassis as a foundation for their often distinctive bodywork, but with the announcement of the twin-carburetter Hornet Special chassis at £175 their prayers were answered further. Swallow, Eustace Watkins (Wittingham and Mitchell), Maltby, Arrow, and other coachbuilders were all quick to bring out dashing open-car designs aimed at appealing to the young, and not-so-young 'speed merchant'. Others saw them as ideal low-priced competition machines - the Eustace Watkins Daytona model could achieve 0-50 mile/h in 17.8 seconds, and a team of three Hornets won the 1932 250-mile

Light Car Club's relay race at Brooklands, averaging 77.57 mile/h. A three-branch exhaust manifold, twin SU carburetters, duplex valve-springs, a higher compression ratio plus an oil

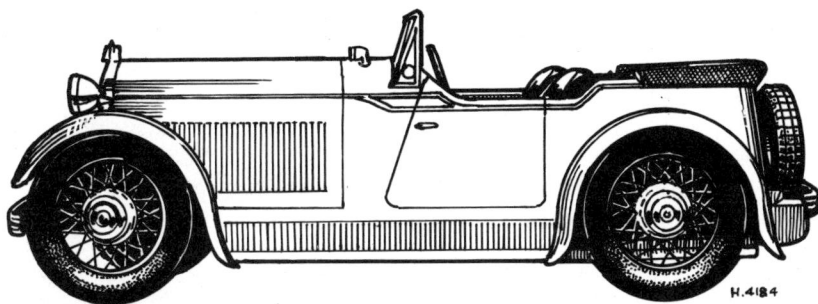

1932 Wolseley Hornet Special Sports Four Seater with bodywork by the Swallow Coachbuilding Company

1934 Wolseley Hornet Saloon owned by Michael Selby-Lowndes

1935 Wolseley Hornet Saloon at the 1973 Wolseley Rally

1934 Wolseley Nine Four Seater Tourer. This very rare version has Eustace Watkins special bodywork coachbuilt by Whittingham and Mitchell. It is owned by Brian W. Young

cooler uprated the Hornet engine significantly. Cycle or swept wings, a raked radiator, masses of louvres, 'cut away' doors etc. made the Hornet Specials at once very appealing, the Daytona costing £298. A supercharger kit was even offered by one firm, and later a new, more efficient cylinder-head became standard.

A three-speed preselector gearbox for the six-light saloon came in 1934, in accord with passing fashion, and in that year the Special chassis was given a 1604 cc engine from the New Fourteen, producing 50 bhp at 4500 rev/min.

Nine (1934–35)

Developed from the Hornet, the four-cylinder ohc Nine of 1018 cc also featured forward engine mounting, which was claimed to give freedom from pitching and afforded useful extra accomodation for the bodywork. Closely resembling its ancestor but for a flared rear panel with small boot, the Nine cost £179 and was of very similar specification to the Hornet.

Wasp (1935–36)

A 9.37 hp four-cylinder car of 1069 cc, the short-lived Wasp took over from the Nine as a smaller edition of the Hornet. Developing 32 bhp at 4000 rev/min and offering 32 mpg, the Wasp's engine had three main bearings. Its chassis incorporating semi-elliptic springing, a four-speed gearbox, spiral-bevel rear axle, hydraulic brakes and grouped lubrication, the Wasp's top speed was 62 mile/h and its acceleration from 0-50 mile/h occupied 28.6 seconds. A stopping distance from 30 mile/h of 29 feet could be expected. A more modern style of body was used, the standard saloon costing £165 and in 'de luxe' form, £178-10s.

Ten (1936–39)

Far closer liaison between Wolseley Motors (1927) Ltd and Morris Motors by 1935 resulted in greater standardization both in the specification and appearance of their models. An ohv design of engine superceded the ohc layout (even the MG TA of 1936 was ohv), and Wolseley cars tended to become luxury versions of the Morris, being often very similar in appearance but for the radiator grille and one or two small details.

The 1292 cc four-cylinder ohv 10/40 of 1936 thus corresponded with the Series II Morris Ten; when a Series III version of the Morris appeared in 1939 a corresponding Wolseley model, the Ten Series III, came on to the market also. While the Wolseley Twenty-five was a 100 mile/h car, the smaller Wolseleys remained in effect prestige models, fairly lavishly equipped and offering silent, above-average performance. The 'Bevelift' jacking system was used on the 10 hp car.

Twelve (1936–39)

A companion to the Ten, the 12/48 shared the same chassis but featured the Jackall jacking system. Developing 48 bhp, its 1547 cc ohv four-cylinder engine incorporated, like that of the Ten, a duplex chain-driven camshaft. steel-skirted pistons and a three-bearing crankshaft. The sturdy box-section frame was further reinforced by the integral construction of the floor. Conventional suspension and transmission were matched by a tastefully traditional body style, the bodywork being served by a system of drain tubes to conduct away rainwater. The maximum speed of the 1936 12/48 was, as tested by the *Autocar*, 62.5 mile/h; 0-50 mile/h through the gears took 26 seconds, and 27-29 mpg could be expected.

A Series III version of the Twelve appeared in 1939, the engine tune being improved and the rear of the larger body rubber-mounted.

New Fourteen (1934–36)

One of the last prewar ohc Wolseleys, the £240 New Fourteen of 1604 cc was distinctive

lighting, charging and ignition switch

mixture

throttle

traffic signals

starter

horn

fog lamp

anti-dazzle

reversing light

1935 Fourteen Saloon

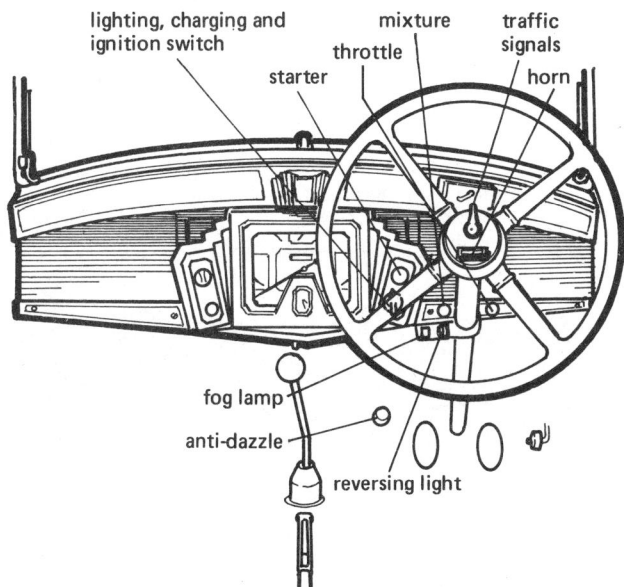

1934 Wolseley Nine Saloon owned by J. C. Barker

BBH 116

CLO 218

1935 Wolseley New Fourteen owned by T. B. Harris (*Photograph by Howard Cooper*)

in its curved waistline, the engine being forward-mounted as in the Nine and Hornet. A deep-section underslung cruciform frame, crossflow cylinder-head, four-bearing crankshaft, accessible engine components, controlled free-wheel and hydraulic brakes and shockabsorbers were important facets of the car's design. The engine's improved gas flow contributing to some 24-28 mpg, the Fourteen could top 66 mile/h, accelerate from 0-50 mile/h in 22.4 seconds and, like all its companions, stop within some 30 feet from 30 mile/h.

The lure of an overhead-camshaft engine makes the pre-1937 Wolseley range desirable vehicles to the enthusiast. The lighter-bodied early versions of the Hornet were lively, serviceable cars, while the 14 hp Hornet Specials had the added bonus of extra power which finally made this model completely viable in competitions.

As for the later ohv saloons, these have a definite dignity of appearance allied to luxurious interior appointments. Overall orthodoxy makes for easier overhaul of the power units, but the semi-unit construction of the chassis will mean that any decay here can put the future of a late-30s Wolseley 'on a knife edge'. Close inspection before purchase is advised.

The enthusiastic Wolseley Register caters for all pre-1948 cars, while a separate Hornet Special Club exists for followers of that particular model.

Wolseley Register: R.S. Burrows, 17 Hills Avenue, Cambridge CB1 4UY.

Wolseley Hornet Special Club: T.Webster, 'Grange View', 39 Anns Hill Road, Gosport, Hants. Gosport 81323.

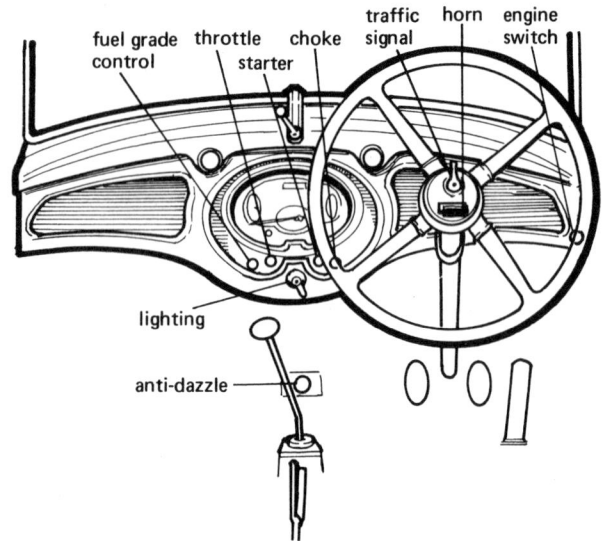

1936 12/48 Saloon

Part Three

Appendix One

The following pages offer technical data on most of the models described in Part 2. The period given under 'years of manufacture' covers the span for which the data is relevant, and not necessarily the model's full dates of manufacture. A code of abbreviations is given below. The author would welcome advice from readers as to inaccuracies or the provision of missing details in the model specifications, so as to improve further editions.

a.	-	aluminium alloy
AA	-	Alford and Alder
a.c.	-	air-cooled
ACM	-	AC mechanical
ah	-	ampere - hours
An.	-	Andre Telecontrol shockabsorbers
Au.	-	Autovac
auto.	-	automatic
b.b.	-	ball bearing
BC	-	Bishop Cam
BD	-	Burman Douglas
BWM	-	Bronze bush, white metal-lined
C	-	cold
cen.	-	central
CF	-	Castrol F
ch.	-	chain
Ch.	-	Champion
CJ	-	compensating jet
CL	-	cam-and-lever
clm.	-	on steering column
CM	-	constant mesh
cn.	-	channel section
co.	-	coachbuilt
com.	-	compensated voltage control
COP	-	chain oiling-pump
CR	-	Castrol R
CrJ	-	correction jet
d.d.	-	downdraught
DP	-	dry-plate
DVS	-	Dewandre vacuum-servo brakes
DWS	-	DWS permanent jacks
EB	-	eccentric bush
ext.	-	external
F	-	front

FA	-	fully advanced
fb.	-	fabric
FF	-	fluid flywheel
flex.	-	flexible
fly.	-	on flywheel
FP	-	full pressure
FR	-	fully retarded
fre.	-	freewheel
G	-	Girling
gen.	-	generator
GL	-	grouped lubrication
H	-	hot
ha.	-	hand-operated air pump
HC	-	half-cantilever
hyd.	-	hydraulic
I	-	inswept
IB	-	'I'-section beam axle
JKO	-	metric Jordan 'knock-on' hub
LB	-	Luvax-Bijour automatic chassis lubrication
Lk	-	Lockheed
Lo	-	Lodge
Lu	-	Lucas
M	-	Magna wire
Ma	-	Marles
mech.	-	mechanical
NA	-	not applicable
neg.	-	negative
n.p.	-	needle position
OSL	-	'one shot' automatic lubrication
p.b.	-	plain bevel
Pi.Sc.	-	pinion-and-sector
PJ	-	pilot jet

PmJ	-	pump jet
pos.	-	positive
PQ	-	pinion and reversed quadrant
pre.	-	preselector
PrJ	-	progression jet
PS	-	pressed steel
QE	-	quarter-elliptic
R	-	rear
r.b.	-	roller bearing
RH	-	right-hand
rig.	-	rigid
Ro	-	Rotax
RP	-	rack-and-pinion
RW	-	Rudge-Whitworth wire
S	-	supercharged
S3	-	silent third
SD	-	spoked disc
s.d.d.	-	semi-downdraught
SDP	-	single dry plate
SE	-	semi-elliptic
sh.	-	steel-backed shell bearings
sp.	-	spiral bevel
SRJ	-	slow-running jet
SUE	-	SU electric fuel pump
syn.	-	synchromesh
TG	-	on timing gears
thi.	-	third brush
TO	-	toe-out
TOE	-	transverse quarter-elliptic
TS	-	on timing sprockets
TSE	-	transverse semi-elliptic
t.sl.	-	throttle slide
TT	-	Torque tube
U	-	unknown historically
und.	-	underslung
up.	-	upswept
V	-	variable
vac.	-	vacuum
W	-	capacity well
w.c.	-	water-cooled
WM	-	white metal
WN	-	worm-and-nut
wo.	-	wooden frame
WP	-	wheel-and-pinion
WS	-	worm-and-sector
WW	-	worm-and-wheel
X	-	friction
Xf.	-	cruciform
3W	-	three-wheeler
—	-	no details

Alvis

Name	Fwd 8/15	Fwd 12/50	Fwd 12/75	12/50	12/60	Firefly
Year(s) of manufacture	1930	1930	1930	1931	1932	1933-34
ENGINE						
Capacity (cc)	1491	1482	1482	1645	1645	1496
Number of cylinders	8	4	4	4	4	4
Bore and stroke (mm)	55 x 78.5	68 x 102	68 x 102	69 x 110	69 x 110	69 x 110
Compression ratio (x:1)	V	5.7	5.0	5.35	5.8	5.8
RAC hp rating	12	12	12	12	12	11.9
Maximum bhp @ rev/min	125 @ 6000	50 @ 4750	75 @ 4750	50 @ 4250	56 @ 4250	50 @ 4250
Firing order	U	U	U	1,2,4,3	1,2,4,3	1,2,4,3
Valve layout	dohc	ohc	ohc	ohv	ohv	ohv
Inlet valve opens (^{o} btdc)	U	5	5	0	0	10
Tappet adjustment (inlet) in.	U	0.006C	0.006C	0.003H	0.003H	0.003H
Tappet adjustment (exhaust) in.	U	0.012C	0.012C	0.003H	0.003H	0.003H
Timing marks location	U	NA	NA	TG	TG	TS
Lubrication pattern	FP	FP	FP	FP	FP	FP
Oil-pump type	4x gear	gear	gear	gear	gear	gear
Optimum oil pressure (lb/in^2)	U	—	—	20-25	20-25	—
Pistons type: number of rings	a;3	a;3	a;3	a;3	a;3	a;3
No. of main bearings	5	3	3	3	3	3
Main bearings	r.b.	WM	WM	WM	WM	WM
Camshaft drive	gear	gear	gear	gear	gear	chain
Sump capacity (pts)	U	—	—	12	12	12-16
Lubricant (summer), SAE	Castrol R	40	40	40	40	30
Lubricant (winter), SAE	NA	40	40	40	40	30
Engine mountings	U	—	—	—	—	—
Exhaust manifold, branches	8	3	3	3	3	3
CARBURATION						
Carburetter	SU	Solex	Solex	Solex	2 x SU	SU
Carburetter type	U	MV	MOHD	30M	HV3HC	HVS
Choke size	U	28 mm	26 mm	26 mm	30 mm	1 5/8 in.
Main jet	U	155	135	125	—	—
Slow-running or pilot jet	U	PJ60	PJ60	PJ52.5	NA	NA
Compensating or correction jet	U	—	—	—	NA	NA
GA and GS jet, or progression jet	U	—	—	—	NA	NA
Capacity well or pump jet	U	—	—	—	NA	NA
Metering needle (standard)	U	NA	NA	NA	AC	KW1
Metering needle (weak)	U	NA	NA	NA	—	SA
Average mpg	—	—	—	27-30	—	26
Fuel feed	U	—	—	SUE	SUE	ACM
Tank capacity (gall)	35	8	8	12	12	14½
IGNITION						
HT supply	magneto	magneto	magneto	coil	coil	coil
Magneto	2 x BTH	BTH-C34	BTH-C34	NA	NA	NA
Distributor	NA	NA	NA	Ro-DJ4A	Ro-DJ4A	Ro-DJ4A
Coil	NA	NA	NA	12v	12v	12v
Contact-breaker gap (in.)	U	U	U	0.012	0.012	0.012
Spark plug gap (in.)	U	0.020	0.015	0.018	0.018	0.018
Spark plug thread (mm)	U	18	18	—	18	18
Spark plug	U	KLG 569	KLG 368	—	—	—
Ignition timing (^{o} btdc)	U	38.6 FA	38.6 FA	28 FA	28 FA	43.5 FA
ELECTRICAL						
Earthing pole	U	—	—	neg.	neg.	neg.
Battery	24v + 12v	12v	12v	12v	12v	12v
Starter motor	dynamotor	—	—	PMO418	PMO418	RMO418
Generator	dynamotor	—	—	C45	C45	C5A BU1

	Fwd 8/15	Fwd 12/50	Fwd 12/75	12/50	12/60	Firefly
CHASSIS						
Chassis-frame pattern	—	—	—	ladder	ladder	ladder
Sidemembers	cn.	cn.	cn.	cn.	cn.	cn.
Crossmembers	cn.	cn.	cn.	cn.	cn.	cn.
Front suspension	ifs	ifs	ifs	SE	SE	SE
Rear suspension	irs	irs	irs	SE	SE	SE
Shockabsorbers	FX, RX	FX	FX	FX, RX	FX, RX	FX, RX
Special chassis features	—	—	—	—	—	—
TRANSMISSION						
Clutch	multi-plate	SDP	SDP	SDP	SDP	SDP
Gearbox action	cr.	cr.	cr.	cr.	cr.	cr. or pre.
No. of forward gears	U	4	4	4	4	4
Gear lever location	U	—	—	RH	RH	cen.
Forward gear ratios (x:1)	U	15.43, 10.18 7.31, 4.77	15.43, 10.18 7.31, 4.77	18.54, 11.04 7.32, 4.77	15.47, 10.16 6.75, 4.77	18.35, 11.9 7.9, 5.22
Gearbox lubricant, SAE	U	40	40	40	40	30 or CF
Gearbox lubricant, quantity (pts)	U	U	U	4-5	4-5	3½
Rear axle bevel; ratio (x:1)	fwd; U	fwd; 4.77V	fwd; 4.77V	sp; 4.77	sp; 4.77	sp; 5.22
Rear axle lubricant, SAE	NA	NA	40	40	40	30
Rear axle lubricant, quantity (pts)	NA	NA	—	—	—	—
STEERING AND FRONT AXLE						
Steering box	U	—	—	Ma-D3	Ma-D3	Ma-L7
Steering box lubricant, SAE	U	140	140	140	140	140
Front axle	ifs	ifs	ifs	IB	IB	IB
Toe-in setting (in.)	U	TO1/8-3/16	TO1/8-3/16	1/8	1/8	1/8
BRAKES						
Type	Alvis	Alvis	Alvis	Alvis	Alvis	Alvis
Actuation	cable	cable	cable	cable	cable	cable
BODYWORK						
Body construction	a.	a. or fb.	co.	co. or fb.	co.	co.
No. of doors	0	2	2	2	2	2
No. of seats	2	2 or 4	2 or 4	2 or 4	2 or 4	4
WHEELS AND TYRES						
Wheels	RW	RW	RW	Alvis W	Alvis W	Alvis W
Tyres, size	U	—	—	4.75 x 30	4.75 x 30	5.00 x 30
Front tyre pressure (lb/in^2)	U	—	—	35	35	35
Rear tyre pressure (lb/in^2)	U	—	—	40	40	40

Armstrong Siddeley

Name	Twelve	Twelve Plus	Fourteen
Year(s) of manufacture	1932 - 35	1936	1936 - 39
ENGINE			
Capacity (cc)	1434	1666	1666
Number of cylinders	6	6	6
Bore and stroke (mm)	56.5 x 95.25	61 x 95.25	61 x 95.25
Compression ratio (x:1)	—	—	—
RAC hp rating	12	14	14
Maximum bhp @ rev/min	—	—	—
Firing order	1,5,3,6,2,4	1,5,3,6,2,4	1,5,3,6,2,4
Valve layout	sv	ohv	ohv
Inlet valve opens (o btdc)	5	5	5
Tappet adjustment (inlet) in.	0.006	0.006	0.006
Tappet adjustment (exhaust) in.	0.008	0.008	0.008
Timing marks location	TS	TS	TS
Lubrication pattern	FP	FP	FP
Oil-pump type	gear	gear	gear
Optimum oil pressure (lb/in^2)	—	—	—
Pistons type; number of rings	a;3	a;3	a;3
No. of main bearings	4	4	4
Main bearings	WM	WM	WM
Camshaft drive	chain	chain	chain
Sump capacity (pts)	—	—	—
Lubricant (summer) SAE	40	40	40
Lubricant (winter) SAE	30	30	30
Engine mountings	—	flex.	flex.
Exhaust manifold, branches	—	—	—
CARBURATION			
Carburetter	Stromberg	Stromberg	Stromberg
Carburetter type	—	—	—
Choke size	—	—	—
Main jet	—	—	—
Slow-running or pilot jet	—	—	—
Compensating or correction jet	—	—	—
GA and GS jet, or progression jet	—	—	—
Capacity well or pump jet	—	—	—
Metering needle (standard)	NA	NA	NA
Metering needle (weak)	NA	NA	NA
Average mpg	24-28	20-24	20-24
Fuel feed	ACM	ACM	ACM
Tank capacity (gall)	8	10	10
IGNITION			
HT supply	coil	coil	coil
Magneto	NA	NA	NA
Distributor	DX6A	DX6A	DX6A
Coil	Q12	Q12	Q12
Contact-breaker gap (in.)	0.012	0.012	0.012
Spark plug gap (in.)	0.018	0.018	0.018
Spark plug thread (mm)	18	14	14
Spark plug	—	Ch. L-10	Ch. L-10
Ignition timing (o btdc)	½ in. atdc, FR	½ in. atdc, FR	½ in. atdc, FR
ELECTRICAL			
Earthing pole	neg.	neg.	pos.
Battery	12v 51ah	12v 51ah	12v 51ah
Starter motor	M418G	M418G	M418G
Generator	C45	C45	C45

	Twelve	Twelve Plus	Fourteen
CHASSIS			
Chassis-frame pattern	F,I;R, up.	F,I;R, up.	F,I;R, up.
Sidemembers	cn.	cn.	cn.
Crossmembers	cn.	cn.	cn.
Front suspension	SE	SE	SE
Rear suspension	SE	SE	SE
Shockabsorbers	F&R, hyd.	F&R, hyd.	F&R, hyd.
Special chassis features	DWS	DWS, OSL	DWS, OSL
TRANSMISSION			
Clutch	auto.	auto.	auto. SDP
Gearbox action	pre.	pre.	pre.
No. of forward gears	4	4	4
Gear lever location	clm.	clm.	clm.
Forward gear ratios (x:1)	—	—	—
Gearbox lubricant, SAE	CF	CF	CF
Gearbox lubricant, quantity (pts)	—	—	—
Rear axle bevel; ratio	sp.; 5.55	TT, sp.; 5.33	TT, sp.; 5.33
Rear axle lubricant, SAE	90	90	90
Rear axle lubricant, quantity (pts)	—	—	—
STEERING AND FRONT AXLE			
Steering box	WW	WW	WN
Steering box lubricant, SAE	140	140	140
Front axle	IB	IB	IB
Toe-in setting (in.)	3/16	3/16	3/16
BRAKES			
Type	mech.	mech.	mech.
Actuation	cable	cable	cable
BODYWORK			
Body construction	co.	co.	co.
No. of doors	4	4	4
No. of seats	4	4	4
WHEELS AND TYRES			
Wheels	wire	wire	disc
Tyres, size	4.75 x 18	5.75 x 16	5.75 x 16
Front tyre pressure (lb/in^2)	30	30	30
Rear tyre pressure (lb/in^2)	35	30	30

Aston Martin

Name	1½ - litre International	1½ - litre Mk II	1½ - litre Ulster	1½ - litre 12/70 Mk II
Year(s) of manufacture	1930 - 33	1934 - 35	1935	1935 - 36
ENGINE				
Capacity (cc)	1488	1496	1496	1496
Number of cylinders	4	4	4	4
Bore and stroke (mm)	69 x 99	66 x 99	66 x 99	66 x 99
Compression ratio (x:1)	—	7.5	8.5	7.5
RAC hp rating	11.9	11.9	11.9	11.9
Maximum bhp @ rev/min	64 @ 4500	70 @ 4750	80 @ 5250	70 @ 4750
Firing order	1,3,4,2	1,3,4,2	1,3,4,2	1,3,4,2
Valve layout	ohc	ohc	ohc	ohc
Inlet valve opens (° btdc)	—	—	—	—
Tappet adjustment (inlet) in.	—	—	—	—
Tappet adjustment (exhaust) in.	—	—	—	—
Timing marks location	TS	TS	TS	TS
Lubrication pattern	dry sump	dry sump	dry sump	dry sump
Oil-pump type	gear	gear	gear	gear
Optimum oil pressure (lb/in^2)	—	—	—	—
Pistons type: number of rings	a; 3	a; 3	a; 3	a; 3
No. of main bearings	3	3	3	3
Main bearings	WM	WM	WM	WM
Camshaft drive	chain	chain	chain	chain
Sump capacity (pts)	tank, 20	tank, 20	tank, 24	tank, 20
Lubricant (summer) SAE	40	40	40	40
Lubricant (winter) SAE	40	40	40	40
Engine mountings	—	—	—	—
Exhaust manifold, branches	4	4	4	4
CARBURATION				
Carburetter	2 x SU	2 x SU	2 x SU	2 x SU
Carburetter type	HV2	HV2		HV3
Choke size	1 1/8 in.	1 1/8 in.	1½ in.	1¼ in.
Main jet	0.090	0.090	0.090	0.090
Slow-running or pilot jet	NA	NA	NA	NA
Compensating or correction jet	NA	NA	NA	NA
GA and GS jet, or progression jet	NA	NA	NA	NA
Capacity well or pump jet	NA	NA	NA	NA
Metering needle (standard)	E4	E4	—	E4
Metering needle (weak)	L	L	—	L
Average mpg	—	—	—	26
Fuel feed	—	2 x SUE	2 x SUE	2 x SUE
Tank capacity (gall)	18	—	15	11 or 15
IGNITION				
HT supply	magneto	magneto	magneto	magneto
Magneto	—	—	—	—
Distributor	NA	NA	NA	NA
Coil	NA	NA	NA	NA
Contact-breaker gap (in.)	0.012	0.012	0.012	0.012
Spark plug gap (in.)	0.018	0.018	0.018	0.018
Spark plug thread (mm)	18	18	18	14
Spark plug	—	—	—	—
Ignition timing (° btdc)	—	—	—	—
ELECTRICAL				
Earthing pole	neg.	neg.	neg.	neg.
Battery	12v	12v	12v 60 ah	12v 60 ah
Starter motor	12v	12v	12v	12v
Generator	12v	12v	12v	12v

	1½ - litre International	1½ - litre Mk II	1½ - litre Ulster	1½ - litre 12/70 Mk II
CHASSIS				
Chassis-frame pattern	ladder	ladder	ladder	cruciform
Sidemembers	cn.	cn.	cn.	cn.
Crossmembers	cn.	cn.	cn.	cn.
Front suspension	SE	SE	SE	SE
Rear suspension	SE	SE	SE	SE
Shockabsorbers	FX, RX	FX, RX	FX, RX	hyd.
Special chassis features	R, und.	R, und.	R, und.	—
TRANSMISSION				
Clutch	SDP	SDP	SDP	SDP
Gearbox action	crash	crash	crash	crash
No. of forward gears	4	4	4	4
Gear lever location	cen.	cen.	cen.	cen.
Forward gear ratios (x:1)	12.18, 7.58, 5.57, 4.75	—	11.15, 7.15, 5.22, 4.11	—
Gearbox lubricant, SAE	40	40	40	40
Gearbox lubricant, quantity (pts)	—	—	—	—
Rear axle bevel; ratio	worm; 4.75	p.b.; —	p.b.; 4.11 or V	sp; 4.66
Rear axle lubricant, SAE	90	90	90	90
Rear axle lubricant, quantity (pts)	—	—	—	—
STEERING AND FRONT AXLE				
Steering box	—	—	—	—
Steering box lubricant, SAE	140	140	140	140
Front axle	IB	IB	IB	IB
Toe-in setting (in.)	—	—	—	—
BRAKES				
Type	mech.	mech.	mech.	mech.
Actuation	cable	cable	cable	cable
BODYWORK				
Body construction	a.	a.	a.	a.
No. of doors	2	2	0	2
No. of seats	2	2 or 4	2	2 or 4
WHEELS AND TYRES				
Wheels	RW	RW	RW	RW
Tyres, size	4.50 x 30	5.25 x 18	5.25 x 18	5.25 x 18
Front tyre pressure (lb/in^2)	35	30	30	28
Rear tyre pressure (lb/in^2)	40	30	30	30

Austin

Name	Seven	7hp Nippy	7hp Speedy	Seven	Big Seven
Year(s) of manufacture	1930 - 36	1936 - 37	1936 - 37	1937	1938 39
ENGINE					
Capacity (cc)	747.5	747.5	747.5	747.5	900
Number of cylinders	4	4	4	4	4
Bore and stroke (mm)	56 x 76	56 x 76	56 x 76	56 x 76	56.77 x 88.9
Compression ratio (x:1)	5.4	–	–	6.31	6.8
RAC hp rating	7.8	7.8	7.8	7.8	7.992
Maximum bhp @ rev/min	10.5 @ 2400	21 @ 4400	21 @ 4400	13.5 @ 3000	25 @ 4000
Firing order	1,3,4,2	1,3,4,2	1,3,4,2	1,3,4,2	1,3,4,2
Valve layout	sv	sv	sv	sv	sv
Inlet valve opens (^{o} btdc)	0	–	–	0	0
Tappet adjustment (inlet) in.	0.004H	0.004H	0.004H	0.004H	0.009H
Tappet adjustment (exhaust) in.	0.004H	0.004H	0.004H	0.004H	0.009H
Timing marks location	fly.	fly.	fly.	fly.	fly. & TS
Lubrication pattern	FP	FP	FP	FP	FP
Oil-pump type	vane	gear	gear	gear	gear
Optimum oil pressure (lb/in^2)	5-7	50	50	20-30	20-30
Pistons type; number of rings	a; 3	a; 3	a; 3	a; 3	a; 3
No. of main bearings	2	3	3	3	3
Main bearings, type	bb. & b.	b.b. & WM	b.b. & WM	WM	sh.
Camshaft drive	chain	chain	chain	chain	chain
Sump capacity (pts)	3	4	4	4	5
Lubricant (summer), SAE	30	30	30	30	30
Lubricant (winter), SAE	30	30	30	30	30
Engine mountings, type	flex.	flex.	flex.	flex.	flex.
Exhaust manifold, branches	unit	4	4	unit	unit
CARBURATION					
Carburetter	Zenith	Zenith	Zenith	Zenith	Zenith
Carburetter type	26VA	VE1	VE1	30VM4	30VM4
Choke size	21 mm	21 mm	25 mm	17 mm	19 mm
Main jet	57	85	120	57	70
Slow-running or pilot jet	SRJ60	SRJ60	SRJ60	SRJ60	SRJ45
Compensating or correction jet	CJ50	CJ 55	CJ 40	CJ 50	CJ 60
GA and GS jet, or progression jet	NA	PrJ 90	PrJ 90	PrJ100	–
Capacity well or pump jet	NA	W2	W2	W2	–
Metering needle (standard)	NA	NA	NA	NA	NA
Metering needle (weak)	NA	NA	NA	NA	NA
Average mpg	38-45	–	–	38	40
Fuel feed	gravity/ACM	ACM	ACM	ACM	ACM
Tank capacity (gall)	4	6	6	5	6
IGNITION					
HT supply	coil	coil	coil	coil	coil
Magneto	NA	NA	NA	NA	NA
Distributor	DJ4A	DJ4A	DJ4A	DK4A	DK4A
Coil	Rotax	6Q6	6Q6	6Q6	6Q6
Contact-breaker gap (in.)	0.012	0.012	0.012	0.012	0.012
Spark plug gap (in.)	0.018	0.018	0.018	0.018	0.015 - 0.018
Spark plug thread (mm)	18	14	14	14	14
Spark plug	KLG-777	–	–	KLG-F50	KLG-F50
Ignition timing (^{o} btdc)	1¼ - 2 in.	–	–	–	5
ELECTRICAL					
Earthing pole	neg.	pos.	pos.	pos.	pos.
Battery	6v	12v 51ah	12v 51ah	6v	6v
Starter motor	–	–	–	–	M35G
Generator	thi.	–	–	–	C45YV3

	Seven	7hp Nippy	7hp Speedy	Seven	Big Seven
CHASSIS					
Chassis-frame pattern	'A'	'A'	'A'	'A'	ladder
Sidemembers	cn.	cn.	cn.	cn.	box
Crossmembers	cn.	cn.	cn.	cn.	cn.
Front suspension	TSE	TSE	TSE	TSE	TSE
Rear suspension	QE	QE	QE	QE	SE
Shockabsorbers	X	X	X	X	hyd.
Special chassis features	—	—	—	—	semi-unit
TRANSMISSION					
Clutch	SDP	SDP	SDP	SDP	SDP
Gearbox action	cr. or syn.	syn.	syn.	syn.	syn.
No. of forward gears	3 or 4	4	4	4	4
Gear lever location	cen.	cen.	cen.	cen.	cen.
Forward gear ratios (x:1)	21,16,9,4.9	23.3,14.4, 9.05, 5.25	23.3, 14.4 9.05, 5.25	23.3, 14.4 9.05, 5.25	22.39, 13.52, 8.52, 5.125
Gearbox lubricant, SAE	30	30	30	30	30
Gearbox lubricant, quantity (pts)	2/3	2/3	2/3	2/3	1
Rear axle bevel; ratio (x:1)	sp.; 4.9	sp.; 5.25	sp.; 5.25	sp.; 5.25	sp.; 5.125
Rear axle lubricant, SAE	140	140	140	140	140
Rear axle lubricant, quantity (pts)	1	1	1	1	1¾
STEERING AND FRONT AXLE					
Steering box	WW	WW	WW	WW	WS
Steering box lubricant	140	140	140	140	140
Front axle	IB	IB	IB	IB	IB
Toe-in setting (in.)	1/8	1/8	1/8	1/8	1/8
BRAKES					
Type	mech./G	mech.	mech.	Girling	Girling
Actuation	cable/rod	cable	cable	rod	rod
BODYWORK					
Body construction	PS	PS	PS	PS	PS
No. of doors	2	2	2	2	4
No. of seats	2 or 4	2 or 4	2 or 4	2 or 4	4
WHEELS AND TYRES					
Wheels	wire	wire	wire	wire	SD
Tyres, size	3.50 x 26V	3.50 x 19	3.50 x 19	4.00 x 17	4.75 x 16
Front tyre pressure (lb/in²)	22	22	22	22	24
Rear tyre pressure (lb/in²)	22	22	22	22	25

Name	Eight	Ten	Twelve-Four	Twelve-Six
Year(s) of manufacture	1939	1932 - 39	1936 - 39	1933 - 36
ENGINE				
Capacity (cc)	900	1125	1535	1496
Number of cylinders	4	4	4	6
Bore and stroke (mm)	56.77 x 88.9	63.5 x 89	69.35 x 101.6	61.25 x 84.83
Compression ratio (x:1)	6.8	6.5	6.2	6.2
RAC hp rating	7.992	9.9	11.9	13.9
Maximum bhp @ rev/min	27 @ 4400	21-28 @ 3000	28 @ 3000	24-31 @ 3000
Firing order	1,3,4,2	1,3,4,2	1,3,4,2	1,5,3,6,2,4
Valve layout	sv	sv	sv	sv
Inlet valve opens (^{o} btdc)	5	10	5	5
Tappet adjustment (inlet) in.	0.012H	0.004H	0.012H	0.004H
Tappet adjustment (exhaust) in.	0.012H	0.004H	0.012H	0.004H
Timing marks location	fly. & TS	fly. & TS	fly. & TS	fly.
Lubrication pattern	FP	FP	FP	FP
Oil-pump type	gear	gear	gear	gear
Optimum oil pressure (lb/in^2)	20 - 30	20 - 30	20 - 30	20 - 30
Pistons type; number of rings	a; 3	a; 3	a; 3	a; 3
No. of main bearings	3	2 or 3	2 or 3	3
Main bearings	sh.	WM or sh.	sh.	WM
Camshaft drive	chain	chain	chain	chain
Sump capacity (pts)	5	6 or 7	8	6
Lubricant (summer), SAE	30	30	30	30
Lubricant (winter), SAE	30	30	30	20
Engine mountings	flex.	flex.	flex.	flex.
Exhaust manifold, branches	3	3	3	5
CARBURATION				
Carburetter	Zenith	Zenith	Zenith	Zenith
Carburetter type	30 VM4	30 VM4	30 VM4	—
Choke size	19 mm	22 mm	23 mm	—
Main jet	70	90	102	—
Slow-running or pilot jet	SRJ 45	SRJ 45	SRJ 50	—
Compensating or correction jet	CJ 60	CJ 50	CJ 55	—
GA and GS jet, or progression jet	—	—	—	—
Capacity well or pump jet	—	—	—	—
Metering needle (standard)	NA	NA	NA	NA
Metering needle (weak)	NA	NA	NA	NA
Average mpg	40	32 - 35	30	28 - 30
Fuel feed	ACM	ACM	ACM	ACM
Tank capacity (gall)	6	6	8	8
IGNITION				
HT supply	coil	coil	coil	coil
Magneto	NA	NA	NA	NA
Distributor	DK4A	DK4A	DK4A	DJ6A
Coil	6Q6	Q12	Q12	12v
Contact-breaker gap (in.)	0.012	0.012	0.012	0.012
Spark plug gap (in.)	0.018	0.018	0.018	0.018
Spark plug thread (mm)	14	18 or 14	14	18
Spark plug	Ch.L-10	Lo.C3 or CN	Ch.L-10	KLG-M50
Ignition timing (^{o} btdc)	0	0	½ in.	1 in. (fly.)
ELECTRICAL				
Earthing pole	pos.	neg. or pos.	pos.	neg.
Battery	6v 63ah	12v 51ah	12v 63ah	12v 63ah
Starter motor	M35G	M418G	M418G	—
Generator	C45YV3	C45YV3	C45YV3	—

	Eight	Ten	Twelve-Four	Twelve-Six
CHASSIS				
Chassis-frame pattern	ladder	ladder	ladder	ladder
Sidemembers	box	cn.	cn.	cn.
Crossmembers	cn.	cn.	cn.	cn.
Front suspension	SE	SE	SE	SE
Rear suspension	SE	SE	SE	SE
Shockabsorbers	hyd.	hyd.	hyd.	hyd.
Special chassis features	—	cruciform	cruciform	cruciform
TRANSMISSION				
Clutch	SDP	SDP	SDP	SDP
Gearbox action	syn.	syn.	syn.	S3
No. of forward gears	4	4	4	4
Gear lever location	cen.	cen.	cen.	cen.
Forward gear ratios (x:1)	21.88, 13.22, 8.31, 5.43	21.1, 12.78, 8.04, 5.25	—	20.8, 13.4, 8.6, 5.5
Gearbox lubricant, SAE	40	40	40	30
Gearbox lubricant, quantity (pts)	1¾	2	3½	3
Rear axle bevel; ratio (x:1)	sp.; 5.43	sp.; 5.25V	sp.; 5	sp.; 5.5
Rear axle lubricant, SAE	140	140	140	140
Rear axle lubricant, quantity (pts)	1¾	2	3½	3
STEERING AND FRONT AXLE				
Steering box	CL	WW or WS	WW	WW
Steering box lubricant, SAE	140	140	140	140
Front axle	IB	IB	IB	IB
Toe-in setting (in.)	1/8	1/8	1/8	3/16
BRAKES				
Type	Girling	mech. or G	mech. or G	mech.
Actuation	rod	cable/rod	cable/rod	cable
BODYWORK				
Body construction	PS	PS	PS	PS
No. of doors	4	2 or 4	2 or 4	4
No. of seats	4	2 or 4	2 or 4	4
WHEELS AND TYRES				
Wheels	SD	wire or SD	wire or SD	wire
Tyres, size	4.50 x 17	4.50 x 18V	4.75 x 19V	4.75 x 19
Front tyre pressure (lb/in^2)	24	26V	25V	25
Rear tyre pressure (lb/in^2)	25	26V	28V	28

British Salmson

Name	S4C 12/55	S4C 12/70	S4D
Year(s) of manufacture	1934 - 36	1934 - 36	1937 - 38
ENGINE			
Capacity (cc)	1470	1470	1596
Number of cylinders	4	4	4
Bore and stroke (mm)	69 x 98	69 x 98	72 x 98
Compression ratio (x:1)	6	6.2	6
RAC hp rating	11.9	11.9	12.8
Maximum bhp @ rev/min	55 @ 4500	70 @ 4500	65 @ 4500
Firing order	1,3,4,2	1,3,4,2	1,3,4,2
Valve layout	dohc	dohc	dohc
Inlet valve opens (^{o} btdc)	14	14	11° 52'
Tappet adjustment (inlet) in.	0.004C	0.004C	0.004C
Tappet adjustment (exhaust) in.	0.006C	0.006C	0.006C
Timing marks location	fly.	fly.	fly.
Lubrication pattern	FP	FP	FP
Oil-pump type	gear	gear	gear
Optimum oil pressure (lb/in^2)	40	60	40
Pistons type; number of rings	a; 3	a; 3	a; 3
No. of main bearings	3	3	3
Main bearings	WM	WM	WM
Camshaft drive	gear	gear	gear
Sump capacity (pts)	10	10	12
Lubricant (summer), SAE	50	50	50
Lubricant (winter), SAE	50	50	50
Engine mountings	flex.	flex.	flex.
Exhaust manifold, branches	4	4	4
CARBURATION			
Carburetter	Solex	2 Solex/2 SU	Solex
Carburetter type	30BFHD	30BFHD/—	35BFHD
Choke size	24 mm	24 mm/1¼ in.	28 mm
Main jet	120 x 51	120 x 51/0.09	1503 x 51
Slow-running or pilot jet	PJ 50	PJ 50/NA	PJ 70
Compensating or correction jet	GA 4.5	GA 4.5/NA	GA 4.5
GA and GS jet, or progression jet	GS 115	GS 115/NA	GS 115
Capacity well or pump jet	—	—/NA	
Metering needle (standard)	NA	NA/BI	NA
Metering needle (weak)	NA	—	NA
Average mpg	30	25 - 30	25 - 30
Fuel feed	SUE	SUE	SUE
Tank capacity (gall)	10	10	11
IGNITION			
HT supply	coil	coil/mag.	coil
Magneto	NA	Scintilla	NA
Distributor	DK4A-0	DK4A-0	DK4A-0
Coil	12v	12v	12v
Contact-breaker gap (in.)	0.016	0.012/015	0.015
Spark plug gap (in.)	0.018	0.018	0.018
Spark plug thread (mm)	18	18	18
Spark plug	KLG-KSS	KLG-KSS	KLG-KSS
Ignition timing (^{o} btdc)	0	0	25 mm (fly.)
ELECTRICAL			
Earthing pole	neg.	neg.	pos.
Battery	12v	12v	12v
Starter motor	dynamotor	dynamotor	M418 A
Generator	—	—	—

	S4C 12/55	S4C 12/70	S4D
CHASSIS			
Chassis-frame pattern	F, I; R, up.	F., I; R, up.	R, up.
Sidemembers	cn.	cn.	box
Crossmembers	cn.	cn.	cn. & box
Front suspension	SE	SE	TSE
Rear suspension	QE	QE	QE
Shockabsorbers	X	X	FX, R, hyd.
Special chassis features	—	—	—
TRANSMISSION			
Clutch	SDP	SDP	SDP
Gearbox action	3 & 4 syn.	3 & 4 syn.	3 & 4 syn.
No. of forward gears	4	4	4
Gear lever location	cen.	cen.	cen.
Forward gear ratios (x:1)	16.2, 10.4, 7.35, 5.2	—	15.4, 9.8, 7, 4.9
Gearbox lubricant, SAE	80	80	80
Gearbox lubricant, quantity (pts)	2½	2½	2½
Rear axle bevel; ratio (x:1)	sp.; 5.2	sp.; 4.75	sp.; 4.9V
Rear axle lubricant, SAE	140	140	140
Rear axle lubricant, quantity (pts)	2½	2½	3
STEERING AND FRONT AXLE			
Steering box	Ma.	Ma.	RP
Steering box lubricant, SAE	grease	grease	grease
Front axle	IB	IB	ifs
Toe-in setting (in.)	1/8 - 3/16	1/8 - 3/16	2 mm
BRAKES			
Type	Bendix	Bendix	Lockheed
Actuation	cable	cable	hyd.
BODYWORK			
Body construction	co., S or a.	co., S or a.	co., S or a.
No. of doors	2 or 4	2	2 or 4
No. of seats	2 or 4	2 or 4	2 or 4
WHEELS AND TYRES			
Wheels	RW	RW	JKO, SD
Tyres, size	5.25 x 18	4.75 x 18	6.25 x 16
Front tyre pressure (lb/in^2)	26	28	18
Rear tyre pressure (lb/in^2)	26	28	20

BSA

Name	Three-wheeler 2-cyl. Scout	Three-wheeler 4-cyl. Scout	Ten	Light Six	10hp Scout Series 4	10hp Scout Series 5
Year(s) of manufacture	1930 - 32	1933 - 36	1933 - 36	1933 - 36	1938	1938
ENGINE						
Capacity (cc)	1021	1075	1330	1380	1203	1203
Number of cylinders	2	4	4	6	4	4
Bore and stroke (mm)	85 x 90	60 x 95	63.5 x 105	57 x 90	63.5 x 95	63.5 x 95
Compression ratio (x:1)	4.6	6	5.75	6.5	5.8	5.8
RAC hp rating	8.9	8.9	10	12	9.9	9.9
Maximum bhp @ rev/min	—	—	—	34 @ 3600	23 @ 4000	23 @ 4000
Firing order	1.2	1,3,4,2	1,3,4,2	1,5,3,6,2,4	1,3,4,2	1,3,4,2
Valve layout	ohv	sv	sv	ohv	sv	sv
Inlet valve opens (^{o} btdc)	16	0	—	—	10	10
Tappet adjustment (inlet) in.	0.0015C	0.004C	0.004C	0.052H	0.004C	0.004C
Tappet adjustment (exhaust) in.	0.0015C	0.006C	0.006C	0.052H	0.008C	0.008C
Timing marks location	TG	fly.	TS	TS	TS	TS
Lubrication pattern	FP	FP	FP	FP	FP	FP
Oil-pump type	gear	gear	gear	gear	gear	gear
Optimum oil pressure (lb/in^2)	2-6	60	—	—	40-50	40-50
Pistons type; number of rings	a; 2	a; 3	a; 3	a; 3	a; 3	a; 3
No. of main bearings	2	2	2	4	2	3
Main bearings	b.b. & r.b.	b.b. & r.b.	WM	WM	b.b. & r.b.	WM
Camshaft drive	gear	chain	chain	chain	chain	chain
Sump capacity (pts)	5	8	8	8	8	8
Lubricant (summer), SAE	30	30	30	30	40	40
Lubricant (winter), SAE	30	30	30	30	30	30
Engine mountings	rigid	rigid	4 x flex.	5 x flex.	3 x flex.	5 x flex.
Exhaust manifold, branches	2	unit	4	3	—	—
CARBURATION						
Carburetter	Solex	Solex	Solex	Solex	Solex	Solex
Carburetter type	26FV d.d.	26FV horiz.	—	—	30BFHG	30HBFG
Choke size	—	—	—	—	23 mm	23 mm
Main jet	—	—	—	—	105	100
Slow running or pilot jet	—	—	—	—	PJ 0.050	PJ 0.050
Compensating or correction jet	—	—	—	—	—	240
GA and GS jet, or progression jet	—	—	—	—	GA 4.5	GA 4.5
Capacity well or pump jet	—	—	—	—	GS 130	GS 130
Metering needle (standard)	NA	NA	NA	NA	NA	NA
Metering needle (weak)	NA	NA	NA	NA	NA	NA
Average mpg	40	40	30 - 35	28 - 30	32 - 40	32 - 40
Fuel feed	gravity	gravity	ACM	ACM	ACM	ACM
Tank capacity (gall)	4½	4½	8	8	6½ or 10	6½ or 10
IGNITION						
HT supply	coil	coil	coil	coil	coil	coil
Magneto	NA	NA	NA	NA	NA	NA
Distributor	Rotax	—	—	—	—	—
Coil	Rotax	6v	12v	12v	404	Q12
Contact-breaker gap (in.)	0.005	0.004	0.012	0.012	0.002 @ tdc	0.002 @ tdc
Spark plug gap (in.)	0.030	0.018	0.018	0.020	0.018	0.018
Spark plug thread (mm)	18	14	14	18	18	18
Spark plug	Lo-C3	Lo-514	Lodge	Lodge	Lo-C3	Lo-C3
Ignition timing (^{o} btdc)	—	0	—	—	see above	see above
ELECTRICAL						
Earthing pole	neg.	neg.	neg.	neg.	pos.	pos.
Battery	6v	6v	12v 57ah	12v 57ah	6v	12v
Starter motor	—	—	—	—	M415A	M35A
Generator	—	—	—	—	C45E	C45E

	Three-wheeler 2-cyl. Scout	Three-wheeler 4-cyl. Scout	Ten	Light Six	10hp Scout Series 4	10hp Scout Series 5
CHASSIS						
Chassis-frame pattern	triang.	triang.	cruciform	cruciform	FI, R und.	FI, R und.
Sidemembers	cn.	cn.	cn.	cn.	cn.	cn.
Crossmembers	cn.	cn.	cn.	cn.	tub.	tub.
Front suspension	4 x QE(ifs)	4 x QE (ifs)	SE	SE	4 x TQE (ifs)	4 x TQE (ifs)
Rear suspension	QE	QE	SE	SE	SE	SE
Shockcbsorbers	X	X	hyd.	hyd.	F, X; R, hyd.	F, X; R, hyd.
Special chassis features	king-post	king-post	—	—	—	—
TRANSMISSION						
Clutch	wet	wet	FF	FF	wet	wet
Gearbox action	crash	crash	pre.	pre.	S3	S3
No. of forward gears	3	3	4	4	3	3
Gear lever location	cen.	cen.	clm.	clm.	dashboard	dashboard
Forward gear ratios (x:1)	16.8, 7.75, 5.16	16.8, 7.75, 5.16	23.54, 11.65, 8.3, 5.5	23.54, 11.65, 8.3, 5.5	17.2, 7.89, 5.2	17.2, 7.89, 5.2
Gearbox lubricant, SAE	30	30	30	30	90	90
Gearbox lubricant, quantity (pts)	—	—	2	2	1	1
Rear axle bevel; ratio	fwd; 5.16	fwd; 5.16	sp.; 5.5	sp.; 5.5	fwd; 5.2	fwd; 5.2
Rear axle lubricant, SAE	NA	NA	90	90	fwd; 90	fwd; 90
Rear axle lubricant, quantity (pts)	NA	NA	1½	1½	NA	NA
STEERING AND FRONT AXLE						
Steering box	PQ	PQ	CL	CL	PS	PS
Steering box lubricant, SAE	140	140	140	140	140	140
Front axle	NA(fwd)	NA(fwd)	tub.	tub.	NA(fwd)	NA(fwd)
Toe-in setting (in.)	—	—	—	—	—	—
BRAKES						
Type	mech.	mech.	mech.	mech.	Bendix	Bendix
Actuation	rod	rod	cable	cable	cable	cable
BODYWORK						
Body construction	a. or fb.	a. or fb.	co.	co.	PS	PS
No. of doors	2	2	2 or 4	2 or 4	2	2
No. of seats	2 or 4	2 or 4	4	4	2 or 4	2 or 4
WHEELS AND TYRES						
Wheels	wire	wire	wire	wire	SD	SD
Tyres, size	4.00 x 19	3.50 x 18	4.75 x 18	4.75 x 18	4.50 x 18	4.50 x 17
Front tyre pressure (lb/in²)	22	22	28	28	20 or 22	24
Rear tyre pressure (lb/in²)	28	26	30	30	20 or 22	24

Crossley

Name	Ten	1½-litre	Twelve Six
Year(s) of manufacture	1931 - 37	1934 - 35	1936 - 37
ENGINE			
Capacity (cc)	1122	1476	1640
Number of cylinders	4	6	6
Bore and stroke (mm)	63 x 90	59 x 90	59 x 100
Compression ratio (x:1)	6	6.2	6.2
RAC hp rating	9.8	12.9	12.98
Maximum bhp @ rev/min	35.5 @ 4000	42 @ 4500	48 @ 4500
Firing order	1,3,4,2	1,5,3,6,2,4	1,5,3,6,2,4
Valve layout	ioe	ioe	ioe
Inlet valve opens (^{o} btdc)	10	10	—
Tappet adjustment (inlet) in.	0.006H	0.006H	0.006H
Tappet adjustment (exhaust) in.	0.006H	0.006H	0.006H
Timing marks location	fly.	fly.	fly.
Lubrication pattern	FP	FP	FP
Oil-pump type	gear	gear	gear
Optimum oil pressure (lb/in^2)	40	40	40
Pistons type; number of rings	a; 3	a; 3	a; 3
No. of main bearings	3	4	4
Main bearings	WM	WM	WM
Camshaft drive	chain	chain	chain
Sump capacity (pts)	9	9	9
Lubricant (summer), SAE	30	30	30
Lubricant (winter), SAE	20	20	20
Engine mountings	rig./flex.	flex.	flex.
Exhaust manifold, branches	3	5	5
CARBURATION			
Carburetter	SU/Solex	Zenith	2 x Zenith
Carburetter type	—	d.d.	d.d.
Choke size	—	—	—
Main jet	—	—	—
Slow-running or pilot jet	—	—	—
Compensating or correction jet	—	—	—
GA and GS jet, or progression jet	—	—	—
Capacity well or pump jet	—	—	—
Metering needle (standard)	—	NA	NA
Metering needle (weak)	—	NA	NA
Average mpg	28 - 30	25	—
Fuel feed	SUE, V	SUE	SUE
Tank capacity (gall)	7 or 8	7 or 8	—
IGNITION			
HT supply	coil	coil	coil
Magneto	NA	NA	NA
Distributor	DK4AJ-0	DLQ6AX17	DLQ6AX17
Coil	Q12	Q12	Q12
Contact-breaker gap (in.)	0.015	0.015	0.015
Spark plug gap (in.)	0.012-15	0.012-15	0.012-15
Spark plug thread (mm)	18	18	18
Spark plug	Ch.16	Ch.16	Ch.16
Ignition timing (^{o} btdc)	—	—	—
ELECTRICAL			
Earthing pole	neg.	neg.	neg.
Battery	2x6v 44ah	2x6v 44ah	12v 44ah
Starter motor	M35A-0/J-2	M418A-3/J4-0	M418A-3/J4-0
Generator	C45/J-1	C45A/J4-0	C45A/J4-0

	Ten	*1½-litre*	*Twelve Six*
CHASSIS			
Chassis-frame pattern	F, I; R, up.	F, I; R. up.	F, I; R, up.
Sidemembers	cn.	cn.	cn.
Crossmembers	cn.	cn.	cn.
Front suspension	SE	SE	SE
Rear suspension	SE	SE	SE
Shockabsorbers	X/hyd.	hyd.	hyd.
Special chassis features	—	—	—
TRANSMISSION			
Clutch	SDP/auto.	auto.	auto.
Gearbox action	S3/pre.	pre.	pre.
No. of forward gears	4	4	4
Gear lever location	cen./clm.	clm.	clm.
Forward gear ratios (x:1)	18.12, 10.66, 7.14, 5.33V	18.12, 10.66, 7.14, 5.33V	16.15, 9.97, 6.36, 4.75
Gearbox lubricant, SAE	90 or CF	CF	CF
Gearbox lubricant, quantity (pts)	4	4	4
Rear axle bevel; ratio	sp.; 5.33V	sp.; 5.33	sp.; 4.75
Rear axle lubricant, SAE	90	90	90
Rear axle lubricant, quantity (pts)	5	5	5
STEERING AND FRONT AXLE			
Steering box	BD	BD	BD
Steering box lubricant, SAE	90	90	90
Front axle	IB	IB	IB
Toe-in setting (in.)	3/16	3/16	3/16
BRAKES			
Type	Bendix	Bendix	Bendix
Actuation	cable	cable	cable
BODYWORK			
Body construction	co.	co.	co.
No. of doors	2 or 4	4	4
No. of seats	4	4	4
WHEELS AND TYRES			
Wheels	wire	wire	wire
Tyres, size	4.75 x 18V	5.50 x 16	5.50 x 16
Front tyre pressure (lb/in^2)	22	22	24
Rear tyre pressure (lb/in^2)	28	28	24

Ford

Name	19Y, Popular, Anglia	CX, Ten, Prefect
Year(s) of manufacture	1932 - 39	1934 - 39
ENGINE		
Capacity (cc)	933	1172
Number of cylinders	4	4
Bore and stroke (mm)	56.6 x 92.5	63.5 x 92.5
Compression ratio (x:1)	6.3	6.16
RAC hp rating	7.96	9.9
Maximum bhp @ rev/min	23.4 @ 4000	30.1 @ 4300
Firing order	1,2,4,3	1,2,4,3
Valve layout	sv	sv
Inlet valve opens (o btdc)	19	19
Tappet adjustment (inlet) in.	0.011 - 0.013	0.011 - 0.013
Tappet adjustment (exhaust) in.	0.011 - 0.013	0.011 - 0.013
Timing marks location	TS	TS
Lubrication pattern	FP	FP
Oil-pump type	gear	gear
Optimum oil pressure (lb/in^2)	30	30
Pistons type; number of rings	a; 3	a; 3
No. of main bearings	3	3
Main bearings	WM or sh.	WM or sh.
Camshaft drive	chain	chain
Sump capacity (pts)	4	4½
Lubricant (summer), SAE	30	30
Lubricant (winter), SAE	20	20
Engine mountings	—	—
Exhaust manifold, branches	3	3
CARBURATION		
Carburetter	Zenith	Ford
Carburetter type	26VF3	d.d.
Choke size	—	—
Main jet	70	85
Slow-running or pilot jet	SRJ 60	SRJ 55
Compensating or correction jet	CJ 65	CJ 75
GA and GS jet, or progression jet	PrJ110	PrJ100
Capacity well or pump jet	—	—
Metering needle (standard)	NA	NA
Metering needle (weak)	NA	NA
Average mpg	35 - 40	33 - 40
Fuel feed	ACM	ACM
Tank capacity (gall)	7	7
IGNITION		
HT supply	coil	coil
Magneto	NA	NA
Distributor	Delco	Delco
Coil	Delco 6v	Delco 6v
Contact-breaker gap (in.)	0.015	0.012
Spark plug gap (in.)	0.022	0.018
Spark plug thread (mm)	18 or 14	14
Spark plug type	Lo-C3 or CN	Ch. L-10
Ignition timing (o btdc)	26 FA	26 FA
ELECTRICAL		
Earthing pole	pos. (1937)	pos. (1937)
Battery	6v 63ah	6v 63ah
Starter motor	Delco	Delco
Generator	Delco	Delco

	19Y, Popular, Anglia	CX, Ten, Prefect
CHASSIS		
Chassis-frame pattern	F, I; R, up.	F, I; R, up.
Sidemembers	cn.	cn.
Crossmembers	cn.	cn.
Front suspension	TSE	TSE
Rear suspension	TSE	TSE
Shockabsorbers	hyd.	hyd.
Special chassis features	—	—
TRANSMISSION		
Clutch	SDP	SDP
Gearbox action	syn.	syn.
No. of forward gears	3	3
Gear lever location	cen.	cen.
Forward gear ratios (x:1)	18.72, 10.76, 5.5	16.89, 9.71, 5.5
Gearbox lubricant, SAE	90	90
Gearbox lubricant, quantity (pts)	1	1
Rear axle bevel; ratio	sp.; 5.5	sp.; 5.5
Rear axle lubricant, SAE	90	90
Rear axle lubricant, quantity (pts)	1	1
STEERING AND FRONT AXLE		
Steering box	WN	WN
Steering box lubricant, SAE	140	140
Front axle	IB	IB
Toe-in setting (in.)	1/16 - 1/8	1/16 - 1/8
BRAKES		
Type	mech.	mech./G
Actuation	rod & cable	cable/rod
BODYWORK		
Body construction	PS	PS
No. of doors	2 or 4	2 or 4
No. of seats	4	4
WHEELS AND TYRES		
Wheels	wire/SD	wire/SD
Tyres, size	4.50 x 17	4.50 x 17
Front tyre pressure (lb/in^2)	28	28
Rear tyre pressure (lb/in^2)	28	28

Frazer Nash

Name	TT Replica Boulogne II Shelsley (S) Nurburg (S)	TT Replica Byfleet II	TT Replica Byfleet I & II Ulster	TT Replica Ulster 100 Colmore Nurburg (S)
Year(s) of manufacture	1930	1934	1933	1936
ENGINE	4ED	Gough	Blackburne	Blackburne
Capacity (cc)	1496	1496	1498	1657
Number of cylinders	4	4	6	6
Bore and stroke (mm)	69 x 100	69 x 100	57 x 98	60 x 98
Compression ratio (x:1)	5.6 or 10	—	—	—
RAC hp rating	12	12	12	14
Maximum bhp @ rev/min	58-62 @ 4500;120(S)	60 @ 4500	65 @ 5000	75-90 @ 5000
Firing order	1,3,4,2	1,3,4,2	1,3,4,2	1,5,3,6,2,4
Valve layout	ohv	ohc	dohc	dohc
Inlet valve opens (º btdc)	—	—	—	—
Tappet adjustment (inlet)	—	—	—	—
Tappet adjustment (exhaust)	—	—	—	—
Timing marks location	TS	TS	TS	TS
Lubrication pattern	FP	FP	FP	FP
Oil-pump type	gear	gear	gear	gear
Optimum oil pressure (lb/in^2)	—	—	—	—
Pistons type; number of rings	a; —	a; —	a; —	a; —
No. of main bearings	3	3	5	5
Main bearings	WM	WM	WM	WM
Camshaft drive	chain	chain	chain	chain
Sump capacity (pts)	8	8	12	12
Lubricant (summer), SAE	40 or CR	40 or CR	40 or CR	40 or CR
Lubricant (winter), SAE	40 or CR	40 or CR	40 or CR	40 or CR
Engine mountings	3-point	3-point	—	—
Exhaust manifold, branches	4	4	3	3
CARBURATION				
Carburetter	2 x SU	2 x SU	2/3 SU; 3 x Zenith	2/3 SU; 3 x Zenith
Carburetter type	—	—	—	—
Choke size	—	—	—	—
Main jet	—	—	—	—
Slow-running or pilot jet	NA	NA	NA	NA
Compensating or correction jet	NA	NA	NA	NA
GA and GS jet or progression jet	NA	NA	NA	NA
Capacity well or pump jet	NA	NA	NA	NA
Metering needle (standard)	—	—	—	—
Metering needle (weak)	—	—	—	—
Average mpg	32	—	—	—
Fuel feed	Ha or SUE	Ha or SUE	Ha or SUE	Ha or SUE
Tank capacity (gall)	12 or 17	12	12	16 or 8
IGNITION				
HT supply	magneto	dual	coil	coil
Magneto	—	—	NA	NA
Distributor	NA	—	—	—
Coil	NA	12v	12v	12v
Contact-breaker gap (in.)	0.015	—	—	—
Spark plug gap (in.)	—	—	—	—
Spark plug thread (mm)	—	—	—	—
Spark plug	—	—	—	—
Ignition timing (º btdc)	—	—	—	—
ELECTRICAL				
Earthing pole	neg.	neg.	neg.	neg.
Battery	12v 72ah	12v 72ah	12v 72ah	12v 72ah
Starter motor	—	—	—	—
Generator	—	—	—	—

	T T Replica Boulogne II Shelsley (S) Nurburg (S)	T T Replica Byfleet II	T T Replica Byfleet I & II Ulster	T T Replica Ulster 100 Colmore Nurburg (S)
CHASSIS				
Chassis-frame pattern	ladder	ladder	ladder	ladder
Sidemembers	cn.	cn.	cn.	cn.
Crossmembers	cn.	cn.	cn.	cn.
Front suspension	QE	QE	QE	QE
Rear suspension	QE	QE	QE	QE
Shockabsorbers	FX, R An.	FX, R An.	FX, R An.	FX, R An.
Special chassis features	COP	COP	COP	COP
TRANSMISSION				
Clutch	SDP	SDP	SDP	SDP
Gearbox action	crash	crash	crash	crash
No. of forward gears	4	4	4	4
Gear lever location	ext. RH	ext. RH	ext. RH	ext. RH
Forward gear ratios (x:1)	10.5, 7, 4.8, 3.8, or V	10.5, 7, 4.8, 3.8, or V	10.5, 7, 4.8, 3.8, or V	10.5, 7, 4.8, 3.8, or V
Gearbox lubricant, SAE	—	—	—	—
Gearbox lubricant, quantity (pts)	—	—		—
Rear axle bevel; ratio	NA; 3.8 or V	NA; 3.8 or V	NA; 3.8 or V	NA; 3.8 or V
Rear axle lubricant, SAE	—			—
Rear axle lubricant, quantity (pts)	—	—	—	—
STEERING AND FRONT AXLE				
Steering box	RP or BC	RP or BC	RP or BC	RP or BC
Steering box lubricant, SAE	140	140	140	140
Front axle	tub.	tub.	tub.	tub.
Toe-in setting (in.)	—	—	—	—
BRAKES				
Type	AA	AA	AA	AA
Actuation	cable	cable	cable	cable
BODYWORK				
Body construction	a. or fb.	a.	a.	a.
No. of doors	1	1	1	1
No. of seats	2	2	2	2
WHEELS AND TYRES				
Wheels	RW	RW	RW	RW
Tyres, size	4.50 x 19	4.50 x 19	4.50 x 19	4.50 x 19
Front tyre pressure (lb/in^2)	35	35	35	35
Rear tyre pressure (lb/in^2)	40	40	40	35

Hillman

Name	Minx	Aero Minx	Minx
Year(s) of manufacture	1932 - 37	1933 - 35	1938 - 39
ENGINE			
Capacity (cc)	1185	1185	1185
Number of cylinders	4	4	4
Bore and stroke (mm)	63 x 95	63 x 95	63 x 95
Compression ratio (x:1)	5.78	6.3	6.5
RAC hp rating	9.8	9.8	9.8
Maximum bhp @ rev/min	27 @ 4200	30 @ 4200	33 @ 4100
Firing order	1,3,4,2	1,3,4,2	1,3,4,2
Valve layout	sv	sv	sv
Inlet valve opens (^{o} btdc)	2	—	2
Tappet adjustment (inlet) in.	0.010C	0.010C	0.010C
Tappet adjustment (exhaust) in.	0.015C	0.015C	0.015C
Timing marks location	fly.	fly.	TS
Lubrication pattern	FP	FP	FP
Oil-pump type	gear	gear	gear
Optimum oil pressure (lb/in^2)	25 - 30	25 - 30	30 - 35
Pistons type; number of rings	a; 3	a; 3	a; 3
No. of main bearings	3	3	3
Main bearings	WM	WM	sh.
Camshaft drive	chain	chain	chain
Sump capacity (pts)	7	7	7
Lubricant (summer), SAE	40	40	40
Lubricant (winter), SAE	30	30	30
Engine mountings	flex.	flex.	flex.
Exhaust manifold, branches	unit	unit	unit
CARBURATION			
Carburetter	Solex	Stromberg	Solex
Carburetter type	horiz.	d.d.	FAI
Choke size	—	—	21 mm
Main jet	—	—	100
Slow-running or pilot jet	—	—	SRJ 45
Compensating or correction jet	—	—	CJ 200
GA and GS jet, or progression jet	—	—	—
Capacity well or pump jet	—	—	—
Metering needle (standard)	NA	NA	NA
Metering needle (weak)	NA	NA	NA
Average mpg	32	27 - 30	30 - 34
Fuel feed	ACM	ACM	ACM
Tank capacity (gall)	7¾	8	7¾
IGNITION			
HT supply	coil	coil	coil
Magneto	NA	NA	NA
Distributor	—	—	DKYH4A
Coil	6v	6v	B12LD
Contact-breaker gap (in.)	0.010	0.010	0.010
Spark plug gap (in.)	0.022	0.022	0.032
Spark plug thread (mm)	14	14	14
Spark plug	Ch.L-10	Ch.L-10	Ch.L-10
Ignition timing (^{o} btdc)	2, FR	2, FR	7, FR
ELECTRICAL			
Earthing pole	neg.	neg.	pos.
Battery	6v 63ah	6v 63ah	6v 51ah
Starter motor	—	—	M35G
Generator	—	—	C45YV

	Minx 1932 - 37	*Aero Minx*	*Minx 1938 - 39*
CHASSIS			
Chassis-frame pattern	F, I; R, up.	F, I; R, up.	F, I; R, up.
Sidemembers	cn./box	cn.	box
Crossmembers	cn.	cn.	cn.
Front suspension	SE	SE	SE
Rear suspension	SE	SE	SE
Shockabsorbers	hyd.	hyd.	hyd.
Special chassis features	—	—	—
TRANSMISSION			
Clutch	SDP or auto.	SDP or auto.	SDP
Gearbox action	crash or syn.	crash or syn.	syn.
No. of forward gears	3 or 4	3 or 4	4
Gear lever location	cen.	cen.	cen.
Forward gear ratios (x:1)	19.6, 13.77, 8.16, 5.44	18.0, 12.65, 7.5, 5	19.6, 13.77, 8.16, 5.22
Gearbox lubricant, SAE	90	90	40
Gearbox lubricant, quantity (pts)	2	2	2
Rear axle bevel; ratio (x:1)	sp.; 5.44	sp.; 5	sp.; 5.22
Rear axle lubricant, SAE	90	90	90
Rear axle lubricant, quantity (pts)	1¾	1¾	1¾
STEERING AND FRONT AXLE			
Steering box	WN	WN	WN
Steering box lubricant, SAE	140	140	140
Front axle	IB	IB	IB
Toe-in setting (in.)	1/8	1/8	1/8
BRAKES			
Type	Bendix	Bendix	Bendix
Actuation	cable	cable	cable
BODYWORK			
Body construction	PS	PS	PS
No. of doors	4	2 or 4	4
No. of seats	4	4	4
WHEELS AND TYRES			
Wheels	wire or SD	RW	SD
Tyres, size	4.50 x 18	4.50 x 18	5.25 x 16
Front tyre pressure (lb/in^2)	28	28	26
Rear tyre pressure (lb/in^2)	30	30	26

HRG

Name	1100	1500
Year(s) of manufacture	1938 - 39	1935 - 39
ENGINE		
Capacity (cc)	1074	1496
Number of cylinders	4	4
Bore and stroke (mm)	60 x 95	69 x 100
Compression ratio (x:1)	7.75	7
RAC hp rating	8.93	11.9
Maximum bhp @ rev/min	40 @ 5200	58 @ 4500
Firing order	1,3,4,2	1,3,4,2
Valve layout	ohc	ohv
Inlet valve opens (^{o} btdc)	20	V
Tappet adjustment (inlet) in.	0.005	—
Tappet adjustment (exhaust) in.	0.007	—
Timing marks location	fly.	fly.
Lubrication pattern	FP	FP
Oil-pump type	gear	gear
Optimum oil pressure (lb/in^2)	—	—
Pistons type; number of rings	a; 3	a; 3
No. of main bearings	2 or 3	3
Main bearings	WM	WM
Camshaft drive	chain	chain
Sump capacity (pts)	13	8
Lubricant (summer), SAE	30	30
Lubricant (winter), SAE	30	30
Engine mountings	flex.	flex.
Exhaust manifold, branches	4	4
CARBURATION		
Carburetter	2 x SU	2 x SU
Carburetter type	—	—
Choke size	—	—
Main jet	—	—
Slow-running or pilot jet	NA	NA
Compensating or correction jet	NA	NA
GA and GS jet, or progression jet	NA	NA
Capacity well or pump jet	NA	NA
Metering needle (standard)	—	—
Metering needle (weak)	—	—
Average mpg	35 - 40	30
Fuel feed	ACM	SUE
Tank capacity (gall)	9	15
IGNITION		
HT supply	coil/mag.	coil/mag.
Magneto	Scintilla	Scintilla
Distributor	DK4A	DK4A
Coil	Q12	Q12
Contact-breaker gap (in.)	0.012	0.012
Spark plug gap (in.)	0.025	0.025
Spark plug thread (mm)	14	18
Spark plug	Ch. L10S	—
Ignition timing (^{o} btdc)	—	—
ELECTRICAL		
Earthing pole	pos.	neg./pos.
Battery	12v	12v
Starter motor	—	—
Generator	—	—

	1100	1500
CHASSIS		
Chassis-frame pattern	F up; R und.	F up; R und.
Sidemembers	cn.	cn.
Crossmembers	tub.	tub.
Front suspension	QE	QE
Rear suspension	SE	SE
Shockabsorbers	F,X; R, X or hyd.	F,X; R,X or hyd.
Special chassis features	—	—
TRANSMISSION		
Clutch	SDP	SDP
Gearbox action	syn.	crash
No. of forward gears	4	4
Gear lever location	cen.	cen.
Forward gear ratios (x:1)	14.88, 9.2, 5.56, 4.0	16.33, 10.33, 6.67, 4.45
Gearbox lubricant, SAE	40	40
Gearbox lubricant, quantity (pts)	2	2
Rear axle bevel; ratio	sp; 4.0	sp; 4.55
Rear axle lubricant, SAE	90	90
Rear axle lubricant, quantity (pts)	—	—
STEERING AND FRONT AXLE		
Steering box	Ma	Ma
Steering box lubricant, SAE	140	140
Front axle	tub.	tub.
Toe-in setting (in.)	—	—
BRAKES		
Type	mech.	mech.
Actuation	cable	cable
BODYWORK		
Body construction	a. on wo.	a. on wo.
No. of doors	2	2
No. of seats	2	2
WHEELS AND TYRES		
Wheels	RW	RW
Tyres, size	5.50 x 16	5.50 x 16
Front tyre pressure (lb/in^2)	26	26
Rear tyre pressure (lb/in^2)	26	26

Humber

Name	Twelve
Year(s) of manufacture	1932 - 37
ENGINE	
Capacity (cc)	1669
Number of cylinders	4
Bore and stroke (mm)	69.5 x 110
Compression ratio (x:1)	6.5
RAC hp rating	11.97
Maximum bhp @ rev/min	42 @ 3800
Firing order	1,3,4,2
Valve layout	sv
Inlet valve opens (° btdc)	6
Tappet adjustment (inlet) in.	0.010C
Tappet adjustment (exhaust) in.	0.015C
Timing marks location	TS
Lubrication pattern	FP
Oil-pump type	gear
Optimum oil pressure (lb/in²)	30 - 35
Pistons type; number of rings	a; 3
No. of main bearings	3
Main bearings	WM
Camshaft drive	chain
Sump capacity (pts)	12
Lubricant (summer), SAE	30
Lubricant (winter), SAE	20
Engine mountings	rig./flex.
Exhaust manifold, branches	unit
CARBURATION	
Carburetter	Stromberg
Carburetter type	—
Choke size	—
Main jet	—
Slow-running or pilot jet	—
Compensating or correction jet	—
GA and GS jet, or progression jet	—
Capacity well or pump jet	—
Metering needle (standard)	NA
Metering needle (weak)	NA
Average mpg	25
Fuel feed	ACM
Tank capacity (gall)	10
IGNITION	
HT supply	coil
Magneto	NA
Distributor	DKYH4A
Coil	LuB12
Contact-breaker gap (in.)	0.010
Spark plug gap (in.)	0.022
Spark plug thread (mm)	18 or 14
Spark plug	—
Ignition timing (° btdc)	7½ mm
ELECTRICAL	
Earthing pole	neg.
Battery	12v 63ah.
Starter motor	Lu
Generator	Lu

	Twelve
CHASSIS	
Chassis-frame pattern	F, I; R, up.
Sidemembers	cn. or box
Crossmembers	cn.
Front suspension	SE
Rear suspension	SE
Shockabsorbers	hyd.
Special chassis features	cruciform
TRANSMISSION	
Clutch	SDP
Gearbox action	S3 or syn.
No. of forward gears	4
Gear lever location	cen.
Forward gear ratios (x:1)	19.2, 13.5, 8.0, 5.33
Gearbox lubricant, SAE	40
Gearbox lubricant, quantity (pts)	2
Rear axle bevel; ratio	sp.; 5.33
Rear axle lubricant, SAE	140
Rear axle lubricant, quantity (pts)	4
STEERING AND FRONT AXLE	
Steering box	WN
Steering box lubricant, SAE	140
Front axle	IB
Toe-in setting (in.)	1/8
BRAKES	
Type	mech.
Actuation	cable
BODYWORK	
Body construction	co. or PS
No. of doors	2 or 4
No. of seats	4
WHEELS AND TYRES	
Wheels	wire
Tyres, size	5.50 x 17
Front tyre pressure (lb/in^2)	26
Rear tyre pressure (lb/in^2)	28

Jowett

Name	7hp	Eight	Ten
Year(s) of manufacture	1930 - 35	1936 - 39	1936 - 39
ENGINE			
Capacity (cc)	907	946	1166
Number of cylinders	2	2	4
Bore and stroke (mm)	75.4 x 101.5	77 x 101.5	63.5 x 92
Compression ratio (x:1)	—	—	—
RAC hp rating	7.04	7.35	9.9
Maximum bhp @ rev/min	16 @ 3000	17 @ 3250	31 @ 4000
Firing order	1,2	1,2	1,4,2,3
Valve layout	sv	sv	sv
Inlet valve opens (^{o} btdc)	0	0	0
Tappet adjustment (inlet) in.	0.002/004C	0.006C	0.006C
Tappet adjustment (exhaust) in.	0.002/004C	0.006C	0.006C
Timing marks location	TS	TS	TS
Lubrication pattern	FP	FP	FP
Oil-pump type	gear	gear	gear
Optimum oil pressure (lb/in^2)	14-16/25-30	30 - 40	45 - 50
Pistons type; number of rings	a; 3	a; 3	a; 3
No. of main bearings	2	2	2
Main bearings	WM	WM	WM
Camshaft drive	chain	chain	chain
Sump capacity (pts)	4½	4½	7
Lubricant (summer), SAE	30	30	30
Lubricant (winter), SAE	30	30	30
Engine mountings	flex./hyd.	hyd.	flex.
Exhaust manifold, branches	2 x 2	2 x 2	2 x 2
CARBURATION			
Carburetter	Zenith	Zenith	Zenith
Carburetter type	V	VM	VM
Choke size	—	25 mm	24 mm
Main jet	—	80	90
Slow-running or pilot jet	—	SRJ 50	SRJ 50
Compensating or correction jet	—	CJ 80	CJ 85
GA and GS jet, or progression jet	—	—	—
Capacity well or pump jet	—	—	—
Metering needle (standard)	NA	NA	NA
Metering needle (weak)	NA	NA	NA
Average mpg	40	30 - 40	45 - 50
Fuel feed	ACM	ACM	SUE
Tank capacity (gall)	6	7	7
IGNITION			
HT supply	coil	coil	coil
Magneto	NA	NA	NA
Distributor	2-cyl.	2-cyl.	DJ4
Coil	6v or 12v	12v 51ah	12v 63ah
Contact-breaker gap (in.)	0.012	0.012	0.012
Spark plug gap (in.)	0.020	0.020	0.020
Spark plug thread (mm)	18 mm	14 mm	14 mm
Spark plug	—	Lo-HN	Lo-HN
Ignition timing (^{o} btdc)	0	0	0
ELECTRICAL			
Earthing pole	neg.	pos.	pos.
Battery	6v or 12v	12v 51ah	12v 63ah
Starter motor	—	—	—
Generator	—	—	—

274

	7 hp	Eight	Ten
CHASSIS			
Chassis-frame pattern	ladder	cruciform	cruciform
Sidemembers	cn.	cn.	cn.
Crossmembers	cn.	cn.	cn.
Front suspension	SE	SE	SE
Rear suspension	SE	SE	SE
Shockabsorbers	X/hyd.	hyd.	hyd.
Special chassis features	—	—	—
TRANSMISSION			
Clutch	DP/auto.	SDP	SDP
Gearbox action	crash	CM & fre.	CM & fre.
No. of forward gears	3 (or 4)	4	4
Gear lever location	cen.	cen.	cen.
Forward gear ratios (x:1)	20.5, 10.35, 5.125V	20.6, 12.3, 7.32, 4.89	20.6, 12.3, 7.32, 4.89V
Gearbox lubricant, SAE	30	30	30
Gearbox lubricant, quantity (pts)	2	2	2
Rear axle bevel; ratio (x:1)	sp.; 5.125V	sp.; 4.89	sp.; 4.89V
Rear axle lubricant, SAE	30	30	30
Rear axle lubricant, quantity (pts)	1	1	1
STEERING AND FRONT AXLE			
Steering box	EB	EB	MW
Steering box lubricant	140	140	140
Front axle	IB	IB	IB
Toe-in setting (in.)	1/8	1/8	1/8
BRAKES			
Type	mech.	Bendix	Bendix
Actuation	rod	cable	cable
BODYWORK			
Body construction	fb or PS	PS	PS
No. of doors	2 or 4	4	4
No. of seats	2 or 4	4	4
WHEELS AND TYRES			
Wheels	wire	SD	SD
Tyres, size	4.40 x 27	4.50 x 19	4.75 x 19
Front tyre pressure (lb/in^2)	30	22	24
Rear tyre pressure (lb/in^2)	32	22	24

Lagonda and Rapier

Name	Lagonda Rapier	Rapier Ten
Year(s) of manufacture	1934 - 35	1935 - 38
ENGINE		
Capacity (cc)	1104	1087
Number of cylinders	4	4
Bore and stroke (mm)	62.5 x 90	62 x 90
Compression ratio (x:1)	7.5	7.5
RAC hp rating	9.69	9.69
Maximum bhp @ rev/min	45 @ 4500	45 @ 4500
Firing order	1,3,4,2	1,3,4,2
Valve layout	ohc	ohc
Inlet valve opens (° btdc)	8	8
Tappet adjustment (inlet) in.	0.006	0.006
Tappet adjustment (exhaust) in.	0.015	0.015
Timing marks location	fly.	fly.
Lubrication pattern	FP	FP
Oil-pump type	gear	gear
Optimum oil pressure (lb/in^2)	—	—
Pistons type; number of rings	a; 4	a; 4
No. of main bearings	3	3
Main bearings	WM	WM
Camshaft drive	chain	chain
Sump capacity (pts)	16	16
Lubricant (summer), SAE	40	40
Lubricant (winter), SAE	30	30
Engine mountings	—	—
Exhaust manifold, branches	4	4
CARBURATION		
Carburetter	2 x SU	2 x SU
Carburetter type	horiz.	horiz.
Choke size	—	—
Main jet	—	—
Slow-running or pilot jet	NA	NA
Compensating or correction jet	NA	NA
GA and GS jet, or progression jet	NA	NA
Capacity well or pump jet	NA	NA
Metering needle (standard)	—	—
Metering needle (weak)	—	—
Average mpg	26 - 28	26 - 28
Fuel feed	SUE	SUE
Tank capacity (gall)	8	8
IGNITION		
HT supply	magneto	magneto
Magneto	BTH-GA4	BTH-GA4
Distributor	NA	NA
Coil	NA	NA
Contact-breaker gap (in.)	0.012	0.012
Spark plug gap (in.)	0.022	0.022
Spark plug thread (mm)	14	14
Spark plug	KLG-F75	KLG-F75
Ignition timing (° btdc)	—	
ELECTRICAL		
Earthing pole	neg.	neg.
Battery	12v 60ah	12v 60ah
Starter motor	—	
Generator	thi.	thi.

	Lagonda Rapier	*Rapier Ten*
CHASSIS		
Chassis-frame pattern	ladder	ladder
Sidemembers	cn.	cn.
Crossmembers	tub.	tub.
Front suspension	SE	SE
Rear suspension	SE	SE
Shockabsorbers	X	X
Special chassis features	—	—
TRANSMISSION		
Clutch	SDP	SDP
Gearbox action	pre.	pre.
No. of forward gears	4	4
Gear lever location	**RH**	RH
Forward gear ratios	17.95, 10.56, 7.18, 5.28V	17.95, 10.56, 7.18, 5.28V
Gearbox lubricant, SAE	30	30
Gearbox lubricant, quantity (pts)	2	2
Rear axle bevel; ratio (x:1)	sp.; 5.28V	sp.; 5.28V
Rear axle lubricant, SAE	90	90
Rear axle lubricant, quantity (pts)	1½	1½
STEERING AND FRONT AXLE		
Steering box	BC	BC
Steering box lubricant, SAE	140	140
Front axle	IB	IB
Toe-in setting (in.)	—	—
BRAKES		
Type	Girling	Girling
Actuation	rod	rod
BODYWORK		
Body construction	a. on wo.	a. on wo.
No. of doors	2	2
No. of seats	2 or 4	2 or 4
WHEELS AND TYRES		
Wheels	RW	RW
Tyres, size	4.50 x 19	4.50 x 19
Front tyre pressure (lb/in^2)	28	28
Rear tyre pressure (lb/in^2)	30	30

Lanchester

Name	Ten	Eleven	Light Six	Roadrider
Year(s) of manufacture	1932 - 36	1936 - 39	1933 - 36	1936 - 38
ENGINE				
Capacity (cc)	1203	1444	1380	1527
Number of cylinders	4	4	6	6
Bore and stroke (mm)	63.5 x 95	66 x 105	57 x 90	60 x 90
Compression ratio (x:1)	6.25	7	7	7
RAC hp rating	10	10.82	12.09	13.4
Maximum bhp @ rev/min	34 @ 4000	38 @ 4000	36 @ 4000	42 @ 4000
Firing order	1,3,4,2	1,3,4,2	1,5,3,6,2,4	1,5,3,6,2,4
Valve layout	ohv	ohv	ohv	ohv
Inlet valve opens (^{o} btdc)	0	0	0	0
Tappet adjustment (inlet) in.	0.058H	0.058H	0.052H	0.052H
Tappet adjustment (exhaust) in.	0.058H	0.058H	0.052H	0.052H
Timing marks location	TS	TS	TS	TS
Lubrication pattern	FP	FP	FP	FP
Oil-pump type	gear	gear	gear	gear
Optimum oil pressure (lb/in^2)	—	—	—	—
Pistons type; number of rings	a; 3	a; 3	a; 3	a; 3
No. of main bearings	3	3	4	4
Main bearings	WM	WM	WM	WM
Camshaft drive	chain	chain	chain	chain
Sump capacity (pts)	8	8	9	—
Lubricant (summer), SAE	30	30	30	30
Lubricant (winter), SAE	20	20	20	20
Engine mountings	flex.	flex.	flex.	flex.
Exhaust manifold, branches	unit	unit	unit	unit
CARBURATION				
Carburetter	SU	SU	SU	SU
Carburetter type	OM or HV2	HV2	HV2	HV3
Choke size	1 or 1 1/8 in.	1 1/8 in.	1 1/8 in.	1¼ in.
Main jet	0.090	0.090	0.090	0.090
Slow-running or pilot jet	NA	NA	NA	NA
Compensating or correction jet	NA	NA	NA	NA
GA and GS jet, or progression jet	NA	NA	NA	NA
Capacity well or pump jet	NA	NA	NA	NA
Metering needle (standard)	DA or DN	07	M6 or MA	BR or BY
Metering needle (weak)	DC or HB	CX	S	D8 or 3
Average mpg	26 - 30	—	28	—
Fuel feed	ACM	ACM	ACM	ACM
Tank capacity (gall)	10	10	10	12
IGNITION				
HT supply	coil	coil	coil	coil
Magneto	NA	NA	NA	NA
Distributor	DVX4A	DVX4A	DX6A	DX6A
Coil	B12	B12	B12	B12
Contact-breaker gap (in.)	0.012	0.012	0.012	0.012
Spark plug gap (in.)	0.020	0.020	0.020	0.020
Spark plug thread (mm)	18	14	18	14
Spark plug	Lodge	Lo-CB14	Lodge	Lo-CLNH
Ignition timing (^{o} btdc)	12 FA	12 FA	—	8 FA
ELECTRICAL				
Earthing pole	neg.	pos.	neg.	pos.
Battery	12v 57ah	12v 57ah	12v 57ah	12v 57ah
Starter motor	M35G	M35G	M35G	M418G
Generator	C45YV/3	C45YV/3	C45	C39PV/2

	Ten	Eleven	Light Six	Roadrider
CHASSIS				
Chassis-frame pattern	R und.	R und.	R und.	cruciform
Sidemembers	cn.	cn.	cn.	box
Crossmembers	cn. & tub.	cn. & tub.	cn. & tub.	cn.
Front suspension	SE	SE	SE	SE
Rear suspension	SE	SE	SE	SE
Shockabsorbers	hyd.	hyd.	hyd.	hyd.
Special chassis features	GL	GL	GL	lattice
TRANSMISSION				
Clutch	FF	FF	FF	FF
Gearbox action	pre.	pre.	pre.	pre.
No. of forward gears	4	4	4	4
Gear lever location	clm.	clm.	clm.	clm.
Forward gear ratios (x:1)	23.33, 12.65, 8.2, 5.43	23.33, 12.65, 8.2, 5.43	23.33, 12.65, 8.2, 5.43	—
Gearbox lubricant, SAE	30	30	30	30
Gearbox lubricant, quantity (pts)	2	2	2	2
Rear axle bevel; ratio	worm; 5.43	worm; 5.43	worm; 5.43	worm; —
Rear axle lubricant, SAE	90	90	90	90
Rear axle lubricant, quantity (pts)	1½	1½	1½	1½
STEERING AND FRONT AXLE				
Steering box	WN	WN	WN	WN
Steering box lubricant, SAE	140	140	140	140
Front axle	IB	IB	IB	IB
Toe-in setting (in.)	1/8	1/8	1/8	1/8
BRAKES				
Type	mech.	Girling	mech.	Girling
Actuation	cable	rod	cable	rod
BODYWORK				
Body construction	co.	co.	co.	co.
No. of doors	2 or 4	2 or 4	2 or 4	4
No. of seats	4	4	4	4
WHEELS AND TYRES				
Wheels	wire	wire	wire	M. wire
Tyres, size	4.50/5.00 x 19/18	5.00 x 18	5.00 x 18	5.00 x 18
Front tyre pressure (lb/in^2)	30/28	28	28	28
Rear tyre pressure (lb/in^2)	30/28	30	30	30

Lea-Francis

Name	12/40 P, V and W types	Hyper Sports S-type	Twelve or 1½-litre	Fourteen
Year(s) of manufacture	1930 - 32	1930 - 32	1937 - 39	1937 - 39
ENGINE	4ED	4ED	Lea-Francis	Lea-Francis
Capacity (cc)	1496	1496	1496	1629
Number of cylinders	4	4	4	4
Bore and stroke (mm)	69 x 100	69 x 100	69 x 100	72 x 100
Compression ratio (x:1)	5.6	—	7.25	7.25
RAC hp rating	11.9	11.9	11.9	12.9
Maximum bhp @ rev/min	38 @ 4000	61 @ 4100	50 @ —	70 @ —
Firing order	1,3,4,2	1,3,4,2	1,3,4,2	1,3,4,2
Valve layout	ohv	ohv	ohv	ohv
Inlet valve opens (º btdc)	—	—	10	15
Tappet adjustment (inlet) in.	—	—	0.004	0.006
Tappet adjustment (exhaust) in.	—	—	0.006	0.008
Timing marks location	fly.	fly.	fly.	fly.
Lubrication pattern	FP	FP	FP	FP
Oil-pump type	gear	gear	gear	gear
Optimum oil pressure (lb/in²)	—	—	—	—
Pistons type; number of rings	a; 3	a; 3	a; 3	a; 3
No. of main bearings	3	3	3	3
Main bearings	WM	WM	BWM	BWM
Camshaft drive	chain	chain	chain	chain
Sump capacity (pts)	8	8	8½	12
Lubricant (summer), SAE	30	40	30	30
Lubricant (winter), SAE	30	40	20	20
Engine mountings	—	—	4 x flex.	4 x flex.
Exhaust manifold, branches	4	4	—	—
CARBURATION				
Carburetter	Solex/SU	Cozette (S)	SU	SU
Carburetter type	—/HV2	—	H4	H4
Choke size	—/1 1/8	—	1½	1½
Main jet	—/0.090	—	0.090	0.090
Slow-running or pilot jet	—/NA	—	NA	NA
Compensating or correction jet	—/NA	—	NA	NA
GA and GS jet, or progression jet	—/NA	—	NA	NA
Capacity well or pump jet	—/NA	—	NA	NA
Metering needle (standard)	NA/M5	NA	AQ	AQ
Metering needle (weak)	NA/M6	NA	AA	AA
Average mpg	28 - 30	20	28 - 30	23 - 28
Fuel feed	grav./Au.	Autopulse	SUE	SUE
Tank capacity (gall)	10	10 or 18	11	11
IGNITION				
HT supply	magneto	magneto	coil	coil
Magneto	—	—	NA	NA
Distributor	NA	NA	DKY4A	DKY4A
Coil	NA	NA	Q12	Q12
Contact-breaker gap (in.)	0.012	0.012	0.012	0.012
Spark plug gap (in.)	0.018	0.018	0.018	0.018
Spark plug thread (mm)	18	18	14	14
Spark plug	Lo-C3	Ch.-KSS1	Lo—H14	Lo-H14
Ignition timing (º btdc)	—	V	—	—
ELECTRICAL				
Earthing pole	neg.	neg.	pos.	pos.
Battery	12v	12v	12v 63ah.	12v 63ah.
Starter motor	Rotax	Rotax	M418G	M418G
Generator	Rotax	Rotax	C45PV	C45PV

	12/40 P, V & W types	Hyper Sports S-type	Twelve or 1½-litre	Fourteen
CHASSIS				
Chassis-frame pattern	F, I; R, up.	F, I; R, up.	F, I; R, up.	F, I; R, up.
Sidemembers	cn.	cn.	cn.	cn.
Crossmembers	cn.	cn.	cn.	cn.
Front suspension	SE	SE	SE	SE
Rear suspension	SE	SE	SE	SE
Shockabsorbers	X	X	hyd.	hyd.
Special chassis features	—	Ki-Gass priming	LB	LB
TRANSMISSION				
Clutch	SDP	SDP	SDP	SDP
Gearbox action	3 & 4 CM	cr.	syn.	syn.
No. of forward gears	4	4	4	4
Gear lever location	RH	RH	cen.	cen.
Forward gear ratios (x:1)	15, 9.4, 6.45, 4.7V	13.03, 7.75, 5.09, 3.91V	20.6, 12.7, 7.6, 5.25	20.6, 12.7, 7.6, 5.25
Gearbox lubricant, SAE	30	30	50	50
Gearbox lubricant, quantity (pts)	—	—	3½	3½
Rear axle bevel; ratio (x:1)	sp.; 4.7V	sp.; 3.91V	sp.; 5.25	sp.; 5.25
Rear axle lubricant, SAE	—	—	140	140
Rear axle lubricant, quantity (pts)	—	—	3	3
STEERING AND FRONT AXLE				
Steering box	WW	WW	BD	BD
Steering box lubricant	140	140	140	140
Front axle	IB	IB	IB	IB
Toe-in setting (in.)	—	—	1/8 − 3/16	1/8 − 3/16
BRAKES				
Type	mech.	DVS	Girling	Girling
Actuation	rod	mech. & vac.	rod	rod
BODYWORK				
Body construction	fb. or a.	fb. or a.	PS or co.	PS or co.
No. of doors	2 or 4	2 or 4	2 or 4	2 or 4
No. of seats	2 or 4	2 or 4	2 or 4	2 or 4
WHEELS AND TYRES				
Wheels	RW	RW	RW	RW
Tyres, size	4.75 x 28V	4.75 x 28	5.25 x 17	5.25 x 17
Front tyre pressure (lb/in^2)	28	28	26	26
Rear tyre pressure (lb/in^2)	30	30	26	26

MG

Name	C	D	F1, F2, F3	J1, J2	J3
Year(s) of manufacture	1931 - 32	1931 - 32	1931 - 32	1932 - 33	1932 - 34
ENGINE					
Capacity (cc)	746	847	1271	847	746
Number of cylinders	4	4	6	4	4
Bore and stroke (mm)	57 x 73	57 x 83	57 x 83	57 x 73	57 x 73
Compression ratio (x:1)	9 or 5.8(S)	5.4	6.2	6.2	6
RAC hp rating	8.05	8.05	12.08	8.05	8.05
Maximum bhp @ rev/min	44-62.5 @ 6500	27 @ 4500	37.2 @ 4100	36 @ 5500	52 @ 6500 (S)
Firing order	1,3,4,2	1,3,4,2	1,5,3,6,2,4	1,3,4,2	1,3,4,2
Valve layout	ohc	ohc	ohc	ohc	ohc
Inlet valve opens (^{o} btdc)	15	0	9	15	15
Tappet adjustment (inlet) in.	0.006 or 8H	0.004H	0.004H	0.006H	0.008H
Tappet adjustment (exhaust) in.	0.006 or 8H	0.004H	0.004H	0.006H	0.012H
Timing marks location	TG	TG	TG	TG	TG
Lubrication pattern	FP	FP	FP	FP	FP
Oil-pump type	gear	gear	gear	gear	gear
Optimum oil pressure (lb/in^2)	—	—	—	—	—
Pistons type; number of rings	3	unit	5	4	4
No. of main bearings	2	2	4	4	4
Main bearings	b.b. & WM	b.b. & WM	WM	b.b. & WM	b.b. & WM
Camshaft drive	via gen.	via gen.	via gen.	via gen.	via gen.
Sump capacity (pts)	8	4 or 8	12	12	12
Lubricant (summer), SAE	40 or CR	30	30	30	30
Lubricant (winter), SAE	40 or CR	30	30	30	30
Engine mountings	flex.	rigid	3 x rigid	3 x rigid	3 x rigid
Exhaust manifold, branches	3	unit	5	5	5
CARBURATION					
Carburetter	SU	SU	2 x SU	2 x SU	SU
Carburetter type	HV3	HV2	OM	OM	HV3
Choke size	1¼ in.	1 1/8 in.	1 in.	1 in.	1¼ in.
Main jet	0.090	0.090	0.090	0.090	0.090
Slow-running or pilot jet	NA	NA	NA	NA	NA
Compensating or correction jet	NA	NA	NA	NA	NA
GA and GS jet, or progression jet	NA	NA	NA	NA	NA
Capacity well or pump jet	NA	NA	NA	NA	NA
Metering needle (standard)	C	M5	M5	D8	RLB
Metering needle (weak)	—	M6	M6	WX1	AE
Average mpg	—	36	30	35 - 40	—
Fuel feed	ha.	SUE	SUE	SUE	SUE
Tank capacity (gall)	10	5	6	8	8
IGNITION					
HT supply	coil	coil	coil	coil	magneto
Magneto	NA	NA	NA	NA	—
Distributor	—	DJ4A	Rotax	DJ4A	NA
Coil	6v	Rotax 6v	Rotax 12v	Rotax 6v	NA
Contact-breaker gap (in.)	0.012	0.012	0.012	0.012	0.012
Spark plug gap (in.)	0.020	0.018	0.018	0.018	0.018
Spark plug thread (mm)	18	18	18	18	18
Spark plug	—	—	—	—	—
Ignition timing (^{o} btdc)	—	30 FA	—	30 FA	—
ELECTRICAL					
Earthing pole	neg.	neg.	neg.	neg.	neg.
Battery	6v	6v	12v	6v	6v
Starter motor	—	—	—	—	—
Generator	—	—	—	—	—

	C	D	F1, F2, F3	J1, J2	J3
CHASSIS					
Chassis-frame pattern	R, und.	R. und.	ladder	R, und.	R, und.
Sidemembers	cn.	cn.	cn.	cn.	cn.
Crossmembers	tub.	cn.	cn.	cn.	cn.
Front suspension	SE	SE	SE	SE	SE
Rear suspension	SE	SE	SE	SE	SE
Shockabsorbers	An.	X	X	X	X
Special chassis features	—	—	R, und; GL	—	—
TRANSMISSION					
Clutch	2DP	SDP	SDP	SDP	SDP
Gearbox action	crash	crash	crash	crash	crash
No. of forward gears	3	3	4	4	4
Gear lever location	cen.	cen.	cen.	cen.	cen.
Forward gear ratios (x:1)	10.78, 7.48, 5.5	17.1, 8.84, 4.89	19.21, 9.56, 6.5, 4.78	19.24, 11.5, 7.31, 5.375	19.24, 11.5, 7.31, 5.375
Gearbox lubricant, SAE	40	30	30	30	30
Gearbox lubricant, quantity (pts)	1½	1½	—	1½	1½
Rear axle bevel; ratio (x:1)	p.b; 5.5	sp.; 4.89	sp.; 4.78	sp.; 5.375	sp.; 5.375
Rear axle lubricant, SAE	90	90	90	90	90
Rear axle lubricant, quantity (pts)	1½	1½	—	1½	1½
STEERING AND FRONT AXLE					
Steering box	WW	WW	WW	WW	WW
Steering box lubricant, SAE	140	140	140	140	140
Front axle	IB	IB	IB	IB	IB
Toe-in setting (in.)	1/8	1/8	1/8	1/8	1/8
BRAKES					
Type	mech.	mech.	mech.	mech.	mech.
Actuation	cable	cable	cable	cable	cable
BODYWORK					
Body construction	racing	S or fb.	a. or fb.	a.	a.
No. of doors	0	2	2	2	2
No. of seats	2	2	4	2	2
WHEELS AND TYRES					
Wheels	RW	RW	RW	RW	RW
Tyres, size	4.00 x 19	4.00 x 19	4.00 x 19	4.00 x 19	4.00 x 19
Front tyre pressure (lb/in^2)	24	24	28	24	24
Rear tyre pressure (lb/in^2)	28	28	30	28	28

Name	J4	K1, K2	KN	K3	L1, L2
Year(s) of manufacture	1933	1932 - 34	1934 - 35	1933 - 34	1933 - 34
ENGINE					
Capacity (cc)	746	1086	1286	1086	1086
Number of cylinders	4	6	6	6	6
Bore and stroke (mm)	57 x 73	57 x 71	57 x 84	57 x 71	57 x 71
Compression ratio (x:1)	—	6.4	6.1	6.2 or 5.4V	6.4
RAC hp rating	8.05	12.08	12.08	12.08	12.08
Maximum bhp @ rev/min	72.3 @ 6000	39-41 @ 5500	56 @ 5500	120 @ 6500 (S)	41 @ 5500
Firing order	1,3,4,2	1,5,3,6,2,4	1,5,3,6,2,4	1,5,3,6,2,4	1,5,3,6,2,4
Valve layout	ohc	ohc	ohc	ohc	ohc
Inlet valve opens (^{o} btdc)	15	0	15	15	15
Tappet adjustment (inlet) in.	0.008H	0.006H	0.008H	0.008H	0.006H
Tappet adjustment (exhaust) in.	0.012H	0.006H	0.008H	0.008H	0.006H
Timing marks location	TG	TG	TG	TG	TG
Lubrication pattern	FP	FP	FP	FP	FP
Oil-pump type	gear	gear	gear	gear	gear
Optimum oil pressure (lb/in^2)	—	—	—	—	—
Pistons type; number of rings	a; 3	a; 3	a; 3	a; 3	a; 3
No. of main bearings	2	4	4	4	4
Main bearings	b.b.; WM	WM & sh.	WM & sh.	WM & sh.	WM
Camshaft drive	via gen.	via gen.	via gen.	via gen.	via gen.
Sump capacity (pts)	—	—	—	20	—
Lubricant (summer), SAE	CR	40	40	CR	30
Lubricant (winter), SAE	CR	30	30	CR	20
Engine mountings	—	flex.	flex.	flex.	rigid
Exhaust manifold, branches	4	2 x 3	2 x 3	2 x 3	5
CARBURATION					
Carburetter	SU	2 or 3 x SU	2 x SU	SU	2 x SU
Carburetter type	horiz.	OM	HV2	HV8	s.d.d.
Choke size	1 5/8 in.	1 in.	1 1/8 in.	1 7/8 in.	1 3/8 in.
Main jet	0.090	0.090	0.090	0.090	0.090
Slow-running or pilot jet	NA	NA	NA	NA	NA
Compensating or correction jet	NA	NA	NA	NA	NA
GA and GS jet, or progression jet	NA	NA	NA	NA	NA
Capacity well or pump jet	NA	NA	NA	NA	NA
Metering needle (standard)	—	D2	3	RM	L
Metering needle (weak)	—	RS	L	—	L
Average mpg	—	—	25	—	—
Fuel feed	2 x SUE	2 Petrolift	SUE	2 SUE or ha.	SUE
Tank capacity (gall)	10	11 or 12	10	23½ or 27½	11
IGNITION					
HT supply	coil	mag./coil	magneto	magneto	coil
Magneto	NA	B.T.H.	B.T.H.	B.T.H.	NA
Distributor	—	—	NA	NA	—
Coil	6v	—/12v	NA	NA	12v
Contact-breaker gap (in.)	0.012	0.012	0.012	0.012	0.012
Spark plug gap (in.)	0.018	0.018	0.018	0.018	0.018
Spark plug thread (mm)	18	14	14	14	18
Spark plug	racing	Ch.L-10S	Ch.L-10S	racing	—
Ignition timing (^{o} btdc)	V	—	—	V	—
ELECTRICAL					
Earthing pole	neg.	neg.	neg.	neg.	neg.
Battery	6v	12v	12v	2 x 6v	12v
Starter motor	—	—	—	—	—
Generator	—	—	—	—	—

	J4	K1, K2	KN	K3	L1, L2
CHASSIS					
Chassis-frame pattern	R, und.	R, und.	R, und.	R, und.	R, und.
Sidemembers	cn.	cn.	cn.	cn.	cn.
Crossmembers	cn.	tub.	tub.	tub.	cn.
Front suspension	SE	SE	SE	SE	SE
Rear suspension	SE	SE	SE	SE	SE
Shockabsorbers	X	X	X	X	X
Special chassis features	—	GL	—	cruciform	—
TRANSMISSION					
Clutch	SDP	auto. or 2DP	2DP	auto.	SDP
Gearbox action	crash	crash or pre.	3rd CM	pre.	crash
No. of forward gears	4	4	4	4	4
Gear lever location	cen.	cen.	cen.	cen.	cen.
Forward gear ratios (x:1)	14.45, 9.98, 7.31, 5.375	19.65, 11.56 7.76, 5.78	24.15, 13.4 7.86, 5.78	V	19.24, 11.5, 7.31, 5.375
Gearbox lubricant, SAE	30	30	30	30	30
Gearbox lubricant, quantity (pts)	6	2	2	6	2
Rear axle bevel; ratio (x:1)	p.b.; 5.375	sp.; 5.78V	sp.; 5.78	p.b.; 4.33V	sp.; 5.375
Rear axle lubricant, SAE	140	140	140	140	140
Rear axle lubricant, quantity (pts)	2	2	2	2	2
STEERING AND FRONT AXLE					
Steering box	WW	MW	MW	MW	MW
Steering box lubricant, SAE	140	140	140	140	140
Front axle	IB	IB	IB	IB	IB
Toe-in setting (in.)	1/8	1/8	1/8	—	1/8
BRAKES					
Type	mech.	mech.	mech.	mech.	mech.
Actuation	cable	cable	cable	cable	cable
BODYWORK					
Body construction	racing	PS & a.	PS & a.	racing	a.
No. of doors	2	2 or 4	2 or 4	0	2 or 4
No. of seats	2	2 or 4	2 or 4	2	4
WHEELS AND TYRES					
Wheels	RW	RW	RW	RW	RW
Tyres, size	4.00 x 19	4.75 x 19V	4.75 x 19	4.75 x 19	4.50 x 19
Front tyre pressure (lb/in^2)	24	28	28	28	28
Rear tyre pressure (lb/in^2)	28	30	30	30	30

Name	M	NA	NE	PA	PB
Year(s) of manufacture	1930 - 32	1934 - 36	1934	1934 - 36	1936
ENGINE					
Capacity (cc)	847	1286	1286	847	939
Number of cylinders	4	6	6	4	4
Bore and stroke (mm)	57 x 83	57 x 84	57 x 84	57 x 83	60 x 83
Compression ratio (x:1)	5.4	6.9	9.5	6.1	—
RAC hp rating	8.05	12.08	12.08	8.05	8.9
Maximum bhp @ rev/min	12 - 27 @ 4500 10	56 @ 5500	68 @ 6500	36 @ 5500	43 @ 5500
Firing order	1,3,4,2	1,5,3,6,2,4	1,5,3,6,2,4	1,3,4,2	1,3,4,2
Valve layout	ohc	ohc	ohc	ohc	ohc
Inlet valve opens (^{o} btdc)	9° atdc or 0	15	25	15	15
Tappet adjustment (inlet) in.	0.004H	0.006H	0.010H	0.006H	0.006H
Tappet adjustment (exhaust) in.	0.004H	0.008H	0.016H	0.008H	0.008H
Timing marks location	TG	TG	TG	TG	TG
Lubrication pattern	FP	FP	FP	FP	FP
Oil-pump type	gear	gear	gear	gear	gear
Optimum oil pressure (lb/in ^{2})	—	—	—	—	—
Pistons type; number of rings	a ; 3	a ; 3	a ; 3	a ; 3	a ; 3
No. of main bearings	2	4	4	3	3
Main bearings	b.b. & WM	WM & sh.	WM & sh.	WM	WM
Camshaft drive	via gen.	via gen.	via gen.	via gen.	via gen.
Sump capacity (pts)	4 or 8	12	12	—	—
Lubricant (summer), SAE	30	40	CR	40	40
Lubricant (winter), SAE	30	40	CR	40	40
Engine mountings	rigid	flex.	flex.	flex.	flex.
Exhaust manifold, branches	unit	2 x 3	2 x 3	4	4
CARBURATION					
Carburetter	SU	2 x SU	2 x SU	2 x SU	2 x SU
Carburetter type	HV2	HV2	HV4	OM	OM
Choke size	1 1/8 in.	1 1/8 in.	1 3/8 in.	1 in.	1 in.
Main jet	0.090	0.090	0.090	0.090	0.090
Slow-running or pilot jet	NA	NA	NA	NA	NA
Compensating or correction jet	NA	NA	NA	NA	NA
GA and GS jet, or progression jet	NA	NA	NA	NA	NA
Capacity well or pump jet	NA	NA	NA	NA	NA
Metering needle (standard)	M5	3	C1	M6	M6
Metering needle (weak)	M6	L	—	S	S
Average mpg	36	26	20 - 24	35 - 38	35
Fuel feed	gravity	SUE	SUE	SUE	SUE
Tank capacity (gall)	4 or 5	10	10	12	12
IGNITION					
HT supply	coil	coil	coil	coil	coil
Magneto	NA	NA	NA	NA	NA
Distributor	Ro. or Lu.	Rotax	Rotax	Rotax	Rotax
Coil	Ro. or Lu. 6v	Rotax 12v	Rotax 12v	Rotax 12v	Rotax 12v
Contact-breaker gap (in.)	0.012	0.012	0.012	0.012	0.012
Spark plug gap (in.)	0.020	0.020	0.020	0.018	0.018
Spark plug thread (mm)	18	14	14	14	14
Spark plug	—	Ch. L10S	racing	—	racing
Ignition timing (^{o} btdc)	30FA	—	—	—	—
ELECTRICAL					
Earthing pole	neg .	neg.	neg.	neg.	neg.
Battery	6v	2 x 6v	2 x 6v	2 x 6v	2 x 6v
Starter motor	—	—	—	—	—
Generator	—	—	—	—	—

	M	NA	NE	PA	PB
CHASSIS					
Chassis-frame pattern	R, up.	R, und.	R, und.	R, und.	R, und.
Sidemembers	cn.	cn.	cn.	cn.	cn.
Crossmembers	cn.	cn.	cn.	cn.	cn.
Front suspension	SE	SE	SE	SE	SE
Rear suspension	SE	SE	SE	SE	SE
Shockabsorbers	X	F,X; R, hyd.	X	F,X; R, hyd.	F,X; R, hyd.
Special chassis features	–	GL	GL	–	–
TRANSMISSION					
Clutch	SDP	SDP	SDP	SDP	SDP
Gearbox action	Cr.	CM or pre.	Cr.	CM	CM
No. of forward gears	3 (or 4)	4	4	4	4
Gear lever location	cen.	cen.	cen.	cen.	cen.
Forward gear ratios (x:1)	17.1, 8.84, 4.89V	21.5, 11.9, 6.98, 5.125	19.43, 17.45, 6.63, 4.875	19.24, 11.51, 7.31, 5.375	19.24, 11.51, 7.31, 5.375
Gearbox lubricant, SAE	30	30	30	30	30
Gearbox lubricant, quantity (pts)	1½	–	–	–	–
Rear axle bevel; ratio (x:1)	sp.;4.89V	sp.;5.125	p.b.;4.875	sp.;5.375	sp.;5.375
Rear axle lubricant, SAE	90	90	90	90	90
Rear axle lubricant, quantity (pts)	1½	–	–	–	–
STEERING AND FRONT AXLE					
Steering box	WW	BC	BC	MW	MW
Steering box lubricant	140	140	140	140	140
Front axle	IB	IB	IB	IB	IB
Toe-in setting (in.)	1/8	1/8	1/8	1/8	1/8
BRAKES					
Type	mech.	mech.	mech.	mech.	mech.
Actuation	cable	cable	cable	cable	cable
BODYWORK					
Body construction	fb. + wo./PS	PS	racing	PS & a.	PS & a.
No. of doors	2	2	0	2	2
No. of seats	2	2 or 4	2	2 or 4	2 or 4
WHEELS AND TYRES					
Wheels	RW	RW	RW	RW	RW
Tyres, size	4.00 x 19	4.00 x 19	4.00 x 19	4.00 x 19	4.00 x 19
Front tyre pressure (lb/in^2)	24	24	24	24	24
Rear tyre pressure (lb/in^2)	28	28	28	28	28

BRITISH LIGHT CARS

Name	Q	R	TA	TB	VA
Year(s) of manufacture	1934	1935	1936 - 39	1939	1937 - 39
ENGINE					
Capacity (cc)	746	746	1292	1250	1548
Number of cylinders	4	4	4	4	4
Bore and stroke (mm)	57 x 73	57 x 73	63.5 x 102	66.5 x 90	69.5 x 102
Compression ratio (x:1)	6.4	6.4	6.5	6.5	12
RAC hp rating	8.05	8.05	10	10.97	12
Maximum bhp @ rev/min	113 @ 7200 (S)	113 @ 7200 (S)	52 @ 5200	54.4 @ 5200	55 @ 4400
Firing order	1,3,4,2	1,3,4,2	1,3,4,2	1,3,4,2	1,3,4,2
Valve layout	ohc	ohc	ohv	ohv	ohv
Inlet valve opens (°btdc)	15	15	11	11	11
Tappet adjustment (inlet) in.	0.008H	0.006H	0.015H	0.019H	0.010H
Tappet adjustment (exhaust) in.	0.014H	0.008H	0.015H	0.019H	0.015H
Timing marks location	TG	TG	TS	TS	TS
Lubrication pattern	FP	FP	FP	FP	FP
Oil-pump type	gear	gear	gear	gear	gear
Optimum oil pressure (lb/in ^{2})	—	—	60 - 70	60 - 70	—
Pistons type; number of rings	a ; 3	a ; 3	a ; 4 or 3	a ; 3	a ; 3
No. of main bearings	3	3	3	3	3
Main bearings	WM	WM	sh.	sh.	sh.
Camshaft drive	via gen.	via gen.	chain	chain	chain
Sump capacity (pts)	—	—	11	11	12
Lubricant (summer), SAE	CR	CR	30	30	30
Lubricant (winter), SAE	CR	CR	30	30	30
Engine mountings	—	—	flex.	flex.	flex.
Exhaust manifold, branches	4	4	3	3	3
CARBURATION					
Carburetter	SU	SU	2 x SU	2 x SU	2 x SU
Carburetter type	HV4	HV4	HV3	HV3	HV3
Choke size	1 3/8 in.	1 3/8 in.	1¼ in.	1¼ in.	1¼ in.
Main jet	0.090	0.090	0.090	0.090	0.090
Slow-running or pilot jet	NA	NA	NA	NA	NA
Compensating or correction jet	NA	NA	NA	NA	NA
GA and GS jet, or progression jet	NA	NA	NA	NA	NA
Capacity well or pump jet	NA	NA	NA	NA	NA
Metering needle (standard)	QA	RA	AC	AC	CO
Metering needle (weak)	—	—	S	S	—
Average mpg	—	—	28	30	27 - 28
Fuel feed	2 x SUE	2 x SUE	SUE	SUE	SUE
Tank capacity (gall)	19	19	15	15	12½
IGNITION					
HT supply	magneto	magneto	coil	coil	coil
Magneto	B.T.H.	B.T.H.	NA	NA	NA
Distributor	NA	NA	DKY4A	DKY4A	DKY4A
Coil	NA	NA	Q12	Q12	Q12
Contact-breaker gap (in.)	—	—	0.012	0.012	0.012
Spark plug gap (in.)	—	—	0.018	0.018	0.018
Spark plug thread (mm)	14	14	14	14	14
Spark plug	racing	racing	Ch. L-10S	Ch. L-10S	Ch. L-10S
Ignition timing (°btdc)	—	—	O,FR	O,FR	—
ELECTRICAL					
Earthing pole	neg.	neg.	pos.	pos.	pos.
Battery	2 x 6v	2 x 6v	2 x 6v	2 x 6v	2 x 6v
Starter motor	—	—	M418G	M418G	M418G
Generator	—	—	C39PV	C39PV	C39PV

	Q	R	TA	TB	VA
CHASSIS					
Chassis-frame pattern	R, und.	'backbone'	R, und.	R, und.	R, und.
Sidemembers	cn.	box	box	box	box
Crossmembers	cn.	box	tub.	tub.	tub.
Front suspension	SE	torsion bars	SE	SE	SE
Rear suspension	SE	torsion bars	SE	SE	SE
Shockabsorbers	F, X; R, hyd.	FX; R, hyd.	hyd.	hyd.	hyd.
Special chassis features	—	—	GL	GL	GL
TRANSMISSION					
Clutch	2DP	2DP	wet	wet	wet
Gearbox action	pre.	pre.	syn.	syn.	syn.
No. of forward gears	4	4	4	4	4
Gear lever location	clm.	clm.	cen.	cen.	cen.
Forward gear ratios (x:1)	15.3, 9, 6.12, 4.5	13.93, 7.59, 5.4, 4.125	19.09, 9.94, 6.43, 4.875	17.32, 9.99, 6.91, 5.125	17.64, 10.18, 7.05, 5.22
Gearbox lubricant, SAE	—	—	30	30	30
Gearbox lubricant, quantity (pts)	—	—	—	—	—
Rear axle bevel; ratio (x:1)	p.b.;4.5V	p.b.;4.125	sp.;4.875	sp.;5.125	sp.;5.22
Rear axle lubricant, SAE	—	—	90	90	90
Rear axle lubricant, quantity (pts)	—	—	—	—	—
STEERING AND FRONT AXLE					
Steering box	—	—	BC	BC	BC
Steering box lubricant	—	—	140	140	140
Front axle	IB	ifs (& irs)	IB	IB	IB
Toe-in setting (in.)	—	—	—	—	—
BRAKES					
Type	mech.	mech.	Lockheed	Lockheed	Lockheed
Actuation	cable	cable	hyd.	hyd.	hyd.
BODYWORK					
Body construction	racing	racing	a. on wo.	co.	PS & a.
No. of doors	0	0	2	2	4
No. of seats	2	1	2	2	4
WHEELS AND TYRES					
Wheels	RW	RW	RW	RW	RW
Tyres, size	4.75 x 18	4.75 x 18	4.50 x 19	5.50 x 19	5.00 x 19
Front tyre pressure (lb/in^2)	30	30	24	24	28
Rear tyre pressure (lb/in^2)	30	30	26	26	26

Morgan

Name	M (3W)	M (3W)	M (3W	M (3W)
Year(s) of manufacture	1931 - 33	1931 - 33	1931 - 33	1931 - 39
ENGINE	J A P,a.c.	J A P, a.c.	J A P, a.c.	J A P, a.c./w.c.
Capacity (cc)	980	1000	1096	990
Number of cylinders	2	2	2	2
Bore and stroke (mm)	—	—	85.7 x 95	85.5 x 85.5
Compression ratio (x:1)	—	—	—	5 or 6.2
RAC hp rating	8	8	8	8
Maximum bhp @ rev/min	28 @ -	43 or 50 @ -	45 or 50 @ -	27 - 42 @ 4200
Firing order	1,2	1,2	1,2	1,2
Valve layout	sv	ohv	sv or ohv	sv or ohv
Inlet valve opens (º btdc)	17	15 - 25	16 - 25	16 or 22
Tappet adjustment (inlet) in.	0.000	0.000	0.000	0.00 (-4, sv)
Tappet adjustment (exhaust) in.	0.000	0.000	0.000	0.00 (-6, sv)
Timing marks location	TS	TS	TS	TS
Lubrication pattern	dry sump	dry sump	dry sump	dry sump
Oil-pump type	plunger	plunger	plunger	plunger
Optimum oil pressure (lb/in ^{2})	5 — 10	5 — 10	5 — 10	6
Pistons type; number of rings	a ; 2 or 3	a ; 2 or 3	a ; 2 or 3	a ; 3
No. of main bearings	2	2	2	2
Main bearings	r.b.	r.b.	r.b.	r.b.
Camshaft drive	gear	gear	gear	gear
Sump capacity (pts)	tank	tank	tank	tank
Lubricant (summer), SAE	30	30	30	30
Lubricant (winter), SAE	30	30	30	30
Engine mountings	rigid	rigid	rigid	rigid
Exhaust manifold, branches	2 x 1	2 x 1	2 x 1	2 x 1
CARBURATION				
Carburetter	Amal	Amal	Amal	Amal
Carburetter type	—	—	—	—
Choke size	t.sl. 4/4	t.sl. 4/4	t.sl. 4/4	6 or 29/4
Main jet	0.1065 (std)	0.1065 (std)	0.1065 (std)	140 or 180
Slow-running or pilot jet	NA	NA	NA	NA
Compensating or correction jet	NA	NA	NA	NA
GA and GS jet, or progression jet	NA	NA	NA	NA
Capacity well or pump jet	NA	NA	NA	NA
Metering needle (standard)	n.p.V	n.p.V	n.p.V	n.p. No. 3
Metering needle (weak)	n.p.V	n.p.V	n.p.V	n.p. No. 2
Average mpg	—	—	—	—
Fuel feed	gravity	gravity	gravity	gravity
Tank capacity (gall)	4	4	4	4
IGNITION				
HT supply	mag./coil	mag./coil	mag./coil	coil
Magneto	Miller	Miller	Miller	NA
Distributor	NA	NA	NA	2 - cyl. type
Coil	NA	NA	NA	6v
Contact-breaker gap (in.)	0.015	0.015	0.015	0.012
Spark plug gap (in.)	0.018	0.018	0.018	0.018
Spark plug thread (mm)	18	18	18	18 or 14
Spark plug	Lo - C3	Ch. 16 or 1·7	V	Ch. L-10 V
Ignition timing (º btdc)	45,FA	45,FA	38 - 40,FA	3/8 in.
ELECTRICAL				
Earthing pole	neg.	neg.	neg.	neg.
Battery	6v	6v	6v	6v
Starter motor	—	—	—	—
Generator	—	—	—	—

	M (980cc)	M (1000cc)	M (1096 cc)	M (990 cc)
CHASSIS				
Chassis-frame pattern	king-post	king-post	king-post	king-post
Sidemembers	tub.	tub.	tub.	tub.
Crossmembers	tub.	tub.	tub.	tub.
Front suspension	coil ifs	coil ifs	coil ifs	coil ifs
Rear suspension	und. QE	und. QE	und. QE	und. QE
Shockabsorbers	none, or X	none, or X	none, or X	none, or X
Special chassis features	—	—	—	—
TRANSMISSION				
Clutch	SDP	SDP	SDP	SDP
Gearbox action	crash	crash	crash	crash
No. of forward gears	3	3	3	3
Gear lever location	cen.	cen.	cen.	cen.
Forward gear ratios (x:1)	—	—	—	—
Gearbox lubricant, SAE	90	90	90	90
Gearbox lubricant, quantity (pts)	—	—	—	—
Rear axle bevel; ratio (x:1)	NA	NA	NA	NA
Rear axle lubricant, SAE	NA	NA	NA	NA
Rear axle lubricant, quantity (pts)	NA	NA	NA	NA
STEERING AND FRONT AXLE				
Steering box	WP, 2 : 1	WP, 2 : 1	WP, 2 : 1	WP, 2 : 1
Steering box lubricant	grease	grease	grease	grease
Front axle	NA (ifs)	NA (ifs)	NA (ifs)	NA (ifs)
Toe-in setting (in.)	1/8	1/8	1/8	1/8
BRAKES				
Type	mech.	mech.	mech.	mech.
Actuation	cable	cable	cable	cable
BODYWORK				
Body construction	S & a. on wo.	S & a. on wo.	S & a. on wo.	S & a. on wo.
No. of doors	0 or 1	0 or 1	0 or 1	2
No. of seats	2	2	2	2 or 4
WHEELS AND TYRES				
Wheels	wire	wire	wire	wire or M
Tyres,size	4.00 x 26	4.00 x 26	4.00 x 26	4.00 x 26V
Front tyre pressure (lb/in^2)	23	23	23	23
Rear tyre pressure(lb/in^2)	25	25	25	25

BRITISH LIGHT CARS

Name	F (3W) 8 or 10 hp (Ford engine)	4/4 (Standard engine)
Year(s) of manufacture	1934 - 39	1938 - 39
ENGINE		
Capacity (cc)	933/1172	1267
Number of cylinders	4	4
Bore and stroke (mm)	56.6 x 92.5 63.5 x 92.5	63.5 x 100
Compression ratio (x : 1)	6.3 or 6.16	7
RAC hp rating	7.96 or 9.9	9.9
Maximum bhp @ rev/min	23 or 30 @ 4300	40 @ 4000
Firing order	1,2,4,3	1,3,4,2
Valve layout	sv	ohv
Inlet valve opens (° btdc)	19	0
Tappet adjustment (inlet) in.	0.011 - 0.013	0.022 C
Tappet adjustment (exhaust) in.	0.011 - 0.013	0.022 C
Timing marks location	TS	fly.
Lubrication pattern	FP	FP
Oil-pump type	gear	gear
Optimum oil pressure (lb/in^2)	30	—
Pistons type; number of rings	a; 3	a; 3
No. of main bearings	3	3
Main bearings	WM or sh.	sh.
Camshaft drive	chain	chain
Sump capacity (pts)	4 or 4½	8
Lubricant (summer) SAE	30	30
Lubricant (winter) SAE	20	20
Engine mountings	—	flex.
Exhaust manifold, branches	3	3
CARBURATION		
Carburetter	Ford/Zenith	Solex
Carburetter type	d.d.	30 FAI
Choke size		26 mm
Main jet	”	125
Slow-running or pilot jet	”	PJ 45
Compensating or correction jet	See 'Ford' data	Cr J 170
GA and GS jet or progression jet	”	—
Capacity well or pump jet	”	—
Metering needle (standard)	”	NA
Metering needle (weak)	”	NA
Average mpg	—	35
Fuel feed	—	ACM
Tank capacity (gall)	5	9
IGNITION		
HT supply	coil	coil
Magneto	NA	NA
Distributor	Delco	—
Coil	Delco 6v	12v
Contact-breaker gap (in.)	0.012 - 0.015	0.012
Spark plug gap (in.)	0.018 - 0.022	0.025
Spark plug thread (mm)	18 or 14	14
Spark plug	Lo. C3 or CN	Ch. NA-8
Ignition timing (° btdc)	26, FA	0, FR
ELECTRICAL		
Earthing pole	neg/pos.	pos.
Battery	6v 63 ah	12v 57ah
Starter motor	—	M35A
Generator	—	C45 NV/L

	F (3W)	*4/4*
CHASSIS		
Chassis-frame pattern	ladder	ladder
Sidemembers	cn.	cn.
Crossmembers	cn.	cn.
Front suspension	coil ifs	coil ifs
Rear suspension	QE	SE
Shockabsorbers	—	hyd.
Special chassis features	Z-section	Z-section
TRANSMISSION		
Clutch	SDP	SDP
Gearbox action	S3 or syn.	syn.
No. of forward gears	3	4
Gear lever location	cen.	cen.
Forward gear ratios (x : 1)	See 'Ford' data	17.6, 12, 6.5, 5.0
Gearbox lubricant, SAE	—	90
Gearbox lubricant, quantity (pts)	—	1½
Rear axle bevel; ratio (x : 1)	—	sp; 5.0
Rear axle lubricant, SAE	NA	140
Rear axle lubricant, quantity (pts)	NA	1½
STEERING AND FRONT AXLE		
Steering box	WP, 2 : 1	WN
Steering box lubricant, SAE	grease	140
Front axle	NA (ifs)	NA (ifs)
Toe-in setting (in)	1/8	1/8
BRAKES		
Type	mech./G	Girling
Actuation	cable/rod	rod
BODYWORK		
Body construction	S & a. or wo.	a. on wo.
No. of doors	2	2
No. of seats	4	2 or 4
WHEELS AND TYRES		
Wheels, type	M	disc
Tyres, size	4.00 x 26V	5.00 x 16
Front tyre pressure (lb/in^2)	23	18
Rear tyre pressure (lb/in^2)	25	20

Morris

Name	Minor	Eight	8 hp E	Ten - Four (Series III)
Year(s) of manufacture	1930 - 34	1934 - 38	1938 - 39	1939
ENGINE				
Capacity (cc)	847	918.6	918.6	1140
Number of cylinders	4	4	4	4
Bore and stroke (mm)	57 x 83	57 x 90	57 x 90	63.5 x 90
Compression ratio (x:1)	—	5.8	6.5	6
RAC hp rating	7.6	8.05	8.05	9.99
Maximum bhp @ rev/min	20 @ 3500 (ohc)	23.5 @ 4000	29.5 @ 4400	31 @ 4000
Firing order	1,3,4,2	1,3,4,2	1,3,4,2	1,3,4,2
Valve layout	ohc or sv	sv	sv	sv or ohv
Inlet valve opens (^{o} btdc)	0	8	8	5
Tappet adjustment (inlet) in.	0.003/4H	0.004H	0.017H	0.017H
Tappet adjustment (exhaust) in.	0.003/4H	0.004H	0.017H	0.017H
Timing marks location	TG or fly.	TS	TS	TS
Lubrication pattern	FP	FP	FP	FP
Oil-pump type	gear	gear	gear	gear
Optimum oil pressure (lb/in ^{2})	20 - 25	30 - 60	30 - 60	30 - 60
Pistons type; number of rings	a ; 3	a ; 3	a ; 3	a ; 3
No. of main bearings	2	3	3	3
Main bearings	WM	WM	sh.	sh.
Camshaft drive	via gen/ch.	chain	chain	chain
Sump capacity (pts)	—	5	6½	8
Lubricant (summer), SAE	30	30	30	30
Lubricant (winter), SAE	20	30	30	30
Engine mountings	—	flex.	flex.	flex.
Exhaust manifold, branches	—	unit	unit	unit
CARBURATION				
Carburetter	SU	SU	SU	SU
Carburetter type	OM	UB	H1	H2
Choke size	1 in.	1 in.	1 1/8 in.	1¼ in.
Main jet	0.090	0.090	0.090	0.090
Slow-running or pilot jet	NA	NA	NA	NA
Compensating or correction jet	NA	NA	NA	NA
GA and GS jet, or progression jet	NA	NA	NA	NA
Capacity well or pump jet	NA	NA	NA	NA
Metering needle (standard)	MR/M9	BA or BD	EK	DJ
Metering needle (weak)	MP/MO	M7	MOW	DM
Average mpg	45 - 48	38 - 45	38 - 45	32
Fuel feed	Petrolift	SUE	SUE	SUE
Tank capacity (gall)	5	5½	5½	7
IGNITION				
HT supply	coil	coil	coil	coil
Magneto	NA	NA	NA	NA
Distributor	DJ4	DK4A	DK4A	DK4A
Coil	6v	6v	6v	Q12
Contact-breaker gap (in.)	0.012	0.012	0.012	0.012
Spark plug gap (in.)	0.022	0.020	0.020	0.022
Spark plug thread (mm)	18	14	14	14
Spark plug	Lo - C3	Ch. L-10	Ch. L-10	Ch. L-10
Ignition timing (^{o} btdc)	—	O,FR	O,FR	O,FR
ELECTRICAL				
Earthing pole	neg.	neg./pos.	pos.	pos.
Battery	6v	6v	6v 51 ah	12v 51 ah
Starter motor	—	—	M35G	M418G
Generator	—	—	C45YV	C45YV

	Minor	Eight	8hp E	Ten-Four (Series III)
CHASSIS				
Chassis-frame pattern	ladder	F, I; R, up.	F, I; R, up.	unitary
Sidemembers	cn.	box	box	box
Crossmembers	cn.	cn.	cn.	floor
Front suspension	SE	SE	SE	SE
Rear suspension	SE	SE	SE	SE
Shockabsorbers	X	hyd.	hyd.	hyd.
Special chassis features	—	—	—	—
TRANSMISSION				
Clutch	SDP	SDP	SDP	SDP
Gearbox action	CM	syn.	syn.	syn.
No. of forward gears	3 or 4	3	4	4
Gear lever location	cen.	cen.	cen.	cen.
Forward gear ratios (x:1)	17.5,8.97,4.88V	17.13,9.73,5.375	20.88, 12.15, 8.14, 5.286	20.88, 12.15, 8.14, 5.286
Gearbox lubricant, SAE	90	90	90	90
Gearbox lubricant, quantity (pts)	1½	1½	1½	1½
Rear axle bevel; ratio (x:1)	sp.;4.88V	sp.;5.375	sp.;5.286	sp.;5.286
Rear axle lubricant, SAE	90	90	140	140
Rear axle lubricant, quantity (pts)	—	1	1	1½
STEERING AND FRONT AXLE				
Steering box	WW/BC	BC	BC	BC
Steering box lubricant	90	90	140	140
Front axle	IB	IB	IB	IB
Toe-in setting (in.)	1/8	1/8	1/8	1/8
BRAKES				
Type	mech/Lk.	Lockheed	Lockheed	Lockheed
Actuation	rod/hyd.	hyd.	hyd.	hyd.
BODYWORK				
Body construction	S or fb.	PS	PS	PS
No. of doors	2	2 or 4	2 or 4	4
No. of seats	2 or 4	2 or 4	4	4
WHEELS AND TYRES				
Wheels	wire	M/SD	SD	SD
Tyres,size	4.00 x 19	4.50 x 17	4.50 x 17	5.00 x 16
Front tyre pressure (lb/in^2)	22 or 24	24	24	23
Rear tyre pressure(lb/in^2)	26 or 27	24 or 27	27	25

	Ten - Six Special Sports	Cowley	Twelve - Four
Name			
Year(s) of manufacture	1934 - 35	1930 - 34	1935 - 37
ENGINE			
Capacity (cc)	1378	1550	1550
Number of cylinders	6	4	4
Bore and stroke (mm)	63.5 x 102	69.5 x 102	69.5 x 102
Compression ratio (x:1)	—	5.8	—
RAC hp rating	12	11.9	11.9
Maximum bhp @ rev/min	42 @ 4200	28 @ 3500	34 @ 3400
Firing order	1,5,3,6,2,4	1,3,4,2	1,3,4,2
Valve layout	sv	sv	sv
Inlet valve opens (^{o}btdc)	—	—	11
Tappet adjustment (inlet) in.	0.015H	0.004H	0.019H
Tappet adjustment (exhaust) in.	0.015H	0.004H	0.019H
Timing marks location	TS	TS	TS
Lubrication pattern	FP	FP	FP
Oil-pump type	gear	gear	gear
Optimum oil pressure (lb/in ^{2})	30—60	25—30	30—60
Pistons type; number of rings	a ; 3	a ; 3	a ; 3
No. of main bearings	4	3	3
Main bearings	WM	WM	WM
Camshaft drive	chain	chain	chain
Sump capacity (pts)	—	12	12
Lubricant (summer), SAE	30	30	30
Lubricant (winter), SAE	30	30	30
Engine mountings	—	4 x flex.	flex.
Exhaust manifold, branches	5	unit	unit
CARBURATION			
Carburetter	2 x SU	SU	SU
Carburetter type	HV2	—	HV2
Choke size	1 1/8 in.	—	1 1/8 in.
Main jet	0.090	—	0.090
Slow-running or pilot jet	NA	NA	NA
Compensating or correction jet	NA	NA	NA
GA and GS jet, or progression jet	NA	NA	NA
Capacity well or pump jet	NA	NA	NA
Metering needle (standard)	AK	—	A1 or AT
Metering needle (weak)	D6	—	M6 or BT
Average mpg	22 - 25	25	28
Fuel feed	SUE	gravity/SUE	SUE
Tank capacity (gall)	6½	7	7
IGNITION			
HT supply	coil	magneto	coil
Magneto	NA	Lucas	NA
Distributor	—	NA	DK4A
Coil	—	NA	12v
Contact-breaker gap (in.)	0.012	0.015	0.012
Spark plug gap (in)	0.020	0.020	0.020
Spark plug thread (mm)	18	18	14
Spark plug	—	Lo - C3	Ch. L-10
Ignition timing (^{o}btdc)	—	—	0
ELECTRICAL			
Earthing pole	neg.	neg.	neg/pos.
Battery	2 x 6v 51 ah	12v	12v 51 ah
Starter motor	—	—	—
Generator	—	—	—

	Ten-Six	Cowley	Twelve-Four
CHASSIS			
Chassis-frame pattern	F,I; R, up.	F,I ; R, up.	F,I ; R, up.
Sidemembers	cn.	cn.	cn.
Crossmembers	cn.	cn.	cn.
Front suspension	SE	SE	SE
Rear suspension	SE	SE	SE
Shockabsorbers	hyd.	X	hyd.
Special chassis features	—	—	—
TRANSMISSION			
Clutch	wet	wet	wet
Gearbox action	CM	CM	syn.
No. of forward gears	4	3	3
Gear lever location	cen.	cen.	cen.
Forward gear ratios (x:1)	—	15.2,8.17,4.75	—
Gearbox lubricant, SAE	90	90	90
Gearbox lubricant, quantity (pts)	1½	—	1½
Rear axle bevel; ratio (x:1)	sp.;	sp.;4.75	sp.;4.875
Rear axle lubricant, SAE	90	90	90
Rear axle lubricant, quantity (pts)	1	1½	1
STEERING AND FRONT AXLE			
Steering box	BC	BC	BC
Steering box lubricant	90	90	90
Front axle	IB	IB	IB
Toe-in setting (in.)	1/8	1/8	1/8
BRAKES			
Type	Lockheed	Lockheed	Lockheed
Actuation	hyd.	hyd.	hyd.
BODYWORK			
Body construction	PS	S & a.	PS
No. of doors	2	2 or 4	2 or 4
No. of seats	2/4	2 or 4	2 or 4
WHEELS AND TYRES			
Wheels	M	wire	wire/SD
Tyres,size	4.75 x 18	4.50 x 19	4.75 x 18
Front tyre pressure (lb/in^2)	30	28	28
Rear tyre pressure (lb/in^2)	30	30	30

Riley

Name	Nine	Nine (Special Series)	Nine Imp
Year(s) of manufacture	1930 - 38	1930 - 38	1935
ENGINE			
Capacity (cc)	1087	1087	1087
Number of cylinders	4	4	4
Bore and stroke (mm)	60.3 x 95.2	60.3 x 95.2	60.3 x 95.2
Compression ratio (x:1)	5.9	6.6	6.6
RAC hp rating	9.01	9.01	9.01
Maximum bhp @ rev/min	26 - 30 @ 4300	35 - 41 @ 5000	41 @ 5000
Firing order	1,2,4,3	1,2,4,3	1,2,4,3
Valve layout	ohv	ohv	ohv
Inlet valve opens (°btdc)	0	0	25
Tappet adjustment (inlet) in.	0.002H	0.002H	0.002H
Tappet adjustment (exhaust) in.	0.003H	0.003H	0.003H
Timing marks location	TS	TS	TS
Lubrication pattern	FP	FP	FP
Oil-pump type	plunger	plunger	plunger
Optimum oil pressure (lb/in ^{2})	40 - 60	40 - 60	40 - 60
Pistons type; number of rings	a ; 3	a ; 3	a ; 3
No. of main bearings	2	2	2
Main bearings	BWM	BWM	BWM
Camshaft drive	gear	gear	gear
Sump capacity (pts)	7	7	7
Lubricant (summer), SAE	30	30	40
Lubricant (winter), SAE	30	30	40
Engine mountings	flex.	flex.	flex.
Exhaust manifold, branches	unit	unit	4
CARBURATION			
Carburetter	SU/Zenith	2 x SU	2 x Zenith
Carburetter type	HV2/26VEH	OM	26 VEH & 26 VEHG
Choke size	1 1/8 in./20 mm	1 in.	21 mm
Main jet	0.090/70	0.090	80
Slow-running or pilot jet	NA/SRJ50	NA	SRJ60
Compensating or correction jet	NA/CJ65	NA	CJ70
GA and GS jet, or progression jet	NA/NA	NA	PrJ 160
Capacity well or pump jet	NA/std.	NA	W std.
Metering needle (standard)	M5/NA	D1/D2/MA/PJ	NA
Metering needle (weak)	M6/NA	PJ/—/S/—	NA
Average mpg	33 - 40	30 - 38	—
Fuel feed	Au./SUE	Au./SUE	SUE
Tank capacity (gall)	7½ or 9½	7½ or 9½	7½ or 9½
IGNITION			
HT supply	mag./coil	mag./coil	coil
Magneto	—	Lucas	NA
Distributor	—	DK4A	DK4A
Coil	12v	12v	12v
Contact-breaker gap (in.)	0.012	0.012	0.012
Spark plug gap (in.)	0.018	0.018	0.018
Spark plug thread (mm)	18	18	18
Spark plug	Ch. 16 or 17	Lo - H2	KLG - KS5
Ignition timing (°btdc)	O,FR	O,FR	O,FR
ELECTRICAL			
Earthing pole	neg/pos.	neg/pos.	neg.
Battery	2 x 6v	2 x 6v	2 x 6v
Starter motor	—	—	—
Generator	—	—	thi.

298

	Nine	*Nine* *(Special Series)*	*Nine Imp*
CHASSIS			
Chassis-frame pattern	F,I ; R, up.	F,I ; R, up.	F,I ; R, up.
Sidemembers	cn./box	cn./box	cn./box
Crossmembers	cn./tub.	cn./tub.	cn.
Front suspension	SE	SE	SE
Rear suspension	SE	SE	SE
Shockabsorbers	X/hyd.	X/hyd.	hyd.
Special chassis features	OSL(1930 - 34)	OSL (1930 - 34)	OSL
TRANSMISSION			
Clutch	SDP/auto.	SDP/auto.	auto.
Gearbox action	S3/pre.	S3/pre.	pre.
No. of forward gears	4	4	4
Gear lever location	cen/clm.	cen/clm.	cen.
Forward gear ratios (x:1)	20.86, 13.5, 8.06, 5.5V	20.86, 13.5, 8.06, 5.5V	21.45, 13.26, 8.06, 5.5
Gearbox lubricant, SAE	30	30	30
Gearbox lubricant, quantity (pts)	3 or 4½	3 or 4½	4½
Rear axle bevel; ratio (x:1)	(TT) sp.; 5.5V	(TT) sp.; 5.5V	(TT) sp.; 5.5
Rear axle lubricant, SAE	90	90	90
Rear axle lubricant, quantity (pts)	3½	3½	3½
STEERING AND FRONT AXLE			
Steering box	WW or WS	WW or WS	WW or WS
Steering box lubricant	140	140	140
Front axle	IB	IB	IB
Toe-in setting (in.)	1/8	1/8	1/8
BRAKES			
Type	mech./G	mech./G	mech.
Actuation	cable/rod	cable/rod	cable
BODYWORK			
Body construction	fb., a. or PS	fb., a. or PS	a. & PS
No. of doors	2 or 4	2 or 4	2
No. of seats	2 or 4	2 or 4	2
WHEELS AND TYRES			
Wheels	wire	wire	wire
Tyres, size	4.50 x 19V	4.50 x 19V	4.50 x 19V
Front tyre pressure (lb/in^2)	34 - 36	34 - 36	34
Rear tyre pressure(lb/in^2)	34 - 36	34 - 36	34

BRITISH LIGHT CARS

Name	4 cyl. 12 hp & 1½-litre	1½-litre (Special Series)	Six - Twelve & 14 hp
Year(s) of manufacture	1935 - 38	1935 - 39	1932 - 34
ENGINE			
Capacity (cc)	1496	1496	1458/1633
Number of cylinders	4	4	6
Bore and stroke (mm)	69 x 100	69 x 100	57/60.3 x 95.2
Compression ratio (x:1)	6.0	6.6	—
RAC hp rating	11.9	11.9	12 or 14
Maximum bhp @ rev/min	45 - 54 @ 4500	61 - 65 @ 5000	45 - 50 @ 4500
Firing order	1,2,4,3	1,2,4,3	1,5,3,6,2,4
Valve layout	ohv	ohv	ohv
Inlet valve opens (^{o}btdc)	0	0	0
Tappet adjustment (inlet) in.	0.003H	0.003H	0.002H
Tappet adjustment (exhaust) in.	0.004H	0.004H	0.003H
Timing marks location	TS	TS	TS
Lubrication pattern	FP	FP	FP
Oil-pump type	plunger	plunger	plunger
Optimum oil pressure (lb/in^2)	30 - 50	30 - 50	40 - 60
Pistons type; number of rings	a ; 3	a ; 3	a ; 3
No. of main bearings	2	2	3
Main bearings	BWM	BWM	BWM
Camshaft drive	gear	gear	gear
Sump capacity (pts)	8	8	16
Lubricant (summer), SAE	30	40	30
Lubricant (winter), SAE	30	30	30
Engine mountings	flex.	flex.	flex.
Exhaust manifold, branches	3	3	5
CARBURATION			
Carburetter	SU/Zenith	2 Zenith/3 SU	SU
Carburetter type	HV3/36VH	36VH/OM	HV3
Choke size	1¼ in./27 mm	25 mm/1 in.	1¼ in.
Main jet	0.090/110	100/0.090	0.090
Slow-running or pilot jet	NA/SRJ65	SRJ55/NA	NA
Compensating or correction jet	NA/CJ85	CJ75/NA	NA
GA and GS jet, or progression jet	NA/PrJ160	PrJ160/NA	NA
Capacity well or pump jet	NA/W,std.	W,std/NA	NA
Metering needle (standard)	RO/NA	NA/CW	RO/RLB
Metering needle (weak)	AM/NA	NA/CX	AM/MME
Average mpg	30	25 - 30	25 - 30
Fuel feed	SUE/ACM	SUE/ACM	Au./SUE
Tank capacity (gall)	9½, 10 or 11½	9½, 10 or 11½	9½, 10 or 11½
IGNITION			
HT supply	coil	coil	mag/coil
Magneto	NA	NA	—
Distributor	—	—	—
Coil	12v	12v	12v
Contact-breaker gap (in.)	0.015	0.015	0.015
Spark plug gap (in.)	0.018	0.018	0.018
Spark plug thread (mm)	14	14	14
Spark plug	Ch. L-10S	Ch. L-10S	Ch. L-10
Ignition timing (^{o}btdc)	O,FR	O,FR	O,FR
ELECTRICAL			
Earthing pole	neg./pos.	neg./pos.	neg.
Battery	12v	12v	12v
Starter motor	—	—	—
Generator	—	—	—

	4 cyl. 12 hp & 1½-litre	*1½-litre (Special Series)*	*Six-Twelve & 14 hp*
CHASSIS			
Chassis-frame pattern	F, I; R, up.	F, I; R, up.	F, I; R, up.
Sidemembers	cn/box	cn/box	cn.
Crossmembers	cn/tub.	cn/tub.	tub.
Front suspension	SE	SE	SE
Rear suspension	SE	SE	SE
Shockabsorbers	X/hyd.	X/hyd.	hyd.
Special chassis features	—	—	OSL
TRANSMISSION			
Clutch	SDP/auto.	SDP/auto.	SDP/auto.
Gearbox action	S3/pre.	S4/pre.	S3/pre.
No. of forward gears	4	4	4
Gear lever location	cen./clm.	cen./clm.	cen./clm.
Forward gear ratios (x:1)	23.91, 19.07, 7.44, 5.22V	23.91, 19.07, 7.44, 5.22V	20.09, 11.64, 7.84, 5.5V
Gearbox lubricant, SAE	2 or 4¾	2 or 4¾	3 or 4½
Gearbox lubricant, quantity (pts)	30	30	30
Rear axle bevel; ratio (x:1)	(TT) sp.; 5.22	(TT) sp.; 5.22	(TT) sp.; 5.5
Rear axle lubricant, SAE	90	90	90
Rear axle lubricant, quantity (pts)	2¾	2¾	3½
STEERING AND FRONT AXLE			
Steering box	WW or WS	WW or WS	WW or WS
Steering box lubricant	140	140	140
Front axle	IB	IB	IB
Toe-in setting (in.)	1/8	1/8	1/8
BRAKES			
Type	mech./G	mech./G	mech./G
Actuation	cable/rod	cable/rod	cable/rod
BODYWORK			
Body construction	a. or PS	a. or PS	S or a.
No. of doors	2 or 4	2 or 4	2 or 4
No. of seats	2 or 4	2 or 4	2 or 4
WHEELS AND TYRES			
Wheels	wire	wire	wire
Tyres, size	4.75 x 18V	4.75 x 18V	4.75 x 18V
Front tyre pressure (lb/in^2)	34V	34V	34V
Rear tyre pressure (lb/in^2)	34V	34V	34V

Rover

Name	Ten	Twelve	14 hp Pilot	Fourteen	Speed Fourteen
Year(s) of manufacture	1935–39	1933–39	1932–33	1932–38	1933–36
ENGINE					
Capacity (cc)	1389	1496	1577	1577	1577
Number of cylinders	4	4	6	6	6
Bore and stroke (mm)	66.5 x 100	69 x 100	61 x 90	61 x 90	61 x 90
Compression ratio (x:1)	—	—	—	—	6.7
RAC hp rating	10.8	11.9	13.84	13.9	13.9
Maximum bhp @ rev/min	44 @ 4200	48 @ 4200	46 @ 4400	48 @ 4400	54 @ 4800
Firing order	1,2,4,3	1,2,4,3	1,5,3,6,2,4	1,5,3,6,2,4	1,5,3,6,2,4
Valve layout	ohv	ohv	ohv	ohv	ohv
Inlet valve opens (^{o} btdc)	10	10	—	10	—
Tappet adjustment (inlet) in.	0.010 H	0.010 H	—	0.010 H	—
Tappet adjustment (exhaust) in.	0.010 H	0.010 H	—	0.010 H	—
Timing marks location	fly.	fly.	fly.	fly.	fly.
Lubrication pattern	FP	FP	FP	FP	FP
Oil-pump type	gear	gear	gear	gear	gear
Optimum oil pressure (lb/in^2)	—	—	—	—	—
Pistons type; number of rings	a; 3	a; 3	a; 3	a; 3	a; 3
No. of main bearings	3	3	4	4	4
Main bearings	WM	WM	WM	WM	WM
Camshaft drive	chain	chain	chain	chain	chain
Sump capacity (pts)	—	—	—	—	—
Lubricant (summer), SAE	30	30	30	30	40
Lubricant (winter), SAE	20	20	20	20	30
Engine mountings	flex.	flex.	flex.	flex.	flex.
Exhaust manifold, branches	unit	unit	unit	3	3
CARBURATION					
Carburetter	SU	SU	SU	SU	3 x SU
Carburetter type	D3	D3	—	D3	HV2
Choke size	1¼ in.	1¼ in.	—	1¼ in.	1^1/8 in.
Main jet	—	—	—	—	—
Slow-running pilot jet	NA	NA	NA	NA	NA
Compensating or correction jet	NA	NA	NA	NA	NA
GA and GS jet or progression jet	NA	NA	NA	NA	NA
Capacity well or pump jet	NA	NA	NA	NA	NA
Metering needle (standard)	CP4 or CN	JM or CN	—	R6	1
Metering needle (weak)	CQ or 5	4 or 5	—	MME	M5
Average mpg	28 - 30	28	25 - 28	25 - 28	22
Fuel feed	ACM	ACM	—	ACM	ACM
Tank capacity (gall)	9½	10½	9	10½	10½
IGNITION					
HT supply	coil	coil	coil	coil	coil
Magneto	NA	NA	NA	NA	NA
Distributor	—	—	—	—	—
Coil	12v	12v	12v	12v	12v
Contact-breaker gap (in.)	0.012	0.012	0.012	0.012	0.012
Spark plug gap (in.)	0.018	0.018	0.020	0.018	0.018
Spark plug thread (mm)	18 or 14	18 or 14	18	18 or 14	14
Spark plug	—	—	—	—	—
Ignition timing (^{o} btdc)	—	—	—	—	—
ELECTRICAL					
Earthing pole	neg./pos.	neg./pos.	neg.	neg./pos.	neg.
Battery	12v 51 ah	12v 51 ah	12v	12v 51 ah	12v 51 ah
Starter motor	Lu.	Lu.	Ro.	Lu.	Lu.
Generator	thi./com.	thi./com.	thi.	thi./com.	com.

	Ten	Twelve	14 hp Pilot	Fourteen	Speed Fourteen
CHASSIS					
Chassis-frame pattern	R und.	R und.	R und.	R und.	R und.
Sidemembers	cn.	cn.	cn.	cn.	cn.
Crossmembers	T	T	T	T	T
Front suspension	SE	SE	SE	SE	SE
Rear suspension	SE	SE	QE	SE	SE
Shockabsorbers	F & R, hyd.	F & R, hyd.	FX, R hyd.	F & R, hyd.	F & R, hyd.
Special chassis features	LB	LB	Startix	LB	LB
TRANSMISSION					
Clutch	SDP & fre.	SDP & fre.	SDP & fre.	SDP & fre.	SDP & fre.
Gearbox action	S3	S3	S3	S3	S3
No. of forward gears	4	4	4	4	4
Gear lever location	cen.	cen.	cen.	cen.	cen.
Forward gear ratios (x:1)	19.8, 11.0, 4.88 7.45	19.8, 11.0, 4.88 7.45	22, 11.5, 5.44 8.27	—	19.8, 11.0, 4.88 7.45
Gearbox lubricant, SAE	30	30	30	30	30
Gearbox lubricant, quantity (pts)	—	—	—	—	—
Rear axle bevel; ratio	sp; 4.88	sp; 4.88	sp; 5.44	sp; 5.22	sp; 4.88
Rear axle lubricant, SAE	90	90	90	90	90
Rear axle lubricant, quantity (pts)	—	—	—	—	—
STEERING AND FRONT AXLE					
Steering box	WN	MW	WN	MW	MW
Steering box lubricant, SAE	140	140	140	140	140
Front axle	IB	IB	IB	IB	IB
Toe-in setting (in.)	1/8	1/8	1/8	1/8	1/8
BRAKES					
Type	Girling	Girling	Lockheed	Girling	Lockheed
Actuation	rod	rod	hyd.	rod	hyd.
BODYWORK					
Body construction	a. & PS	a. & PS	co.	a. & PS	a. & PS
No. of doors	2 or 4	2 or 4	4	2 or 4	2
No. of seats	2 or 4	2 or 4	4	2 or 4	2 or 4
WHEELS AND TYRES					
Wheels	RW	RW	wire	RW	RW
Tyres, size	4.75 x 18	5.25 x 17	4.75 x 18	5.25 x 17	4.75 x 18
Front tyre pressure (lb/in^2)	30	30	30	30	30
Rear tyre pressure (lb/in^2)	32	32	32	32	32

Singer

Name	Junior	Nine	9 hp Le Mans	9 hp Bantam
Year(s) of manufacture	1930 - 32	1932 - 36	1935 - 37	1937 - 39
ENGINE				
Capacity (cc)	848	972	972	1074
Number of cylinders	4	4	4	4
Bore and stroke (mm)	56 x 86	60 x 86	60 x 86	60 x 95
Compression ratio (x:1)	—	—	—	—
RAC hp rating	8	8.93	8.93	8.93
Maximum bhp @ rev/min	26.5 @ 4000	26.5 @ 4000	39 @ 5200	
Firing order	1,3,4,2	1,3,4,2	1,3,4,2	1,3,4,2
Valve layout	ohc	ohc	ohc	ohc
Inlet valve opens (^{o}btdc)	—	10	—	10
Tappet adjustment (inlet) in.	0.005H	0.005H	0.005H	0.005H
Tappet adjustment (exhaust) in.	0,005H	0.005H	0.005H	0.005H
Timing marks location	fly.	fly.	fly.	fly.
Lubrication pattern	FP	FP	FP	FP
Oil-pump type	gear	gear	gear	gear
Optimum oil pressure (lb/in ^{2})	—	—	—	—
Pistons type; number of rings	a ; 3	a ; 3	a ; 3	a ; 3
No. of main bearings	2	2	2	3
Main bearings	WM	WM	WM	WM
Camshaft drive	chain	chain	chain	chain
Sump capacity (pts)	—	—	—	—
Lubricant (summer), SAE	30	30	40	30
Lubricant (winter), SAE	20	20	40	20
Engine mountings	rigid	3 flex.	3 flex.	3 flex.
Exhaust manifold, branches	—	4	4	unit
CARBURATION				
Carburetter	Solex	Solex	2 x SU	Solex (1937)
Carburetter type	—	horiz.	HV2	30FAI
Choke size	—	22 mm	1 1/8 in.	22mm
Main jet	—	105 x 41	—	115
Slow-running or pilot jet	—	PJ 0.060	NA	PJ 0.045
Compensating or correction jet	—	GS 110	NA	GS 115
GA and GS jet, or progression jet	—	GA4	NA	GA4
Capacity well or pump jet	—	—	NA	—
Metering needle (standard)	NA	NA	WX1	NA
Metering needle (weak)	NA	NA	AK	NA
Average mpg		33 - 38	—	33 - 38
Fuel feed	Autovac	Au. or SUE	SUE	SUE
Tank capacity (gall)	7	7	13½	7
IGNITION				
HT supply	coil	coil	magneto	coil
Magneto	NA	NA	Scintilla	NA
Distributor	—	—	NA	—
Coil	—	12v	NA	12v
Contact-breaker gap (in.)	0.012	0.012	0.012	0.012
Spark plug gap (in.)	0.018	0.018	0.018	0.018
Spark plug thread (mm)	18	18	14	14
Spark plug	—	—	—	—
Ignition timing (^{o}btdc)	—	—	20	—
ELECTRICAL				
Earthing pole	neg.	neg./pos.	neg.	pos.
Battery	—	12v 51 ah	12v 51 ah	12v 51 ah
Starter motor	—	—	—	—
Generator	—	—	—	—

CHASSIS	Junior	Nine	9 hp Le Mans	9 hp Bantam	
Chassis-frame pattern	ladder	ladder	ladder	ladder	
Sidemembers	cn.	cn.	cn.	cn.	
Crossmembers	cn.	cn.	cn.	cn.	
Front suspension	SE	SE	SE/ifs	SE	
Rear suspension	SE	SE	SE	SE	
Shockabsorbers	F,X;R,X	F,X;R,X	F,X;R,X	F,X;R hyd.	
Special chassis features	—	—	—	—	
TRANSMISSION					
Clutch	SDP	SDP	SDP or FF	SDP	
Gearbox action	S3	S3	syn.	syn.	
No. of forward gears	4	4	4	3	
Gear lever location	cen.	cen.	cen.	cen.	
Forward gear ratios (x:1)	—	—	10.25,7.15,5.36,	—	4.77
Gearbox lubricant, SAE	30	30	30	30	
Gearbox lubricant, quantity (pts)	—	—	—	—	
Rear axle bevel; ratio (x:1)	sp.;—	sp.;5.57	sp.;4.77	sp.;—	
Rear axle lubricant, SAE	90	90	90	90	
Rear axle lubricant, quantity (pts)	—	—	—	—	
STEERING AND FRONT AXLE					
Steering box	—	—	—	—	
Steering box lubricant	140	140	140	140	
Front axle	IB	IB/ifs	IB	IB	
Toe-in setting (in.)	1/8	1/8	1/8	1/8	
BRAKES					
Type	mech.	Lock./mech.	Lockheed	Girling	
Actuation	cable	hyd./cable	hyd.	hyd.	
BODYWORK					
Body construction	PS	Co. or PS	a.	PS	
No. of doors	2 or 4	2 or 4	2	4	
No. of seats	2 or 4	2 or 4	2	4	
WHEELS AND TYRES					
Wheels	M	M	RW	SD	
Tyres, size	4.00 x 27	4.50 x 17	4.50 x 18	—	
Front tyre pressure (lb/in^2)	—	—	35	—	
Rear tyre pressure (lb/in^2)	—	—	35	—	

Name	Ten	Eleven	Twelve	1½-litre Le Mans
Year(s) of manufacture	1937 - 39	1934 - 35	1936 - 39	1934 - 36
ENGINE				
Capacity (cc)	1185	1384	1525	1493
Number of cylinders	4	4	4	6
Bore and stroke (mm)	63 x 95	65 x 105	68 x 105	59 x 91
Compression ratio (x:1)	—	—	—	—
RAC hp rating	9.8	10.95	11.47	12.95
Maximum bhp @ rev/min	35 @ 4200	37 @ 4000	43 @ 4200	63 @ 4800
Firing order	1,3,4,2	1,3,4,2	1,3,4,2	1,5,3,6,2,4
Valve layout	ohc	ohc	ohc	ohc
Inlet valve opens (^{o}btdc)	10	10	10	—
Tappet adjustment (inlet) in.	0.005H	0.005H	0.005H	—
Tappet adjustment (exhaust) in.	0.005H	0.005H	0.005H	—
Timing marks location	fly.	fly.	fly.	fly.
Lubrication pattern	FP	FP	FP	FP
Oil-pump type	gear	gear	gear	gear
Optimum oil pressure (lb/in ^{2})	—	—	—	—
Pistons type; number of rings	a ; 3	a ; 3	a ; 3	a ; 3
No. of main bearings	3	3	3	4
Main bearings	WM	WM	WM	WM
Camshaft drive	chain	chain	chain	chain
Sump capacity (pts)	—	—	—	—
Lubricant (summer), SAE	30	30	30	40
Lubricant (winter), SAE	20	20	20	30
Engine mountings	3 flex.	3 flex.	3 flex.	—
Exhaust manifold, branches	unit.	unit.	unit.	3
CARBURATION				
Carburetter	SU (1939)	Solex	Solex	3 x SU
Carburetter type	D2	—	—	—
Choke size	1 1/8 in.	—	—	—
Main jet	—	—	—	—
Slow-running or pilot jet	NA	—	—	NA
Compensating or correction jet	NA	—	—	NA
GA and GS jet, or progression jet	NA	—	—	NA
Capacity well or pump jet	NA	—	—	NA
Metering needle (standard)	07	NA	NA	—
Metering needle (weak)	CX	NA	NA	—
Average mpg	—	—	—	21 - 26
Fuel feed	SUE	SUE	SUE	SUE
Tank capacity (gall)	8	8	10	15
IGNITION				
HT supply	coil	coil	coil	coil/mag.
Magneto	NA	NA	NA	—
Distributor	—	—	—	—
Coil	12v	12v	12v	12v
Contact-breaker gap (in.)	0.012	0.012	0.012	0.012
Spark plug gap (in.)	0.018	0.018	0.018	0.020
Spark plug thread (mm)	14 ^{²}	18	14	14
Spark plug	—	—	—	—
Ignition timing (^{o}btdc)	—	—	—	—
ELECTRICAL				
Earthing pole	pos.	neg.	pos.	neg.
Battery	12v 51 ah	12v 51 ah	12v 51ah	12v 51ah
Starter motor	—	—	—	—
Generator	—	—	—	—

CHASSIS	Ten	Eleven	Twelve	1½-litre Le Mans
Chassis-frame pattern	ladder	ladder	ladder	low-slung
Sidemembers	cn.	cn.	cn.	cn.
Crossmembers	cn.	cn.	cn.	cn.
Front suspension	SE	SE/ifs	SE	SE
Rear suspension	SE	SE	SE	SE
Shockabsorbers	hyd.	X orhyd.	hyd.	F, An; R, An
Special chassis features	—	—	—	—
TRANSMISSION				
Clutch	SDP	SDP or FF	SDP	SDP
Gearbox action	syn.	syn.	syn.	S3
No. of forward gears	4	4	4	4
Gear lever location	cen.	cen.	cen.	cen.
Forward gear ratios (x:1)	—	—	—	17.7, 9.08, 5.64, 4.44
Gearbox lubricant, SAE	30	30	30	30
Gearbox lubricant, quantity (pts)	—	—	—	—
Rear axle bevel; ratio (x:1)	sp. ; —	sp. ; 5.22	sp. ; —	sp. ; 4.44
Rear axle lubricant, SAE	90	90	90	90
Rear axle lubricant, quantity (pts)	—	—	—	—
STEERING AND FRONT AXLE				
Steering box	—	—	—	—
Steering box lubricant	140	140	140	140
Front axle	IB	ifs or IB	IB	IB
Toe-in setting (in.)	—	—	—	—
BRAKES				
Type	Lockheed	Lockheed	Lockheed	Lockheed
Actuation	hyd.	hyd.	hyd.	hyd.
BODYWORK				
Body construction	PS	PS	PS	a.
No. of doors	4	4	4	2
No. of seats	4	4	4	2
WHEELS AND TYRES				
Wheels	SD	wire	SD	RW
Tyres, size	—	5.00 x 17	—	4.75 x 18
Front tyre pressure (lb/in^2)	—	—	—	30
Rear tyre pressure (lb/in^2)	—	—	—	30

Squire

Name	1½-litre
Year(s) of manufacture	1934 - 36
ENGINE	
Capacity (cc)	1496
Number of cylinders	4
Bore and stroke (mm)	69 x 120
Compression ratio (x:1)	6.5
RAC hp rating	11.9
Maximum bhp @ rev/min	110 @ 5000
Firing order	1,3,4,2
Valve layout	dohc
Inlet valve opens (^{o} btdc)	—
Tappet adjustment (inlet) in.	0.030
Tappet adjustment (exhaust) in.	0.040
Timing marks location	—
Lubrication pattern	FP
Oil-pump type	gear
Optimum oil pressure (lb/in ^{2})	—
Pistons type; number of rings	a ; —
No. of main bearings	4
Main bearings	WM
Camshaft drive	gear & chain
Sump capacity (pts)	16
Lubricant (summer), SAE	40
Lubricant (winter), SAE	40
Engine mountings	flex.
Exhaust manifold, branches	2 x 2
CARBURATION	
Carburetter	SU
Carburetter type	—
Choke size	—
Main jet	—
Slow-running or pilot jet	NA
Compensating or correction jet	NA
GA and GS jet, or progression jet	NA
Capacity well or pump jet	NA
Metering needle (standard)	—
Metering needle (weak)	—
Average mpg	—
Fuel feed	2 x ACM
Tank capacity (gall)	12½
IGNITION	
HT supply	coil
Magneto	NA
Distributor	—
Coil	12v
Contact-breaker gap (in.)	—
Spark plug gap (in.)	—
Spark plug thread (mm)	—
Spark plug	—
Ignition timing (^{o} btdc)	—
ELECTRICAL	
Earthing pole	pos.
Battery	12v 90ah
Starter motor	dynamotor
Generator	dynamotor

CHASSIS	*1½-litre*
Chassis-frame pattern	F,I;R,up./und.
Sidemembers	cn.
Crossmembers	cruciform
Front suspension	SE
Rear suspension	SE
Shockabsorbers	hyd.
Special chassis features	DSL
TRANSMISSION	
Clutch	none
Gearbox action	pre.
No. of forward gears	4
Gear lever location	clm.
Forward gear ratios (x:1)	14.4, 8.2, 5.7, 4.25V
Gearbox lubricant, SAE	–
Gearbox lubricant, quantity (pts)	–
Rear axle bevel; ratio (x:1)	sp. ; 4.25V
Rear axle lubricant, SAE	90
Rear axle lubricant, quantity (pts)	–
STEERING AND FRONT AXLE	
Steering box	CL
Steering box lubricant	140
Front axle	IB
Toe-in setting (in.)	–
BRAKES	
Type	Lockheed
Actuation	hyd.
BODYWORK	
Body construction	co.
No. of doors	2
No. of seats	2 or 4
WHEELS AND TYRES	
Wheels	RW
Tyres, size	5.00 x 18
Front tyre pressure (lb/in^2)	30
Rear tyre pressure (lb/in^2)	32

S.S.

Name	II	II	Jaguar
	10 hp	12 hp	1½-litre
Year(s) of manufacture	1933 - 36	1933 - 36	1936 - 37
ENGINE			
Capacity (cc)	1343	1609	1609
Number of cylinders	4	4	4
Bore and stroke (mm)	63.5 x 106	69.5 x 106	69.5 x 106
Compression ratio (x:1)	6.2 or 7	6.2 or 7	7
RAC hp rating	9.9	11.98	11.98
Maximum bhp @ rev/min	32 @ 3600	38 @ 3600	44 - 50 @ 4500
Firing order	1,3,4,2,	1,3,4,2	1,3,4,2
Valve layout	sv	sv	sv
Inlet valve opens (^{o}btdc)	10	10	10
Tappet adjustment (inlet) in.	0.006H	0.012H	0.012H
Tappet adjustment (exhaust) in.	0.006H	0.012H	0.012H
Timing marks location	fly.	fly.	fly.
Lubrication pattern	FP	FP	FP
Oil-pump type	gear	gear	gear
Optimum oil pressure (lb/in^2)	30 - 50	30 - 50	30 - 50
Pistons type: number of rings	a ; 3	a ; 3	a ; 3
No. of main bearings	3	3	3
Main bearings	WM	WM	WM
Camshaft drive	chain	chain	chain
Sump capacity (pts)		13	13
Lubricant (summer), SAE	30	30	30
Lubricant (winter), SAE	20	20	20
Engine mountings	flex.	flex.	flex.
Exhaust manifold, branches	3	3	3
CARBURATION			
Carburetter	R.A.G./2 x SU	R.A.G./2 x SU	Solex
Carburetter type	—	—	35FIL/30FI
Choke size	—	—	—
Main jet	—	—	—
Slow-running or pilot jet	—	—	—
Compensating or correction jet	—	—	—
GA and GS jet, or progression jet	—	—	—
Capacity well or pump jet	—	—	—
Metering needle (standard)	—	—	NA
Metering needle (weak)	—	—	NA
Average mpg	27	25	25 - 27
Fuel feed	ACM	ACM	ACM
Tank capacity (gall)	8	8	10
IGNITION			
HT supply	coil	coil	coil
Magneto	NA	NA	NA
Distributor	DKY4A	DKY4A	DKY4A
Coil	Q12	Q12	Q12
Contact-breaker gap (in.)	0.012	0.012	0.012
Spark plug gap (in.)	0.018	0.018	0.018
Spark plug thread (mm)	18	18	18
Spark plug	—	—	—
Ignition timing (^{o}btdc)	O,FR	O,FR	O,FR
ELECTRICAL			
Earthing pole	neg.	neg.	pos.
Battery	12v 51 ah	12v 51 ah	12v 51 ah
Starter motor	M35G	M418G	M418G
Generator	C35YV	C35YV	C35YV

CHASSIS	10 hp	12 hp	1½-litre
Chassis-frame pattern	cruciform	cruciform	cruciform
Sidemembers	cn.	cn.	cn.
Crossmembers	cn.	cn.	cn.
Front suspension	SE	SE	SE
Rear suspension	SE	SE	SE
Shockabsorbers	X or hyd.	X or hyd.	hyd.
Special chassis features	R, und.	R, und.	R, und.
TRANSMISSION			
Clutch	SDP	SDP	SDP
Gearbox action	syn.	syn.	syn.
No. of forward gears	4	4	4
Gear lever location	cen.	cen.	cen.
Forward gear ratios (x:1)	20.85, 12.84, 7.68, 5.29V	19.18, 11.8, 7.06, 4.86	19.18, 11.8, 7.06, 4.86
Gearbox lubricant, SAE	30	30	30
Gearbox lubricant, quantity (pts)	2	2	2
Rear axle bevel; ratio (x:1)	sp. ; 5.29V	sp. ; 4.86	sp. ; 4.86
Rear axle lubricant, SAE	90	90	90
Rear axle lubricant, quantity (pts)	—	—	—
STEERING AND FRONT AXLE			
Steering box	CL	CL	WN
Steering box lubricant	140	140	140
Front axle	IB	IB	IB
Toe-in setting (in.)	1/8	1/8	1/8
BRAKES			
Type	Bendix	Bendix/G	Girling
Actuation	cable/rod	cable/rod	rod
BODYWORK			
Body construction	a. on wo.	a. on wo.	PS
No. of doors	2 or 4	2 or 4	4
No. of seats	4	4	4
WHEELS AND TYRES			
Wheels	RW	RW	RW
Tyres, size	4.75 x 18	4.75 x 18	4.75 x 18
Front typre pressure (lb/in^2)	26	26	28
Rear tyre pressure (lb/in^2)	28	28	30

Standard

Name	Eight	Little Nine & Big Nine	Flying Nine
Year(s) of manufacture	1938–39	1931–34 & 1930–33	1936–39
ENGINE			
Capacity (cc)	1021	1005/1287	1131
Number of cylinders	4	4	4
Bore and stroke (mm)	57 x 100	60.25 x 88/63.5 x 102	60 x 100
Compression ratio (x:1)	6.7	5	6.7
RAC hp rating	8	8.99 or 9.9	8.93
Maximum bhp @ rev/min	31 @ 4000	22/25 @ 3600	33 @ 4000
Firing order	1,3,4,2	1,3,4,2	1,3,4,2
Valve layout	sv	sv	sv
Inlet valve opens (º btdc)	10	10	10
Tappet adjustment (inlet) in.	0.015 C	0.004 C	0.015 C
Tappet adjustment (exhaust) in.	0.015 C	0.004 C	0.015 C
Timing marks location	fly.	fly.	fly.
Lubrication pattern	FP	FP	FP
Oil-pump type	gear	gear	gear
Optimum oil pressure (lb in^2)	40	30	40
Pistons type; number of rings	a; 3	a; 3	a; 3
No. of main bearings	3	2	3
Main bearings	sh.	WM	sh.
Camshaft drive	chain	chain	chain
Sump capacity (pts)	7½	5	10
Lubricant (summer), SAE	30	30	30
Lubricant (winter), SAE	20	20	20
Engine mountings	flex.	flex.	flex.
Exhaust manifold, branches	3	unit	unit
CARBURATION			
Carburetter	Solex	Solex	Solex
Carburetter type	26AIC	26FH	26FAI
Choke size	21 mm	23 mm	24 mm
Main jet	95	85	85
Slow-running or pilot jet	PJ45	PJ50	PJ55
Compensating or correction jet	Cr J220	–	Cr J220
GA and GS jet or progression jet	GA4, GS95	–	–
Capacity well or pump jet	–	–	–
Metering needle (standard)	NA	NA	NA
Metering needle (weak)	NA	NA	NA
Average mpg	45 - 48	40	40
Fuel feed	ACM	grav./ACM	ACM
Tank capacity (gall)	6	5	6
IGNITION			
HT supply	coil	coil	coil
Magneto	NA	NA	NA
Distributor	DKYH4A-0	DJ4	DKYH4-0
Coil	R6	6v	12v
Contact-breaker gap (in.)	0.015	0.012	0.015
Spark plug gap (in.)	0.025	0.018	0.025
Spark plug thread (mm)	14	18	14
Spark plug	Ch. N-8	AC-K5	Ch. L-10
Ignition timing (º btdc)	0, FR	0, FR	0, FR
ELECTRICAL			
Earthing pole	pos.	neg.	pos.
Battery	6v 51 ah	6v	12v 51 ah
Starter motor	M35G	–	M35G
Generator	C35YV	–	C35YV

312

	Eight	*Little Nine & Big Nine*	*Flying Nine*
CHASSIS			
Chassis-frame pattern	F, I; R, up.	F, I; R, up.	F, I; R, up.
Sidemembers	box and cn.	cn.	box and cn.
Crossmembers	cn. and tub.	cn.	cn. and tub.
Front suspension	TSE	SE	SE or TSE
Rear suspension	SE	SE	SE
Shockabsorbers	hyd.	X	hyd.
Special chassis features	—	—	—
TRANSMISSION			
Clutch	SDP	SDP	SDP
Gearbox action	syn.	S2	syn.
No. of forward gears	3	3	4
Gear lever location	cen.	cen.	cen.
Forward gear ratios (x:1)	18.75, 8.63, 5.14	19.05, 9.61, 5.22	21.42, 13.18, 7.88, 5.43
Gearbox lubricant, SAE	40	90	40
Gearbox lubricant, quantity (pts)	1¼	2	2
Rear axle bevel; ratio	sp.;5.14	sp.;5.22	sp.;5.43
Rear axle lubricant, SAE	140	90	140
Rear axle lubricant, quantity (pts)	1½	¾	1½
STEERING AND FRONT AXLE			
Steering box	BD	WN	BD
Steering box lubricant, SAE	140	90	140
Front axle	NA (ifs)	IB	IB or ifs
Toe-in setting (in.)	TO, 1/8	1/8	TO, 1/8 (ifs)
BRAKES			
Type	Bendix	Bendix	Bendix
Actuation	cable	cable	cable
BODYWORK			
Body construction	PS	PS	PS
No. of doors	2	4	2
No. of seats	4	4	4
WHEELS AND TYRES			
Wheels	SD	wire	SD
Tyres, size	4.75 x 16	4.00 x 27	5.00 x 16 V
Front tyre pressure (lb/in^2)	24	24	28
Rear tyre pressure (lb/in^2)	26	27	28

BRITISH LIGHT CARS

Name	Flying Ten	Flying Twelve	Little Twelve & Big Twelve
Year(s) of manufacture	1936–39	1936–39	1932–34
ENGINE			
Capacity (cc)	1267	1609	1337/1497
Number of cylinders	4	4	6
Bore and stroke (mm)	63.5 x 100	69.5 x 106	57 x 87.3/60.25 x 87.3
Compression ratio (x:1)	6.5	6.5	—
RAC hp rating	9.99	11.98	12 or 13.5
Maximum bhp @ rev/min	36 @ 4000	44 @ 4000	—
Firing order	1,3,4,2	1,3,4,2	1,5,3,6,2,4
Valve layout	sv	sv	sv
Inlet valve opens (^{o} btdc)	10	10	10
Tappet adjustment (inlet) in.	0.015 C	0.015 C	0.004 C
Tappet adjustment (exhaust) in.	0.015 C	0.015 C	0.004 C
Timing marks location	fly.	fly.	fly.
Lubrication pattern	FP	FP	FP
Oil-pump type	gear	gear	gear
Optimum oil pressure (lb/in^2)	40	40	30
Pistons type; number of rings	a; 3	a; 3	a; 3
No of main bearings	3	3	2
Main bearings	Sh	sh.	sh.
Camshaft drive	chain	chain	chain
Sump capacity (pts)	10	13	—
Lubricant (summer), SAE	30	30	30
Lubricant (winter), SAE	20	20	20
Engine mountings	flex.	flex.	—
Exhaust manifold, branches	3	3	unit
CARBURATION			
Carburetter	Solex	Solex	Solex
Carburetter type	30 FAI	30 FAI	30 FH
Choke size	25 mm	27 mm	—
Main jet	105	125	—
Slow running or pilot jet	PJ50	PJ45	—
Compensating or correction jet	CrJ230	CrJ290	—
GA and GS jet or progression jet	NA	NA	—
Capacity well or pump jet	—	—	—
Metering needle (standard)	NA	NA	NA
Metering needle (weak)	NA	NA	NA
Average mpg	38 - 40	30 - 32	—
Fuel feed	ACM	ACM	ACM
Tank capacity (gall)	6	10	—
IGNITION			
HT supply	coil	coil	coil
Magneto	NA	NA	NA
Distributor	DKYH4-0	DKYH4-0	DJ4
Coil	R6	B12	—
Contact-breaker gap (in.)	0.015	0.015	0.012
Spark plug gap (in.)	0.025	0.025	0.018
Spark plug thread (mm)	14	14	18
Spark plug	Lo-CN	Lo-CN	Lo-C3
Ignition timing (^{o} btdc)	0, FR	0, FR	0, FR
ELECTRICAL			
Earthing pole	pos.	pos.	neg.
Battery	12v 51 ah	12v 51 ah	12v
Starter motor	M35G	M418G	—
Generator	C35YV	C45YV/3	—

	Flying Ten	*Flying Twelve*	*Little Twelve & Big Twelve*
CHASSIS			
Chassis-frame pattern	F, I; R, up.	F, I; R, up.	F, I; R, up.
Sidemembers	box and cn.	cn.	cn./box
Crossmembers	cn. and tub.	cn.	cn. and tub.
Front suspension	TSE	TSE	SE
Rear suspension	SE	SE	SE
Shockabsorbers	hyd.	hyd.	An.
Special chassis features	—	cruciform	GL
TRANSMISSION			
Clutch	SDP	SDP	SDP
Gearbox action	syn.	syn.	S3 or pre.
No. of forward gears	4	4	4
Gear lever location	cen.	cen.	cen.
Forward gear ratios (x:1)	20.86, 12.84, 7.68, 5.29	19.18, 11.8, 7.06, 4.86	—
Gearbox lubricant (SAE)	40	40	90
Gearbox lubricant, quantity (pts)	2	2	—
Rear axle bevel; ratio	sp.;5.29	sp.;4.86	—
Rear axle lubricant, SAE	140	140	90
Rear axle lubricant, quantity (pts)	1½	2	—
STEERING AND FRONT AXLE			
Steering box	BD	BD	WN
Steering box lubricant (SAE)	140	140	90
Front axle	IB or ifs	IB or ifs	IB
Toe-in setting (in.)	TO, 1/8 (ifs)	TO, 1/8 (ifs)	1/8
BRAKES			
Type	Bendix	Bendix	Bendix
Actuation	cable	cable	cable
BODYWORK			
Body construction	PS	PS	PS or co.
No. of doors	4	4	4
No. of seats	4	4	4
WHEELS AND TYRES			
Wheels	SD	SD	wire
Tyres, size	5.25 x 16	5.25 x 16	4.50 x 19
Front tyre pressure (lb/in^2)	28	28	26
Rear tyre pressure (lb/in^2)	28	28	28

Sunbeam Talbot

Name	Talbot 65	Talbot Ten	Sunbeam-Talbot Ten
Year(s) of manufacture	1933 - 35	1935 - 38	1939
ENGINE			
Capacity (cc)	1666	1185	1185
Number of cylinders	6	4	4
Bore and stroke (mm)	61 x 95	63 x 95	63 x 95
Compression ratio (x:1)	—	6.8	6.8
RAC hp rating	13.8	9.8	9.8
Maximum bhp @ rev/min	65 @ 4800	40 @ 4400	40 @ 4400
Firing order	1,5,3,6,2,4	1,3,4,2	1,3,4,2
Valve layout	ohv	sv	sv
Inlet valve opens (^{o}btdc)	—	2	8
Tappet adjustment (inlet) in.	—	0.010C	0.010C
Tappet adjustment (exhaust) in.	—	0.015C	0.015C
Timing marks location	TS	TS	fly.
Lubrication pattern	FP	FP	FP
Oil-pump type	gear	gear	gear
Optimum oil pressure (lb/in^2)	—	30 - 35	—
Pistons type; number of rings	a ; 3	a ; 3	a ; 3
No. of main bearings	4	3	3
Main bearings	WM	WM	sh.
Camshaft drive	chain	chain	chain
Sump capacity (pts)	—	7	7
Lubricant (summer), SAE	30	40	30
Lubricant (winter), SAE	30	30	30
Engine mountings	—	flex.	flex.
Exhaust manifold, branches	5	3	3
CARBURATION			
Carburetter	Stromberg	Zenith	Stromberg
Carburetter type	—	VIG	DBA36
Choke size	—	—	31/32 in.
Main jet	—	—	0.045
Slow-running or pilot jet	—	—	SRJ 75 - 70
Compensating or correction jet	—	—	CJ 0.034
GA and GS jet, or progression jet	—	—	—
Capacity well or pump jet	—	—	—
Metering needle (standard)	NA	NA	NA
Metering needle (weak)	NA	NA	NA
Average mpg	22	28 - 30	30 - 32
Fuel feed	ACM	ACM	ACM
Tank capacity (gall)	16	8	8
IGNITION			
HT supply	coil	coil	coil
Magneto	NA	NA	NA
Distributor	—	—	DKYH4A
Coil	12v	12v	B12
Contact-breaker gap (in.)	0.012	0.018	0.015
Spark plug gap (in.)	0.018	0.022	0.028 - 0.032
Spark plug thread (mm)	18	14	14
Spark plug	—	Ch.L-10	Ch.N-8
Ignition timing (^{o}btdc)	—	1°atdc,FR	5,FR
ELECTRICAL			
Earthing pole	neg.	neg.	pos.
Battery	12v	12v5lah	12v5lah
Starter motor	dynamotor	—	M35G
Generator	thi.	—	—

	Talbot 65	Talbot Ten	Sunbeam-Talbot Ten
CHASSIS			
Chassis-frame pattern	—	F, I; R, up.	F,I;R,up.
Sidemembers	—	cn.	box
Crossmembers	—	cn.	cn.
Front suspension	SE	SE	SE
Rear suspension	HC	SE	SE
Shockabsorbers	hyd.	hyd.	hyd.
Special chassis features	OSL	—	—
TRANSMISSION			
Clutch	SDP/auto.	SDP	SDP
Gearbox action	syn/pre.	syn.	syn.
No. of forward gears	4	4	4
Gear lever location	cen/clm.	cen.	cen.
Forward gear ratios (x:1)	23.5, 13.33, 8.69, 5.87	19.6, 13.77, 8.16, 5.44	19.6, 13.77, 8.16, 5.22
Gearbox lubricant, SAE	30	30	30
Gearbox lubricant, quantity (pts)	—	2	2
Rear axle bevel; ratio (x:1)	sp.;5.87	sp.;5.44	sp.;5.22
Rear axle lubricant, SAE	—	140	140
Rear axle lubricant, quantity (pts)	—	1¾	1¾
STEERING AND FRONT AXLE			
Steering box	—	WN	WN
Steering box lubricant	—	140	140
Front axle	IB	IB	IB
Toe-in setting (in.)	—	1/8	1/8
BRAKES			
Type	mech.	Bendix	Bendix
Actuation	rod & cable	cable	cable
BODYWORK			
Body construction	co.	co.	PS
No. of doors	4	2	4
No. of seats	4	4	4
WHEELS AND TYRES			
Wheels	RW	wire/disc	disc
Tyres, size	5.50 x 29	5.25 x 16	5.25 x 16
Front tyre pressure (lb/in^2)	28	24	24
Rear tyre pressure (lb/in^2)	30	26	26

Triumph

Name	Super Seven & Super Eight	Super Nine	9.5 hp Popular Ten Gloria Ten Southern Cross	Scorpion
Year(s) of manufacture	1930 - 34	1931 - 34	1934 - 35	1931 - 33
ENGINE				
Capacity (cc)	832	1018	1087	1202
Number of cylinders	4	4	4	6
Bore and stroke (mm)	56.5 x 83	60 x 90	62 x 90	56.5 x 80
Compression ratio (x:1)	—	6.1	6.2	5.5
RAC hp rating	7.9	8.9	9.5	11.9
Maximum bhp @ rev/min	20.93 @ 4000	29.8 @ 4000	40 @4500	27.2 @ 4000
Firing order	1,3,4,2	1,3,4,2	1,3,4,2,	1,5,3,6,2,4
Valve layout	sv	ioe	ioe	sv
Inlet valve opens (° btdc)	5	10	10	5
Tappet adjustment (inlet) in.	0.006 H	0.004 H	0.004 H	0.006 H
Tappet adjustment (exhaust) in.	0.006 H	0.006 H	0.006 H	0.006 H
Timing marks location	TS	TS	fly.	TS
Lubrication pattern	FP	FP	FP	FP
Oil-pump type	gear	gear	gear	gear
Optimum oil pressure (lb/in^2)	—	—	—	—
Pistons type; number of rings	a; 3	a; 3	a; 3	a; 3
No. of main bearings	3	3	3	4
Main bearings	WM	WM	WM	WM
Camshaft drive	chain	chain	chain	chain
Sump capacity (pts)	4	7	7	9
Lubricant (summer), SAE	30	30	30	30
Lubricant (winter), SAE	30	30	30	30
Engine mountings, type	—	—	—	—
Exhaust manifold, branches	4	4	4	—
CARBURATION				
Carburetter	Solex	Solex	Solex/Zenith	Solex
Carburetter type	horiz.	horiz.	—/—	horiz.
Choke size	19 mm	22 or 26 mm	30-21/25 mm	21 mm
Main jet	85 x 41	100 x 51A	115-100/105	100 x 51
Slow-running or pilot jet	PJ60	PJ50	PJ55-60/SRJ50	PJ60
Compensating or correction jet	—	—	— /CJ70	—
GA and GS jet or progression jet	—	—	— / —	—
Capacity well or pump jet	—	—	— / —	—
Metering needle (standard)	NA	NA	NA	NA
Metering needle (weak)	NA	NA	NA	NA
Average mpg	35 - 40	—	—	—
Fuel feed	grav./Au.	Autovac	SUE	Petrolift
Tank capacity (gall)	5½	5½	7½ or 9	7½
IGNITION				
HT supply	coil	coil	coil	coil
Magneto	NA	NA	NA	NA
Distributor	D41/DJ4	DJ4	DJ4A/DK4A-0	DL6A
Coil	P4/4Q6	4Q6	Q12	P68
Contact-breaker gap (in.)	0.018	0.018	0.018	0.018
Spark plug gap (in.)	0.018	0.018	0.018	0.018
Spark plug thread (mm)	18	18	18	18
Spark plug	—	—	Ch. 16	—
Ignition timing (° btdc)	—	—	—	—
ELECTRICAL				
Earthing pole	neg.	neg.	neg.	neg.
Battery	6v	6 or 12v	2 x 6v 53 ah	6v or 12v
Starter motor	M/MO418F	M418AF	M35A	M418AF
Generator	C45DF	C45DF	C45A or H	C45DF

	Super Seven & Super Eight	Super Nine	Popular Ten Gloria Ten Southern Cross	Scorpion
CHASSIS				
Chassis-frame pattern	ladder	ladder	ladder	ladder
Sidemembers	cn.	cn.	cn.	cn.
Crossmembers	cn.	cn.	cn.	cn.
Front suspension	SE	SE	SE	SE
Rear suspension	QE	QE	QE/SE	QE
Shockabsorbers	X	X	X/hyd.	X
Special chassis features	R, und.	R, und.	Glor - Xf.	—
TRANSMISSION				
Clutch	SDP	SDP	SDP	SDP
Gearbox action	cr.	S3 (& fre.)	S3 (& fre.)	S3
No. of forward gears	3 or 4	4	4	4
Gear lever location	cen.	cen.	cen.	cen.
Forward gear ratios (x:1)	22.4, 13.6, 8.8, 5.75V	20.4, 12.5, 8, 5.25	20.4, 12.5, 8, 5.25V	22.4, 13.6, 8.8, 5.75
Gearbox lubricant, SAE	90	90	90	90
Gearbox lubricant, quantity (pts)	—	—	2½	—
Rear axle bevel; ratio (x:1)	worm; 5.75V	worm; 5.25	w/sp; 4.8/5.25	worm; 5.75
Rear axle lubricant, SAE	—	—	140	140
Rear axle lubricant, quantity (pts)	—	—	3	—
STEERING AND FRONT AXLE				
Steering box	WW	WW	WW or WN	WW
Steering box lubricant, SAE	140	140	140	140
Front axle	IB	IB	IB	IB
Toe-in setting (in.)	—	—	1/8	—
BRAKES				
Type	Lockheed	Lockheed	Lockheed	Lockheed
Actuation	hyd.	hyd.	hyd.	hyd.
BODYWORK				
Body construction	a. & fb.	a. on wo.	a. on wo.	a. on wo.
No. of doors	2 or 4	2 or 4	2 or 4	4
No. of seats	2 or 4	4	4	4
WHEELS AND TYRES				
Wheels	wire	wire	wire	wire
Tyres, size	4.00 x 27V	4.50 x 19	4.50 x 19V	4.50 x 19
Front tyre pressure (lb/in^2)	23 or 27V	34	34 or 31	34
Rear tyre pressure (lb/in^2)	23 or 27V	34	34 or 31	34

Name	10.8 hp Gloria & Southern Cross	Gloria Fourteen	1½-litre Dolomite & Gloria	New Twelve
Year(s) of manufacture	1934 - 37	1933 - 34	1937 - 39	1939
ENGINE				
Capacity (cc)	1232	1476	1496	1496
Number of cylinders	4	6	4	4
Bore and stroke (mm)	66 x 90	59 x 90	69 x 100	69 x 100
Compression ration (x:1)	6.2 or 6.8	—	7	7
RAC hp rating	10.8	12.9	11.8	11.8
Maximum bhp @ rev/min	42/50 @ 5000	50 @ 4500	50 @ 4500	50 @ 4500
Firing order	1,3,4,2	1,5,3,6,2,4	1,3,4,2	1,3,4,2
Valve layout	ioe	ioe	ohv	ohv
Inlet valve opens (^{o} btdc)	10	10	12	12
Tappet adjustment (inlet) in.	0.004H	0.004H	0.003H	0.003H
Tappet adjustment (exhaust) in.	0.006H	0.006H	0.003H	0.003H
Timing marks location	fly.	fly.	fly.	fly.
Lubrication pattern	FP	FP	FP	FP
Oil-pump type	gear	gear	gear	gear
Optimum oil pressure (lb/in ^{2})	—	—	20	20
Pistons type; number of rings	a ; 4	a ; 3	a ; 3	a ; 3
No. of main bearings	3	4	3	3
Main bearings	WM	WM	WM	WM
Camshaft drive	chain	chain	chain	chain
Sump capacity (pts)	12	-	13	13
Lubricant (summer), SAE	30	30	40	40
Lubricant (winter), SAE	30	30	30	30
Engine mountings	—	—	flex.	flex.
Exhaust manifold, branches	4	—	4	4
CARBURATION				
Carburetter	2 x SU	2 x Zenith	Solex	Solex
Carburetter type	HV2/OM/D3	30VE1	horiz.	horiz.
Choke size	1-1/8/1/1¼ in.	—	26 mm	26 mm
Main jet	0.090	—	120	120
Slow-running or pilot jet	NA	—	PJ55	PJ55
Compensating or correction jet	NA	—	CrJ210	CrJ210
GA and GS jet, or progression jet	NA	—	—	—
Capacity well or pump jet	NA	—	—	—
Metering needle (standard)	1/CX/4	NA	NA	NA
Metering needle (weak)	M5/D2/S4	NA	NA	NA
Average mpg	27 - 30	26	—	—
Fuel feed	SUE	SUE	SUE	SUE
Tank capacity (gall)	10½ or 13	13	12	12
IGNITION				
HT supply	coil	coil	coil	coil
Magneto	NA	NA	NA	NA
Distributor	DK4A-0	DJ6A-0	DKY4A	DKY4A
Coil	Q12	Q12	Q12-L	Q12-L
Contact-breaker gap (in.)	0.012	0.012	0.015	0.015
Spark plug gap (in.)	0.020	0.020	0.020	0.020
Spark plug thread (mm)	18	18	14	14
Spark plug	Ch. 16 or R7	—	—	—
Ignition timing (^{o} btdc)	—	—	O,FR	O,FR
ELECTRICAL				
Earthing pole	neg./pos.	neg.	pos.	pos.
Battery	2 x 6v 53ah	2 x 6v	2 x 6v 63ah	2 x 6v 63ah
Starter motor	M35A-O	M418G	M418G-L	M418G-L
Generator	C45H-O	C45H	C45PV-L	C45PV-L

	10.8 hp Gloria & Southern Cross	Gloria Fourteen	1½-litre Dolomite & Gloria	New Twelve
CHASSIS				
Chassis-frame pattern	cruciform	cruciform	cruciform	cruciform
Sidemembers	cn.	cn.	cn.	cn.
Crossmembers	cn.	cn.	cn.	cn.
Front suspension	SE	SE	SE	SE
Rear suspension	SE	SE	SE	SE
Shockabsorbers	hyd.	hyd.	hyd.	hyd.
Special chassis features	R, und.	R, und.	R, und.	R, und.
TRANSMISSION				
Clutch	SDP	SDP	SDP	SDP
Gearbox action	S3 & fre.	S3 & fre.	syn.	syn.
No. of forward gears	4	4	4	4
Gear lever location	cen.	cen.	cen.	cen.
Forward gear ratios (x:1)	20.4,12.4,8,5.22	20.4,12.4,8,5.22	U, 10.8, 6.9, 5.0	U, 10.8, 6.9, 5.0
Gearbox lubricant, SAE	90	90	90	90
Gearbox lubricant, quantity (pts)	2½	2½	3	3
Rear axle bevel; ratio (x:1)	sp. ; 5.22	sp. ; 5.22	sp. ; 5.0	sp. ; 5.0
Rear axle lubricant, SAE	140	140	140	140
Rear axle lubricant, quantity (pts)	3	3	3	3
STEERING AND FRONT AXLE				
Steering box	WN	WN	WN	WN
Steering box lubricant	140	140	140	140
Front axle	IB	IB	IB	IB
Toe-in setting (in.)	1/8	1/8	1/8	1/8
BRAKES				
Type	Lockheed	Lockheed	Lockheed	Lockheed
Actuation	hyd.	hyd.	hyd.	hyd.
BODYWORK				
Body construction	a. on wo.	a. on wo.	a. on wo.	a. on wo.
No. of doors	2 or 4	4	4	4
No. of seats	2 or 4	4	4	4
WHEELS AND TYRES				
Wheels	wire	wire	wire/disc	disc
Tyres,size	4.75 x 17V	4.75 x 17V	5.00 x 17V	5.00 x 17V
Front tyre pressure (lb/in²)	22	22	28	28
Rear tyre pressure(lb/in²)	27	27	28	28

Vauxhall

Name	Light Six	Ten	Twelve
Year(s) of manufacture	1933 - 38	1937 - 39	1939
ENGINE			
Capacity (cc)	1531	1203	1442
Number of cylinders	6	4	4
Bore and stroke (mm)	57 x 100	63.5 x 95	69.5 x 95
Compression ratio (x:1)	5.5 or 6.25	6.5	6.8
RAC hp rating	12.08	10	12.08
Maximum bhp @ rev/min	32 - 36 @ 4000	31.5 @ 3600	35 @ 3600
Firing order	1,5,3,6,2,4	1,3,4,2	1,3,4,2
Valve layout	ohv	ohv	ohv
Inlet valve opens (^{o}btdc)	—	4	4
Tappet adjustment (inlet) in.	—	0.006H	0.006H
Tappet adjustment (exhaust) in.	—	0.013H	0.013H
Timing marks location	TS	TS	TS
Lubrication pattern	FP	FP	FP
Oil-pump type	gear.	gear.	gear.
Optimum oil pressure (lb/in^2)	—	—	—
Pistons type; number of rings	a ; 3	a ; 3	'squish' ; 3
No. of main bearings	4	3	3
Main bearings	WM	sh.	sh.
Camshaft drive	chain	chain	chain
Sump capacity (pts)	—	5½	5½
Lubricant (summer), SAE	30	20	20
Lubricant (winter), SAE	20	20	20
Engine Mountings	flex.	flex.	flex.
Exhaust manifold, branches	—	3	3
CARBURATION			
Carburetter	Zenith	Zenith	Zenith
Carburetter type	—	30VIG/-2	30VIG-2
Choke size	—	25 mm	25 mm
Main jet	—	85 or 75	75
Slow-running or pilot jet	—	—	—
Compensating or correction jet	—	CJ70 or 90	CJ90
GA and GS jet, or progression jet	—	—	—
Capacity well or pump jet	—	PmJ60	PmJ50
Metering needle (standard)	NA	NA	NA
Metering needle (weak)	NA	NA	NA
Average mpg	26 - 28	40	35
Fuel feed	ACM	ACM	ACM
Tank capacity (gall)	9	6¾	6¾
IGNITION			
HT supply	coil	coil	coil
Magneto	NA	NA	NA
Distributor	DJ6A	DK4A	DK4A
Coil	Q12	Q12	Q12
Contact-breaker gap (in.)	0.012	0.012	0.012
Spark plug gap (in.)	0.018	0.038 - 40	0.038 - 40
Spark plug thread (mm)	18	14	14
Spark plug	—	Lo-CAN	Lo-CAN
Ignition timing (^{o}btdc)	—	2 - 9	2 - 9
ELECTRICAL			
Earthing pole	neg.	pos.	pos.
Battery	12v57ah	6v	6v
Starter motor	—	—	—
Generator	—	—	—

322

CHASSIS	*Light Six*	*Ten*	*Twelve*
Chassis-frame pattern	F, I; R, up.	unitary	unitary
Sidemembers	cn.	box	box
Crossmembers	cn.	NA	NA
Front suspension	SE or coil	torsion b.	torsion b.
Rear suspension	SE	SE	SE
Shockabsorbers	hyd.	hyd.	hyd.
Special chassis features	cruciform		
TRANSMISSION			
Clutch	SDP	SDP	SDP
Gearbox action	syn.	syn.	syn.
No. of forward gears	4	3	3
Gear lever location	cen.	cen.	cen.
Forward gear ratios (x:1)	18.7, 11.02, 7.18, 4.77	17.66, 8.42, 5.14	16.19, 7.72, 4.71
Gearbox lubricant, SAE	90	90	90
Gearbox lubricant, quantity (pts)	—	1	1
Rear axle bevel; ratio (x:1)	sp. ; 4.77	sp. ; 5.14	sp. ; 4.71
Rear axle lubricant, SAE	90	90	90
Rear axle lubricant, quantity (pts)	—	2	2
STEERING AND FRONT AXLE			
Steering box	WS	WN	WN
Steering box lubricant	140	140	140
Front axle	IB or ifs	ifs	ifs
Toe-in setting (in.)	—	—	—
BRAKES			
Type	mech.	Lockheed	Lockheed
Actuation	cable	hyd.	hyd.
BODYWORK			
Body construction	PS	PS	PS
No. of doors	4	4	4
No. of seats	4	4	4
WHEELS AND TYRES			
Wheels	wire or SD	SD	SD
Tyres, size	5.50 x 16	5.00 x 16V	5.25 x 16
Front tyre pressure (lb/in^2)	30	25	25
Rear tyre pressure (lb/in^2)	28	30	30

Wolseley

Name	Hornet	Hornet Special Chassis	Nine	Wasp
Year(s) of manufacture	1930–36	1932–36	1934–35	1935–36
ENGINE				
Capacity (cc)	1271/1378	1271/1604	1018	1069
Number of cylinders	6	6	4	4
Bore and stroke (mm)	57 x 83/57 x 90	57 x 83/61.5 x 90	60 x 90	61.5 x 90
Compression ratio (x:1)	5.6	6	—	—
RAC hp rating	12.08	12.08 or 14	8.95	9.37
Maximum bhp @ rev/min	32 - 35 @ 4500	37/50 @ 4500	30 @ 4000	32 @ 4000
Firing order	1,5,3,6,2,4	1,5,3,6,2,4	1,3,4,2	1,3,4,2
Valve layout	ohc	ohc	ohc	ohc
Inlet valve opens (^{o} btdc)	0	9	0	0
Tappet adjustment (inlet) in.	0.004 H	0.004 H	0.003 C	0.003 C
Tappet adjustment (exhaust) in.	0.004 H	0.004 H	0.003 C	0.003 C
Timing marks location	TG	TG	fly.	fly.
Lubrication pattern	FP	FP	FP	FP
Oil-pump type	gear	gear	gear	gear
Optimum oil pressure (lb/in^2)	—	—	—	—
Pistons type; number of rings	a; 3	a; 3	a; 3	a; 3
No. of main bearings	4	4	3	3
Main bearings, type	WM	WM	WM	WM
Camshaft drive	via gen./ch.	via gen./ch.	chain	chain
Sump capacity (pts)	12	12	8	8
Lubricant (summer), SAE	30	30	30	30
Lubricant (winter), SAE	30	30	30	30
Engine mountings	—	—	rigid	rigid
Exhaust manifold, branches	unit	3	unit	unit
CARBURATION				
Carburetter	SU	2 x SU	SU	SU
Carburetter type	HV2	HV2	HV2	HV2
Choke size	$1^1/8$ in.	$1^1/8$ in.	$1^1/8$ in.	$1^1/8$ in.
Main jet	0.090	0.090	0.090	0.090
Slow-running or pilot jet	NA	NA	NA	NA
Compensating or correction jet	NA	NA	NA	NA
GA and GS jet or progression jet	NA	NA	NA	NA
Capacity well or pump jet	NA	NA	NA	NA
Metering needle (standard)	H4	WX1/62/WX	W3	AV
Metering needle (weak)	V2	AK/AJ/WX1	MA	HA
Average mpg	28 - 35	—	—	32
Fuel feed	grav./SUE	SUE	SUE	SUE
Tank capacity (gall)	8	5	8	8
IGNITION				
HT supply	coil	coil	coil	coil
Magneto	NA	NA	NA	NA
Distributor	DJ6A	DJ6A	DK4A	DK4A
Coil	Q12	Q12	12v	12v
Contact-breaker gap (in.)	0.012	0.012	0.012	0.012
Spark plug gap (in.)	0.018	0.018	0.018	0.018
Spark plug thread (mm)	18	18	18	18
Spark plug	ch. 17	—	—	—
Ignition timing (^{o} btdc)	—	—	0	0
ELECTRICAL				
Earthing pole	neg.	neg.	neg.	neg.
Battery	12v	12v	12v	12v
Starter motor	—	—	—	—
Generator	—	—	thi.	thi.

	Hornet	Hornet Special Chassis	Nine	Wasp
CHASSIS				
Chassis-frame pattern	ladder	ladder	cruciform	cruciform
Sidemembers	cn.	cn.	cn.	cn.
Crossmembers	cn.	cn.	cn.	cn.
Front suspension	SE	SE	SE	SE
Rear suspension	SE	SE	SE	SE
Shockabsorbers	hyd.	hyd.	hyd.	hyd.
Special chassis features	—	—	—	GL
TRANSMISSION				
Clutch	SDP (& fre.)	SDP	SDP	SDP
Gearbox action	CM or pre.	CM	syn.	syn.
No. of forward gears	3 or 4	4	4	4
Gear lever location	cen./clm.	cen.	cen.	cen.
Forward gear ratios (x:1)	15.22, 8.76, 4.78V	17.5, 10.5, 6.64, 4.89	—	—
Gearbox lubricant, SAE	90	90	90	90
Gearbox lubricant, quantity (pts)	1¾	1¾	1¾	1¾
Rear axle bevel; ratio (x:1)	sp; 4.78V	sp; 4.89	sp; 5.29	sp; 5.28
Rear axle lubricant	90	90	90	90
Rear axle lubricant, quantity	1¼	1¼	1¼	1¼
STEERING AND FRONT AXLE				
Steering box	WW	WW	WW	WW
Steering box lubricant	140	140	140	140
Front axle	IB	IB	IB	IB
Toe-in setting (in.)	1/8	1/8	1/8	1/8
BRAKES				
Type	Lockheed	Lockheed	Lockheed	Lockheed
Actuation	hyd.	hyd.	hyd.	hyd.
BODYWORK				
Body construction	S or PS	NA	PS	PS
No. of doors	4	NA	4	4
No. of seats	4	NA	4	4
WHEELS AND TYRES				
Wheels	M	M or RW	M	wire/SD
Tyres, size	4.40 x 27V	4.75 x 18V	4.50 x 18	5.25 x 16
Front tyre pressure (lb/in^2)	30	28	28	26
Rear tyre pressure (lb/in^2)	30	28	28	26

BRITISH LIGHT CARS

Name	Ten-Forty & Ten Series III	Twelve-Forty-eight & Twelve Series III	New Fourteen
Year(s) of manufacture	1936 - 39	1936 - 39	1935 - 36
ENGINE			
Capacity (cc)	1292	1547	1604
Number of cylinders	4,	4	6
Bore and stroke (mm)	63.5 x 102	69.5 x 102	61.5 x 90
Compression ratio (x:1)	6.8	6.6	—
RAC hp rating	9.9	11.98	14
Maximum bhp @ rev/min	40 @ 4500	48 @ 4500	50 @ 4500
Firing order	1,3,4,2	1,3,4,2	1,5,3,6,2,4
Valve layout	ohv	ohv	ohc
Inlet valve opens (^{o} btdc)	5	11	—
Tappet adjustment (inlet) in	0.015H	0.015H	0.003C
Tappet adjustment (inlet) in.	0.015H	0.015H	0.003C
Tappet adjustment (exhaust) in.	fly.	fly.	fly.
Lubrication pattern	FP	FP	FP
Oil-pump type	gear	gear	gear
Optimum oil pressure (lb/in ^{2})	—	—	40 - 60
Pistons type; number of rings	a ; 3	a ; 3	a ; 3
No. of main bearings	3	3	4
Main bearings	WM or sh.	WM or sh.	WM
Camshaft drive	chain	chain	chain
Sump capacity (pts)	8	13 or 9½	10
Lubricant (summer), SAE	40	40	40
Lubricant (winter), SAE	30	30	30
Engine mountings	flex.	flex.	—
Exhaust manifold, branches	—	—	—
CARBURATION			
Carburetter	SU	SU	SU
Carburetter type	D3 or H2	D3	HV3
Choke size	1¼ in.	1¼ in.	1¼ in.
Main jet	0.090	0.090	0.090
Slow-running or pilot jet	NA	NA	NA
Compensating or correction jet	NA	NA	NA
GA and GS jet, or progression jet	NA	NA	NA
Capacity well or pump jet	NA	NA	NA
Metering needle (standard)	5 or FC	5 or 4	S6
Metering needle (weak)	AJ or DQ	AJ or S4	AM
Average mpg	30 - 32	27 - 29	24 - 28
Fuel feed	SUE	SUE	SUE
Tank capacity (gall)	7	7 or 10	8
IGNITION			
HT supply	coil	coil	coil
Magneto	NA	NA	NA
Distributor	DKY4A	DKY4A	—
Coil	Q12	Q12	12v
Contact-breaker gap (in.)	0.012	0.012	0.012
Spark plug gap (in.)	0.022 - 0.025	0.022	0.018
Spark plug thread (mm)	14	14	18
Spark plug	Ch. L-10	Ch. L-10	—
Ignition timing (^{o} btdc)	O,FR	O, FR	—
ELECTRICAL			
Earthing pole	pos.	pos.	neg.
Battery	12v 51 ah	12v 51 ah	12v 51 ah
Starter motor	M418G	M418G	—
Generator	C45YV-3	C45YV-3	—

	Ten-Forty & Ten Series III	Twelve-Forty-eight & Twelve Series III	New Fourteen
CHASSIS			
Chassis-frame pattern	ladder/unit	ladder/unit	cruciform
Sidemembers	cn./box	cn./box	cn.
Crossmembers	cn.	cn.	cn.
Front suspension	SE	SE	SE
Rear suspension	SE	SE	SE
Shockabsorbers	hyd.	hyd.	hyd.
Special chassis features	Bevelift	Jackall	GL
TRANSMISSION			
Clutch	SDP	SDP	SDP
Gearbox action	syn.	syn.	syn.
No. of forward gears	4	4	4
Gear lever location	cen.	cen.	cen.
Forward gear ratios (x:1)	20.88, 12.33, 7.98, 5.22	20.98, 12.33, 7.98, 5.22	21.32, 11.83, 8.11, 5.1
Gearbox lubricant, SAE	30	30	30
Gearbox lubricant, quantity (pts)	2	2	1¾
Rear axle bevel; ratio (x:1)	sp. ; 5.22	sp. ; 5.22	sp. ; 5.1
Rear axle lubricant, SAE	90	90	90
Rear axle lubricant, quantity (pts)	2	2	2¼
STEERING AND FRONT AXLE			
Steering box	BC	BC	CL
Steering box lubricant	140	140	140
Front axle	IB	IB	IB
Toe-in setting (in.)	1/8	1/8	1/8
BRAKES			
Type	Lockheed	Lockheed	Lockheed
Actuation	hyd.	hyd.	hyd.
BODYWORK			
Body construction	PS	PS	S on wo.
No. of doors	4	4	4
No. of seats	4	4	4
WHEELS AND TYRES			
Wheels	SD	SD	SD
Tyres, size	5.75 x 16	5.75 x 16	5.75 x 16
Front tyre pressure (lb/in^2)	22	22	22
Rear tyre pressure (lb/in^2)	25	25	22 - 26

Appendix Two

Specialist services and suppliers, references mentioned in Part 1

Tyres and tubes for the older car: Vintage Tyre Supplies Ltd, Hackman Mews, North Circular Road, Neasden, London N W 10.

ABV automatic bleed valves: Patent Enterprises Ltd, 143 - 145, View Road, Richmond, Surrey.

Any components made to pattern: PES, Nipsells Chase, Mayland, Chelmsford, Essex.

Compression gauge: Silhill Products, 226 Mary Street, Birmingham B12 9RJ.

Dashboard instrument repairs: John E. Marks, 4 Whybourne Crescent, Tunbridge Wells, Kent.

Engine-lifting tackle and tripod: Gantry and Hoist (Manufacturing) Co, 52 Bell Green, Sydenham, London SE 26.

Engine-lifting crane: The Old Hill Co Ltd, Powke Lane, Rowley Regis, Warley, Worcs.

Exhaust systems in stainless steel: Langford and Knight, Oldknows Factory, Egerton Street, Nottingham.

General 1930s spares: Motolympia, Welshpool, Montgomeryshire, Wales.

Home arc-brazing kits: Kellers Welding Centre, 32 - 33 Cattle Market Street, Norwich NOR 27B.

Magneto repairs: Donald Day, 31 Goddard Avenue, Swindon, Wilts. SN1 4HR.

Radiator repairs: Raymond Radiators Ltd, 60 Chalk Farm Road, London NW1.

For a very extensive list of specialist services, sources of spares, etc., the reader is recommended to obtain a copy of the *Veteran and Vintage Directory,* published at 55p (inc p&p) by Pioneer Publications Ltd, 3 Wyndham Place, London W1.

Spare Parts
The most ready source of spares for a particular prewar model is the appropriate Car Club. Other sources are listed in the *Veteran and Vintage Directory.*

Bibliography

1929–39 editions of *Autocar, Motor, The Light Car, Practical Motorist* and *Motor Sport*
The Light Car — C. F. Caunter, Science Museum (HMSO)
Motor Cars, Descriptive Catalogue Part II — C. F. Caunter, Science Museum (HMSO)
Car Profiles Nos 39, 45, 51, 52, 58, 64, 65, 70, 76, 82 and *83*
Alvis in the Thirties   (Enthusiast Publications)
S. S. Cars, 1931–37   "   "
MG Cars in the Thirties   "   "
Book of the BSA Scout   "   "
Book of the Morgan   "   "
Handbook of the Austin 7   "   "
Riley Maintenance Manual — S. V. Haddleton (Foulis)
British Sports Cars — G. Grant (Foulis)
Vintage Years of the Morgan Three-wheeler — W. Boddy (Grenville Publishing Co)
Practical Automobile Engineering (Odhams)
The Autocar Handbook, 18th Edition (Iliffe and Sons Ltd)
The Book of the Riley Nine   (Pitman)
The Book of the Standard Car   "
The Book of the Jowett   "
The Book of the Wolseley   "
The Book of the Morris Eight   "
The Book of the Hillman Minx   "
The Book of the Ford Eight   "
The Book of the Ford Ten   "
The Book of the Vauxhall Ten, Twelve and Wyvern   "
The Book of the Austin Ten   "
The Book of the Austin Seven   "
The Book of the JAP   "
Standard Cars — T. D. Postlethwaite and I. Walton (Pearson)
Ford Facts (Ford Motor Company)
Manufacturers' manuals and handbooks

Index